THE INFORMATION SOCIETY:
EMERGING LANDSCAPES

IFIP – The International Federation for Information Processing

IFIP was founded in 1960 under the auspices of UNESCO, following the First World Computer Congress held in Paris the previous year. An umbrella organization for societies working in information processing, IFIP's aim is two-fold: to support information processing within its member countries and to encourage technology transfer to developing nations. As its mission statement clearly states,

> *IFIP's mission is to be the leading, truly international, apolitical organization which encourages and assists in the development, exploitation and application of information technology for the benefit of all people.*

IFIP is a non-profitmaking organization, run almost solely by 2500 volunteers. It operates through a number of technical committees, which organize events and publications. IFIP's events range from an international congress to local seminars, but the most important are:

• The IFIP World Computer Congress, held every second year;
• Open conferences;
• Working conferences.

The flagship event is the IFIP World Computer Congress, at which both invited and contributed papers are presented. Contributed papers are rigorously refereed and the rejection rate is high.

As with the Congress, participation in the open conferences is open to all and papers may be invited or submitted. Again, submitted papers are stringently refereed.

The working conferences are structured differently. They are usually run by a working group and attendance is small and by invitation only. Their purpose is to create an atmosphere conducive to innovation and development. Refereeing is less rigorous and papers are subjected to extensive group discussion.

Publications arising from IFIP events vary. The papers presented at the IFIP World Computer Congress and at open conferences are published as conference proceedings, while the results of the working conferences are often published as collections of selected and edited papers.

Any national society whose primary activity is in information may apply to become a full member of IFIP, although full membership is restricted to one society per country. Full members are entitled to vote at the annual General Assembly. National societies preferring a less committed involvement may apply for associate or corresponding membership. Associate members enjoy the same benefits as full members, but without voting rights. Corresponding members are not represented in IFIP bodies. Affiliated membership is open to non-national societies, and individual and honorary membership schemes are also offered.

THE INFORMATION SOCIETY: EMERGING LANDSCAPES

IFIP International Conference on Landscapes of ICT and Social Accountability, Turku, Finland, June 27-29, 2005.

Edited by

Chris Zielinski
Senior Consultant, World Health Organization, Geneva, Switzerland

Penny Duquenoy
Senior Lecturer, Middlesex University, London, United Kingdom

Kai Kimppa
Lecturer, University of Turku, Finland

 Springer

The Information Society: Emerging Landscapes
Edited by Chris Zielinski, Penny Duquenoy, and Kai Kimppa

p. cm. (IFIP International Federation for Information Processing, a Springer Series in Computer Science)

ISSN: 1571-5736 / 1861-2288 (Internet)

Printed on acid-free paper

ISBN: 978-1-4419-4030-8   e-ISBN: 978-0-387-31168-5

springeronline.com

Contents

3   Social Aspects

4   Politics and Regulation

5   Economics and Work

6   Technology, Virtual Reality and Emerging Technologies

INTRODUCTION

Penny Duquenoy, Chris Zielinski and Kai Kimppa
Respectively Chair, Vice Chair and Secretary of IFIP WG9.2

In 1990, members of IFIP Working Group 9.2 were instrumental in producing one of the first books to describe the 'Landscape' of the new phenomena created by the uptake of computerization – the so-called Information Society[1].

Ten years on, at the annual Namur meeting of our Working Group, in January 2000, a proposal was made to produce a second book and the brainstorming began. In the ten years that had passed the developments in computer technology had brought the Internet within reach of ordinary citizens, and the World Wide Web had spawned a new 'e-industry'. The landscape of the information society had changed dramatically, and it continues to change at a breathtaking pace.

This book is the result of our discussions at that July meeting, and the culmination of our "Landscapes" Conference in July 2005 held at Turku University, Finland. The themes chosen for the conference – philosophy, ethics and sociological aspects, culture and education; social aspects; politics and regulation; economics and work; technology and emerging technologies – represent the many perspectives we can adopt from which to view this landscape. The papers reproduced here illustrate the diverse impacts of the information society and the changing paradigms within education, law, health care, the workplace and on future societal infrastructures through

---

[1] Berleur, J., A. Clement, R. Sizer, & D. Whitehouse (editors). *The Information Society: Evolving Landscapes. Report from Namur*. Springer-Verlag: New York & Captus University Publications: North York. 1990

research initiatives and the development of new technologies. In other words, we have attempted to capture the new 'emerging landscape' of the Information Society.

A picture of profound technological and social change emerges from this holistic approach. We believe it offers a key to understanding the ramifications of computer technologies within the information society, and of the social accountability of all those working with and affected by them.

Finally, we would like to thank the University of Turku for providing us with the space for discussion and information exchange, and Turku Centre for Computing Science (TUCS) for their valuable support.

Penny Duquenoy   **Chris Zielinski**   **Kai Kimppa**
Chair   *Vice Chair*   *Secretary*

on behalf of IFIP WG9.2

PART 1

PHILOSOPHY, ETHICS AND SOCIOLOGICAL ASPECTS

INFORMATION CULTURES AND COUNTER-CULTURES

Colin Beardon
Department of Computer Science, University of Waikato, Hamilton, New Zealand
cbeardon@cs.waikato.ac.nz

Abstract: The Arts and Sciences have always been considered distinct, but have played differing roles with respect to significant ethical, humanitarian and political issues of the day. Computers were first introduced within a culture of data processing, which gave rise to a number of social issues. As computers developed, the concept of 'information' became more important, yet it is very difficult to say what is meant by that term. Despite this, the concept of 'information' has been instrumental in promoting free-market economics. However, the introduction of mixed media computing raises some serious questions about the adequacy of the concept of 'information' and suggests that the current mainstream ideology of computing is under some pressure. People who worked in computing in the early decades frequently held libertarian views that were often described as counter-cultural. Many of these views were absorbed within the dominant culture of free-market liberalisation, but different counter-cultures have emerged (e.g., hackers and political activists). Some digital artists and designers can also be considered counter-cultural and it is from this direction that we might see an emerging positive ethical response to contemporary issues.

> *Data, data, everywhere and not a thought to think.*
> *Jesse Shera*

1.   INTRODUCTION: ARTS AND SCIENCES

The Royal Albert Hall in London is nowadays used almost entirely for entertainment purposes but when it was erected over one hundred years ago it was, according to the engraving upon its outside,

...erected for the advancement of the Arts and Sciences, and works of industry of all nations...

In the true spirit of the late nineteenth century, differences between the Arts and Sciences were acknowledged, but also their cooperation was considered a matter for practical action. When the Hall opened in 1871 it soon became a venue for events as diverse as demonstrations of Morse Code and electric lighting, exhibitions of bicycles and motor cars, music concerts and readings of poetry. One hundred years ago, the bringing together of the Arts and Sciences was a significant practical project.

Nearly ninety years later, in 1959, the novelist C. P. Snow delivered a famous lecture in Cambridge entitled 'The Two Cultures' in which he also talked about the Arts and Sciences —in Snow's terminology, *intellectuals* and *scientists,* or more precisely *literary intellectuals* and *physical scientists* (Snow, 1964). Snow claimed that the two groups had "...almost ceased to communicate at all, [and] in intellectual, moral and psychological climate had so little in common...". It appears that in those 90 years the Arts and Sciences, rather than coming closer together, had drifted further apart.

Snow's lecture received plenty of publicity that at time, and has continued to receive considerable attention right up to today. For example, a recent search for "Two Cultures" on Google (25/1/05) yielded 39,400 hits: to put this in perspective, Stephen Hawking's "A Brief History of Time" yielded 72,600 hits and Francois Lyotard's "Postmodern Condition" yielded 25,800 hits.

From the standpoint of the early 1960s, Snow was projecting a strong modernist belief that (in the words of Harold Wilson, a future Prime Minister of the UK) "the white heat of the technological revolution" was the only progressive response to the unimaginative conservatism that had been in power, certainly in Britain, for over a decade.

Moving forward another 20 years to the 1970s we find that such popular optimism for science and technology had all but evaporated and science was frequently perceived as too large and dangerous. The development of nuclear weapons, the unreliability of nuclear power, the over-use of pesticides, fertilisers and other chemicals, the misuse of drugs and medicines, the depletion of natural resources – these had done much to deflate the idea that unbridled science will inevitably lead to global happiness. They brought about a refocusing on questions of what kind of science was needed, what limitations should placed upon it, and how its benefits should be distributed.

The response of many scientists was to retreat into a claimed 'neutrality of science' which was then posed as the opposite of 'ideology'. In 1973, Daniel Bell (the author of 'The End of Ideology' (1960)) described the scientific community as universal and disinterested with "no set of postulated formal beliefs" (Bell 1973). But in the eyes of many young people the traditional physical sciences started to decline in popularity (though this was not the case in newer, non-material sciences such as computer science and psychology). By contrast to the 'neutral' stance adopted by physical scientists, it was social scientists and literary intellectuals who increasingly expressed political commitment to working class and Third World issues and were significant among the supporters of the left. Many novelists, dramatists and poets, (not to forget also artists, actors and musicians, who were omitted from Snow's analysis) were prominent in left-of-centre political campaigns. Left-leaning governments have generally enjoyed (and usually still enjoy) the support of the artistic communities and are seen as being good for creativity. So, within another 20 years, while the gap that Snow alerted us to still existed, the roles played by the respective parties had almost completely reversed.

2. THE CULTURE OF INFORMATION

2.1 Two Early Cultures of Computing

Snow would have been only vaguely aware in 1959 of the future exponential growth of the computer (though, no doubt, he would have approved). At that time, the evolving nature of computing was still in the balance with two opposing cultures ranged against each other. As Stephen Heims (1980) has documented, there was real ideological conflict in the early days about the deep relationship of computers to their societal context. The ideology of cybernetics, as championed by Norbert Wiener, saw the computer as one element of a larger and more holistic system in which it would play a useful regulatory role. Against this was the more formalized model of computing proposed by John von Neumann in which, working within a strict positivist philosophy, the computer plays a more abstract, functional role, and within which it is largely insulated from the wider consequences of its use.

Von Neumann's view received overwhelming political and economic support at that time, and, probably as a result, the type of computing that developed engendered an aura of mistrust. Newspapers described early computers as 'Giant Brains'. A famous protester in the 1960s carried a placard reading: "I am a human being: do not bend, fold, staple or mutilate". IBM became synonymous with conformity of the worst kind. The computer became a symbol of unemployment, deskilling, the sexual division of labour, lack of privacy and bureaucracy. Computer ethics emerged as a humanist response to the concept of the computer as a machine for anonymous, large-scale processing of data. It was the 'data processing' model that became the first ideological face of the computer for most people.

The concept of 'Data Processing' represented a major epistemological realignment whereby the social language of computing was moulded to the form of logical positivism. This system of thought held out the hope that systems of symbols might reflect the totality of the world and, therefore, that processing such symbols might yield legitimate knowledge and enable us to exercise legitimate control over the real world, either with or without human intervention (Toulmin, 1991). From it flowed a number of socio-economic developments, from the routinization of office work through to more speculative projects such as artificial intelligence.

The computer's emergence as a data processing machine involved a new language promulgated to make legitimate activities such as corporate and bureaucratic computing. From the late 1960s through to the 1980s numerous textbooks were published that sought to explain data and information processing, all in strictly positivist terms (e.g. Arnold, 1978; Davis, 1969; Frates & Moldrup, 1983; Gore, 1979; Verzello, 1982). These books told us that data processing is about the transformation of *data* into *information* and that the key difference between the two is that information has a *meaning* or *purpose*. This, of course, implies that the generation of meaning is a process that is universal, does not rely on people and does not relate to the context of use.

2.2   Problems with 'Information'

Philosophically, this distinction between 'data' and 'information' is very unclear. Armand Mattelart (2003) refers to "the fuzziness of the notion of information" and I have argued that such attempts to define this distinction do not stand up to analysis (Beardon, 1994).

'Data' is a noun and does not have a verbal form; whereas the noun 'information' is derived from the verb 'to inform'. According to the Oxford English Dictionary (www.dictionary.oed.com):

To inform

... To impart knowledge of some particular fact or occurrence to (a person); to tell (one) of or acquaint (one) with something; to apprise. (OED)

This is a human social action—someone informs someone else of something—and is the root from which all other transformations seem to have been made. It should be noted that any instance of the verb 'to inform' requires an agent who does the informing, a particular fact that is being told, and a person or persons who are the recipients. There are no real problems with our use of this verb.

Our ability to create new words by transformation of existing words has led to many philosophical-linguistic problems. Initially, the transformed word "information' was harmless,

Information

... Knowledge communicated concerning some particular fact, subject, or event; that of which one is apprised or told; intelligence, news. (OED)

That is to say, it refers to the 'something' that is communicated in any particular act of informing. Had it stayed at this there would still be no real problem as it remained rooted in actual social events but, from the 1940s, an alternative way of thinking about information was promoted as the Mathematical Theory of Information (Shannon and Weaver, 1949). This notion defines information as,

... a mathematically defined quantity ...; now especially one which represents the degree of choice exercised in the selection or formation of one particular symbol, sequence, message, etc., out of a number of possible ones. (OED)

This sense of 'information' introduces a new idea: information that can exist without there being any act of informing; thus the context, content and purpose of the communication is all put to one side and we are invited to concentrate only on the formal and functional aspects of communication.

Of course, there is nothing wrong with introducing a new sense of a word for a specific purpose but problems can occur when specialist senses get confused with traditional senses.

Charlie Gere is clear that this has happened with the mathematical concept of information:

...it is from Shannon's concept of information that we owe the idea of information technology and by extension the information society it helped to bring about. (Gere 2002 50)

This did not happen without opposition, and we can observe another clash of cultures within computing over this issue. The economist, Fritz Machlup, refused to assign any special status to the new notion of 'information' and he argued that 'information' and 'data' are in most practical respects complete equivalents; further, they form no natural hierarchy or sequence and can, in most cases, be used interchangeability (Machlup 1983). To attempt to build a science upon their separation (i.e. 'Information Science') was, in his view, bogus and ill-informed.

Despite his formidable reputation, Machlup's satisfaction with the traditional concept of 'information' was politically unacceptable. First the US Government, and then the OECD, preferred a concept of information based upon the idea of 'quantities of data that are organized and communicated' (Porat, 1977). Thus, the mathematical notion of information was allowed to dominate in social and political policy discussions and issues of the content and context of information were made secondary. In this debate over the future of computing and society we were led to pay less attention to the social use (or 'use-value') of information and more attention to the value to be extracted from its mass processing (its 'exchange value').

Porat's analysis was very influential in the thinking that led to many nation states formulating policies for the 'information society'. In 1971 Japan adopted the goal to become an 'information society' by the year 2000. In 1977 the US Senate Foreign Relations Committee for the first time adopted the definition of information as a "new national resource" and proposed The New World Information Order and there followed a plethora of national reports and policies from other countries (France, India, Brazil, etc.). These reports and policies were domestic responses by each nation-state, as industrialized nations around the world responded to the decline of their manufacturing sectors. International coordination was to quickly follow, through developments such as the European FAST programme in 1980. The implications were clear: the computer was to be seen as a processor of 'information', and this was going to herald an 'information revolution' leading to a new 'information society' though, in truth, no-one was sure what these words meant.

2.3   The Limitations of Symbols

The one weakness in this growing ideology of 'information' is a fundamental weakness of logical positivism itself. Logical positivism is a philosophy based around symbolic knowledge. It is about facts encoded in a language, and as such has very little to say about things that are not facts, for example, images or sounds. For the logical positivists such forms of experience are considered 'emotional' and discounted, along with religion and other unformalized belief systems. Daniel Bell wrote: "Technical decision-making can, in fact, be viewed as the diametric opposite of ideology; the one calculating and instrumental, the other emotional and expressive" (Bell 1973).

It was the advent of the multimedia computer that began to open up some of the contradictions within this shaky ideology of computing. The languages of symbolic computing have proved to be lacking when confronted with experiences such as digital photography, digital drawing, electronic music, multimedia, virtual reality, digital animation, digital film production, computer games, mobile telephony and digital radio. Of course, there is a level at which the mathematical notion of information applies and is useful, but as a general model of communication, the 'information processing' paradigm has nothing interesting to say. When dealing with such objects of popular media, the content and context are paramount concerns: the need for a new ideology of computing, a new 'digital culture', becomes pressing.

We can see early traces of this in the 1980s when there were again two very publicly competing 'cultures' within computing. The personal computer — a complete computer for every person — had becoming economic and popular and a battle emerged between the Macintosh and the IBM PC that was ideological at least as much as it was economic. The IBM PC with its DOS operating system and ASCII screen insisted that the computer was a symbol manipulator. The Apple Macintosh, with its new graphical interface and its mouse had a vision that the computer was a visual and aural medium (Bolter and Gromola, 2003). There were many computer experts at that time who predicted that people would not want to use the unnecessary and inefficient interfaces introduced by Apple and that command-line interfaces were far more 'logical' and would therefore prevail: but they did not. The PC finally gave up the ideological fight and 'Windows for PC' was launched: at this point the basic relationship of people to the computer changed. The pure data processing / information processing model began to lose its grip. The logic of the market had determined this change: 'users' were no longer just 'workers', they were now 'customers'.

> Computer technology is not mainly used for production, it is used for all kinds of work and leisure (and changing the relations between work, leisure, and education) ... the focus has slowly, but steadily moved away from workers towards customers ... computer technology has developed from being mainly production technology to being communication technology. (Bjerknes & Bratteteig, 1995)

Ironically, the new vision of the consumer-led information revolution— as espoused by Bill Gates and others— is a truly cybernetic one: it is of a frictionless capitalism, which is borderless and leaderless, and for which no-one is accountable (Mattelart, 2003). Thus, in 1997, and in terms highly reminiscent of C.P. Snow, we were presented with the concept of the 'Digital Citizen' who would be

> ...knowledgeable, tolerant, civic-minded, and radically committed to change. Profoundly optimistic about the future, they're convinced that technology is a force for good and that our free-market economy functions as a powerful engine for good. (Katz 1997)

Despite this vision of dystopia, there still remains the question of power. Information represents power and whichever nation has the best 'information processing systems' supposedly has the most power. But, as part of the redefinition of 'information' it has become emptied of content, and so we can (and do) no longer talk about its veracity: in the brave new world, 'information' and 'truth' very rarely have anything to do with each other for value of 'information' is in its exchange and not its use. The power of information is derived from the processing of information, true or false, and in recognition of this we find talk of 'soft power':

> the ability to arouse in others the desire for whatever it is you want them to desire, and the faculty of leading them to accept the norms and institutions that produce the desired behaviour. (Mattelart, 2003, 130)

Suddenly, the content and social dynamics of information has become important again, but this time without any necessary relationship to truthfulness.

Interlude

> In her recent novel, 'The Autograph Man' (2002), Zadie Smith has a father taking his 12 year-old son to a professional wrestling match at the Royal Albert Hall. Reading the inscription (quoted in the first paragraph of this paper), the father wonders whether professional

wrestling is an Art or a Science. He suggests to his son that there are reasons to think that it is probably a little of each. "Rubbish", says his son and when challenged as to which it is, replies, "Neither. It is TV".

3.   MIXED MEDIA: MIXED CULTURES

3.1   Computers and Art

Art has been part of the evolution of computing almost from the beginning. From the early 1960s artists who were interested in kinetic art (as pioneered by Naum Gabo, László Moholy-Nagy, Jean Tinguely, Len Lye and others) had became especially interested in the idea of adaptive systems and the relationship of information to control. A formal interest in cybernetics was behind Roy Ascott's 1963 show 'Diagram Boxes and Analogue Structures' (Molton Gallery, London). Writing in 1966, Ascott described an "art of cybernetics" which referred not to any obvious relationship between the two terms, but rather to "the spirit of cybernetics, which may inform art and in turn be informed by it" (Ascott [1966] 2003, p.126). More material expressions of the relationship of cybernetics to art can be found in the work of David Medalla, for example, who in 1966 built cybernetic art works involving mud, bubbles and sand, or the theatre director, Gordon Pask, who developed adaptive lighting systems for the theatre. In 1970 Pask built an adaptive cybernetic art piece that involved communication between the different parts of the sculpture and the human spectator. In 1967, Robert Rauschenberg and Billy Klüver in New York formed a group called Experiments in Art and Technology (EAT). EAT was very influential and was also concerned with technology as a subject for art, rather than just a medium. One artist who was associated with EAT was Edward Kienholz, whose sculpture 'The friendly grey computer' in 1965 addressed a more subjective side of the relationship to the computer.

At the same time that artists were becoming interested in the concepts of cybernetics and computing, there were a number of engineers who explored the computer as a medium or as an instrument for producing more conventional forms of art. Frieder Nake produced very early graphical 'artworks' using a computer-controlled plotter ('Rectangular hatchings', 1965) and was soon followed by others who employed a variety of novel techniques to produce visual imagery (e.g. Michael Noll, Katherine Nash, Leon Harmon and Kenneth Knowlton, Charles Csuri and others). These represent technical approaches to 'computer art', which we can describe as the production of objects that look like traditional art works and are produced by using the computer as an instrument (Lovejoy, 2004).

The growing interest in art and the computer led, in the late 1960s, to three international exhibitions that were fairly eclectic, attracted cross-disciplinary participation and are generally seen as significant and successful:

1968   Cybernetic Serendipity: The Computer and the Arts, ICA, London
1968   The Machine as Seen at the End of the Mechanical Age. MOMA, NY
1970   Software, Information Technology: Its New Meaning for Art; Jewish Museum, NY

This early interest of both artists and the art world in the potential of computers proved difficult to sustain. For those who were using the computer as an instrument, it proved to be a rather limited one once the novelty had worn off. Technically, the computers of the 1970s and 1980s lacked sufficient storage capacity and processing power, and they lacked devices that could produce good quality output. There were only a few artists who pursued computer art through the 1970s and 1980s. William Latham, for example, worked with IBM in the UK to develop complex graphical algorithms which resulted in organically inspired images and animations. Harold Cohen used learning algorithms from cognitive science to produce themed sketches, but such work rarely showed sufficient creative development to gain artistic attention or acceptance.

For the cyberneticians, who wanted to include computing devices in live exhibitions and events, the issue was not so much lack of computing power but rather lack of computer reliability. Many early works were technically very fragile and in real exhibition conditions failed to meet the reliability standards expected. In the 1970 exhibition "Software, Information Technology' many of the exhibits "did not actually work due to technical difficulties" and experiences such as this contributed to a number of artists abandoning the use of computer technology in their work (Gere 2002).

Some of these artists retained an interest in computing, but tended to explore other approaches to interactive experience, through alternative contemporary forms such as performance art and video art. Those who retained a more philosophical or intellectual involvement in the idea of cybernetics tended to move into one of the main art movements of recent decades, Conceptual Art. Early Conceptual Art was very much about the relationship of objects to signs and symbols and strong parallels can be found between the concerns of these artists and the emerging concept of 'information'. Arguably, the interest of artists in the computer was sustained through the 1970s and 1980s but engaged with the new concept of 'information' rather than with computer technology itself.

3.2 Information, Art and Users

It is easy to form a compound noun by putting the words 'information' and 'art' together but in doing so we have not necessarily created an interesting category. In fact, the term 'information art' is rather barren. There are no books published on the subject (the one with this title actually amounts to a catalogue of science and art collaborations). I have asked several curators what they would make of the term and they either have no response, or they suggest conceptual artists such as Jenny Holzer. The term seems to have very little currency which reinforces the view that perhaps it marks some deep schism in our contemporary culture.

There is a definition of 'art' that is central to our concerns:

Art is truth without facts

(this is very similar to Picasso's famous dictum, "Art is a lie that tells the truth"). These definitions directly address the gulf between the logical positivist 'information processing' culture and the mixed media culture of the creative arts. The latter accepts that the positivist systems of knowledge may be consistent, but claims that they are not complete. There is knowledge that exists outside of the formal system and is very interesting. Because artists are not bound by any formal semantic code they are able (at least some of them) to find more direct ways of expressing this reality.

From the 1960s, Umberto Eco began writing about 'the open work': "works which the performer and the audience both help complete, through different kinds of engagement" (Eco, 1989). Perhaps one of the earliest and most seminal of pieces of art to express this idea was John Cage's 1952 performance of *4' 33"*, featuring a pianist and consisting of three short movements of silence. Part of Cage's point was that any sound performance always takes place within an environment in which there are other noises and he was in a sense arguing, albeit in an extreme form, that these need not be drowned or filtered out. A second, perhaps stronger, point was that the meaning of a performance does not depend solely upon the author or performer, but it is also created by the active participation of the audience.

This has implications for the whole dialogue of computing. If the computer is seen as a processor of universal meanings, then the human beings who surround it are passive appendages—they are simply 'users'. On the other hand, if the person who receives the information, and the context in which they receive it, are significant in the creation of meaning, then the computer cannot be assigned this abstract, universal role.

With the advent of the personal computer, the individual who sits in front of it became a customer who chooses not only which machine to purchase, but also which software to purchase and use. That put a new concept of usability high on the list of desirable features. Bill Buxton has long been concerned with comparisons between the computer and other more traditional technologies.

> I use the analogy with brushes and instruments because they are the intermediaries between what is in the mind and its realization in the external world. Like computers, these technologies also have "users," *but it is almost an insult to describe them as such.* (Buxton, 1992)

Buxton makes clear that the ideology that surrounds the computer is different from the ideology that surrounds other everyday instruments. It is less empowering, binding us to abstract languages and concepts.

> The term *user* is unfortunate (but now unavoidable), as if we were habituated or addicted to the artefact. Good digital designs do not addict; they invite us to participate, to act and react. (Bolter and Gromola, 2003)

Gradually, the impact of mixed media computing is causing the whole ideology of 'information' to begin to unravel.

4.   INFORMATION COUNTER-CULTURES

4.1   Freedom of Information?

Though the computer emerged in the 1960s as a major symbol of conformity, many people working within computing at that time felt that they were part of a counter-culture (radicals within "the white heat of the technological revolution"). Computing techniques represented a new rationality—an instant way of replacing established procedures which were frequently based on prejudice and class superiority. The new technology had the potential for a new equality based upon freedom of speech, logic, transparency and empowerment.

At times this got very 'counter-cultural'. In 1965 Ted Nelson published a book 'Computer Lib/Machine Dreams'. The 1968 Fall Joint Computer Conference in the US was compared in its advance publicity to a "trippy rock concert". Computers were being seriously discussed in publications such as the *Whole Earth Catalog* and the magazine *Rolling Stone* and Timothy Leary even proclaimed the personal computer as "the LSD of the '90s". Whether expressed in such extrovert ways or in more introverted forms, such as informal dress and unusual working hours, people who worked with computers had a strong association with notions of personal freedom.

The notion of counter-culture is, however, relative to an historical context: what is counter-culture at one time may well become mainstream culture later. At first the personal libertarian ideology of people around computing was a counter-cultural position, but external political events were to change this. Ever since the beginnings of the Cold War in the late 1940s, the US State Department had promoted the doctrine of the free flow of information. It did this largely in opposition to the Soviet Bloc who often felt that cross-border information flow was equivalent to outside interference or aggression. For Cold War ideologists in the West, a particular notion of 'freedom' was central and, though this did not coincide with the personal libertarianism of the counter-culture, the distance between them was not great.

With the coming to power of Ronald Reagan and Margaret Thatcher, and the associated ideological shift towards free-market economics, a major realignment of computing occurred. Computer people do not like external authorities, external controls and restrictions on what can be done and often these sentiments led them to actively support free-market thinking. It may seem strange, but an early significant contributor to the very counter-cultural *Whole Earth Catalog* was Milton Friedman, one of the principle advocates of neo-liberal economic theory. Today, much of the counter-cultural elements of computing have been absorbed into the dominant economic libertarian culture.

From the standpoint of 2005, what can we say of the counter-culture of computing today? It is certainly ideologically fragmented in that it has no clear focus or unity. I can point to at least three separate loci of counter-cultures in computing.

4.2   Hackers and Anarchists

In the early days of computing the verb 'to hack' had a slightly different sense from what it has today. Up until the 1980s, 'to hack' meant to develop software in a manner that did not necessarily have a single rational organizing principle. A 'hacked' solution often worked but did not lead to elegant code. On the more positive side, it tended to exploit aspects of the machinery that more formal methods overlooked. It was this latter aspect, when taken in the context of communications systems, that led to the contemporary sense of the word,

To hack
To gain unauthorized access to (computer files, etc., or information held in one). (OED)

Despite many crackdowns by authorities, and many new laws and prosecutions, 'hacking' (in the contemporary sense) continues and has a vein of tacit support running right through the computing community. In the 1980s a number of hackers groups were formed (414s, Legion of Doom, Chaos Computer Club) and some not only still exist today, but are quite strong.

In 1990, a seemingly unlikely combination of people (a lyricist of a famous rock group, a Republican Party politician, the founder of a major software company and the founder of the *Whole Earth* project) came together to start the Electronic Frontier Foundation (EFF) dedicated to the preservation of free speech and freedom of expression in the new media (www.eff.com). It describes itself as "a modern group of freedom fighters" and adds "we fight measures that threaten basic human rights. Only the dominion we defend is the vast wealth of digital information, innovation, and technology that resides online". It extends this to defending hackers who have run foul of the law.

On the one hand, hacking is very negative and causes a great deal of frustration and expense; on the other, many people within computing see hacking as having a counter-cultural aspect that engenders some sympathy. We do not want to see the system win every time; we support the lonely underdog against the system. Given a chase between the police and someone they are chasing, there is (as the O.J. Simpson example showed) still a strong cultural identification with the person being chased.

4.3 Political Activism

On February 11, 1995 a letter was distributed widely throughout electronic networks containing an appeal from the "The Indigenous Clandestine Revolutionary Committee, General Command of the EZLN". It read:

> Brothers and sisters, the government of Ernesto Zedillo is killing us, it is killing children, it is attacking women and raping them. We ask the people of Mexico and all the people of the world to do something to stop this war.

This is often cited as the first major example of the use of Internet to raise international support for a political struggle. The EZLN has been involved in a civil insurrection against the Mexican government in the region of Chiapas since 1994 and made this use of the Internet to gain international support to stop an intensive military campaign against them. It was a tactic that was largely successful.

On 27 June 2002 thousands of trade unionists around the world took part in protest action calling for the immediate release of imprisoned trade unionists in South Korea. In the run-up to Korea co-hosting the football World Cup, a total of 52 trade unionists were in prison on account of legitimate activities, including the president of the Korean Confederation of Trade Unions. A concerted international day of action was organized directly through the use of digital communications technology. It was successful in getting several unionists released from prison (http://www.imfmetal.org/main/index.cfm?id=47&l=2&cid=7204 also http://www.global-unions.org/korea2002.asp).

These are but two of many examples of the Internet being used for political action that is counter to state power. It had long raised concerns within the US Military,

> ... an insurgent or drug trafficking group's access to and utilization of electronic media technology for exploiting the information superhighway will bolster their support networks and enhance their command and control. (U.S. Army intelligence, 1994)

The US Dept of Defense, working within the paradigm of the free-flow of information, saw the Internet as a potential new medium for the extension of Cold War policies:

The Internet is clearly a significant long term strategic threat to
authoritarian regimes, one that they will be unable to counter
effectively. News from the outside world brought by the Internet into
nations subjugated by such regimes will clash with the distorted
versions provided by their governments, eroding the credibility of their
positions and encouraging unrest. (Swett, 1995)

It was then but a short step to argue that freedom of information provides
the context for a new type of human intervention. To ensure that US foreign
policy prevails, the Report suggests that the Internet may be used
'offensively',

The U.S. might be able to employ the Internet offensively to help
achieve unconventional warfare objectives. ...Just as the U.S. could be
vulnerable to disinformational e-mail, politically active groups using
the Internet could be vulnerable to deceptive messages introduced by
hostile persons or groups. ...

Some of its uses might include...Cultivating political and even
operational support for the U.S. side and opposition to the other side.
(Swett, 1995)

Faced with such blatant political use of the Internet, the counter-culture
has developed more imaginative responses. One example of such political
activism is the activities of the 'Yes Men', recently recorded in a full-length
documentary film. The 'Yes Men' have been involved in a number of
actions aimed at what they term, 'Identity Correction'. For example, through
their ownership of the domain name for GATT (the precursor of the World
Trade Organization) they occasionally receive requests to send speakers to
conferences in the belief that they are the real WTO. On occasions they have
responded and sent a speaker who, in a creative way, tries to give a more
'correct' view of the organization, i.e., one as seen from a counter-cultural
perspective (see www.theyesmen.org). For an example of their activities, see
the following announcement on their website.

WTO to announce schedule for disbanding

After a protracted and detailed review of current trade policy and its
effects on developing countries, the World Trade Organization has
decided to effect a cessation of all operations, to be accomplished over
a period of several months. The WTO will eventually reintegrate as a
new trade body whose charter will be to ensure that trade benefits the
poor. (www.gatt.org)

4.4 Digital Artists and Designers

The work of digital artists has also, at times, been seen in opposition to mainstream culture. In 1971 a retrospective exhibition by the cybernetic artist Hans Haacke at the Guggenheim Museum in New York was cancelled because one of the proposed works was a list of the real-estate holdings of the trustees of the museum.

Artists were part of the large Internet campaign to organize opposition to the latest war against Iraq. On Monday, 3 March 2003, artists and performers in 59 countries co-ordinated 1,029 readings of *Lysistrata*, Aristophanes' anti-war comedy, to protest the Bush Administration's unilateral war on Iraq (www.lysistrata.com) in what was billed as the "First-Ever Worldwide Theatrical Act Of Dissent".

A few artists have chosen to directly address the computer interface as the content of their art and produce works that make us feel uncomfortable because what we take as basic and given—the operating system, or common applications software—no longer behaves as we expect. For example, in 1995, Jeff Instone used the Macintosh WIMP interface as the vehicle for an 'interactive text' ('The Word Beyond Speech', 1995); or more recently Adrian Ward created 'Auto-Illustrator', a seeming copy of Adobe Illustrator with some unexpected responses and which he describes as a "parody of commercial software" (www.signwave.co.uk). Part of the purpose of these works is to demonstrate that the computer need not always be as it appears, that the operating system and software you use are the result of conscious design and could have been, and could be, different.

While such interventions are still, in a sense, oppositional, as we move from considering art to design, we move to a different set of issues (Winograd and Flores, 1987). In their book *Windows and Mirrors*, Bolter and Gromola point to a contemporary debate within the digital design community. On the one side there are the so-called 'structuralists' who believe that the ultimate aim of good design is the invisibility or transparency of the designed object. Hence, Donald Norman wrote a book entitled *The Invisible Computer* (Norman, 1998) in which he argued that computers will disappear into 'information appliances', in just the same way as electric motors have disappeared into vacuum cleaners, power tools and DVD-players.

A similar viewpoint to Norman's has been put forward by Jakob Nielsen (2000) with respect to web design. Nielsen argues that web pages should be transparent vehicles for information delivery. The information exists outside the system and the web page design should simply, efficiently and effectively deliver the required information to the user. It is a classical position from within the 'information processing' paradigm. There is a strict distinction between form and content; the design of digital interfaces is part of the 'form' and its role should be to provide access to the content without distortion of any kind. This is an inherently conservative position as it requires complete adherence to the cultural norm of representation. One is not allowed to question, or even embellish, the coded information within the system.

Against this viewpoint is the influence, within multimedia computing, of a growing number of film makers, graphic designers, artists and performers who simply do not accept that the 'message' is separate from the 'medium' and who see the process of narration, of telling, of revealing as being "to fascinate, exhilarate, and sometimes provoke us" (Bolter and Gromola, 2003). These designers do not accept that the technology works within an 'information processing' paradigm, and they produce works that at least open up a more engaging and open relationship between the computer and the person who experiences it.

Many of today's digital artists and designers are challenging the intention of software designers and finding unexpected new uses for the technology. Artists are using networking to establish working co-operatives that exchange work and enable many artists to contribute to the same work. Performers are using the Internet as a stage upon which to create novel performance work. Within these and other works it is possible to see elements of disrespect for the supposed functionality of the software, but also a disruptive element that can be traced back to Brecht.

5.   CONCLUSION

We have seen how discourses of the Arts and Sciences are not only different but that, at different historical stages, they have had different relationships to questions of accountability, responsibility, ethics, values and politics. From the 1930s to the 1960s the sciences were seen as progressive within Western societies, but by the 1970s they had retreated to a claimed neutrality and by the twenty-first century the word 'technical' has conservative connotations, signifying a lack of fundamental questioning. It is only be 'breaking the rules', by 'thinking outside the box' and by being 'creative' that progress is now made.

Insofar as we can consider the digital computer as a focus for a description of society, then we may observe that while it initially thrived upon an alternative and libertarian culture, this has become absorbed in the new dominant culture of the free-market, through which concepts such as 'information' and 'information society' have become accepted uncritically as part of the common system of thought.

From the beginnings of computing there have always been alternative views, the earliest probably being that of cybernetics. These have been put aside in the social and political shaping of computing and it is only recently that the conditions have been such for new alternatives to emerge. These have often been in the guise of the Arts and have been associated with anti-capitalist political movements which currently form about the only ideological opposition from within Western societies.

So, while it is important to pursue ethics and accountability from within the dominant cultural perspective that will always be, in my view, 'negative ethics', which is to say that it will attempt to respond to particular issues that have arisen in agendas such as globalization, the information society and the global free-flow of information. It is work that, of course, has to be undertaken, but it is not the only work. There is also the work of daring to imagine how things might be different, of helping to design an alternative future, one that is positive and one that a person can believe in. The inspiration for this will come from artists, from counter-cultures, and many others, but the work itself is that of designers. It is time to reassert the politics of design and time that scientists, in the broadest sense, attempted to return to the position they held over 50 years ago – as optimists who believed that they could tackle and solve major problems in the world, such as the division between the rich and the poor.

REFERENCES

Arnold, R.R., Hill, H.C. & Nichols, A.V. (1978) Modern Data Processing, 3rd edition. John Wiley, Santa Barbara.

Ascott, R. (2003) Telematic Embrace. University of California Press, Berkeley, CA.

Beardon, C. (1994) Computers, postmodernism and the culture of the artificial. AI & Society, 8, 1-16.

Bell, D. (1960) The End of Ideology. The Free Press, New York.

Bell, D. (1973) The Coming of Post-Industrial Society: A Venture in Social Forecasting. Basic Books, NY.

Bjerknes, G. & Bratteteig, T. (1995) User participation – a strategy for work life democracy? In R. Trigg, S.I. Anderson & E. Dykstra-Erikson (ed.) PDC'94 Proceedings of the participatory design conference, Chapel Hill, NC, 27-28 October 1994, pp.3-11. Computer Professionals for Social Responsibility (CSPR), Palo Alto, CA.

Bolter, J.D. and Gromola, D. (2003) Windows and mirrors: interaction design, digital art, and the myth of transparency. MIT Press, Camb, Mass.

Buxton, W. (1992) Snow's two cultures revisited. In L. Jacobson (Ed.), Cyberarts: Exploring art & technology, Miller Freeman, San Francisco, pp. 24 – 31.

Davis, G.B. (1969) Computer Data Processing. McGraw-Hill, New York.

Eco, U. (1989) The Open Work. Harvard University Press.

Frates, J. & Moldrup, W. (1983) Computers and Life: an integrative approach. Prentice-Hall, Englewood Cliffs, NJ.

Gere, C. (2002) Digital Culture. Reaktion Books, London.

Gore, M.R. & Stubbe, J.W. (1979) Computers and Data Processing. McGraw-Hill, New York.

Heims, S. (1980) John von Neumann and Norbert Weiner: from mathematics to the technologies of life and death. MIT Press, Camb, Mass.

Katz, J. (1997) The Digital Citizen. Wired, 5:12, Dec 1997.

Lovejoy, M. (2004) Digital Currents. Routledge, New York.

Machlup, F. (1983) Semantic Quirks in Studies of Information. In Machlup, F. & Mansfield, U. (eds.) The study of information. John Wiley & Sons, New York, p. 641-671.

Mattelart, A. (2003) The Information Society: An Introduction. Sage, London.

Nielsen, J. (2000) Designing Web Usability. New Riders, Indianapolis.

Norman, D. (1998) The Invisible Computer: Why Good Products Can Fail, the Personal Computer is So Complex, and Information Appliances Are the Solution. MIT Press, Camb, Mass.

Porat, M. (1977) The Information Economy: Definition and Measurement. US Government Printing Office, Washington, DC.

Jared Sandberg (1994) Fringe Groups Can Say Almost Anything And Not Worry About Getting Punched, The Wall Street Journal, December 8, 1994, pp. B1-B4.

Shannon, C. and Weaver, W. (1949) The Mathematical Theory of Communication. University of Illinois Press, Urbana-Champaign, IL.

Smith, Z. (2002) The Autograph Man. Hamish Hamilton, London.

Snow, C. P. (1964) The two cultures: and a second look. Cambridge University Press.

Swett, C. (1995) Strategic Assessment:The Internet. US Department of Defense, Office of the Assistant Secretary of Defense for Special Operations and Low-Intensity Conflict.

http://www.fas.org/cp/swett.html#Abstract, accessed 17/2/05

Toulmin, S. (1991) The dream of an exact language. In: B. Göranzon & M. Florin (eds) Dialogue and technology: art and knowledge. Springer-Verlag, London.

U.S. Army Intelligence (1994) Technical Applications For Insurgents (unclassified) (3 August 1994).

Verzello, R.J. & Reutter III, J. (1982) Data Processing: systems and concepts. McGraw-Hill, London.

Winograd, T. and Flores, F. (1987) Understanding computers and cognition: a new foundation for design. Addison-Wesley, Reading, Mass.

WHEN IS IT GOOD TO STEAL? A MORAL REFLECTION ON CURRENT TRENDS IN INTELLECTUAL PROPERTY

J.J. Britz, S.R. Ponelis

Britz is with the School of Information Studies, University of Wisconsin-Milwaukee, USA and Ponelis is with the² School of Information Technology, University of Pretoria, South Africa

Abstract: This paper explores the role of intellectual property rights in the distribution of information in the marketplace. It is argued that the current trends in IP legislation bring an imbalance between access to scholarly information and its control. It is further argued that scholarly information is essential in nature and that people cannot be excluded from it. It therefore poses a moral concern. Based on the work of John Rawls general guidelines are proposed that can be used directly by policymakers with regard to the fair distribution of scholarly information in the marketplace.

1. INTRODUCTION

Intellectual property rights (IPRs) constitute a legal mechanism to make information excludable, i.e. to legally protect the economic value of information. Information plays an important role in the education of members of a society. A major source of information for this purpose are scholarly publications, the intellectual property rights of which are generally held by the publishers of the journals. The increasingly stricter control of access exercised by these publishers on scholarly information gives rise to a moral question, namely, is the extent of the high pricing of scholarly information justifiable? It is well known that many scholars, particularly in the developing world, cannot afford access to scholarly journals. The moral question is even more applicable to information that is electronically available – considering that the marginal cost of electronic information is nearly zero.

In order to answer the aforementioned question, the paper will be structured as follows: first, we will provide a broad introduction to the problem, namely the imbalance between access to and control of intellectual property; second, the moral concerns will be discussed together with the associated complexity of moral reasoning; and last, general guidelines will be formulated based on the Rawlian perspective of social justice.

1.1   Control of Versus Access to Information

Information has played an increasingly important role in several economies, particularly in those of industrialized countries. Given this development in these economies, information has increasingly become a commodity; as a result, the value of information is of paramount importance. The value that information can have varies and the same information can have more than one type of value, which is determined by its use. Broadly speaking, these kinds of value can be related to either the domain of common or public good, or to private good. The kinds of value together with the applicable category are indicated in **Table 1**.

Table 1: Kinds of value of information (from Lor and Britz, 2005)

Competitive value	Lies in possessing information that others do not (yet) have that can be exploited to gain a livelihood or competitive advantage.	Private good
Instrumental value	Found in the application of information to improve the capacity of humankind to cope with the environment.	Common or public good
Accumulative value	Lies in being used to build upon the contributions of others in order to create and generate new information.	
Educational value[1]	Equipping successive generations of humans to improve the quality of their lives and the quality of their environment.	
Cultural value	Strengthening the cohesion of communities and societies/enhancing the quality of communal living.	
Transcendent value	Relates to satisfaction of aesthetic, religious, spiritual or higher needs, i.e., non-material quality of life.	

---

[1] Closely linked to accumulative value for the educational value of information enables accumulative value.

Information, furthermore, has certain characteristics that distinguish it from other economic goods, namely:

- An information good must be used or consumed in order to demonstrate the good and to determine the associated value;
- Information goods are typically non-rival (that is, one person's consumption does not diminish another's ability to consume the same information good) and sometimes non-excludable (that is, one person's consumption cannot exclude another person from consuming the information – or as Barlow (1993) put it: "information can be transferred without leaving the possession of the original owner"); and
- The cost structure of information goods comprises a high fixed cost but low variable and marginal costs (Varian, 1998).

The atypical cost structure of information goods in competitive markets results in the price of information goods tending to zero since these markets drive prices towards marginal costs. In order to counter this, the competitive value must be protected so that the act of creation of information in economies and societies can be supported and stimulated through compensation for creation. This is done legally by means of the concept of intellectual property (IP) and intellectual property rights (IPRs).

Intellectual property is defined as a means of acquiring ownership over a particular resource that is intangible in nature and usually involves the protection of some of invention that is created by the human mind. As such IP includes music, novels, medicines, computer software and products obtained from the use of indigenous knowledge (Prakash, 1999). Du Plessis (1999) defines intellectual property as incorporeal or intangible property that comes into existence through the mental or intellectual activity and creativity of a person; once created, the property has an independent existence separate from and outside of the person of the creator and has commercial value and thus merits legal protection. IPRs are traditionally divided into statutory and common law rights, with the former constituting the majority of the rights. These comprise the four major categories: patents, trade marks, industrial designs and copyright. Other IPRs include plant breeders' rights, heraldic rights and performers' rights (Du Plessis, 1999).

Scholarly publication is a major source of information creation. Compensation in the scholarly arena goes to the publishers who hold the copyright to the journals, and in the case of other academic publications in which academic work is presented, compensation is shared rather then going to the authors (although authors are sometimes paid a modest amount). However the authors, are funded either by their institutions, governments, research institutions, normally but not exclusively in the form of grants[2]. Upon examination of the major scholarly publishers it is clear that handsome profits are to be had by these information intermediaries: In 2003 Reed Elsevier's pre-tax profits totalled £222 million compared with £216 million the previous year (Sabbagh, 2004). In addition, Sabbagh (2004) reports that Elsevier also proposed a 5.5% price increase because it was "increasing the content it was producing and investing in new electronic features." The UK's Commons Science and Technology Committee furthermore reported that the price of scientific publications had increased by 58% since 1998 and accuses Reed Elsevier of "not being transparent" about its costs and "ripping off the academic community" (Sabbagh, 2004), which is in essence a captive audience.

Information contained in scholarly publications plays a vital role in education. Education is seen as having a positive ancillary social value for a society (Bates, 1988). Bates (1988) is of the opinion that where ancillary social value is concerned, real-life markets do not seem economically efficient nor generate maximum social welfare thus resulting in sub-optimal markets. According to him it will threaten the sustainability of information-based societies and contribute to the digital divide and widen the gap between the so-called information 'haves' and the 'have-nots'.

Shapiro and Varian (1998) noted that the unique and atypical cost structure of information leads to a propensity for monopolies to be created in the marketplace. Most countries try to prevent monopolistic tendencies since control of a market results in the very real possibility for prices to be set without much or any cognizance being taken of the market's willingness (or ability) to pay. Having the economic control in the scholarly publishing industry therefore makes it far more likely for prices to be beyond the reach of those in developing countries, who are unable to pay the prices thus set, due to unfavourable exchange rates, etc.

It is important to note that the recognition and application of IPRs *per se* is not being disputed. Based on the Lockeian labour theory and the Hegelian personality theory it is argued that individuals have property rights and that this extends to intangible IPRs. These rights need to be protected by government and individuals have the right to benefit from them. As

---

[2] "Generally applicable to basic or sometimes applied research, it is based on the principle of cost reimbursement rather than on the value of the output since the form of new knowledge can obviously not be predicted. To manage costs, monitoring and performance is usually built in" (Ponelis and Britz, 2004).

Hamelink (1999:158) correctly points out, intellectual property regimes are developed to:

- Protect the moral rights of authors (moral justification);
- Recognize and protect the right to fair compensation for the creation and distribution of information goods (economic justification); and
- Enhance, to the benefit of the common good, the creation and accessibility of new knowledge (social justification).

It is, however, clear from the above that there is a tension between control and access[3]: publishers need to control distribution of information in order to protect their interests but access to scholarly information is needed for education and development. The increase in pricing of scholarly publications led to the marginalization of many scholars and even from preventing them access to information. IPRs in effect is allowing the private good to partially eclipse the common or public good, as depicted in **Error! Reference source not found.**. This increasing imbalance in the tension between control and access gives rise to a moral question which begs for a moral response.

Figure 1: The private good's partial eclipse of the common/public good

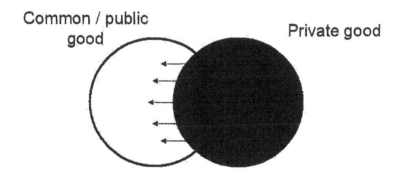

[3] Access does not also imply accessibility; accessibility is a broader concept and encompasses, for example, understanding the language in which information is conveyed, sharing the context in which it is created, etc. The argument here is about access and not accessibility.

2.   COMPLEX NATURE OF THE MORAL ARGUMENT

The moral response to this tension is complicated by the complexity of the moral argument. There are a number of factors that contribute to the complex nature, namely:

Complexity of information—Information can be used for many different purposes, for example, education at primary, secondary and tertiary levels; entertainment; and marketing. Educational use differs from entertainment and marketing in the sense that it can be considered as essential information. It can be argued that the paradigm for legal protection of information should be based on the uses of information rather than on the control of the making of copies (Branscomb, 1994:6) and that information considered essential should be treated differently in terms of IPRs.

Publishers argue that they need to cover costs of production—but is it acceptable to push all these costs to the end-user/consumer? Several movements, for example, copyleft and the Creative Commons (and its offshoot the Scientific Commons) aim to make electronic information available freely to end-users under a number of licensing arrangement; the costs of production is borne by the author(s), thereby preventing entry into the private good domain by means of IPRs legislation. Both scientific authors and their funding bodies are also increasingly endeavouring to provide freer access to scholarly information, with the medical sciences acting as pioneers – possibly a result of the controversial nature of denial of access leading to loss of, if not lives, then at least quality of lives in both developed and developing countries. For example, in the medical sciences, the National Institute of Health (NIH) in the United States requires all publications of research to which it had contributed funds be made available for free one year after publication in a journal. Although journal publishers are not pleased about this, refusing to comply could well result in the loss of around 60,000 papers annually, many of which are considered to be the best in the field (The Economist, 2005). There are also a number of electronic peer-reviewed academic journals that charge authors to publish and make content available to end-users at no cost; these journals are being included on Thomson's ISI listings.

Instrumental, accumulative and educational value of information eroded—Higher education institutions, in a bid to increase ever-decreasing funding from traditional sources are attempting to move their scholarly research outputs out of the common good domain into the private good domain through IPRs in order to benefit financially. For example, Columbia University patented a process, the validity of which is now being disputed by seven biotechnology firms in the United States (The Economist, 2004). As a result the traditional "experimental use" exception for non-commercial research granted to universities to bypass IPRs compensation is also being challenged.

Economic choices—End-users make choices in terms of consumption based on their priorities. For example, many students have a mobile phone but argue that textbooks are too expensive to buy. Price is an economic mechanism through which resources are allocated as such is a measurement or function of the value that a consumer places on the good exchanged (Du Toit, 1994; Rowley, 1997). According to Rowley (1997), price plays a central role in the availability and access to information goods. IPRs provide the legal instruments to protect these economic interests.

Price discrimination exists when sales of identical goods are transacted at different prices from a single vendor. Vendors use price discrimination for a variety of reasons. A customer may have to pay more if the seller determines that he or she is willing to – for example, because of the customer's wealth, carelessness, lack of knowledge, or eagerness to buy. The practice of taking advantage of a state of imbalance between two (or possibly more) markets where price discrimination is exercised is called arbitrage. Sellers of goods and services often attempt to prohibit or discourage arbitrage.[4]

Discouraging arbitrage entails either keeping the different price groups separate, making price comparisons difficult, or restricting pricing information; these mechanisms result in a boundary between segments known as a rate fence. With e-commerce on the Internet, however, it is easy to compare prices from different vendors or the same vendor in different geographic locations and to make an economically prudent buying decision, thereby eroding the effectiveness of the rate fence. For example, students in the United States regularly buy textbooks from the book retailer Amazon's UK website[5] for £40 rather than for US$80 on the US website[6]. Using price discrimination as a mechanism to ensure access to information goods to developing countries may result in a similar situation arising.

---

[4] Note that over time arbitrage tends to reduce price discrimination through, for example, adjustments in exchange rates for currency.

[5] URL http://www.amazon.co.uk

[6] URL http://www.amazon.com

Global trade requires control—agreements such as the World Trade Organization's (WTO) Trade-Related Aspects of Intellectual Property Rights (TRIPS) and bodies like the World Intellectual Property Organization (WIPO) are necessary to regulate global trade, but who is advantaged and who disadvantaged through the exercise of control? Branscomb (1994) is of the opinion that information technology can be used as a solution to offer universal access, but she expresses doubt as to the collective will worldwide to do so. Poor developing countries are voiceless with regard to decisions that directly affect them although there are efforts to counter this, for example, the proposal by a number of developing countries including Brazil and Argentina with regard to a new development agenda on IP (WIPO, 2004).

By using simulation, Maxwell (2004) showed that "the same policy options have different effects depending on the condition of the publishing industry at any stage of development." For example, during the early stages of development, adequate capitalization is far more critical than the recognition of copyright. This is contrary to the view advocated by many in favour of strong copyright protection in developing countries saying that it is beneficial to development because it attracts overseas capital investment (Maskus, 2000): strong international IPRs may in fact impair the developing countries' ability to develop local publishing capability, thus slowing the growth and health of publishing and authorship in these countries. Maxwell's model therefore suggests that "developing country trade protectionism, coupled with moderate copyright protection and initial price controls, might be more beneficial to the development of domestic publishing in Third World countries" which is of course heavily opposed by the US and WIPO. As Barlow (1993) has stated, laws developed prior to consensus in a society usually favour the already established few who get them passed and not society as a whole.

Progression in knowledge production determine a country's response to IP—Varian (1998) indicates the positive relationship between per capita income in a country and recognition of IPRs: as the demand for local content increases when consumers have more disposable income, the protection of local as well as other content is increasingly recognised in order to stimulate creation. This has been the case in India. Thus, overall economic security should automatically result in recognition for IPRs but in its absence, one can expect there to be little incentive to create information goods or to respect the IP of others.

IP is based on individual property rights, a hallmark of the Western intellectual tradition; China (Lara, 1998) and countries in Africa do not have an inherent culture of IP and therefore of its protection. Confucianism and the emphasis on the good of society at the expense of personal reward gives rise to the notion in China that it is an honour to copy someone's work (Lara, 1998); however, Chinese cultural conceptions as justification for industrial scale piracy in China are not as easily defended nor accepted.

Lehman (2002) is one among many who argue that developing countries must use IPRs as a tool for economic growth; but if the concept is culturally alien, is it possible for them to do so without any assistance from outside which again raises the question of dependence or whether it is acceptable to expect them to do so? Furthermore, the nature of indigenous knowledge (IK), which is a valuable source for development and scientific research, is frequently such that it does not allow for protection by IPRs, since for example, it may not meet the criteria of uniqueness, or of having an identified creator or author, etc.

If one accepts Maxwell's conclusions from his simulation on the effects of IPRs in a society, then some interesting questions arise: are the IPRs enforced on developing countries appropriate to the state of development of their respective publishing industries? In other words, will sufficient new creators join the marketplace to reach the critical mass necessary for Varian's argument to hold true? And, if the publishing industries in developed countries are indeed mature and if aggressive market expansion into developing countries is advised, will this not flood the developing countries markets with culturally alien goods (which again raises the question of access as opposed to accessibility)? Again, there is a tension between access to the private good and destruction of cultural diversity as common good.

UNESCO's *Convention on the Protection of the Diversity of Cultural Contents and Artistic Expressions* aims to allow countries to implement policies that foster cultural diversity. However, some governments have proposed revisions that would transform this Convention into an instrument that further extends corporate ownership of culture. The US is particularly concerned that the Convention might be used to support trade barriers against it. The Communication Rights in the Information Society (CRIS) campaign points out that references to IPRs (private good) protection in the Convention must be balanced with protection of the cultural commons (common good), which is not currently the case. Negotiations are continuing on various aspects of this Convention (Media Trade Monitor, 2005).

3.   USING RAWLS' PRINCIPLES OF SOCIAL
JUSTICE TO DEVELOP GENERAL GUIDELINES

According to Britz (1999) justice viewed from an Aristotelian perspective can be broadly defined as giving a person or group what they deserve. Justice has a two-fold objective: preventing harm and demanding treatment that is respectful of humanity. As such it can be said to be a virtue of a moral agent. Rawls re-established social justice in contemporary moral reasoning in his work Theory of Justice (1973) and is of the opinion that justice is "the first virtue of social institutions, as truth is in systems of thought" (Rawls, 1973).

Rawls views justice as fairness and argues for the fair distribution of social goods in a society. Approaching justice as fairness is necessary to ensure that the basic rights and liberties of all are protected and that should social and economic inequalities exist these should still be to the benefit of all. Rawls (1973) formulated two principles of justice to ensure fair distribution of social goods in a society. These principles state that:

1.   "Each person is to have an equal right to the most extensive total system of basic liberties compatible with a similar system of liberty for all".
2.   Social and economic inequalities that do exist are to be arranged so that they can be reasonably expected to be to everyone's advantage and be attached to positions and office that are open to all.

The authors propose that these two principles of Rawls be used as a moral tool to develop general guidelines for resolving the tension between control and access to scholarly information with specific reference to developing nations.

According to the first principle all people are fundamentally equal, have equal intrinsic human rights together with the freedom to exercise them without infringement on the similar rights of others. These basic rights ought to form the foundation of the fair distribution of social goods in society. The right to access to essential information (i.e. the common or public good category) can be seen as such a basic right because of its essential nature in satisfying all basic rights and as such should be taken into account in the development of any IPRs system. IPRs must therefore ensure that each person at least has access to the minimum information to satisfy essential needs. Failure to do so can be said to be a form of information injustice. According to Kingma (2001), there are various mechanisms to ensure fair distribution of essential information, including government subsidies through taxation, donations, and advertising. For poor and developing nations this normative guideline is of even more relevance in order to ensure access to essential information.

The second principle implies that certain information goods can be treated as commodities, i.e. as private goods, and be distributed and used unequally in a society. Thus fair compensation for authors through IPRs is accommodated and the inequalities arising out of the competitive value of information justified. But there are some provisos: first, such information ownership rights are allowed only when it is to the benefit of all (Rawls, 1973). Should this not be the case, it is unjust. Second, there should at least be equal opportunities for everyone to access essential information and have the opportunity to contribute as a creator of information goods. Last, the permissible inequalities are always secondary to the first principle (Rawls, 1973). The authors are therefore arguing that the right to access to essential information (common good) can and must take precedence over the right to ownership of information (private good).

Applying Rawls' two principles the imbalance between the common and private good, or access and ownership, must be restored in terms of information goods. This would reflect the dual purpose of IPRs and will allow for a more equitable intellectual property regime appropriate for developing nations. In terms of the earlier metaphor, the ground conceded to the common good need to be reclaimed as depicted in
Figure 2.

Figure 2: Restoring balance between common/public & private good
The following two guidelines can be presented to ensure the fair and just distribution of essential information to developing countries:

- Since the right of access to essential information is more important than the right to ownership, IPRs should protect information as a common good (also referred to as the information commons) and ensure that the

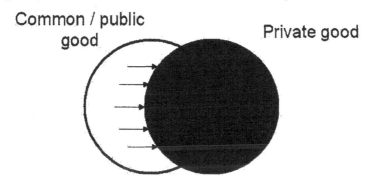

Common / public good   Private good

information needed to satisfy basic needs, such as agriculture and education, is distributed in such a manner that everyone has access to it and an equal opportunity to benefit from it. In developing countries, this aspect is of particular importance in the cases of indigenous knowledge that have become subject to IPRs.

- Creators and distributors of information goods can claim moral and economic rights on the conditions that these rights:
  - Do not prevent creativity;
  - Shrink the gap between the information rich and poor; and
  - Ensure fair compensation for the original creators. Again, this is of vital importance to developing countries when it comes to indigenous knowledge.

4. CONCLUSION

In this paper, it was argued that the distribution of scholarly information must be fair in the marketplace. It is based on the view that education is essential and that people cannot be excluded from access to educational material, including scholarly publications. It was furthermore argued that the current trend in IP legislation favours the stricter control of access to scholarly material. This poses the moral question of the fair distribution of scholarly information in the marketplace. Based on the social justice theory of John Rawls it was argued that access to scholarly information is essential and more important than the right to own or protect it.

REFERENCES

Bates, B.J. (1988), Information as an Economic Good: Sources of Individual and Social Value. In: The Political Economy of Information, ed. Mosco, V. and Wasko, J. Madison, Wisconsin: The University of Wisconsin Press, pp. 76-94.

Branscomb, A. W. (1994), The Economics of Information—Public and Private Domains of Information: Defining the Legal Boundaries (adapted from the keynote address presented at the 1994 ASIS annual Meeting in Alexandria, Virginia), online at http://www.asis.org/Bulletin/Dec-94/branscom.html accessed 17.02. 2005

Britz, J. J. (1999), Access to Information: The ethical challenges to the information era. In: The Ethics of Electronic Information in the Twenty-First Century. Century. Ed. Pourciau, L. West Lafayette: Purdue University Press, pp. 9-29.

Lor, P.J. & Britz, J.J. (S.a.), Knowledge production, international information flows and intellectual property: an African perspective. International Information and Library Review. In press.

Du Plessis, E. (1999), Intellectual property and intellectual freedom. The Moral and Legal Challenges of the Information Era, University of Pretoria, Pretoria, South Africa, 24-25 May 1999.

Du Toit, A.S. (1994), Developing a price strategy for information products. South African Journal of Library and Information Services, 62 (4): 162 – 167.

Hamelink, C. J. (1999), Digitaal Fatsoen: Mensenrechten in Cyberspace. Amsterdam: Boom.

Kingma, B. R. (2001), The Economics of Information: A Guide to Economic and Cost-Benefit Analysis for Information Professionals. Littleton, Colorado: Libraries Unlimited.

Lara, G. (1998), The Piracy of American Films in China: Why the U.S. Art Form is not Protected by Copyright Laws in the People's Republic of China, UCLA Journal of International Law And Foreign Affairs 2(2):343-352.

Lehman, B. (2002), Key Report Sends Developing Countries a Distorted Message on IP Rights. Legal Times, accessed online 12.02.2005 at http://www.IPRscommission.org/graphic/Views_articles/Legal_Times.htm

Maskus, K.E. (2000), Intellectual property rights in the global economy. Washington, D.C.: Institute for International Economics.

Maxwell, T. (2004), Is copyright necessary? First Monday 9(9), online at http://firstmonday.org/issues/issue9_9/maxwell/index.html accessed 15.02. 2005.

Media Trade Monitor. (2005), UNESCO Convention on Cultural Diversity, online at http://www.mediatrademonitor.org/taxonomy/page/or/30 accessed 21.01.2005

Ponelis, S. R. and Britz, J. J. (2004), Teaching Information Economics to Undergraduate Information Science Students at the University of Pretoria. South African Journal of Information Management, December 2004, 6(4).

Prakash, S. (1999), Towards a synergy between biodiversity and intellectual property rights. Journal of World Intellectual Property, 2(5).

Rawls, J. (1973), A Theory of Justice. Cambridge: The Belknap Press of Harvard University Press.

Rowley, J. (1997), Principles of price and pricing policies for the information marketplace. Library Review, 46 (3): 179 – 189.

Sabbagh, D. (2004), Reed Elsevier chief hits back in scientific publishing row. Times Online, online at http://business.timesonline.co.uk/article/0,,9071-1204570,00.html accessed 17.01.2005

Scholars for dollars. (2004), The Economist, December 11th 2004, p. 55.

Shapiro, C. and Varian, H. R. (1998), Versioning: The Smart Way to Sell Information. Harvard Business Review, November-December 1998: 106-114.

The triumph of the commons. (2005), The Economist, February 12th 2005, pp. 55-56.

Varian, H. R. (1998), Markets for Information Goods, online at http://www.sims.berkeley.edu/~hal/Papers/japan/index.html accessed 17.02.2005

Who pays the piper… (2005), The Economist, February 12th 2005, pp. 70-72.

WIPO. (2004), Proposal by Argentina and Brazil for the Establishment of a Development Agenda for WIPO (WO/GA/31/11). WIPO General Assembly, Thirty-First (15th Extraordinary) Session, Geneva, September 27 to October 5, 2004.

SOCIALLY RESPONSIBLE INTERNATIONAL INTELLECTUAL PROPERTY RIGHTS IN SOFTWARE AND OTHER DIGITALLY DISTRIBUTABLE MATERIAL

Kai K. Kimppa
Lecturer, LABORIS research laboratory, Department of Information Technology, University of Turku

Abstract: In this paper relativistic ethical theories are handled in relation to intellectual property rights (IPRs). Different cultural traditions are a descriptive fact, and many such traditions—past and present—will be presented. It will be shown that the current Western versions of IPRs are offered as the only viable options in negotiations in international organisations such as the World Trade organization (WTO) and the World Intellectual Property Organization (WIPO) as well as in uni-, bi- and other multilateral negotiations by most Western countries. Free and open source software (F/OSS) and IPR systems similar to it are offered as a possibilities to respect the local traditions, although any local traditions are encouraged to be tried as options to the cultural homogenisation which the international treaties offer instead.

Key words: Social responsibility, IPRs, immaterial, tolerance, relativism, F/OSS

1. INTRODUCTION

First, relativism and its relationship—if any—to tolerance will be looked at. It will be shown that relativism *per se* does not promote tolerance, but since tolerance is an important value of liberal Western democracies and at least cultural relativism an established fact, it will be claimed that other IPR traditions should be given a chance to show whether they promote the good of mankind or not.

Intellectual creations make a post-industrial nation. If a nation has poor access to and poor levels of intellectual creativity in the form of immaterial creations, it is unlikely that the nation in question will rise even to an industrialized, let alone post-industrial level. There are many historical examples of how the access to immaterial creations has been handled by various strategies, ranging from a no-IPR policy, through government control of IPRs, to a policy of enforcing IPRs strongly within a country, but not respecting external IPRs (i.e., those in other countries) – In Western and other countries during their industrialization. Some of those will be examined in this paper. A surprising similarity can be found between the current IPR traditions of developing countries and those countries which have developed recently, with approaches that could be of benefit to the developing countries. Countries in similar situations to recently industrialized Western countries today include nations such as Brazil, China and other Second World countries that have been working on rising from the status of a Second World country to that of a First World country for some time. Third World countries generally do not have the infrastructure to fully exploit either a strong IPR policy or to benefit from the possibilities a no-IPR policy would grant them, if it was possible to establish such a policy. Even the poorest nations could benefit some, however, and could possibly enhance their best and brightest possibility to be included in the global society of immaterial creations.

Subsequently, the international treaties and organizations will be examined and their undoubted one-sidedness discussed. Finally, alternative possibilities to the system of IPRs promoted by Western countries will be considered. Some problems and possible future directions of IPRs are mapped in the concluding sections.

2.   RELATIVISM

It is difficult to define what constitutes a culture. A typical first example would be a nation (state). Nations are not, however, homogenous groups but are constituted from various different groups which may interact with one another. Nor are cultures limited within national boundaries. The groups within and between nations can be native tribes, hacker communities, business leaders, university students, religious groups, etc. These groups do, however, typically share at least some values to some degree. Nonetheless, empirical facts from sociological and anthropological studies verify that different societies with different values exist. Empirical facts do not mean normative, ethical truths nor does tolerance necessarily emerge from acknowledging that different cultures have differing values. (See, e.g., Feldman, 1978; Pietarinen and Poutanen, 1997 or Weggert and Al-Saggaf, 2003, among many others.)

Tolerance for different value sets has, however, been one of the most treasured Western values (based on the liberal tradition of the Western democracies). Different values are considered as enriching societies. It is strange how this does not seem to hold between societies when it comes to the values associated to immaterial creations. Tolerance should, however, be taken into account as an ethical way to function when designing IPR systems which are worldwide. It is known as a descriptive fact that various different traditions in regard to IPRs exist in different societies (Alford, 1995; Spinello, 1995; Chang, 2001a). Why should others be not allowed to find their own ways when it comes to creating ways to handle IPRs? This of course does not mean that the Western societies ought to let other cultures dominate their thinking either. Nonetheless, if tolerance is a Western value, the Western societies should let other cultures define their ways of dealing with IPRs and respect that decision instead of forcing all societies to adopt the same IPR systems through organisations such as WTO and WIPO (TRIPS coming into effect even to the poorest nations in 2006, see Chang, 2001a). In addition, the other systems could be examined: maybe something could be learned from the choices made. These decisions might actually aid the creation of intellectual woks in Western societies as well.

Even if relativistic moral theory is accepted, moral utterances of other groups or societies can be critiqued (Pietarinen and Poutanen, 1997). In relativistic moral thinking (be it conventionalism or cultural relativism) values are thought to come from the values of the group with which the values are shared (Feldman, 1978). Thus the values are not objective nor are they claimed to be right for those belonging to other groups. Other groups should not be forced to share the views of the first through international treaties or pressure by uni- or bilateral negotiations, but rather by convincing them that the expressed moral opinions are true even on the basis of their own moral premises.

Western societies are participating in cultural imperialism when forcing their own IPR systems onto other countries. As Weckert and Al-Saggaf (2003) put it: "A culture might dominate, not because it is 'better' as a culture, but because it is the culture of a group who are economically and militarily strong." This does not mean that cultures with lesser or more free IPRs would be morally wrong in their attitudes towards immaterial creations even if the differing view would not necessarily survive the 'fight' between different views on IPR laws. They might still promote a better and more ethical way to treat the users and even the creators of the immaterial than the Western-promoted ones do.

Freedom of choice in how the IPR laws are made should be the norm instead of the exception. Now the various IPR legislations are forced in place by bilateral (or rather unilateral) negotiations by the stronger (See, e.g., Alford, 1995 on how China (both continental and Taiwan) has been treated). If we are worried about being ethical, cultural imperialism "cannot be defended simply on the grounds of 'survival of the fittest'" (Weckert and Al-Saggaf, 2003).

Different interpretations of IPRs should be respected. This would be both tolerant and respecting others' views about the way they want to build their societies. Some societies, such as that of China, have had a culture in which plagiarism is seen as the (sometimes only) way to give credit for a worthy thought (Alford, 1995). Other societies, often native ones, see the societal ownership of immaterial creations as being the right way (Shiva, 2003).

3.   HISTORY

Until very recently, the idea behind IPRs in the Western societies has also been to promote the advancement of the societies. Examples of this are the recent practices of the patent applications of "first to file" instead of "first to invent". The Western societies have copied intellectual capital such as the technologies of printing, paper, powder, etc. from various other cultures. The result has often been that the IPRs have been claimed by those who introduced the technologies in the countries to which they were copied, instead of by the inventor in the countries where they were created. As Chang (2001a) puts it: "patenting of *imported inventions* by their nationals was often explicitly allowed" (emphasis in original). Nor have the inventions been introduced to public domain in the society to which they were introduced, were the original inventors or their descendants not eligible for the protection any more.

Throughout history, countries in the process of industrialization have tried their best to ignore at least any foreign IPRs (see, e.g., Alford, 1995 or Drahos, 1996). Originally patent rights were not given to IPR creators in UK (and elsewhere in Europe, see Chang 2001a), but rather to anyone who brought forth new inventions in the country. A similar situation prevailed in the US regarding copyrights (as foreign copyrights were not acknowledged), until the US was no longer a net benefactor of copyright (foreign copyrighted materials did not receive, even formally let alone in reality, protection in US until 1891) (Alford, 1995; Chang, 2001a and 2001b). At the same time, however, the US was strongly driving for stronger international patent rights (Chang, 2001b). Many Western countries either did not have effective IPR laws during large parts of the years of their industrialization (e.g., Netherlands and Switzerland, which for a long period had no patent laws at all) or did not respect at least foreign IPRs (for a more detailed description see Chang 2001a). Japan after the Second World War did not enforce strong IPRs until its own rate of IPR creation rose to a level similar to that in other industrialized nations, turning it into a net benefactor in granting IPRs (See, e.g., Pirages, 1996, or Chang, 2001a).

In these examples of Western countries and their attitudes to IPRs throughout history, IPRs were not granted to foreigners or even to nationals of the countries themselves or were considerably shorter in duration and more narrow in scope (see, e.g., Spinello, 1995 or Lessig, 2001) in the field they protected, for the specific reason that this benefited the society at that time. Such examples show that the moral (and economic) grounds for IPRs can and do change over time. In US, the original term of copyright was 14 years, renewable once for another 14 years. This was changed in 1831 to 28 years, once renewable for another 14 years and so forth until in the Bono Copyright Extension Act it was lengthened to the lifetime of the creator plus 70 years (for a more detailed description, see Henderson, 2003).

It would be absurd to claim that, were Japan, Taiwan or South Korea still Third or Second World countries, this would be better for the rest of the world, let alone for the people living there. One of the reasons this is not the case, is that, well before the aggressive bilateral negotiations started in the early 80s, these countries were able to use the intellectual capital created in the more-industrialized countries (Granstrand, 1999; Chang, 2001a). They were able to establish their own production of cars, electronics, clothing etc. by performing what could be called industrial espionage in Western factories and searching through filed patents in patent offices, building their own factories, producing similar products and then excelling in many of the fields to get on par with and then overtake the American or European producers.

Today, IPRs cannot be copied similarly due to the emergence of the post-industrial era, Most of the actual useful material is not in the form of factories or machines anymore. Now it is in the form of immaterial creations; software, inventions, and chips which cannot be copied just by looking at them, as well as digitally distributable material. It is especially difficult to copy the way software works since only the object code is released in commercial creations. We are already seeing problems with countries such as China which are trying to reach the industrial state of Western countries—with factory conditions reminding us of the industrialization of UK – industrialization causing both local and global pollution, with much of the benefits flowing to Western capital owners instead of benefiting the local economy etc. It might be possible to bypass some of that industrialization in at least the Third World countries (if not in China or India anymore). This would consume fewer natural resources, since it would lead straight into the post-industrial situation where intellectual capital could be more valuable to all societies combined and use less resources needed industrial production like oil through enhanced products and at least partly bypass industrialization. This would also benefit the Western world in polluting less, creating less global warming and other non-beneficial effects in the world and yet raise the living standard of people living in these countries. It would create a situation of raw-material production (which already exists in developing countries) combined with post-industrial and some industrial production.

4.   OTHER SOLUTIONS TO THE IMMATERIAL

Until recently, countries such as Brazil (see, e.g., Stallman, 2004 on how Brazil still seeks measures for curing the digital divide through using F/OSS and how the US voted against including such solutions in the World Summit on the Information Society (WSIS)), China and other Second World countries have tried to oppose the enforcement of foreign IPRs. This was partly a result of their own national histories in regard to IPRs and of course because they consider acknowledging foreign IPRs as being detrimental to their own development. This holds even more true for Third World countries, which have virtually no IPRs of their own, yet are expected to follow international treaties supporting the existing IPRs of industrialized and post-industrial countries.

Many societies, especially in the developing countries, see the need to spread new innovations in the society as being more important than granting IPRs (Steidlmeier, 1993; Spinello, 1995). Malaysia, for example, still sees the good of the society important enough to override IPR holders' rights to software in some situations, such as for educational use in schools or for encouraging computer use in general. They have as recently as 2002, considered letting pirated software to be used in schools and social organizations. (Weckert and Al-Saggaf, 2003) As Weckert and Al-Saggaf put it: "This suggests a quite different view of the importance of intellectual property." Intellectual property is not considered as valuable as other goals in society. The learning to use and create immaterial products is considered to be, at least in these cases of a higher value.

A recent example of non-Western countries wishing not to have the international Western-type IPRs applied universally and questioning the idea of strong IPRs resulting to strong development can be found in the motion proposal tabled at WIPO by Argentina, Bolivia, Brazil, Cuba, the Dominican Republic, Ecuador, Egypt, Iran, Kenya, Peru, Sierra Leone, South Africa, Tanzania and Venezuela (WIPO, 2005). This "Group of Friends of Development" called for "promoting development and access to knowledge for all" exactly in the form of lesser and more localized IPR laws.

F/OSS groups have chosen to license their immaterial creations under various licenses (for the actual licenses, see Free Software Foundation, 2001) which enable anyone to use both the source and object code and documentation for the software once it is released. There is a large group of software creators who see this as the correct way of treating immaterial creations. The same is made possible for other forms of immaterial creations by the Creative Commons (www.creativecommons.org) licenses.

Contemporary examples would include plant patents for which the knowledge is often considered the socially owned intellectual capital of a tribe. After being introduced in pharmaceutical form, even the tribe's members, who often are at best paid baubles for the information, must pay to use it even though they were the original inventors of the information (on 'biopiratism', see e.g., George, 2003 or Shiva, 2003). The current international IPR treaties which the countries in which this happens have been forced to accept do not take into account communal ownership of knowledge. Nor could it be taken into account in a fair way due to the imbalance of the negotiation situation even if the communal patent or communal copyright were introduced. The situation is in a way very similar and yet the opposite of the former introducing of an invention. It is similar in the sense that it allows the one who introduces the invention to use it (and even excludes the original inventors). It is the opposite in the sense that it now applies also to the country from which the knowledge was gathered. Now that the exploiter is a beneficiary also in the country which is being robbed of its intellectual capital, the introducer can gain even wider access to IPRs which even now should belong to others.

An analogy with the HIV/AIDS cures in South Africa illustrates the situation. Western societies have ensured (to varying, but mainly functional, degrees) that their citizens have access to HIV/AIDS cures, but intellectual property rights have (in part) seen to it that nations with lesser capabilities to purchase IPR protected medicines have few alternatives. Counter to treaties in IPRs (TRIPS, George, 2003) signed by the South African government, South Africa none the less decided not to pay licensing fees to Western pharmacy companies if they didn't lower the prices of the medicines to a more acceptable level, which they then did. Drug production in various other countries such as India or Brazil also breaks these IPR treaties. Many of the drugs used in South Africa are imported from these countries. Even though some of the medicines produced in these countries end up in the markets of industrialized countries, the amount is negligible compared to the potential rises of up to 99% in the prices of the medicines (see, e.g., IPS, 2004).

The same is apparent in access to information. Those with fewer resources have less access to information but are expected to follow the rules of the "haves". This results in a situation where the advances gained by the "haves" do not benefit the "have-nots" even in the long run as is claimed by those subscribing to the 'trickle down theory' of the benefits eventually reaching the poor as well (see Kimppa, 2004a for a more thorough handling of the issue).

The percentages of so-called software piracy (another very loaded word) in countries which have or have had lesser or no IPRs in place and among population groups such as students (notably having less income than many other groups of the society) promotes the thought that maybe there is something wrong with our IPRs rather than with the people they drive to use 'pirated' software. A more moderate approach in IPRs might well propel the economies of developing countries to rise.

5.   INTERNATIONAL TREATIES

To the best of their ability, organizations such as WTO (through TRIPS), international monetary fund (IMF) and WIPO have tried to fight for the privileges of the IPR holders. WTO and IMF for example are strongly promoting the neo-liberal thinking which has as one of its main components strong IPR legislation as global solution to the problems of the Third World (Chossudovsky; 2001, for the problems of justifying IPRs based on the liberal tradition, see Kimppa, 2004b, 2005a and 2005b). It does not seem that these organizations are be interested in the rights of the creator of the immaterial, nor of the user of immaterial creations, but rather in the interests of the organizations that hold and distribute the immaterial and the interests of the countries which create most of the immaterial at the moment (against those who do not have IPRs).

The strengthening, lengthening and enlarging of the area of protection of IPRs benefits the industry, but does not enlarge the distribution of the products. It protects the IPR owners' rights instead of the IPR creators' rights. For the creators, the wider distribution which shorter IPRs would enable, could in many cases be of more benefit than the longer protection. The software business in any case hardly ever grants any rights to the creator of the immaterial but rather they are transferred directly to the employer.

This leads to a one-sided view, which hardly can be called socially responsible in the global scale. The rights of the people of the countries which do not hold immaterial creations and rights in large amounts are not taken into account. The rights of these people to do with as they please with their material based on that immaterial is strictly limited due to them not being able to use the immaterial to improve their situation. In a Lockean liberal sense, this would seem wrong (Kimppa, 2005a). Also, the consequences of this kind of politics seems to strengthen the current divide in the prosperity that would be available (Kimppa, 2004a and Kimppa, 2005b). Finally, the ethical aspect of relying on laws and regulations in a situation which would rather call for ethical behaviour in the part of the potential users and respecting their rights seems to be forgotten (Kimppa, 2005b).

It should be noted that the 'democracy' of WTO (where, it is claimed, all the countries are in similar situation when each has a vote), is subverted by the fact that the numbers of lobbyists from the industrialized countries seems to be equal or even exceeds the amount of country representatives, while 40 countries either do not even have one regular representative or share a representative with another country (George, 2003). If the negotiation situation would be more equal, we might be able to find a globally acceptable solution to IPRs, although, owing to different values in different societies, even that is doubtful.

The situation is similar within WIPO. Lessig (2001) provides us with an example on how the lobbying in these organizations works:

> "It is an iron law of modern democracy [which WIPO and WTO theoretically are!] that when you create a regulator, you create a

target for influence, and when you create a target for influence, those in the best position to influence will train their efforts upon that target." "Thus, commercial broadcasters—NBC and CBS in particular—were effective in getting the government to allocate spectrum according to their view of how spectrum should be used. (This was helped *by the broadcasters' practice of offering free airtime to members of Congress.*)" (Lessig, 2001.)

It seems, thus, that expecting the current Second and Third World countries to respect the IPRs of the industrialized and post-industrial nations is only a way to keep the status quo by limiting the possibilities of these countries to climb to an equal level in the world. This might—in the short run—be beneficial to certain groups in the Western world. But even for the Western world it is clearly not beneficial in the long run. For who would seriously think anyone better off if, for example, Japan, Taiwan or South Korea had been held back from using the Western IPRs during their (re)industrialization after the Second World War? This does not even begin to consider all the negative aspects this kind of development holds for the currently industrializing or Third World countries.

6.   ALTERNATIVE WAYS

To a large degree, the Eastern and other Second World IPR creators in the software business now sell their creativity to IPR holders in Western societies. Through this practice they are not helping their own societies nearly as much as they could if the creations and their profits stayed in their own societies. The situation is similar to that in tourism development where a company brings all the materials and even workers to construct and operate a holiday resort from abroad and then also takes all the profits back abroad. The local economy hardly sees a difference except in its resources being exploited.

There is a similar trend with the creation of software and other digitally distributable material (DDM) as well. In the F/OSS movement the situation would be different. If local programmers create software—and luckily they are—for F/OSS instead of for the proprietary software companies, even local software can be used anywhere. Any local software can be modified to benefit any society or social group, whether the software is made in India or in Finland. This is clearly not true for the proprietary software in the same amounts as it is true for F/OSS.

If all software would function as F/OSS we would not have this problem, for all software—or other DDM for the matter—could be used to benefit the local needs and wants instead of the large corporations and their shareholders it is benefiting now. Unfortunately for this kind of creativity, the various forms of digital millennium copyright act (DMCA, 1998; European Copyright Directive, 2001) and software patents are trying to stifle this as are the lengthening and strengthening of IPRs in other ways.

This is also why the ideological basis behind F/OSS and especially FSS (Free Source Software) is more important than it first appears. This is why we should try to encourage ideological thinking about software creation and DDM creation instead of just plain practical thinking. If we are not ideological, we do not care about the good of the people but only about what happens to be good for us right now, and this can hardly be considered as being much more ethical than the thinking of proprietary companies in which the only aim is to increase the shareholder value. This kind of behaviour cannot in good conscience be considered socially responsible.

Just releasing constraints on IPRs will of course not bring about the change for better. Other measures, including some which are actually being taken at the moment (such as forgiving the debts of at least the poorest Third World countries) must be taken. Unfortunately that does not help the Second World countries, nor does it help countries to bypass the industrialization stage.

Other measures must be taken as well if we want to improve the situation in the long run – one of which would be to release all restrictions on using IPRs by the poorest countries.

Even though the no-IPR policy might produce the best results, whatever method is chosen by the countries should be respected. This is true, whether the chosen way is to adopt an IPR policy similar to the current Western one, or rather one that resembles the way countries that are currently post-industrial treated other countries' IPRs during their industrialization, or the no-IPR policy suggested here.

7. CONCLUSION

Most countries either did not have strong internal IPRs nor did they exhibit much respect for international IPRs during their industrialization. The European countries and US were in the first wave of such IPR behaviour. The second wave included the East Asian 'new tigers', such as Japan, South Korea, Taiwan and Singapore, refining the practices the previous industrializing countries used. (Chang, 2001a)

The current situation differs from both of these. Copying production methods and processes has become ever harder in general, due to their complexity and, in software in particular, due to the object code being released but the source code being held as a trade secret. Fortunately, the use of digitally distributable material (DDM), be it software or anything else, is easy.

If treaties such as TRIPS were not forced on Third World countries, this could be used to the advantage of developing countries in many ways. Some of these, like the IPR policy adopted in Iran, would closely follow the practice of previous times where internal IPRs were enforced but external ones where generally ignored. Others would surely adapt ways closer to the ideas in practice in countries like Malaysia, where the social good is considered more important, and thus the usage of IPR protected material at least in selected parts of the society could be free.

Why would software and DDM specifically be of benefit to the development of immaterial creations in Second and Third World countries? The copying of such materials is the easiest form of copying—any DDM can be copied and recopied if it is not specifically obstructed by digital rights management software. On top of this, we have a thriving F/OSS culture which is already doing things similar to what is suggested in this paper. The F/OSS movement could offer some ways to handle IPRs in these new situations.

The concept of being paid for work done, instead of being granted rights to the intellectual material could be taken up. This would produce local jobs enhancing and implementing software and creating other digitally distributable material. The way to support this kind of action should be through proving that it would work rather than forcing the developing societies to accept any particular way of using and creating their own immaterial creations.

A moratorium on the enforcement of the IPRs of the industrialized countries would be one of the necessary steps for the Third World to be able to catch up with the industrialized countries while by-passing some of the problems inherent in industrialization. During the moratorium, an analytical discussion should be conducted to determine which would be the best way for the developing country to move towards IPRs, whether it would be the current one-for-all system proposed through the WTO, or whether it would be something different depending on the needs of the given society. Honouring the IPR systems others choose to implement would be ethical, tolerant and socially responsible in helping the developing countries to develop their own immaterial creations.

REFERENCES

Alford, William P. (1995). To steal a book is an elegant offence: Intellectual property law in Chinese civilization. Stanford, California: Stanford university press.

Chang, Ha-Joon (2001a). Intellectual Property Rights and Economic Development: historical lessons and emerging issues, Journal of Human Development, Vol. 2, No. 2, 2001, pp. 287—309.

Chang, Ha-Joon (2001b). A background paper prepared for World Industrial Development Report of the UNIDO. https://www.unido.org/userfiles/hartmany/IDR-chang-draftpaper2.pdf accessed 11.4.2005.

Chossudovsky, Michel (2001). Köyhyyden globalisointi: Maailmanpankin ja IMF:n uudistusten vaikutuksia (originally printed in 1999, Globalisation of Poverty), Otavan Kirjapaino Oy, Keuruu.

DMCA (1998). The Digital Millennium Copyright Act. http://www.gseis.ucla.edu/iclp/dmca1.htm accessed 15.02.2004.

Drahos, Peter (1996). A Philosophy of Intellectual Property. Dartmouth Publishing.

European copyright directive of 2001 (2001). http://europa.eu.int/cgi-bin/eur-lex/udl.pl?REQUEST=Seek-Deliver&COLLECTION=oj&SERVICE=all&LANGUAGE=en&DOCID=20011167p0010 accessed 15.02.2004.

Feldman, Fred (1978). Introductory Ethics, Prentice-Hall Inc. New Jersey.

Free Software Foundation (2001). Categories of Free and Non-Free Software, http://www.gnu.org/philosophy/categories.html accessed 15.4.2005.

George, Susan (2003). Maailmankauppajärjestö kuriin (originally printed in 2001, Remettre l'OMC à sa place), Gummerus Kirjapaino Oy, Jyväskylä, Finland.

Granstrand, O (1999). Corporate Management of Intellectual Property in Japan, *International Journal of Technology Management,* Special Issue on Patents, edited by Edwin Mansfield.

Henderson, K. A. (2003). J.Lo and the Intellectual Commons: An exposition on copyright expansion in the digital age, Proceedings for CEPE 2003 and Sixth Annual Ethics and Technology Conferences, Boston College, June 25-28, 2003 pp. 120—127 of Sixth Annual Ethics and Technology Conference proceedings.

IPS (2004) Health: Global Poor to Suffer If Denied Indian Generic Drugs – Experts http://www.ipsnews.net/interna.asp?idnews=27563 accessed 27.02.2005.

Kimppa, Kai K. (2004a). Consequentialist Considerations of Intellectual Property Rights in Software and other Digitally Distributable Media. Proceedings of the Seventh International Conference, Ethicomp 2004, Challenges for the Citizen of the Information Society, University of the Aegean, Syros, Greece, 14 to 16 April 2004.

Kimppa, Kai K. (2004b) Redistribution of Power from Government to Intellectual Property Rights Owners and Organizations Looking After Their Interests: Justifiable from a Liberalist Position? – The Free Software Foundations Position Compared to John Locke's

Concept of Distributable Rights. Second Summer School by IFIP WG 9.2, 9.6/11.7, 9.8, Risks and Challenges of the Network Society. 4-8 August 2003, Karlstad University, Sweden. Preceedings available at: http://www.cs.kau.se/IFIP-summerschool/preceedings/Kimppa.pdf In Penny Duquenoy, Simone Fishcer-Hübner, Jan Holvast & Albin Zuccato (eds.) Risks and Challenges of the Network Society. Karlstad University Press, Karlstad, Sweden.

Kimppa, Kai K. (2005a). Intellectual Property Rights in Software—Justifiable from a Liberalist Position? Free Software Foundation's Position in Comparison to John Locke's Concept of Property. In Richard A. Spinello and Herman T. Tavani, (eds.) Intellectual Property Rights in a Networked World. Information Science Publishing (an imprint of Idea Group Inc.), Hershey, PA, USA.

Kimppa, Kai K. (2005b) (in print). Intellectual Property Rights – or Rights to the Immaterial – in Digitally Distributable Media Gone All Wrong? Lee A. Freeman and Graham Peace (eds.) Information Ethics: Privacy and Intellectual Property. Information Science Publishing (an imprint of Idea Group Inc.), Hershey, PA, USA.

Lessig, Lawrence (2001). The Future of Ideas: The Fate of the Commons in a Connected World, Vintage Books, New York.

Pietarinen Juhani and Poutanen, Seppo (1997). Etiikan teorioita (Theories of ethics, not translated), Turun yliopiston offsetpaino, Turku.

Pirages, Dennis (1996). Intellectual Property in a Post Industrial World, *Science Communication*, Vol. 17, No. 3, March 1996, pp. 267—273.

Shiva, Vandana (2003). Voiko tietoa omistaa? Patentit kehitysmaiden uhkana (originally printed 2001, Protect or Plunder? Understanding Intellectual Property Rights), Dark Oy, Vantaa.

Spinello, Richard A. (1995). Ethical Aspects of Information Technology, Prentice-Hall, Inc. New Jersey, USA.

Stallman, Richard (2004). World Summit on the Information Society, Originally published on Newsforge, available at http://www.gnu.org/philosophy/wsis.html accessed 27.02.2005.

Steidlmeier, P. (1993). The Moral Legitimacy of Intellectual Property Claims: American Business and Developing Country Perspectives, *Journal of Business Ethics*, February: 157—164.

Weckert, John and Yeslam Al-Saggaf (2003). Online Cultural Imperialism: Is it an Ethical Issue? Information, Communication & Ethics in Society, Vol 1, Issue 1, 21—29, Jan 2003.

WIPO (2005). Proposal to establish a development agenda for WIPO: an elaboration of issues raised in document WO/GA/31/11, Inter-sessional intergovernmental meeting on a development agenda for WIPO, First Session, Geneva, April 11 to 13, 2005, available at http://www.wipo.int/edocs/mdocs/mdocs/en/iim_1/iim_1_4.pdf accessed 4.5.2005.

ACCOUNTABILITY AND REFLECTIVE RESPONSIBILITY IN INFORMATION SYSTEMS

Bernd Carsten Stahl
Centre for Computing and Social Responsibility, Faculty of Computer Science and Engineering, De Montfort University, The Gateway, Leicester LE1 9BH, UK
bstahl@dmu.ac.uk

Abstract: This paper discusses the role of accountability in responsibility ascriptions regarding information and communication technology (ICT). It starts with a definition of responsibility as the social construct representing the ascription of an object to a subject. Recounting the traditional responsibility, the paper will point out the weaknesses of responsibility with regards to ICT. It will then propose an alternative way of dealing with responsibility under the heading of "reflective responsibility". Accountability will be defined as the structures and institutions that establish a link between object and subject. As such it is a necessary condition of successful responsibility ascriptions. The paper will discuss the influence of ICT on the construction of accountability and consequently on responsibility. It will highlight the problem of pathological accountability where accountability becomes reified and solidified and in effect goes counter to the social aim of responsibility. The paper will conclude with a discussion of how problems and pathologies of accountability can be overcome in order for reflective responsibility to be able to fulfil its purpose.

Key words: Responsibility, accountability, ICT, pathological accountability, reflective responsibility

1.   INTRODUCTION

What is the meaning of the metaphor of "landscapes of ICT and social accountability"? It would seem to imply several things. First, there is the assumption that ICT and accountability are related in some way and that this accountability is of a social nature. Furthermore, it implies that there is no unambiguous picture of the relationship of accountability and ICT. Instead, the metaphor of the landscape suggests that there are different types of relationships and that there are different approaches to these landscapes just as there are different types of landscapes (hills, mountains, deserts, ...) and one can approach them differently (walk, fly, drive, ride,...). When walking through such different landscapes it is important to know where one is and wants to go in order to ascertain that one has the right equipment and the right companions.

This paper will explore the overlap of a number of different landscapes. On one hand, it is based on the debate within the field of computer and information ethics. It is informed by what the philosophical interest in information and communication technology has to say about possible approaches to ethical issues. On the other hand, it is interested in the organisational use of ICT and thus in the subject area of the discipline of information systems (IS).

2.   RESPONSIBILITY AND ICT

Accountability describes the structures that need to be in place to facilitate responsibility. In order for this concept to be convincing, we need to make it clear what is meant by responsibility. Since the concept of responsibility presented here will no doubt be somewhat different from what most readers may understand by that term, a brief literature review will be provided on the concept of responsibility. This will lead to a discussion of the traditional understanding of responsibility and the answer to these problems, namely reflective responsibility. In this short conference paper, it will not be possible to do justice to all of the niceties of the debate on responsibility. The interested reader can find a more comprehensive discussion of the topic in Stahl (2004).

2.1   Definition of Responsibility

"Responsibility" is a term with many meanings. Very briefly, responsibility can best be defined as the ascription of an object to a subject.

The subject is the entity, usually a person, who is responsible. The object is that which the subject is responsible for. A responsibility ascription thus renders the subject answerable for the object. The ascription that is the heart of responsibility is a social process. It socially constructs realities out of the perceptions of the agents involved (Hart, 1948). In order to understand such an ascription, it is important to take into account its underlying motivation. There are a number of possible aims that can be intended through the ascription of responsibility. These include retribution (Fauconnet, 1997) and revenge (Nietzsche, 1987) but are usually of a more positive nature.

Responsibility ascriptions generally aim to improve the individual and social existence of the individuals who are involved. They do so by determining whether consequences of an action are desirable and accordingly deciding on sanctions for certain actions. This means that the attribution of sanctions, be they positive or negative, are of central importance for responsibility (Bayertz, 1995). Responsibility aims to affect social change for the benefit of those involved in the ascription. It is important to keep this fundamental tenet of responsibility in mind because it can explain some of the dimensions of responsibility and it will also allow us to identify instances where accountability becomes counterproductive to responsibility.

A complete ascription of responsibility involves a number of other aspects and dimensions in addition to the subject and the object. Chief among them are the authority and normative basis. In order for responsibility to be ascribed, there must be a normative rule to which the ascription can refer. In some cases such rules are relatively easy to determine, such as the law in legal responsibility. In other cases they may be less simple to find, for example in the case of moral responsibility. However, a responsibility ascription that is to be successful in improving social reality must be based on acceptable rules that the individuals involved are ready to adhere to. The existence of rules is not enough, since they need to be applied and interpreted in specific situations. This is where the authority finds its place. A responsibility ascription needs to define a relationship between an object and a subject and it needs to do so by imputing sanctions to the subject depending on the object. Such a theoretical definition must be translated into reality and it must be executed, which is the job of the authority. In legal responsibility the authority is the judge or the jury but in other types of responsibility it is often less clear who or what constitutes the authority.

Apart from these main aspects of responsibility, every real ascription must consider a number of other issues. These include the type of responsibility (legal, moral, role, …) the temporal dimension (prospective or retrospective), the type of ascription (transitive, reflexive, vicarious, …) as well as limits and exemptions. It should be clear that all ascriptions are unique combinations of these aspects that require careful negotiation and implementation. In order to demonstrate the role of accountability in this concept of responsibility, some of the problems of responsibility ascriptions will next be described, and will be used to develop a theory of reflective responsibility.

Finally, the above definition of responsibility may seem a bit dry and the reader may wonder what the relevance to ICT is. The argument will therefore be supported through the use of a hypothetical case: Let us imagine a large multinational organization that decides to introduce an Enterprise Resource Planning (ERP) software. The purpose of the installation of this system is to streamline operations and to provide all the data to important decision makers in real time. At the same time, it can be linked to other organizational systems, such as a Customer Relationship Management (CRM) system and the combined data can be used for strategic purposes such as data mining.

The case should look sufficiently familiar to anybody who has done research in information systems recently. ERP systems were the latest fashion for a while (they may by now have been overtaken by even larger systems such as Supply Chain Management (SCM) or others). The case is thus realistic. At the same time, there is enough literature that is highly critical of ERP systems because they often do not deliver what managers hope they will. They also tend to raise a number of moral issues. The case should not be misunderstood as "proving" anything; rather, it is meant to provide a plausible context for some of the issues of responsibility and accountability in information systems.

2.2   Problems of Responsibility and ICT

Problems of responsibility ascriptions can arise with regard to all three of the main dimensions; the subject, the object, and the authority. Responsibility becomes problematic where it cannot fulfill its social role, where it cannot have the desired effects. This is the case where either the relationship between subject and object cannot be established or where the establishment of the relationship does not have any tangible results.

Problems of the subject are those that preclude a possible subject from being successfully seen as responsible and thus being ascribed the object.

The majority of such problems of the subject are related to a lack of fulfillment of the conditions of responsibility, which will be introduced. The literature on responsibility names a number of conditions, the most important will therefore be supported of which are causality, freedom, power, knowledge, and personal qualities. Causality means that there must be some sort of causal relationship between subject and object. This relationship may be indirect in that the subject did not cause the object but could have had the opportunity to avoid it. A subject may thus be responsible for someone's death because the subject caused it directly, but there could also be an ascription if the subject could have saved the person in question but failed to do so. Causality in our example might be given when the CEO of the company decides to implement the ERP, which means that she is a crucial part of the causal chain that leads to the object. However, it could also be an external expert who knows the situation but fails to inform the CEO of the possible downside and thus gives up the chance to affect the development.

Another typical condition of responsibility is freedom of the subject. The subject not only has to play a causal role in the outcome but he or she must also be in a position to change this outcome. It is usually seen as problematic to ascribe responsibility to subjects who did not possess the freedom to affect the object. This is linked closely to the next condition, namely knowledge. The freedom to affect the outcome of the causal chain resulting in the object requires that the subject be aware of the subject and his or her own role in the development of matters. Without knowledge, there can be no intentional action. The same can be said about power. It is no use for the subject to be causally involved as well as sufficiently free and aware of the situation if it is outside of the subject's power to affect the object. Finally, one can find a number of authors who discuss the importance of personal characteristics for the ascription of responsibility. These personal characteristics include emotions, intentionality and rationality, the ability to act a number of traits that render us sociable such as education and formation, self-control and a bodily existence. These latter personal requirements are important for the subject to react appropriately to the ascription of responsibility. In order for responsibility to be successful, the subject must want to react to the threat of punishment or promise of reward. If this is not given, causality, freedom, power, and knowledge have no purpose.

The philosophically versed reader will have noticed that the conditions of responsibility are deeply problematic and touch on some of the most contentious issues that philosophy has been grappling with for the last few millennia. Since Hume, philosophers have recognized that causality is not a natural occurrence, that it is nothing that can ever be observed. We can only observe before and after states but the causal link always remains obscure. A similar, possibly worse concept is that of freedom. In the physical description of the world there is no place for freedom. Natural occurrences follow natural and scientifically recognizable laws. Every state of nature is a necessary consequence of prior states. Since we as humans are part of the natural world, this description applies to us as well. As a result we seem to be completely determined. If, consequentially, there is no freedom, then it is questionable whether responsibility ascriptions can fulfill any purpose (cf. Wallace 1996). Other fundamental problems of these conditions are that we can never know the internal states of persons. That means we cannot know whether they are aware of things and whether they intend certain consequences.

For the purposes of this paper, we will ignore the fundamental philosophical problems. It will suffice to work with the everyday and common sense notions of causality and freedom. We can assume that causal relationships can in many cases be reliably established and that agents have the freedom to act, albeit often within constraints. We can also assume that most of the persons involved in responsibility ascription for the use of ICT are adult and reasonably rational. And yet, even when accepting these ideas, the subject of responsibility for ICT remains problematic.

To demonstrate the point, let us return to the example: the prime exponent of responsibility in organizations tends to be the formal head of the organization, usually the CEO. We could thus say that the CEO is responsible for everything that happens in the company, including the introduction of the ERP. The CEO is well placed to make decisions but she usually lacks the necessary knowledge. She may take the decision to implement the system but she will not normally be able to assess the results in any detail. On the other end of the organizational spectrum, there will be data workers who input and use the system, who may have a better understanding of specific parts of the system but they will usually lack an overview as well as the power to affect things.

It is thus problematic to find subjects who can be ascribed responsibility. However, the subject is not the only dimension producing problems. The object, the thing or fact that the subject is responsible for, can also be problematic. Three problems are cumulative effects, side effects, and the question of doing and omitting. In traditional responsibility ascription the person as the subject is ascribed the clearly identifiable consequences of an intentional act. In many cases the morally problematic aspect of ICT is not related to a single intentional act but to the accumulation of a large number of acts. Where the single act is fundamentally unproblematic, the accumulation represents a problem. A nice example of this is the use of a car. While a single use of a car by an individual is typically of no moral interest, the accumulation of uses of cars has a huge range of consequences including many thousands of people killed every year but also a change in social and technical infrastructure that favours the well-off. It is not clear how responsibility for the cumulative effect can be broken down to individual responsibility. A related problem is that of side effects. Responsibility aims to affect intentional acts. However, most, if not all, acts have other effects than those that are intended. How can we ascribe responsibility for these?

A final problem of the object is that of doing and omitting. Traditionally, responsibility is ascribed for acts, not for omissions. I have, however, already mentioned the case of a subject letting someone die despite a chance to intervene. This is a good example of responsibility for omissions. The practical problem this raises is that the inclusion of omissions into the objects of responsibility leads to an infinity of ascriptions. Coupled with the potential infinity of causality, this means that a subject at any time is responsible for an infinite number of consequences, independent of whether the subject acts or not. This is clearly not manageable and will lead to the end of responsibility.

A final problem of responsibility worth mentioning is that of the authority. I have said earlier that the authority is the entity that can determine and enforce the sanctions associated with the responsibility ascription. For this purpose it needs to be based and rely upon a generally accepted normative framework. In the case of moral responsibility, both are hard to come by. There is no generally accepted morality, there is no universal ethical theory and there is no person and no institution that can be relied upon to attribute sanctions and to enforce them.

These general problems can also be detected in our ERP case. A problem of cumulative effect may be that of customer data protection. Noting down the preferences of a customer on a piece of paper is something that merchants have always done in order to please their customers. When the ERP system is supplemented with a customer relationship management (CRM) system, this practice can easily lead to the accumulation of large amounts of information on individual customers. This, in turn, can lead to legal as well as ethical questions.

Similarly, unintended consequences of systems introduction are frequent. The intention of the ERP system is presumably to increase efficiency, control, and agility. It is easily imaginable, though, that the system will have other consequences. The organization may have to be restructured and some employees made redundant because of this. Some may find their jobs enriched, others impoverished. These are consequences nobody intended, even thought they may have foreseen them. Can we hold the CEO responsible? And to which consequences will this lead? Finally, which are the moral rules that the organization agrees on and who can hold subjects responsible?

2.3   Reflective Responsibility for ICT

Because of these problems that preclude a straightforward application of responsibility to many of the problems of ICT, the present author has elsewhere (Stahl, 2004) suggested a concept of reflective responsibility. The idea of reflective responsibility is to determine the core of the concept and to apply this reflexively to itself. Or, to put it differently, it is the question whether a responsibility ascription is indeed an expression of responsibility. In order to do this, it is important to identify the core of responsibility ascriptions. There are three characteristics that most ascriptions share: openness, an affinity to action, and a teleological basis.

Openness stands for the fact that responsibility ascriptions are not closed and not predictable but, as social constructs, they are open to change. That means that it is not possible to exclude stakeholders from the ascription process and that the outcome of the ascription is always in some doubt. This is true for the most formalized of responsibility ascriptions, legal responsibility, where external stakeholders may appear as experts or witnesses in a court of law. Also, it is impossible to predict the outcome of a case even though one may in many cases guess what it will be. For less formalized types of responsibility such as moral responsibility, the aspect of openness is even stronger.

The second characteristic of reflective responsibility is the affinity to action. This stands for the fact that responsibility ascriptions always carry the promise that they will lead to a manifest change of some description. Holding someone responsible means that that person will change their ways and that social reality will be affected as a result. This is closely linked with the purpose of responsibility, namely to make life better for those involved.

The final characteristic is that of teleology. This teleological orientation has two aspects: consequentialism and the "good life". The good life represents the above mentioned property of responsibility to improve social reality. Such an improvement is only possible if there is a vision as to what a desirable society or social life would look like. Responsibility ascriptions therefore aim, explicitly or implicitly, to achieve some sort of social result. Furthermore, responsibility ascriptions are based on consequences rather than intentions. In many cases these consequences may not (yet) be known but the consequentialist direction is something that seems to the general rule for responsibility ascriptions.

Reflective responsibility takes these three characteristics, (openness, affinity to action, and teleology), and applies them to responsibility ascriptions. It asks whether an ascription is open, whether it is likely to lead to action and manifest changes and whether it is based on a tenable vision of the good life and considers relevant consequences. There are several ways such reflective responsibility can be realized. What they have in common is that they must be reflective about their nature as social constructs and therefore actively consider the process of construction. This, in turn, coupled with the ethical necessity to recognize the equal dignity of all human beings, means that responsibility ascriptions should be participative endeavours that aim to allow all those who are affected to voice their opinions. Reflective responsibility will therefore in practice look somewhat like a Habermasian (1981) discourse and the present author has argued elsewhere that the Habermasian ideal speech situation is part of what renders such participative responsibility ascriptions ethically legitimate.

To return to our example of the introduction of an ERP system, reflective responsibility would look quite different from the type of responsibility that we usually encounter in commercial organizations. Instead of trying to link given subjects to given or presumed objects and imposing sanctions according to the instrumental rationality of the organization, reflective responsibility would start prior to these steps. In order to be successful it would have to identify the stakeholders. In practice this would mean that someone with a sufficient interest and organizational power, i.e., the CIO, a project manager, or maybe the CEO would have to start the process. During the stakeholder deliberations, all aspects of the ascription would have to be debated. That means that during the process of ascription the subject, object, rules, and authority would have to be identified, and in some cases even constructed. This means that most of the problems of traditional responsibility enumerated earlier can be overcome. Responsibility will be ascribed for those objects that the subjects are in control of and the sanctions will be measured in such a way as to facilitate the attainment of the shared goal. Therefore, it is possible that subjects are defined for specific purposes. These would include subjects that are problematic from a traditional responsibility point of view such as collective bodies (Stahl, 2004b) or information processing machines (Stahl. 2004c). Similarly, the process of ascription would comprise the definition and delimitation of the object. This would be done in conjunction with the definition of the subject as well as the norms and sanctions. Problems of cumulative or side effects can thus be addressed as well as the question whether doing and omitting need to be treated differently. Unintended effects of the ERP system could thus be incorporated into the responsibility ascription as long as at least one of the stakeholders raises the prospect. It should be relatively easy to see that the result of such reflective responsibility will not be a single responsibility ascription but a web of interrelated and interdependent responsibilities. This web can easily become quite complex and thereby add to the problems of responsibility, namely the lack of awareness and knowledge of subjects regarding objects. At this point, accountability gains its importance in the concept of reflective responsibility.

3.   RESPONSIBILITY AND ACCOUNTABILITY

In this section the concept of accountability and its relevance in the area of ICT will be will be defined.

3.1   Accountability

Accountability and responsibility are often used synonymously (Johnson, 2001; Weckert & Adeney, 1997). The etymology suggests that the term has a dual origin, from the Latin *accomputare*, meaning to compute and the French *a conter*, to tell a story (Yakel, 2001). The etymology is thus compatible with the "response" of responsibility (Giddens, 1984). Furthermore, the term "account" in "accountability" suggests that people will be taken to account, an accountability can thus refer "to the perception of defending or justifying one's conduct to an audience that has reward or sanction authority, and where rewards or sanctions are perceived to be contingent upon audience evaluation of such conduct" (Beu & Buckley, 2001)

Here a slightly different definition will be suggested – one that views accountability as one aspect of responsibility. Where responsibility refers to the entire process of ascription of object to subject, accountability is concerned with the way in which this relationship can be established and verified. Laudon & Laudon (1999, 457) express this idea in the following way: " Accountability is a feature of systems and social institution: It means that mechanisms are in place to determine who took responsible action, who is responsible." Where "responsibility has to do with tracing the causes of actions and events, of finding out who is answerable in a given situation" (Goodpaster & Matthews, 1982 p. 133), accountability is the set of mechanisms that allow such tracing of causes, actions, and events. This means that accountability is a necessary but not a sufficient condition of responsibility (Spinello, 1997). Without accountability, that means without the means of attributing the subject to the object, there can be no full process of responsibility ascription. However, even if accountability is unproblematic, responsibility may not be forthcoming because some other aspect of the ascription is not feasible.

The nature of accountability is similar to that of responsibility. It is a social construction. Accountability is easier to handle than responsibility because it concentrates on one aspect of responsibility, namely the link between subject and object. On the other hand, this means that accountability can only be considered when subject and object are defined. For a given subject and object accountability considers the conditions under which they can be linked. It thus has to find solutions or proxies for the problems of responsibility such as lack of knowledge, power, or influence

Let us take a look at our example. A possible set of subject and object might be the CIO and the cost of the project. In this case, accountability can be simple. It will require the provision of information of project benefits and costs to the CIO in such a way that he or she can influence them. In organizational practice this may turn out to be complicated but theoretically it seems quite straightforward.

Another set of subject and object could be the implementation group and customer privacy. This is more complex, because the subject is a collective and the object is a fuzzy area of ethics and law whose stakeholders are located outside of the organizational boundaries. Accountability would require ways for the implementation group to assess the users' privacy needs and rights. These would have to be fed back into the implementation process. Accountability could thus be constructed with the help of social research tools such as surveys, focus groups user involvement or others. The important thing is that the subject is in such a relationship to the object that the ascription of responsibility is convincing to the stakeholders involved.

Accountability is of central importance for reflective responsibility. One of the reflective aspects was that of affinity to action. This means that reflective responsibility must ask whether an ascription will lead to action and thus to the desired social change. Responsibility ascriptions to subjects who have no influence or no knowledge of the objects usually cannot make a difference. From the reflective point of view they are therefore useless. Holding the CIO responsible for data input when she knows nothing about it, is not likely to be successful. Accountability is therefore a central part of every reflective ascription of responsibility. It needs to be considered and made explicit so that the different stakeholders agree on the ascription. If they do not agree, then sanctions are unlikely to fulfil their aims.

3.2   Accountability and ICT

There are several possible links between accountability and ICT. A salient one is the use of ICT for the purpose of establishing accountability. ICT is used for establishing accountability where the technology helps identify the relationship between subjects and objects of responsibility. The fundamental idea here is that an essential part of accountability is information and the distribution of information to the relevant stakeholders. Since ICT is designed to capture and disseminate information, it can easily support such processes. In business organizations this can be done by using ICT to mirror movements of money or material.

The detailed inventory tracking systems that ERP systems contain, for example, allow for the ascription of individual pieces to individual persons. Similarly, financial information systems allow for the linking of movements of money to individual actions. These ways of establishing accountability are not new (in fact, they are at least as old as the field of accounting) but they can be greatly helped and improved through ICT use. More generally, one can say that ICT can help track behaviour of all sorts of entities (Skovira, 2003) and thereby allows ascriptions of responsibility.

One can find numerous examples for this sort of accountability-enhancing use of ICT. In some way most electronically created files can be interpreted in this way. This is true for the above-mentioned business records but it is at least as true in other areas such as health care and related records (Yakel, 2001). Another set of examples is that of public administration and politics.

Political responsibility is a type of responsibility that has not been mentioned here so far. The reason is that it is an exception in many respects.

For example, it is not necessary to play a causal role in order to be politically responsible. Also, political systems tend to be highly complex, which makes the discursive processes of responsibility ascription difficult and hard to understand. Every government, or at least every democratic government, should be accountable to its citizens. This is one more reason to search for means of creating accountability and ICT can be one. ICT can be used to publish information that allows the citizens to scrutinize the public use of funds and thereby identify good policy and avoid corruption (Barata & Cain, 2001).

There is thus a good point to be made that ICT can be used for the purposes of accountability. However, at the same time ICT requires new responsibility ascriptions and can become a contentious problems for accountability.

3.3   Problems of Accountability and ICT

While ICT can thus be invaluable for providing accountability, it can also have the opposite effect. Nissenbaum (1995) identifies four areas where computers can lead to a dispersion or dissolution of accountability. These are the problem of "many hands", which is created by the fact that computers are complex machines consisting of software and hardware which often renders it practically impossible to establish a link between individuals and functions of a computer (cf. Johnson & Mulvey, 1995). Part of these problems are software malfunctions or "bugs", which are commonly accepted as inevitable but which again make it difficult to attribute subject and object. A frequent problem is that of the computer as scapegoat, where the technology is used for the express purpose of deflecting accountability and thus responsibility. Finally, Nissenbaum sees a problem in the distribution of property because, on the one hand, ownership rights in intellectual property are asserted strongly but, on the other, no corresponding move to accountability for the property seems to be established. These are issues of the deflection of accountability through ICT that most of us will be familiar with and that should be plausible to most readers.

There tend to be deeper issues of accountability hidden within the makeup of ICT. A fitting example that links nicely with the ERP example I have used throughout the paper is that of accounting information systems. The very name suggests strongly that such systems are meant to establish links of accountability. They link costs to individuals or processes that produce them and thereby establish financial accountability that can be used for the purpose of responsibility ascription. The consequences are often manifest. If a unit or a division does not live up to the expected level of profit or other measures then individuals or even the whole unit may be made redundant or outsourced. Similarly, a good fulfilment of financial goals as demonstrated by the accounting system can result in promotions or bonuses. This generally accepted model of accountability through accounting hides the fact that there are a number of value choices on which the whole idea of accounting is based and which, by necessity, have to be coded into the system. This means that the accounting practices, which themselves could be objects of responsibility ascriptions become reified and hidden within the system (Meijer, 2001). This is problematic in the context of our concept of reflective responsibility because it is not open to discursive inquiry. This means that there are accountability practices implicit in ICT which are not subject to accountability.

A related problem is a simplistic understanding of the accountability-establishing faculties of ICT. It is often supposed that transparency, here making data or information available, e.g., via the Internet, will lead to accountability. Barat and Cain (2001) discuss this problem with regard to public sector financial accountability. They state that the relationship between accountability and ICT is often oversimplified, which, in turn, may lead to a decrease of accountability rather than an increase.

4. PATHOLOGIES OF ACCOUNTABILITY

When writing this paper and thinking about the problems and disadvantages of accountability and ICT, it became increasingly clear to me that there are two fundamentally different disadvantages. One group comprises the above problems where accountability can become problematic because of the use of ICT. Instead of providing structures of accountability, such problems inadvertently have an opposite effect. However, these problems can be overcome by introducing new accountability structures or other measures.

However, there seems to be a different type obstacle to accountability as a supporting mechanism of responsibility, which the present author terms the "pathology of accountability". Such pathologies are given when accountability, despite fulfilling its original purpose, becomes an obstacle to responsibility ascriptions. The point here is that accountability, originally meant to be a support for responsibility ascriptions, becomes independent of the underlying responsibility and produces effects that run counter to the social purpose of responsibility. A fitting example is probably the practice of employee surveillance (cf. Stahl et al., 2005). A possible justification of employee surveillance is that it is a measure meant to support or establish accountability within the context of the responsibility ascription that has been agreed on in the work contract. In reality, employee surveillance is often not used as a measure to implement discursive agreement but as a usually one-sided exertion of power. The debate surrounding surveillance suggests that it should itself be viewed as an object of responsibility. This is generally recognized in academia but workplace surveillance is seldom the object of debates in commercial organizations. It has thus turned into a pathological case of accountability through ICT that is reified, changes the original responsibility context and is not open to revision. Instead of supporting responsibility ascription, surveillance as a measure of accountability undermines them.

The final example of such pathological accountability can be our ERP system. One can see the ERP system as an attempt to create accountability. It is meant to collect data from all parts and aspect of the organization which is at least partly used to facilitate responsibility ascriptions. At the same time there is a good probability that the ERP system will be removed from the realm of discourse and function as a tool of power and authority. The underlying responsibility relationships may change over time but reflecting these changes in the system is quite difficulty. Similar to the other examples of pathological accountability, this one also has the potential to fundamentally change the original responsibility ascription without itself being subject to scrutiny. The introduction of a far-reaching system such as an ERP system in a company will usually affect the structure and business processes thereby changing the basis of responsibility ascriptions. These changes will in many cases have moral importance but the ERP system as the cause of change is usually not questioned.

5. CONCLUSION

This paper has put forward the argument that responsibility is an important concept to address ethical and moral issues that arise because of the use of ICT. It has discussed the shortcomings of traditional theories of responsibility and suggested the idea of reflective responsibility as a possible solution. Using this as a basis, the concept of accountability was introduced as a supporting structure for reflective responsibility. Accountability was defined as structures and procedures that allow establishing links between responsibility subjects and objects. Without accountability, reflective responsibility is not feasible. In a final step, the influence of ICT on the process of constructing accountability was discussed. It turned out that ICT can be used as a support of accountability but that there are also cases where ICT leads to a reduction in accountability.

The most interesting aspect of the problems of ICT and accountability were discussed under the heading of pathologies of accountability. Those are instances where accountability, originally meant to support responsibility, runs counter to the purposes of responsibility and renders the responsibility ascription impossible. The question is what should be done under such circumstances.

One part of the answer to this question will be to return to the nature of responsibility and accountability and keep in mind that both are social constructs. Neither of them is naturally given and both rely on social interaction to become effective. Whenever they become reified, solidified, sedimented, and out of reach of those who are involved, there is good reason to suspect that they need to be reconsidered. This seems to be the main problem of accountability becoming pathological. It happens when the process of establishing a link between a subject and an object is divided from the responsibility context that originally required it. It is then easy for accountability to take on a life of its own and to go counter to the original intention of responsibility. A frequent occurrence of this is the quantification of accountability information. Our ongoing example of the ERP system is based on the idea that accountability information can be quantified. The quantification of accountability is widely spread in modern societies. One can often find an underlying assumption that relevant information is numerical and that responsibility ascription can and should be based on such quantification. It is part of responsibility ascriptions to agree on what constitutes a relevant object and it is thus not problematic if numerical representations of reality are seen as relevant. However, if those representations are translated into accountability systems and if the original meaning of the quantitative data is lost, then we can easily come to the pathological situation where accountability processes require the production of numbers which are not related to the original responsibility context.

How should we react? The general, if possibly not satisfying, answer is that we, as members of collectives that ascribe responsibility and define accountability need to be aware of the ongoing nature of these social constructs. Responsibility ascriptions need to be updated and continued, just like accountability procedures. For large responsibility projects this will be a complex issue. It is nevertheless necessary to keep working on it if we want to avoid the danger of accountability becoming reified and pathological.

John Stuart Mill famously put forward the argument that truth must remain open to scrutiny and critique, otherwise it will become dogma. I believe that a similar approach should be taken to responsibility. Responsibility ascriptions and the related accountability structures must remain open to discursive challenges, otherwise they run the risk of objectification and thereby of failing to fulfil their purpose or, worse, of having effects that are opposed to the social purpose of responsibility.

REFERENCES

Barata, K. & Cain, P. (2001), Information, Not Technology, Is Essential to Accountability: Electronic Records and Public-Sector Financial Management, *The Information Society* 17, pp. 247 – 258

Bayertz, K. (1995), Eine kurze Geschichte der Herkunft der Verantwortung. In: Bayertz, K. (ed.) (1995), *Verantwortung: Prinzip oder Problem?* Darmstadt, Wissenschaftliche Buchgesellschaft, pp. 3 – 71

Beu, D. & Buckley, M. R. (2001): The Hypothesized Relationship Between Accountability and Ethical Behavior, *Journal of Business Ethics* 34, pp. 57 – 73

Fauconnet, P. (1997), La responsabilité: étude de sociologie, In: Neuberg, Marc (ed.) (1997), *La responsabilité – questions philosophiques,* Paris, Presses Universitaires de France, pp. 141 – 152

Giddens, A. (1984), *The Constitution of Society – Outline of the Theory of Structuration,* Cambridge: Polity Press

Goodpaster, K. E. & Matthews, J. B. Jr. (1982), Can a corporation have a moral conscience? *Harvard Business Review* (Jan – Feb 1982), pp. 132 – 141

Habermas, J. (1981). *Theorie des kommunikativen Handelns* – Band I+II. Frankfurt a. M.: Suhrkamp Verlag

Hart, H. L. A. (1948), The Ascription of Responsibility and Rights, *Proceedings of the Aristotelian Society* 1948: 171 – 194

Johnson, D. G. (2001), *Computer Ethics,* 3rd edition Upper Saddle River, New Jersey: Prentice Hall

Johnson, D. G. & Mulvey, J. M. (1995), Accountability and Computer Decision Systems, *Communications of the ACM* (38:12), pp. 58 – 64

Laudon, K. C. & Laudon, J. P. (1999), *Essentials of Management Information Systems.* 4th edition London et al., Prentice Hall

Meijer, A. (2001), Electronic Records Management and Public Accountability: Beyond an Instrumental Approach, *The Information Society* 17, pp. 259 – 270

Nietzsche, F. (1987), Argumente gegen Vergeltung und Abschreckung, In: Hoerster, N. (ed.) (1987): *Recht und Moral – Texte zur Rechtsphilosophie,* Stuttgart, Philip Reclam jun., pp. 229 – 231

Nissenbaum, H. (1995), Computing and Accountability, in: Johnson, D. G. & Nissenbaum, H. (eds.) (1995), *Computers, Ethics & Social Values.* Upper Saddle River: Prentice Hall, pp. 526 – 538

Skovira, R. J. (2003), The Social Contract Revised: Obligation and Responsibility in the Information Society. In: Azari, R. (ed.) *Current Security Management & Ethical Issues of Information Technology.* Hershey et al.: IRM Press, pp. 165 – 186

Spinello, R. (1997), *Case studies in information and computer ethics*, Upper Saddle River, NJ: Prentice Hall

Stahl, B. C. (2004), *Responsible Management of Information Systems,* Idea Group Publishing, Hershey PA

Stahl, B. C. (2004b), Reflective Responsibility: Using IS to Ascribe Collective Responsibility,: *Philosophy of Management* (formerly Reason in Practice) (4:1), Special Issue on Organisation and Decision Processes, edited by Leonard Minkes and Tony Gear, pp. 13 – 24

Stahl, B. C. (2004), Information, Ethics, and Computers: The Problem of Autonomous Moral Agents,: *Minds and Machines* 14, Special Issue on the Philosophy of Information, edited by Luciano Floridi, pp. 67 – 83

Stahl, B. C.; Prior, M.; Wilford, S. & Collins, D. (2005), Electronic Monitoring in the Workplace: If People Don't Care, then What is the Relevance? In: Weckert, J. (ed.), *Electronic Monitoring in the Workplace: Controversies and Solutions*. Idea-Group Publishing, Hershey PA, pp. 50 – 78

Wallace, R. J. (1996), *Responsibility and the Moral Sentiment*, Cambridge, Massachusetts / London, England, Harvard University Press

Weckert, J. & Adeney, D. (1997), *Computer and Information Ethics*, Westport, Connecticut / London: Greenwood Press

Yakel, E. (2001), The Social Construction of Accountability: Radiologists and Their Record-Keeping Practices, *The Information Society* 17, pp. 233 – 245

PART 2

CULTURE AND EDUCATION

ON THE SEDUCTIVE LIGHTNESS OF BEING: INSIGHTS INTO CYBERSPACE

Julia Fauth
Coordinator for Youth Interaction, International Council for Caring Communities, and MA Student, London School of Economics

Abstract: Since the 1980s, the continuing developments, changes and hybridisations in information and communication technologies have essentially influenced our ways of perceiving, thinking and behaving. The media revolution in the Internet Age affects all areas of our society. Today we are living far beyond McLuhan's Gutenberg Galaxy, but nevertheless we can see the points of reference for at least structural comparisons between both phenomena – that of the Internet revolution and that of the emergence of printing. In addition to "place-centric" knowledge perspectives, historical approaches also seem not only possible, but also necessary. The present paper offers a thought project for a kind of macro-philosophy of media, which could be defined as a reflective consideration of global media praxis and media politics, and thus a media ethics with a claim to global validity. Such a thought-project could fill a gap in the scientific discourse on media, which cannot be tackled so broadly by using the differentiated concepts surrounding the "Global Village", which were developed from sociological and macro- or micro-economic perspectives.

1. BEYOND POST-MODERNITY

1.1 An Unprecedented Generation of Internet Users

In a recent article in a well-known computer magazine, a commentary was provided on an development, which is both socially and economically interesting, in South Korea, where e-mail is slowly but surely becoming "snail mail". South Korean teenagers are obviously some way beyond the average users of modern telecommunications offerings and thus the best examples of "earliest adopters"; they are consumers in the Information Age par excellence.

The teenagers said that they now only used e-mail when they wanted to communicate with older people. Otherwise they only used Instant Messenger, or mini-Homepages, or Internet blogs, for fast communication.

What realities are coming together here? In a world where 80 percent of the population does not even have access to communications devices like fixed or mobile phones, the post-post-modern communications consumers no longer deal in seconds, but in milliseconds. Obviously, this raises key issues that are not only economic and infrastructural in nature, but also social and ethical. But, along with questions of equal treatment and equal rights in the context of globalization, when one reads about such phenomena as only the Internet Age can bring about, the question arises as to what kind of world view (or world views) are we going to leave behind with this rapid pace of communications, and towards what kind of new views are we moving?

1.2   A Thousand and One Approaches to the Media Revolution – Which is the Right One?

The problem areas arising in the media revolution in the broader context of globalization are spread across various branches of knowledge, from macroeconomics, sociology and on to philosophy. The media revolution in the Internet Age affects all areas of our society. To echo Niklas Luhmann, it integrally penetrates and modifies every single subsystem in our society, whether it is agriculture, culture or politics, with an intensity that can only be compared with the invention of printing and its consequences on trade, culture and science.

Today we are living far beyond the Gutenberg Galaxy (McLuhan, 1986) of yore but nevertheless we can see the points of reference for at least structural comparisons between both phenomena – that of the Internet revolution and that of the emergence of printing. In addition to "place-centric" knowledge perspectives, historical approaches also seem not only possible, but also necessary.

This thought project of a kind of macro-philosophy of media could fill a gap in the scientific discourse on media, which cannot be tackled so broadly by using the differentiated concepts surrounding the "Global Village", which were developed from sociological and macro- or micro-economic perspectives.

1.3 Introducing the Thought Project of a "Macro-Philosophy of Media"

A macro-philosophy of media could be defined as a reflective consideration of global media praxis and media politics, and thus a media ethics with a claim to global validity. In the discourse to date, relatively little significance has ever been attributed to this in orthodox philosophy, let alone the comparatively young branch of media studies.

This is a gap that should not be underestimated: When modern communications media are accessed through global networks, what has happened and happens is always in the framework of the communications and media politics of the various nations or of the private sector operating with the gold rush mentality of the "New Economy". Both are areas that offer notoriously little space for media-ethical questions.

Thus, the example of the South Korean teenagers highlights the need to develop new perspectives and approaches to the "Global Village" and its largest knowledge resource, the Internet, that include the amazing performers of the internet generation themselves. The youth as earliest adopters and fastest users of information technologies could provide perspectives in a dialogue on global media that would open spaces to ask the questions and pose the problems which the New Economy would prefer to leave unaddressed.

Phenomena like the South Korean teenagers and their relationship to communications should not be seen in isolation, but in the context of a world which is certainly not universally networked. This encourages us to look at such examples, which lead us deeper and deeper into cyberspace, in the search for new categories for space, time and human identity.

A macro-philosophy of media would address precisely such problems. It would take as its theme not the New Economy, but the people in the New Economy, the "digital consumers", the people of the Information Age and equally those on the other side – the people who are excluded from looking into cyberspace – and that is the majority of the world.

A macro-philosophy of media would be equivalent to a humane and ethically driven look into cyberspace.

2.   MAN AND MEDIA

The media-focused world parades in front of us every day, consisting of many different geographical, political and economical dimensions. Just as the ambivalence of our economic description certainly increases, the more conventional description criteria fail. So it is up to us to find new description criteria. We have to facilitate a discourse on nothing less than us and the media.

Naturally there are already forums in which such a discourse is under way, but these are mostly discussion spaces operating in the traditional culture- and social-critical way, as literature, but without a direct approach to political praxis.

The Norwegian author Jostein Gaarder has been conducting a media-philosophical discourse since the beginning of the nineties through his works of fiction: "The Time Scanner" (Gaarder, 1997) is one of his literary future dystopias, which cleverly show where the actual problems of cyberspace lie, or to put it better, could lie, when it eventually really will become commonplace to consider e-mail as snail mail, and to circle the world in record times through the Net.

He considers the kind of human that might exist in the future. In his short story, he depicts the image of humans hundreds of years after us, so networked that every activity away from the computer terminal, which of course every household would own, would be a lapse from the normal form of existence. Time and space are overcome with the help of the groundbreaking developments of quantum physics. A so-called time scanner can measure, and through its display make accessible, every place and every time in the past – with the result that, by taking constant historical cyber tours, the present is no longer created, with the exception of the one that takes place in front of the computer terminal. In the truest sense of the words, history stops. A bold idea.

Gaarder's fictional excursion into the future makes it only too clear which basic categories of human life are suddenly open to discussion and reconstitution, when it comes to the influence of the new media on human life, or rather the constant increase of this influence – an influence which is so profound that, before our very eyes, it revolutionizes the concepts of time, space and work, the basic social and economic determinants of our human coexistence.

Naturally Gaarder is not the first to conceive of a media-philosophical dystopia. Rather, he takes his place in the tradition of a whole series of thinkers who from the beginning, and in a very targeted way, have reflected with critical distance on the relationship between "Man and Media".

2.1 The Impact of Media on Social and Political Structures

Going back more than two thousand years, even in Plato's "Πολιτεια", the Republic (Plato, 1999), there are reflections on the changes in humans and their social and political contexts in the transition from oral to written culture. This critically reflected position on the emergence of new forms of media passes through history schematically and blossoms again as it arrives in the twentieth century with the conquest of television.

In the post-modern era, 2,500 years after Plato, Neil Postman delineated the fundamental influence of television on humanity. Joshua Meyrowitz (1985) even attributed to it true witchcraft in its presentation of social role models. Marshall McLuhan (1995) saw it as the extension of our five senses and the sociologist Pierre Bourdieu (1996) uncompromisingly made the point that "Television has a kind of factual monopoly in the training of the brains of most people: "Television increasingly decides who and what exists, in a social and political sense."

2.2 Humans of the Internet Age have many faces

The "Digital Age" has already found its media critics, who try to get to the bottom of what "Being Digital" (Negroponte, 1995) means and explain the radical transformation of the world of atoms to the world of weightless bits – and the demand for explanations is large.

As is now perfectly clear, this transformation has initiated a fundamental recoding of our daily life. But why does the media-critical man in the Media Age address both sides of the mirror so faint-heartedly – himself and technology in a new interdisciplinary domain of understanding?

The changes in our society, our economy and our access to knowledge brought about by digital media should set in motion a discourse that should not be reducible to technical, economic or political aspects of the media revolution.

Manuel Castells (2003) has performed the best spade-work for such a discourse: with his concept of Network Society he is able to express how greatly the recoding of our daily life in the course of the "Digital Age" has brought technology and society in parallel and how both domains have been networked into a completely new culture of behavioural goals and options.

These do nothing less than bring about a new kind of human being: not the computer-steered cyborg of horror films, but a far subtler and more ambivalent creature, a creature with many faces: that of the Korean high-speed Internet user, as well as that of 80 percent of the earth's inhabitants, who have no access to the instantaneity of the software world. Up to now, this new orientation of humans in the "Digital Age" in a global context of increasing social heterogeneity and discontinuity could not be made completely comprehensible with the individual measuring rods of economic, sociological, philosophical or even media studies thought-models.

To encapsulate this point: even a macro-philosophy of media will not be able to offer a holistically comprehensive approach to "Digital Age" man, although it would be able to analyse the concept in the media context in an as-yet unknown manner and perspective. This is urgently needed in the array of current analytical approaches to digital being.

2.3   The benefits of a macro-philosophy of media

This new model of philosophy could address what have seemed up to now fringe events: the permanent data flow of the Information Society and the continual addressability of everyone locked into the global village and its effects on our thinking in the categories of time, space and the basic concept "work", but also the ever-more extreme effects of discrepancies between an networked and an un-networked world.

A macro-philosophy of media would be able to reflect on why the categories of knowledge and information suddenly find themselves in a controversial discussion process in the Internet Age, on one hand being treated as economic resources and on the other, from the perspective of the Information Society, fatally over-valued.

A macro-philosophy of media is bound to ask why knowledge and information couldn't be democratized in the spirit of educational tradition and as a result of its increasing digitization and availability.

A media-ethical question: since digital technology is capable of facilitating easy access to knowledge and information, shouldn't every human have the right to this information and knowledge?

From this perspective, media are an ethically contentious good, and in a sense reality, which can develop political and economic thought models. The phrase "can develop" is deliberately used here, since we have to accept the notion that basic cultural-historical concepts like knowledge and information in a digital age run through the process of a disengagement of thought models that are drawn from both purely the humanities as well as purely economics and politics. It becomes a challenge to allow the individual fields and disciplines to be considered in an innovative and interdisciplinary discourse and exchange of opinions.

3. PUTTING MACRO-PHILOSOPHY OF MEDIA INTO PRACTICE

In order to be able to speak of a global framework, we need to have forums that can bring together the different interest groups of global civil society, the private and governmental sectors, under the umbrella of internationalism, state community and with a basis of principles of democratic agreement.

Macro-economics and the macro-philosophy of media should meet wherever political, economical and social changes can be discussed at a transnational level and where their implementation can be initiated. With such a framework, the macro-philosophy of media will be seen as an essential element within a praxis-oriented media ethics.

To date, only a few international bodies dealing with communication politics have included media philosophy in their proceedings.

As the community of policy negotiators in international communication politics is currently endeavoring to define a new international body which could fill the gap of an open and transparent, globally serving multi-stakeholder forum on harnessing information and communication technologies for development, all entities which are being included in that transition process should challenge themselves to not only think about the definition of a new shape in which a global discussion forum could be incorporated but rather move towards a thinking in genuine new patterns in order to create an authentically interdisciplinary discourse and heterogeneous collaboration of partners in the domain of Information and Communications technologies (ICT) for development.

3.1   Thinking Communication Policies in New Patterns in an Innovative Forum

A purely political-economic think-tank can do without media ethics, but a heterogeneous community of interests, envisaged as multi-stakeholder forum of Information and Communications Technologies and their policies cannot, if it seeks to fulfill its decent responsibilities and mandate: to ensure inclusive and transparent discussion about the digital divide, the potential that ICT have for development and the models and ways in which ICT can be harnessed to bridge the digital divide and to make the benefits of the new technologies accessible to all. This includes dealing with the teleological question of where a human in the Digital Age, with the plurality of faces that he now has, can go, and where he wants to go.

As a young citizen of the "Global Village" the present author cannot avoid challenging herself with this question whenever she encounters other young citizens of the Information Age through the Internet using technologies like instant messengers or e-mail. It is still stunning how the new information and communication technologies are able to dispel distances within milliseconds and open unprecedented opportunities for global dialogue and exchange.

Young people, as tireless users and promoters of those new ways of "Communication without Borders" are capable of providing meaningful input to both policy-making and philosophical reflection in the area of ICT. Thus they should be included formally in all discussion processes aimed at creating a new, transparent and inclusive body, a multi-stakeholder forum to advance ICT for development and harness them as a valuable tool for the next generation in particular.

Such a body is going to be further defined within the scope of forthcoming events such as the Summit examining the progress after five years towards achieving the Millennium Development Goals, originally set by Kofi Annan in his Millennium Declaration in 2000, and the ninth meeting of the UN ICT Task Force.

The UN ICT Task Force, established by Kofi Annan on request of the Economic and Social Council in 2002 attempts to add a forum with global reach and extent to the multitude of efforts to bridge the digital divide. The

Task Force is officially being supported by the Heads of State and Government of all UN member states who endorsed the ECOSOC Ministerial Declaration at the Millennium Summit in 2000.

The Task Force seeks to enhance partnerships between the United Nations system, Governments, the private sector and financing trusts and foundations, donors and programme countries in order to define and develop mechanisms to unleash the potential of ICT as key tool for development.

As the mandate of the UN ICT Task Force ends in December 2005, a vivid discussion has been launched in the ICT for development community about the needs and definitions for possible follow-up models to the Task Force.

The most common vision that has been shared so far favors an inclusive, transparent and in its structure lighter multi-stakeholder forum than the Task Force forum has been. However, those new ideas are being exposed to the different, both critical and supportive views of the various stakeholders in ICT for development.

Remarkably, the discussion process has highlighted less the general aspects which could form a Global Alliance in the best imaginable way for the global community and rather pointed to the political issues which constrain the creation of this new forum on ICT for development.

However, everybody who believes in ICTs and their potential for human development should try to imagine a global forum on ICT which follows the prerequisites of equal access to all stakeholders, of democratic rules and legitimacy.

The following section is a response to three basic ideas which dominated the Global Alliance discussion in the beginning, from the prospective of their relevance to youth:

3.2 Stronger Linkage between MDGs and ICT

First of all, the needs for a stronger linkage between the action lines in ICT for development and those declared and identified in the Millennium Development Goals (MDGs) could be fulfilled through a Global Alliance on ICT for development. Such a linkage would address youth as meaningful stakeholders and contributors to effective discussion and policy making in particular.

Young people around the globe have shown their strong interest and commitment to the fulfilment of the Millennium Development Goals, have strongly engaged themselves in the Millennium Campaign and have contributed with fresh ideas to the Millennium project as students or members of youth organizations. Furthermore, they have already implemented such a required linkage between the MDGs and ICT for development in communities like the World Summit on Information Society Youth Caucus. Members of the Youth Caucus have contributed to the Millennium Project and the Millennium Campaign, were members of the ad hoc working group for youth and the MDGs, but have also actively been involved in the World Summit on Information Society and the Global Forum of the UN ICT Task Force.

Against this background, youth participation should be warmly welcomed both in the Global Alliance and in events around the MDG + 5 that are going to deal with ICT as tool for implementing the MDGs.

How fruitful such an inclusion of young people can be, has become clear at the recently held eighth meeting of the UN ICT Task Force where the Youth Caucus of the World Summit on Information Society had been asked to officially intervene and interact with other stakeholders of the ICT for development domain in the UN ICT Task Force forum. Given the success of youth interventions in the preparatory stages and first leg of the World Summit on Information Society, the involvement of youth in the Task Force forum has been considered as being both unprecedented and indispensable for future discussion processes on ICTs for development.

A frequent criticism voiced in the World Summit on Information Society process is that the private sector has only been insufficiently involved in the ICT for development agenda. However, where interaction between private sector and civil society has proven to be particularly beneficial to the development aspect of ICT, was when it occurred between youth and the private sector: in the form of sponsorships for youth projects, campaigns or youth discussions. The private sector has supported the inclusion of young people in ICT for development and this activity should be even further enhanced. Young people are both a repository of creativity and idealism when it comes to the new technologies of the information age and the group of earliest adopters and consumers of ICT. These facts should define new action lines in the private sector when it comes to youth and ICT. The private sector is being asked increasingly to recognize the financial as well as the social potential which lies in its interaction with the youth sector. To perceive youth as one of the most lucrative groups of consumers should at the same time lead the private industry to undertake a decent commitment to empower youth not only as consumers but also as social entrepreneurs, youth activists in development and by doing so enhance the idea of human development and shared social responsibility among the generations.

3.3 Intergenerational Dialogue

South Korean youth provide the best example of the needs for intergenerational dialogue. As the fastest adopters of ICT, they provide hoards of experience and thinking that are different from the former generation. Clearly, this should be the best argument to share those different experiences and approaches in an intergenerational dialogue and by doing so move on to a decent understanding of social coherence and integration. This should not be only a prerequisite for the Global Alliance but for all community driven bodies, whether they act on a local or global level.

4. CONCLUSION

The inclusion of youth in the yet-to-be-established Global Alliance has to begin in the phase of its definition. Young people can be seen as meaningful contributors to linkages and bridges between ICT and MDGs. Consequently, youth stakeholders need to be empowered so that they can fully and formally participate in that process to make their voices have that impact they deserve.

REFERENCES

Bourdieu, Pierre (1996): Sur la télévision. Paris: Raisons d'Agir.
Castells, Manuel (2003): Das Informationszeitalter. Wirtschaft – Gesellschaft – Kultur. Band I-III. Stuttgart.
Gaarder, Jostein (1997): "The Timescanner" and "Arbitrary Consciousness". In: A Rare Bird. German Translation. Munich.
McLuhan, Marshall (1986): The Gutenberg Galaxy. The Making of Typographic Man. Toronto: University of Toronto
McLuhan, Marshall (1995): The Magic Channels. Understanding Media. Dresden. Verlag der Kunst.
Meyrowitz, Joshua (1985): "No Sense of Place": The Impact of Electronic Media on Social Behavior. Oxford.
Negroponte, Nicholas P. (1995): „Being Digital". New York. Toronto. Random House.
Plato: The Republic. Leipzig, Reclam. 1999.

EVOLVING LANDSCAPES FOR EDUCATION

Juana M. Sancho
Department de Didàctica i Organització Educativa, Universitat de Barcelona

Abstract: Education is one of the most changing and sensitive landscapes of today's
              society. Anything that has an impact on any part of society (the economy,
              work, technology or culture, etc.) has an influence on education in the short,
              medium or long term. This paper first deals with how processes of change and
              no change in society are having fundamental consequences for education. In
              acknowledgement of the importance of ICT in teaching and learning processes
              it then argues that the real challenge of education today lies in our
              understanding of the nature of knowledge and its modes or production, the
              need to evolve from a disciplinary to a cross-disciplinary approach to the
              curriculum and students' experience, and the way we approach people's
              learning processes, including both emotional and biographical issues.

1.   A CHANGING WORLD?

In the 15 years since the publication of *The Information Society: Evolving Landscapes*, edited by Jacques Berleur, many fundamental changes have taken place. Although the essence of life is change, human beings never seem to be prepared to cope with change. However, what seems to be even more distressing and creates greater turmoil are not the aspects that change, but those that remain unchanged. Thus, as suggested by Pareto (1966), a way of understanding social phenomena is the identification of elements of change and no change that compel people to deal with situations of conflict and to confront turmoil in their personal, professional and emotional lives. When related to education, these situations seem particularly conflictive and difficult.

In the following paragraphs several factors of change and no change in contemporary society along with their consequences for education will be identified.

Elements of change	Elements of no change
Developments in information and communication technologies have exacerbated processes of production, storage and transmission of information and, thus, of exogenous knowledge.	Individuals have not significantly increased their capacity to receive information and give it meaning (ontogenous knowledge).

Chen (1992) proposes a distinction between ontogenous knowledge (namely the knowledge that grows in the individual) and exogenous knowledge, which is interwoven intimately with technology. Ontogenous knowledge grows in the subject as a result of complex processes that relate innate knowledge that comes from the expression of the development of the genetic load to knowledge acquired through learning in the environment. All knowledge and processes involved in it are endogenous, regardless of whether they are located in the central nervous, the limbic or the genetic system. The development of the time scale of ontogenous knowledge is equal to the living space of an individual. This consideration raises some questions such as: Can individuals indefinitely increase their capacity to receive information and give it meaning? Are there technologies that allow for an increase in individuals' *storage* and *processing* capacity?

Exogenous knowledge defines the knowledge external to the body. It refers to public knowledge that has been accumulated by humanity in different ways and by complex social processes. Social institutions and information and communication technologies are the best bearers of this knowledge. The unit of analysis for examining exogenous knowledge is the social system as a whole and includes science, technology, the education system, cultural systems, the media, and different ideological institutions (religious and political), etc. The time scale for this knowledge type is around three million years for humanity, a hundred thousand years for *homo sapiens*, and ten thousand years for modern civilization. It is exogenous knowledge that has woven the closely-knit connection with technology and has done so in three stages.

The first stage involved the appearance of *writing* and *numeration systems* (around 3000 BC). These technologies allowed representations of knowledge to be conserved and transferred the ephemeral oral language of an acoustic body to a longer-lasting physical artefact. Writing systems gave two new dimensions to exogenous knowledge: the transfer of knowledge would no longer be limited to factors of time or place. Knowledge could be communicated horizontally with all those places where someone may need it, or vertically to future generations.

In the Western world, the second stage began in the 16th Century with the *printing press*, which provided for mass reproduction of exogenous knowledge and allowed access to this form of knowledge by a greater number of society's members.

The third stage involves the emerging information and communication technologies. The most remarkable feature of these technologies is that, for the first time, they allow for the exogenous *processing* of knowledge outside the human brain. Meanwhile, digital information and communication technologies have meant improvements in the conservation and accumulation functions of the first stage and the reproduction functions of the second. In short, information and communication technology is focused on the social structure involved in the creation, accumulation, conservation and distribution of exogenous (public) knowledge.

There is no evidence of any significant increase in human beings' memory capacity, learning rate or higher cognitive skills. This led Chen (1992) to state that a young person in Athens in 200 BC would probably do as well at school as one in Boston in 1991 AD. The person from Boston would perhaps even do far worse and would certainly know much less about his or her world than the Athenian. This is because the huge production of public knowledge exercises enormous pressure on individuals who wish to have access to it.

This statement entails the paradox that men or women of today, despite greater access to information, may indeed know considerably less about their world than their ancestors knew about theirs. This is because, proportionally, what they do not know is a lot greater than what they know (Sotelo, 1987). This phenomenon has weighty implications for education that have not been sufficiently assessed to date.

Elements of change	**Elements of no change**
Exponential growth of technological knowledge.	For most human beings, life has not only not improved but in many cases has worsened. Inequality, hunger, new and *old* illnesses continue to strike.

Some years ago in an interview that appeared in the Spanish journal *El País*, a Nobel prize winner for Physics argued that since the Second World War science had been trying to answer questions that had already been raised and resolve problems that were already known, new questions needed to be asked. Two things were required in particular.

The first involves the orientation of decisions regarding research programmes that are considered to be priority and the allocation of resources for scientific and technological developments. If, instead of focusing all effort on achieving results that can be turned into patents, commercialised, and geared to the war industry and unsustainable mass consumption, science and technology focused on a search for knowledge and techniques for the real improvement of the lives of all human beings, the world could become an unimaginable place. Perhaps more effort would be put into solving real, everyday problems that make people suffer.

The second is connected with the political and economic will to redistribute the results of technological developments and make them truly and equally accessible to all. However, as environmental groups argue, the model of wellbeing upon which Western society is based can only be maintained at the cost of a large part of the population.

The created situation has very clearly implications for education as schools reflect the enormous gap between technologically rich and poor individuals and groups.

Elements of change	Elements of no change
Income and concentration of capital in the last 10 years of the twentieth century were spectacular.	Economic power is still concentrated in the hands of a few who hold increasing power.

For Ramonet (1995), Tapscott *et al* (2000) and Ontiveros (2001) today, more than ever, the highest form of power is economic, which is increasingly concentrated in the hands of fewer people and produces increasingly harsh and unaffordable rules for most countries and groups. Then comes the media. For Ramonet (1995), none of Ted Turner, President of CNN, Rupert Murdoch, of News Corporation Limited, Bill Gates of Microsoft, Jeffrey Vinik, of Fidelity Investment, Robert Allen, of ATT, or, of course, speculators such as George Soros or many other true owners of the world have subjected their economic and information and communication projects to universal suffrage. Democracy does not apply to them. They are above the interminable debates in which concepts such as the public good, social welfare, freedom and equality are still meaningful. These types of individuals do not have time to lose. Unhindered, their money, their products and their ideas cross the borders of a globalized market. In their eyes, political power is simply the third highest power. However, electoral results like those in the last elections in Italy mean that barriers among financial, media and political power have diluted up to the point that they become confused. The current president, Silvio Berlusconi, is one of the richest men in Italy and the world and owns a powerful media corporation. The consequences of this phenomenon for aspects such as the knowledge, skills and values to be encouraged in education are considerable.

Elements of change	Elements of no change
Information and communication technologies allow access to a huge amount of information from anywhere on the planet.	The world is still structured and presented by the owners of the media (from local newspapers to Internet portals).

This change and continuity is closely related to the previous argument. The accumulation of power and capital cannot occur without the control of the media, which creates images of the world to suit those who have power. Individuals and groups with no power have little or no chance of expressing themselves, explaining their views of the world or staking their claims. This phenomenon leads to an increase in the gap between the info-rich and the info-poor, who are now not only those who do not have access to information sources, but also those who do not *control* these sources. This situation is also found in educational systems where the difference between information rich and information poor schools is constantly growing.

Elements of change	Elements of no change
The organizational, symbolic and artefactual systems of most jobs and professions have experienced profound change.	The systems of exploitation of workers still apply (temporary employment agencies, child labour, etc.) and are on the increase.

Since the 1980s, growing organizational, financial and technological changes in the workplace have led to even more complex demands on employees. The first skill considered to be necessary in societies in which profound technological changes are occurring is the capacity to deal with change itself. There is a need to be prepared to change work when a job becomes obsolete, to adapt to new software and hardware and to a way of understanding labour relations and the business world. This capacity to adapt to change requires general skills that can be used in different situations, which means that schools and universities must teach relatively general skills and leave the acquisition of specific skills to on-the-job training.

Another demand in work is the capacity to think critically and communicate effectively through the mastery of language. Problem-solving abilities and critical thought seem to be essential in many jobs. However, *critical thinking* and *higher order thinking skills* do not include the capacity to be critical of social and economic institutions, of superiors, of social standards and of cultural rules. At work, even for top executives, higher thought is more of a conformist phenomenon than a feature of dissidence. It is the aptitude to solve the problems of an engineer who sees a technical problem as something specific and not that of a reformer's tendency to identify a social problem, analyse its causes and seek to eradicate it.

The above seems to be both coherent with and contradictory to employment policies based on employee instability and unfair working conditions while it is an element of demotivation and discouragement for young people in education and training.

Elements of change	Elements of no change
Politicians, business owners and scientists now more than ever consider education to play an essential role throughout life.	In state schools, and in some private ones, there are still administrative shortfalls and limitations.

Politicians, business owners and intellectuals have never before shown so much concern for education. However, their explicit interest yields neither clear, determined policies nor significant investment for the introduction of substantial reforms in education systems and the provision of diversified learning environments adapted to the educational needs of the whole population. Hence, schools, and particularly state schools, continue to face chronically scarce resources and bureaucratic limitations that makes it difficult for them to meet the needs of an increasingly diverse and impoverished school population.

2.   CHANGE AND *NO CHANGE* IN THE EDUCATION SYSTEM

In direct relation to the above argument, in education the orientation of the elements of change/no change is to be found at different levels of the education system.

Insofar as students are concerned, the factors of change are directly related to the fact that they are individuals being educated, even though there is a current trend to assume that everyone is being educated throughout life. In addition to natural elements of change in childhood and adolescence, today's children and young people encounter quite a different situation to that of a few years ago.

- Because of the process of individuation that has occurred since the eighteenth century, children and adolescents are expected to develop their own interests, which are considered in relation to those of their family, the community, school, media, political, economic and religious systems, laws of the market, etc.
- Because of the explosion of knowledge and information, children and adolescents are expected to assume not only the traditional curriculum's content, but also, and particularly, new languages (audio-visual, IT, virtual, etc.), which do not replace any curriculum requirement, but complement it, thus multiplying learning demands and at the same time expression and communication options.
- The education system that traditionally valued students' capacity to assimilate standards and reproduce the information provided by teachers or text books, is beginning to require students to develop independent, creative thinking and problem-solving ability, to prioritise understanding over and above mechanical reproduction and, in short, to take responsibility for their learning as they will have to continue learning throughout life (OECD, 2004).

For teachers, the situation produced by elements of change is not significantly different from that of the students. However, the most significant specific transformations in their work revolve around:

- *Student characteristics.* The interests, lifestyle, expectations, values and attitudes of today's children and adolescents who attend schools have little to do with today's teachers and even with their childhood and adolescence. These differences are even evident in comparison with students of 10 or 15 years ago. The diversification of social environments provided by information and communication technologies has stripped traditional nuclei of socialization such as the family and school of their exceptional role as transmitters of values, social standards and information. Today, students need more frameworks of reference and interpretation, more intellectual tools and emotional resources than they need information. They need more items for judging and evaluation than pre-directed, factual knowledge.

- *Teacher identity.* Up to now, teachers, and particularly secondary school teachers, have been defined by the subject they teach. However, the extension of the compulsory school age (to 16 in Spain and 18 in some countries), an ever complex daily life and the delegation of many aspects of family education to schools, has made *what* is taught less and less important and *how* it is taught and *what for* much more so. This situation is seen by many teachers to mean a *decrease in standards* and a *degradation* of their function. This phenomenon, which Goodson (1998) called *repositioning* in the workplace, is also occurring place in many other jobs of a social kind, such as the health-related professions.

In an institution such as the school, which is not transformed merely by passing decree-laws, these elements of change coexist with deeply rooted elements of *no change* such as:

- *The compartmentalization of school knowledge.* As has been repeatedly shown, the choice and structure of school curricular content are still based on the nineteenth-century notions of scientific disciplines (Goodson, 2000), with repeated attempts to introduce emerging subjects, albeit on a *cross-disciplinary* basis (Yus, 1994 and Sancho, 1998). This way of understanding knowledge affects how the aim of school, particularly in the period of compulsory education, and its operation as a whole are not only perceived (Hargreaves et al, 1996) but *naturalised* (Tyack and Tobin, 1994)
- *The organization of the schools' physical and symbolic space.* In close relation to the above point, the physical, symbolic and artefactual organization of schools is designed to *transmit* to *homogeneous* groups a knowledge that is considered to be valuable, the main repository of which are teachers and text books. If this is not the case, why remove students from other learning experiences and other stimuli and interactions to have them around six or seven hours per day sitting, listening and copying, with a greater or lesser degree of understanding, what the teacher is saying, demonstrating or writing on the board?
- *Teaching practice.* In continuation of the above points, if teachers find they must *cover, give, teach* and *deliver* a syllabus full of subjects within a specific period of time, then methodological options are substantially reduced. Encouraging understanding by the students and getting their active participation in the learning process requires time, implies mutual trust, and a capacity to negotiate meanings and ways of ensuring a certain coherence between ends, means and quality in the process and the result of learning. Neither the current design of schools, nor teacher training provides the conditions for encouraging these processes and situations. In

this background, the use of resources other than the board, chalk, textbooks, the odd informative video and computer program that substitutes class or laboratory exercises is not envisaged at all.

- *Assessment.* Despite virtually constant questioning of assessment practices and their very often negative role in the process of student learning, assessment is still mainly focused on learning results shown by students in pencil and paper tests. Indeed, in spite of all reform efforts, this assessment system seems to fit most current education systems perfectly (see Fig. 1).

Figure 1. Representation of the standard sequence of the teaching and learning process.

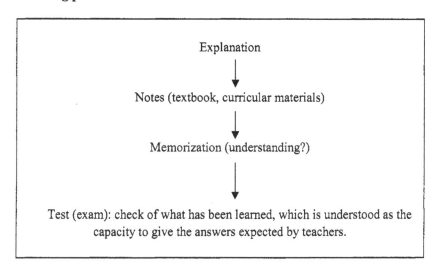

- *Teacher professional development.* A recurring theme in the history of educational renewal, innovation and reform is the need to train teachers, change their attitudes and expectations, encourage their capacity to learn, argue, make founded professional judgements and increase and extend their pedagogical baggage in order to put into practice alternative and improved forms of educational intervention. The persistent failure to provide initial and in-service training to teachers that promotes and enhances these attitudes and capacities does not facilitate elements for change in teaching practices. It also leaves intact the basic problems in today's education, which are partly reflected in the above paragraphs.
- *Professional development of teacher trainers.* The, attendance of future primary and secondary teachers at a university lacking depth in its teaching innovations can be a significant restraint on their professional

development. The retraining of trainers is a longstanding issue that urgently needs to be tackled.

- *Professional development of civil servants and politicians.* In some countries, the constant increase in regulations and bureaucratisation of education systems means that policy makers and administrative bodies are one of the greatest obstacles for schools in rising to educational challenges in today's society (Sancho, 2003 and Hargreaves, 2003).
- *Training of families.* Not all families have the training, the predisposition and the material conditions to enable them to understand the best way to use their time. To continue learning means relearning with one's child and having the self-esteem and responsibility to be able to do so. One of the factors of no change in schools is the lack of training opportunities for families to acquire and develop the emotional capacities, the knowledge and the skills that enable them to assume their paternal and maternal responsibilities.

This network of change and no change is the main stage for the education system-perplexity, disorientation and lack of references are some of the basic problems in education.

3.   FROM COMPUTERS IN EDUCATION TO EDUCATING FOR THE KNOWLEDGE SOCIETY

Technological advancement has traditionally come together with demands for the reform of school systems. Knowledge and skills, and even predisposition and motivation, required by individuals and societies are very different in different historical, social, economic and technologic contexts.

At the start of the 1960s, the general concern for the effects of technological developments on skills required and on employment levels led to an examination of many areas that are once again topical (National Commission on Technology, Automation, and Economy Progress, 1966; Jaffe and Froomkin, 1968).

In the 1980s some guidelines that were the basis for a large number of educational reforms at the end of the decade, were set out in the report *A Nation at Risk*[1], which considered that society in the United States was being eroded by a growing tide of mediocrity that was threatening the people's future and even its own future as a nation. Hence, the need to improve the

---

[1] *National Commission on Excellence in Education* (1983)

curriculum and to give a more important role to mathematics, science and technology. This was based on the argument that *basic learning* in the twenty-first century must include communication and higher problem-solving skills and scientific and technological literacy: *tools of thinking* that help us understand the technological world that surrounds us. The role of science and mathematics would not only have professional purposes, but also the development of students' problem-solving capacities and critical thinking in all areas of learning. Meanwhile other reports pointed to the need to recover humanities and placed special emphasis on critical thought as crucial in all the areas of a person's development (Broudy, 1984; Botstein, 1984). The elements involved in higher-order thinking skills generally include the capacity to use abstract systems (different types of language and representations), the capacity to build logical arguments, deductive skills, problem-solving skills and the capacity for independent learning. For Grubb (1987) this learning type is not only necessary to do well-paid jobs, but also to favour independent political thinking and a real understanding of cultural differences, something that seems basic in democratic and globalized societies, where the growing blending of cultures is a fact.

The real problem at the beginning of the 21st Century, as shown by the result of PISA (OECD, 2004) is young peoples' capacity (or incapacity) to use school knowledge and skills to solve everyday problems.

"This approach represents a change in the goals and objectives of curricula themselves, which are increasingly concerned with what students can do with what they learn and not only whether they can reproduce what they have learnt" (OECD, 2004: 20).

This is where the problem lies. In an increasingly competitive world, in which growing effectiveness in the use of public resources to meet the needs of the public and society is demanded and in which changes in work require flexible individuals, with the capacity to continue learning and a predisposition to deal with new situations, basic sound education for the great majority of people seems essential. This will enable them to understand the complexity of today's world, while following their learning path during their life. It is also necessary because there is a growing belief that countries without workers who are skilled to perform jobs in knowledge intensive companies, which require considerable intellectual work by staff, will be reduced to the category of service countries without the capacity to produce added value. Leadership on the other hand is where added value is created, nourished and developed[2].

---

[2] In Reich (1991), quoted by Tedesco (1995).

Meeting all these educational and societal challenges seems to need much more than sophisticated digital technologies.

4.   INFORMATION AND COMMUNICATION TECHNOLOGY AS A SET OF TOOLS TO TRANSFORM EDUCATION

As the present author has have discussed elsewhere (Sancho, 2004) the impressive development and application of ICT in practically all fields of human endeavour and the unbelievable power and the magnificent wealth and glamour generated by some ICT-related companies and people have aroused great interest and excitement in the realm of education. However, lessons learnt in over 40 years of research on the application of different media to improve teaching and learning processes have made well-informed educators and scholars aware that the use of any new tool does not automatically mean:

• The development and implementation of new approaches to school or academic knowledge.
• The transformation or improvement of existing teaching and learning methods or the development and implementation of better ones[3].
• The solution to all educational problems.

For practitioners, educators and researchers, the real meaning of the social transformations arising from political, economic and technological changes and the appearance of new tools is the need to meet new educational challenges, and find new kinds of practical issues and new research topics. Because political, economic and technological transformations have an impact on the construction of society and shape the inclusion/exclusion processes with their related consequences for people's learning opportunities. New information and communication technologies alter the structure of our interests (the things we think about), change the nature of symbols (the things about which we think) and modify the nature of the community (the area in which we develop our thought)[4].

This new scenario is faced by primary, secondary and higher education and vocational training and gives rise to a need for a deep rethink of teaching

---

[3] See Zammit (1992), Fabry and Higgs (1997) Richardson (2000), Burbules and Callister (2001), Cuban (2001), Pelgrum (2001), Schofield and Davidson, 2001; Zhao et al (2002), Ringstaff and Kelley, 2002; Kozman, 2003.
[4] Inis (in Tudesco, 1995).

and learning processes as a whole. This means not only reconsidering the content to be taught, the way of teaching it and of assessing student learning, but also the characteristics of the learning environments provided and the quality of the feasible learning experience. In this context, digital technologies can be considered as new learning settings in which students find an extension of their learning experience. However, the real challenge for education in today's society lies in the way educational systems are planned and implemented so they may connect with people's real educational needs.

Currently, in any education system cycle, the need both to use the available information and communication technologies and to consider the knowledge generated from the extremely wide fields of general science, technology and culture is more than accepted.

When planning and implementing the curriculum in this context, education systems find it necessary to establish the most suitable means to encourage students' understanding, problem-solving capacities and willingness to learn. If widespread use of the printing press made textbooks essential, it seems logical that widespread use of ICT, with their enormous culture-enhancing power (Steinberg and Kincheloe, 1997) will make these tools also essential.

It is sometimes argued that ICT will take longer to become involved in education as it is much more versatile that previous technologies and requires much more training to use it. This posture is backed by a large number of studies that reveal the scant impact of this technology on education, despite the large resources that are invested (Cuban, 2001; Ringstaff and Kelley, 2002; Kozman, 2003).

Nevertheless, there are currently a wide range of media to choose from in teaching. In addition, in the case of digital information and communication technologies, user options are multiplied (see Table 1)

Table 1. Educational use of ICT (OECD, 2001).

Type of application	Examples	Educational use
General tools	Word processing, presentation, spreadsheet, multimedia authoring, including Internet publishing.	Becoming increasingly important; require innovative and creative thinking from the teacher; the quality lies in the application and not the tool itself as such tools are not dependent on particular content.
Teacher tools	On-line lesson outlines; computer-projector systems; whiteboards.	Lesson preparation; whole class teaching with shared view of screen; interaction managed by teacher.
Communications	e-mail, e-learning; video conferencing, Internet browsers.	Require a view of education as something reaching beyond school, family in the out-of-school context.
Resources	Especially Web-based and either general or specifically educational.	Used according to availability, however required; for resource-based, skills-oriented learning.
Computer-assisted instruction (CAI)	Drill-and-practice, related to a certain kind of content and relatively unsophisticated.	Offers individual learning opportunities without expensive development: appears to go well with transmission models of teaching and learning.
Integrated learning systems (ILS)	Individualized task assignment, assessment and progression, including CAI, with recording and reporting of achievement.	These appear to lie outside teacher-led instruction and learning, but are only truly effective as an integrated part of the learning process, which may have to be re-thought.
Computer-based assessment tools	Examination boards are developing computer-based examinations, intended to mimic paper-based tests.	Components give advantage to the computer literate: teachers will need to incorporate some elements of similar tasks in their teaching, in order to prepare students adequately.
Management tools	Classroom procedures School administration Publication of results Communication	Students' progress, deficiency analysis, etc. Financial, personnel and educational resources. Parents, governors. Inspectorate, general public. *e.g.* between school and home

Furthermore, continuous development of communication tools is leading to an extension of the concept of space and time in education as they provide for permanent access to information and digital tutoring, which are theoretically increasingly suited to learners' needs. Upon fulfilment of the "forecasts" of the inevitable prophets that accompany all new technology, these virtual environments are already transforming ongoing professional training and will also change both primary and secondary schools. However, nearly 40 years after computers were introduced in education, the presence of these tools in classrooms is still the exception and educational planning and implementation continue to have the same organizational and symbolic structures.

For McClintock (2000:76) "digital technologies are very powerful forces that are deeply shaping our culture, education included. That is said from the perspective of a historical observer. From the perspective of people acting, trying to shape practice through the intentional use of digital technologies, we must recognize that educational change happens very slowly, that schools constitute a vast, far-flung system of practice. At best we will work reform slowly. But like iron, once wrought, it will hold its shape for ages".

The basic hypotheses upon which all McClintock's projects at the Institute of Learning Technologies at Teachers' College were based led to the following *axioms* that set out the basic conditions for ICT to act as a trigger for educational innovation.

- High-speed WAN to LAN connectivity is essential and should reach all classrooms.
- Schools should integrate new media into all aspects of the curriculum for students of all ages.
- Diffusion of the use of new media in a school should not be mandatory, but the result of the responsive support of voluntary efforts – constructivism in school management.
- Schools should design their technological implementation as investments in students' power to acquire their education.
- Educators should abandon the premise that they can predict what a good student should have learned as a result of an educational experience.
- Classrooms should become places from which students and teachers communicate interactively, among themselves, and with specialists and peers throughout the locality, culture, and globe.
- Under emerging conditions, precepts of pedagogical common sense may need substantial review, particularly with respect to what is and is not

age appropriate, who is entitle to make sound pedagogical choices, and how feedback controlling the educational process should work.

In McClintock's own account, the results so far have been disappointing. Progress has been good only with regard to the first axiom of practice: it has proven feasible to link schools via high-speed wide area networks to the Internet and to provide widespread access to that connectivity through local area networks reaching multiple workstations in each classroom. Such connectivity is expensive, but the resources available for it are increasing while its cost is diminishing. Insofar as the other axioms of practice are concerned, we have learned a well-established truth – significant historical change in complex institutions takes place on a time-scale of extended duration.

This situation is highly similar in most education systems that make considerable investment in ICT.

5.   CHANGING THE FOCUS AND THE PRIORITIES

As argued above, some proposals for reform initiated in many countries in the 1990s, interpreted in a strict sense, would require a deep, sometimes radical (from the root) transformation of the way in which schools operate. The effects of such transformation could range from architecture and the use of human and material resources inside and outside the centre to the use and distribution of time and space (Sancho, 2000).

Elsewhere, reports drawn up by influential bodies with very diverse interests such as the Organisation for Economic Co-operation and Development (OECD, 1998), UNESCO (Delors et al, 2003), the European Commission (Study Group on Education and Training, 1996), the European Roundtable of Industrialists (ERT, 1995) have defined what have come to be called the educational needs of the Information Society. All support the need to educate a citizen who:

- Is integrally developed.
- Is able to make reflective judgements.
- Has developed research-like skills.
- Is able to attain self-fulfilment and the option of finding out what he or she really is.
- Is able to overcome the tension between which is world-wide and local, universal and particular, between tradition and modernity, the long-term

and short-term, indispensable competence and the concern for equal opportunity, the exceptional development of knowledge and their assimilation skills, and that which is spiritual and material,

- Has a broad range of skills that include the capacity to work with numbers, to read and write, critical judgement and basic knowledge of mathematics, science and technology, humanities, economic and social sciences,
- Knows how to think and not only to accumulate facts,
- Has the self-discipline to adapt to constant change and deal with continuous challenges.
- Has developed his or her communication capacity, linguistic skills, creativity, capacity for teamwork, and problem-solving capacity.
- Is qualified to work and use new technologies, exercises responsibility as a citizen, enjoys individual self-satisfaction, maintains an independent investigative spirit, is aware of his or her social rights and duties, and has a sustained disposal to work.

One item common to most of these views is the need to foster the development of higher order thinking skills. This is not only because it may be considered a professional skill for a small group of elite workers in jobs that involve freedom and creativity. It is rather because for most workers or the unemployed the capacity of independent political thinking and real understanding of cultural differences is still necessary. There is also broad consensus that a technological society requires greater powers of abstraction and independence in daily life so that complexity may be mastered and not be a source of confusion and exclusion.

6. WHERE SHOULD THESE CITIZENS BE EDUCATED?

It seems evident that this entails much more than the use of the most outstanding digital technology. The series of actions required to educate this type of pupil, student or citizen is far removed from the physical, intellectual and emotional potential of current schools. The education system must change a great deal to favour a learning environment that encourages this type of education. Moreover, the most important changes will not only be related to the incorporation of information and communication technologies in schools but are of a social and pedagogical nature and are related to:

- The need to transform the way in which the nature, the methods of production and types of knowledge are understood.

- A change from the disciplinary vision of the curriculum towards a more cross-disciplinary and experiential approach, which takes into consideration the evolution of knowledge and the need to interpret the world.
- The way of representing the forms of learning of different individuals and the factors involved therein. More comprehensive views of cognition that are aware of all the items involved in learning (emotions, likes, feelings, motivation, expectations, context, and biographies, etc.) are required.
- The way of conceiving education and learning scenarios. The basic organizational metaphor of the school must undergo a profound transformation. The class, as an exceptional place for education must become a multiple series of learning environments in which students can develop and acquire the skills, knowledge and attitudes necessary to live in society. In such environments information and communication technologies will probably have an important place. This will bring with it a need to generate new pedagogical know-how with regard to the planning and monitoring of student learning in diverse situations.

Many things must change in today's education system if a better future for the individuals and society is to be attained. Most are not within the reach of teaching professionals or the most appealing digital technologies. They are associated with legislative decisions, investment in material and human resources, training plans, working conditions, general social conditions, etc. Others are connected more with those people most directly involved in practice, and with their knowledge, predisposition and attitude. Hence, teachers' professional development is repeatedly mentioned as crucial in education.

In short, the education system as a whole needs to be rethought. There is a need to try out other ways of understanding contexts for teaching and learning, the content of learning itself, and the role of those involved in the process and of the means used.

7.   CONCLUSION

Education is one of the most changing and sensitive landscapes of today's society. Anything that has an impact on any part of society (the economy, work, technology or culture, etc.) has an influence on education in the short, medium or long term. From this perspective, a more complex and holistic view of education is required in order truly to meet the challenges of current education systems. Only an approach capable of taking into account the consequences of change and no change at different levels of society will prove to be the theoretical and practical basis upon which to develop teaching and learning scenarios for all kinds of learners. Taking into account this should be done in an ever-evolving political, economic, social, cultural, technological and educational landscape.

REFERENCES

Botstein, L. (1984) Lenguage reasoning and the Humanities. En C.E. Finn, Jr., D. Ravitch y R. T. Fancher (Eds.) *Againts Mediocrity : The Humanities in America's High School*. New York: Holmes and Meier Pu.

Broudy, H. S. (1984) The uses of humanistic schooling. En C.E. Finn, Jr., D. Ravitch y R. T. Fancher (Eds.) *Againts Mediocrity : The Humanities in America's High School*. New York: Holmes and Meier Pu.

Cuban, L. (2001). *Oversold and Underused. Computers in Classrooms*. Cambridge, MA: Harvard University Press.

Chen, D (1992) An Epistemic Analysis of the Interaction between Knowledge, Education, and Technology. En E. Barrett (Ed.) *Sociomedia. Multimedia, Hypermedia and the Social Construction of Knowledge*. Cambridge, Ma.: MIT Press.

Delors, J. et al. (2003) *Learning, the treasure within: report to UNESCO of the International Commission on Education for the Twenty-first Century*. Paris: UNESCO.

ERT (1995) *Education for Europeans. Towards the Learning Society. A report from the European Round Table of Industrialists*. Polycopied.

Fabry, D. L., & Higgs, J. R. (1997). Barriers to the effective use of technology in education: current status. *Journal of Educational Computing Research*, 17(4), 385-395.

Goodson, I. F. (1998) The Educational Researcher as Public Intelectual. *British Journal of Educational Research*., Vol. 25, 3, pp. 277-297.

Goodson, I. (2000) *The changing curriculum: studies in social construction*. New York: Peter Lang Inc.

Grubb, W. N. (1987) Responding to the Constancy of Change: New Technologies and Future Demands on US. En G. Burke y R.W. Rumberger (Eds.) *The Future of Technology on Work and Education*. The Falmes Press.

Hargreaves, A. (2003) Teaching in the knowledge society: education in the age of insecurity. Buckingham: Open University.

Hargreaves, A., Earl, L. and Ryan, J. (1996) *Schooling for change: reinventing education for early adolescents*. London: Falmer Press.

Jaffe, A. J. y Froomkin, J. (1968) *Technology and Jobs: Automation in Perspective*. New York: Praeger Pu.

Kincheloe, J. L. and Steinberg , S. R. (Eds.) (1997) *Kinderculture : the corporate construction of childhood*. Boulder, Colo. : WestviewPress.

Kozman, R. B. (2003). *Technology, Innovation, and Educational Change –A Global Perspective*. Washington, DC: ISTE

McClintock, R. (2000) Prácticas pedagógicas emergentes. *Cuadernos de Pedagogía*, 290, pp. 74-76.

National Commition on Technology, Automation, and Economy Porgress (1966) *Technology and American Economy*. Washington, DC: US Government Printing Office.

OECD (1998) *Education Policy Analysis 1998*. Paris: CERI.

OECD (2001) *Learning to Change embracing: ICT at Schools*. París: OCDE.

OECD (2004) *Learning for Tomorrow's World. First Results from PISA 2003*. París: OECD.

Ontiveros, E. (2001) *La economia de la red*. Madrid: Taurus.

Pareto, W. (1966) *Sociological Writings*. London: Pall Mall Press.

Pelgrumn, W. J. (2001) Obstacles to the integration of ICT in education: results from a worldwide educational assessment. *Computers & Education, 37, 163-187.*

Ramonet, I. (1997) *Un mundo sin rumbo*. Madrid: Temas de debate.

Richardson, J. (2000): *ICT Implementation in Education. An analysis of implementation strategies in Australia, Canada, Finland and Israel*. Final Report. Ministry of Education, Luxembourg.

Ringstaff, and C. Kelley, L. (2002). *The Learning Return on Our Educational Technology Investment*. WestEd. http://www.wested.org/cs/we/view/rs/619.

Sancho, J. M. (1998) Misturar água e azeite ou procurar uma nova "solução"? *Pátio. Revista Pedagógica*, 5, pp. 12-17.

Sancho, J. M. (2000) Diversificar los espacios de enseñanza. *Cuadernos de Pedagogía*, 290, pp. 54-57.

Sancho, J. M. (2003) 2nd European conference on Information Technology in Education and Citizenship: a critical insight. *Education, Communication and Information (ECi)*, 3(3), pp. 281-286.

Sancho, J. M. (2004) Expanding Learning Experiences: Possibilities and Limitations of Virtual Learning Environments. En J. Bento, J. P. Duarte, M. V. Heitor, y W, J. Mitchell (Eds,) *Collaborative Design and Learning Competence Building*. Westport, CT: Praeger. Pp. 55-78.

Schofield, J.W., & Davidson, A.L. (2002). *Bringing the Internet to school: Lessons from an urban district*. San Francisco, CA: Jossey-Bass. Sotelo, I. (1987) Poder y técnica. *Revista de Occidente*, 71, pp. 5-16.

Study Group on Education and Training (1996) *Accomplishing Europe through Education and Training*. Brussels: European Commission. DG XII.

Tapscott, D., Ticoll, D. and Lowy , A. (2000) *Digital capital. Harnessing the Power of Business Webs*. Boston : Harvard **Business** School Press.

Tyack, D. & Tobin, W. (1994) The "grammar" of schooling: Why has it been so hard to change? *American Educational Research Journal*, 31, 453-479.

Tedesco, J. C. (1995) *El nuevo pacto educativo*. Madrid: Anaya.

Yus, R. (1994) Dos mundos contradictorios. *Cuadernos de Pedagogía*, 227, pp. 25-39.

Zammit, S. A. (1992). Factors facilitating or hindering the use of computers in schools. *Educational Research*, 34(1),57-66.

Zhao et al. (2002). Conditions for classroom technology innovations: Executive summary. *Teachers College Record, 104* (3) 482-515.

ABDUCTIVE REASONING AND ICT ENHANCED LEARNING: TOWARDS THE EPISTEMOLOGY OF DIGITAL NOMADS

Erkki Patokorpi
IAMSR, Åbo Akademi University, Finland

Abstract: The core features of mobile technology are said to be mobility, interactivity, contextuality, ubiquity, pervasiveness, personalization and collaboration. These features seem to tally surprisingly well with the ideals of constructivist pedagogy. Information and communication technology -enhanced learning in general and mobile learning in particular seem to favour the abductive form of reasoning. I suggest that abduction is the mobile (or "pedestrian") form of reasoning *par excellence* because it meets the demands of a mobile learner envisioned by constructivist pedagogues. However, knowledge by abduction has its limitations. In addition to abduction, tacit knowledge and aura are concepts that help exploring the limits of ICT-enhanced knowledge and learning. It is suggested further that there are certain features connected to advanced mobile technologies by which one may overcome some limitations of ICT-enhanced education and edutainment. These features are multisensoriality, context-awareness and vireality (i.e. mixtures of the real and the virtual).

Key words: Technology enhanced learning, edutainment, mobile technology, nomadicity, constructivist pedagogy, abduction

1.   INTRODUCTION

Mobile and wireless technologies are the new cutting-edge of modern information and communication technology (ICT). Educators have embraced ICT and are trying to find ways of integrating it in the curriculum as well as in their day-to-day teaching. Concepts like mobility and edutainment challenge the old pedagogical principles and practices as educators combine modern ICT with constructivist ideals of learning. Some visionaries claim that we are all turning into nomads (Keen and Mackintosh, 2001; Carlsson and Walden, 2002; Kleinrock, 2001; Sørensen, 2002; 2003). In a nomadic culture learning does not take place in the classroom but wherever one is in need of relevant information or new skills. Yet it is not clear how the new ICT will (if at all) change the ways we perceive the world around us, and how educators could or should use the new tools?

This paper is the first approximation of a larger research project, consisting of five research articles. The topic of each individual article belongs to a well-established field of scientific research. Each numbered section in this paper corresponds to one future research article. The first section discusses the claim, made by some influential computer science and information systems researchers, that we are on the threshold of a new paradigm of digital communication and computing – true digital nomadicity. Section two presents the *credo* of constructivist pedagogy, and its relation to technology enhanced learning. The third section introduces abductive reasoning, and argues that it is the most central inferential mechanism at work in interaction taking place in advanced ICT environments in general and in mobile environments in particular. Section four charts the limits of digital objects and interaction with the assistance of three philosophical concepts: abduction, tacit knowledge and aura. Section five briefly examines the features of the emerging paradigm of digital interaction. The features examined are: context-awareness, multisensoriality and vireality. Taken together these topical fields make up a motley crew whose mutual implications are hard to account for or verify. Abduction is the primary unit of analysis, tying all these topics together. Abduction enables crossing over disciplinary boundaries and at the same time retaining an acceptable level of scientific rigour. In summary the paper proposes a focal area of future enquiry along with tentative methodological recommendations.

2.   WHAT DO THE TECH VISIONARIES MEAN WHEN THEY TALK ABOUT DIGITAL NOMADS?

It is becoming extremely clear that some key concepts used in computer science and information systems literature – most notably those of nomadicity, mobility and interaction – cannot any more satisfactorily capture the present-day reality of advanced mobile technology environments. Although we are still partly trapped in the old world of fixed computing platforms, accessed by users with the same (personal) device from the same IP address, the world of radical mobility – true nomadicity – is just round the corner (see esp. Kleinrock, 2001). Peter Wegner (1997), Carsten Sørensen (2002; 2003) and Leonard Kleinrock (2001), among others, have aspired to describe and explain the workings of this paradigm shift from a strapped mobility to truly nomadic digital environments.

"We are all nomads," says Leonard Kleinrock in an article that was published in 1996. And he continues: "but we lack the systems support to assist us in our various forms of mobility" (p. 351). For Kleinrock, nomadicity means two different things. First, nomadicity implies the technological capability to deal with temporary disconnectedness, caused by movement from one connected place to another connected place, and second, the seamless and transparent technological support for nomads, for whom being on the move is the normal state of affairs. In a more recent paper, Kleinrock (2001) starts off with the assumption that most users of computing, communication and services are people on the move, and here he systematically uses the word nomadicity to refer to a phenomenon in which the state of being on the move is the normal state and not a break from the normal. Kleinrock underlines the need for a better infrastructure and a more advanced system support for nomadic users so that the computing environment adjusts itself to the user rather than the other way round. Computing should become as transparent and convenient a product as electricity (on the utility model see Rappa, 2004). According to Kleinrock, we are on our way to a world of true nomadicity.

Portable computing – in the form of laptops, mobile phones, PDAs and handheld computers – set the so-called knowledge workers free from the physical confines of the office. Along this line of thought, mobility has traditionally meant the ability of the user to move anywhere, anytime and yet stay connected, independently of the geographical constraints. For instance, Kopomaa (2000) talks about urban nomads and their "placeless use" of mobile devices. This kind of mobility Kakihara and Sorensen (2001; 2002) call spatial mobility: people in the post-industrial era are geographically independent "nomads" supported by various technologies.

Let us call it contextual mobility when context is, in some form, taken into account. Positioning (e.g. GPS, GLONASS, Galileo) is the single most important technology that makes contextual mobility possible (see e.g. Spriestersbach and Vogler, 2002; Priyantha et al., 2001; Liljedal, 2002). In other words, the location where the device is being used has an important impact on the nature of the information presented and on the whole interaction. All the same, this type of discussion focuses on the technological aspects of mobility. Some writers take a step further, trying for instance to make sense of both persons and devices moving in space (see e.g. O'Hare and Gregory, 2000; Floch et al., 2001), and of the value that such technologically supported connectedness while moving creates in m-commerce or in work (Anckar and Eriksson, 2003).

To sum up so far, in the early days of mobility, most mobile applications still sought to hide the location of use. Mobility implied first of all being able to move anywhere, anytime and still staying connected – to be able to stay happily oblivious about location. In contrast, context-aware design, to name one example, tries to exploit location, making some aspects of it an integral part of the interaction between the user, the mobile system and the mobile device. Sørensen and his associates (2002; 2003; Kakihara and Sørensen, 2001; 2002; Pica and Kakihara, 2003) have vigorously propagated for an even more expanded view on mobility, one which would better take into account the fact that not just devices and persons move but that also objects, spaces and symbols do so. This fact entails that over and above the spatial context, we consider the social and virtual contexts of use.

Researchers consistently stress the importance of personalization as the key to enhanced usability of mobile services. When machines universally talk to one another, personalized user interfaces seem to be the only way to reasonably well cater for individual information and service needs (Omojokun and Isbell, 2003). Unfortunately, at the same time as context is becoming more important than ever, our personalization techniques have seen little progress (Lyytinen and Yoo, 2002; Sørensen, 2002).

Traditionally computability is seen in line with the algorithmic model. According to Peter Wegner (1997), equating computability with the behaviour that Turing machines are able to do (i.e. to compute mathematical functions), falls short of satisfactorily describing the behaviour of object-oriented and distributed or decentralized multiagent systems. Peter Wegner and Dina Goldin (1999; Goldin and Wegner, 2004) say that the interaction of this sort of advanced computing systems is similar to dialogue, question-answering and two-person games in the sense that inputs are dynamically dependent on prior outputs, whereas in a Turing machine the inputs are history-independent and reproducible. Keil and Goldin (2003) characterize decentralized multiagent systems as open systems that are constructed and constrained by the environment rather than designed. A termite colony is an example of a decentralized multiagent system in nature. Without design (i.e., an internal representation of a shared goal) as well as without a capacity for planning and coordination, the termites as a colony are capable of building a nest. If Wegner and his colleagues are right, we have to revise our thinking not only of human-computer interaction but also of interaction within computers and computing systems.

The term ubiquity (Lat. *ubique*, everywhere) conveys the idea that computing will be available in all places and at all times. Ubiquitous computing and communication means intelligent environments in which various distributed computing units are linked together by heterogeneous communication links (see e.g. Abowd and Mynatt, 2000). Ubiquitous mobile computing, in order to be really ubiquitous, entails that different networking technologies work seamlessly together (see e.g. Chen and Petrie, 2003). Ubiquitous computing is not the same thing as nomadic computing. The term nomadicity implies that the user carries the technology with him/her, whereas ubiquity implies that the world itself is computerized. Presently, these two lines of development are converging. Other terms related to ubiquitous and nomadic computing are for instance ambient intelligence, distributed and context-aware systems, tangible interaction, mobile informatics and pervasive computing (Lyytinen and Yoo, 2002).

It seems plausible that the recent developments described above constitute a new paradigm, although we are still missing a common theoretical ground, by the help of which to make sense of it. It means that the epistemological conditions have changed or are changing, too. As I try to argue in the course of the project, abduction will play a central part in the new world of digital nomads.

3. CONSTRUCTIVIST PEDAGOGY AND ICT ENHANCED LEARNING – A MATCH MADE IN HEAVEN?

It is generally claimed by educationalists that ICT mediated, and especially mobile, learning realizes the central ideals of constructivist pedagogy. In modern constructivist learning theories, knowledge is seen essentially as a social phenomenon; a social construct. Because the learner builds on his prior knowledge and beliefs as well as on the knowledge and beliefs (and actions) of others, learning needs to be scrutinized in its social, cultural and historical context (Piaget, 1975; Piaget and Inhälder, 1982; Vygotsky, 1969; Leontjev, 1977; Engeström, 1987; Tynjälä, 1999; Järvinen, 2001). According to Järvinen (2001), technology-enhanced learning supports "naturally" learning by manipulation (e.g. trial and error), comparison and problem solving in a non-prescriptive real-world-like context that leaves room for creative thinking and innovation.

Recent research literature indicates that there is a fairly clear consensus on the central features of modern constructivist methodology (see e.g. Järvinen, 2001; Tynjälä, 1999; Ahtee and Pehkonen, 1994; Johansson, 1999; Poikela, 2002). First of all, constructivist pedagogues underline the importance of *a larger goal* that organizes smaller tasks into a sensible whole, giving an incentive to take care also of the less exciting intermediate routines. Consequently, constructivist learning usually takes the form of a project (e.g. Pehkonen, L., 1994). Learning is not focused on separate facts but on *a problem*. The learner needs to feel that the problem in some way concerns him (i.e. to *own the problem*) in order to be motivated to try to solve it. The problem should be *close to a problem in the real world*. When dealing with a real-world problem the student turns straight to information sources in the real world instead of trying to figure out what one would do *if* this were a real situation (see e.g. Kanet and Barut, 2003; Leino, 1994). Unlike in traditional teaching, in constructivist learning there is no one right answer but *many possible solutions to a problem* or at least if there is one right solution, there are many alternative routes to it.

It follows from what has been said above that it is the learner and not the teacher who needs to take in a significant degree the *responsibility for gathering knowledge*. The learning environment, too, should be in some sense *similar to a real-world environment*. This usually means going out from the traditional classroom, and learning things in their authentic environment (see e.g. Lehtonen, 2002). The learner's prior knowledge, experience and skills should be taken into account. Even if the learning materials was not something practical but facts or abstract concepts, the learner will better understand and remember them if they are *built on his prior knowledge and experience* (e.g. Ahtee, 1994; Haapasalo, 1994). People are different, with different experiences, skills, interests and goals. Constructivist education seeks to take this fact into account by leaving *room for alternative individual learning strategies*.

Constructivists underline the social aspect of learning; *all forms of interaction are encouraged*, and usually assignments involve teamwork or other forms of cooperation. Consequently, communication with peers and outsiders is also encouraged, unlike in traditional teaching where consulting one's neighbor is usually considered cheating. The demand for *iteration* is based on the conception that knowledge is not something ready-made and static but an ongoing process. The learners need to retrace their steps and constantly revise their knowledge and skills in interaction with their environment. Constructivist learning is thus usually constructed in a form that allows a cyclic movement, that is, a possibility to return to earlier stages or to review intermediate results. When the learning process itself is more important than the outcome, it follows that evaluation should focus on the process rather than the outcome (Björkqvist, 1994). The final feature stressed by constructivist pedagogues is *guidance*. In constructivist learning methodology traditional teacher monologue ex cathedra is replaced by guidance, in which the teacher's role is to facilitate learning by giving pieces of advice and guiding onto the right direction.

A cursory look at what teachers say about the practical use of ICT in education indicates that ICT enhanced learning seems exceptionally well to tally with the constructivist ideals. According to Sotillo (2003), "[n]ew developments in wireless networking and computing will facilitate the implementation of pedagogical practices that are congruent with a constructivist educational philosophy. Such learning practices incorporate higher-order skills like problem-solving, reasoning, and reflection". Arja Puurula (2002) claims that teaching by virtual environments (or telematic teaching) has a number of advantages over more conventional methods. It seems that the students cooperate more, work more intensively and are more motivated than in conventional classroom teaching. Telematic teaching is an efficient equalizer, leveling regional and social inequalities (see also e.g. Hussain et al., 2003). Langseth (2002) stresses creativity and the fact that the pupils take responsibility for their own work, and, instead of using their logical and linguistic faculties, use a "broader range of intelligences according to their personal preferences" (pp. 124-125). Langseth continues: "The web offers individuality in the sense that you can choose your own pace, your own source of information, and your own method; in a group or alone" (p. 125; see also e.g. Kurzel et al., 2003). One more general point made by teachers is that the focus is on collaborative work, not on the final product. These views are probably representative of the enlightened popular idea of the matter. All in all, ICT-enhanced teaching is supposed to be more democratic, more personal, give broader skills, more creative, more interactive, and so forth. We could say that constructivist pedagogy and ICT mediated knowledge and learning seem to have at least the following general features in common: the construction of personal meaning; an incentive to collaboration; the learner is mainly responsible over the information seeking process; learning by doing (i.e. praxis over theory).

In recent literature, the earlier claims that e-learning saves time and makes learning more efficient have been challenged (see e.g. Eales, 2004;

Judge, 2004). Nevertheless, the general opinion among constructivist pedagogues seems to be that the ICT-mediated learning and the constructivist educational doctrine is a match made in heaven. And, at least on the surface, so it seems. Furthermore, it seems that the features associated with both constructivist learning and the new technologies used for supporting that learning – democratic, personal, skilled, creative and interactive – are also used for describing knowledge by abduction.

4. THE LOGIC OF SHERLOCK HOLMES IN LEARNING THROUGH TECHNOLOGY

Sherlock Holmes, the hero of Arthur Conan Doyle's novels, often amazed his loyal friend Dr. Watson by drawing a correct conclusion from an array of seemingly disparate and unconnected facts and observations. The method used by Sherlock Holmes is abduction. Abduction is inference to the best explanation. Here is an example of abduction from Charles Sanders Peirce (1996; 2001):

All beans from this bag are white.

These beans are white.

Therefore, these beans come from this bag.

The inference is not formally (i.e., deductively or analytically) valid – because the beans could come from somewhere else – but this form of reasoning conveys the manner in which people reason when making discoveries in the sense of coming up with new ideas. Abduction is considered a logic of discovery.

As a logic of discovery, abduction is essentially a matter of finding and following clues. However, a clue alone is not enough (Peltonen, 1999). A clue leads the reasoner to something that he already knows. The observation of a clue is in relation to the observer's background knowledge. In other words, clues without models or theories are useless. Abduction, in contrast to the mere following of clues, aims at eliciting new knowledge. One cannot become an adept detective, that is, skilful in finding clues, by following rules. The semiotic (i.e., dealing with signs , symbols, clues) paradigm of knowledge does not deal with a disciplined regulation of coded knowledge, yet the clues are there for all to see. However, the clues that are there for all to see are qualitative and unique. They cannot be measured and regulated. This sets the stage for knowledge that is essentially personal. It is personal in the sense that individuals differ in their ability to detect clues, due to individual differences in their prior knowledge and experience as well as logical acumen (see e.g., Ginzburg, 1989; Peltonen, 1999).

Abduction seems to be central to the form of knowledge used in ICT enhanced learning. According to the Italian microhistorian Carlo Ginzburg, certain sciences or disciplines typically allow or call for interpretation and the searching of clues. Ginzburg calls them symptomatological sciences. Medicine, history, physical astronomy, geology, palaeontology, physical anthropology, ethnography, archaeology belong to the symptomatological sciences. These disciplines could also be called – at least in their 19th-Century form – private detective sciences (Ginzburg, 1989). These disciplines embraced the semiotic paradigm based on the searching of clues or symptoms.

So, there seems to be an area of knowledge that suits or calls for the form of reasoning called abduction and for the way of retrieving knowledge that accompanies it. It seems that abduction is also admirably suitable for describing and explaining the special epistemological circumstances of modern ICT mediated learning. Abduction is not yet fully understood but it certainly seems a better conceptual tool than descriptive adjectives like "mobility" and "ubiquity" that are presently used in mobile technology research. It is better because: First, abduction is a single (as well as rigorous and well-defined) unit of analysis, allowing one to analyse and compare diverse phenomena with good scientific accuracy. Second, abduction catches the gist of how humans reason under uncertainty in a context. Abduction, as a scientific tool, brings to mind fuzzy logic, which was at first an outcast but has by now proved its scientific worth and practical potential. An advanced mobile computing situation calls for, or even compels to, the use of abductive reasoning.

The use of abduction offered here is twofold. First, abduction is an analytical tool that will explain certain features of mobile technology. Second, abduction is probably the central inferential mechanism at work when learners learn in an ICT or mobile context.

5. WHAT OBJECTS MADE OF BITS AND BYTES CANNOT DO: ABDUCTION, AURA AND TACIT KNOWLEDGE

In the same way as traditional classroom teaching sets boundaries to what and how learners can learn there seem to be some limitations to ICT-enhanced and mobile knowledge, that is, limitations or conditions set by e-learning and m-learning environments. A brief look will be taken below at these limitations with the help of three well-known philosophical concepts: abduction, aura and tacit knowledge.

The armchair approach of Sherlock Holmes (i.e., abduction) does not work in all cases but has its limitations. Some avenues of investigation require systematic observations and induction; or deduction; or experiments, using expensive special machinery or other equipment; special skills, and so forth. The construction of a personal meaning goes at times against the objectives of more traditional educational principles, which include the dissemination of uniform knowledge and eradication of false conceptions. Especially as a result of the immense increase in information, the eradication of erroneous conceptions has become one of the most important and most difficult tasks of today's teachers.

Aura, in turn, gives expression to the intuition that a copy (even a perfect copy) of Leonardo Da Vinci's Mona Lisa is not the same thing as the original. The concept of aura is Walter Benjamin's attempt to put a finger on the inimitable qualities that an original object has (or is supposed to have). Walter Benjamin's defence of the unique was a reaction to the expansion of the reproductive industries into art in the early 20th Century. He tried to find the unique features of a work of art in photography, too, so that photography could enter the realm of the unique. Reproduction, or copying, destroys the unique in things, that is, it destroys their aura. An object has a history and a patina. Patina is a number of physical traces which can be detected for instance by chemical analysis. A history of an object consists for instance of a known record of the people that have owned the object and places that it has been in. Unique traces guarantee an object's authenticity. With technical reproduction like photography authenticity cannot be ascertained. To have an aura is to be unique (Benjamin, 1991).

Benjamin posits aura in the things themselves. This is difficult to accept. Following Matti Peltonen (1999), the present writer unceremoniously rejects Benjamin's habit of positing meanings in objects themselves. It is rather human beings that posit meanings in objects. The romantic idea of the uniqueness of artefacts and the uniqueness of individual artists and their genius lies at the bottom of this thought construction. Its heyday was especially in the Renaissance and the modern era. Aura is rather a historical construction; an idea, an attitude, and a practice that has a historical origin, and therefore a historical end as well. The idea of aura rests on the well-known social and economic structures of the art market. Quite as easily the unique features (aura) may lose their value in the eyes of the beholder and in the social and economic system. Photography, Warhol's reproductive art, digital products which can be copied and reproduced perfectly may be steps towards a different way of seeing works of art and other "unique" objects. The young generations may well constitute a public with a different sensibility.

Some knowledge is tacit, i.e. knowledge that cannot be communicated verbally: we know more than we are able to tell. According to Michael Polanyí (1964; 1967), knowledge is a human construction, and although it is public, it is at the same time to a great extent personal. Knowledge is personal in the sense that our emotions and experiences are an important and inescapable part of our knowledge. However, the language, concepts and intellectual tools we use when processing our experiences come from the social and linguistic community (i.e., from other people) whose members we are. The concepts we inherit and use always have a tacit dimension. Some knowledge, like special skills, has a large proportion of tacit knowledge. It follows that to mediate tacit knowledge, practical or physical interaction with people, machines and objects in time and place are required.

Especially in terms of its collaborative potential, ICT-mediated learning enhances the mediation of skills (and thus the transference of tacit knowledge) whenever the learner gets practical guidance by a human collaborator (via a computation element) or built-in machine guidance. It seems plausible that there is a limit (which can be approached but never quite reached) to how well tacit knowledge can be mediated purely by ICT without the subject being on the spot in flesh and blood. Shapin and Schaffer (1989) as well as Collins and Kusch (1998) have illuminated the immense difficulties in repeating from a distance – that is, without hands-on guidance – a scientific experiment that involves more or less complicated equipment. Online shopping is another example. It is common knowledge that online customers need to feel the fabric, smell the flowers and kick the tyres in order to be persuaded to buy something.

6.   THE NEW-PARADIGM FEATURES: CONTEXT-AWARENESS, VIREALITY AND MULTISENSORIALITY

Context-awareness, multisensoriality and vireality force us rethink especially the effects of mobile technologies in various walks of life. The present author has coined the word "vireality" to refer to a certain kind of mixture of the real and the virtual. The above, selected features seem to mark the beginning of a second era (a new paradigm) of very advanced ICT in general and mobile technology in particular, transgressing the earlier limits. Although the current infrastructure does not support such advanced (especially mobile) environments on any larger scale, it is possible to envision such an environment being fully functional. Consequently, this part of the paper is futuristic in nature, and will focus on the key enabling technologies of nomadic and ubiquitous computing environments.

Context-awareness refers to the knowledge that can be read from the user's environment, including all sorts of devices and information that are to be found in that environment. Context-aware systems are thus systems in which the devices are to some extent aware of their own status, the user status, the surroundings, and (possibly) other devices in the surroundings (Bellavista *et al.*, 2003). Intuitively the demands of context are not too difficult to grasp. Robert Filman in his editorial in *IEEE Internet Computing* puts it nicely:

> If someone approaches you in Times Square and asks if you know how to get to Carnegie Hall, for example, you don't answer, "Yes." Rather, you take account of the question's context. You might consider the weather or seek information (or infer from age and dress) on whether the questioner prefers the subway, a taxi, or walking. People are context-aware in their service responses – and more concerned with intent than literal interpretation (Filman, 2003).

The conclusion one can draw from this is that future systems will need to be able to have conversations. This pressure to make systems increasingly human-like is particularly felt in context-aware mobile systems. Examples of context-aware applications include active maps that automatically change as the user moves (Schilit *et al.*, 1994); applications for the orientation of device position indoors (Bahl *et al.*, 2000) and outdoors (Priyantha *et al.*, 2000) or for both, as the Cyberguide (Abowd *et al.*, 1996) and the REAL (Baus *et al.*, 2001).

Virtual reality is "a computer generated interactive, three-dimensional environment in which a person is immersed" (Aukstakalnis, 1992). To take a step further towards virtuality, systems or environments that extend parts of the real world with virtual elements are called augmented realities or augmented reality systems. It is possible to create virtual environments that are based on metaphors instead of scientific theories or models. These virtual models can be realized in the computer environment without any need to verify them against the physical reality (Turoff, 1997). The ability to "opportunistically" and at will to mould virtual environments is seen as the most valuable function of virtuality in computing systems (see e.g. O'Hare, 2000).

The tangible User Interface (TUI) is a major step towards a more advanced digital environment with a more balanced combination of the real and the virtual. TUI combines physical objects and physical space with virtual elements. So-called Tangible Bits allow haptic (i.e., grasp and manipulate) interaction with physical objects, exploiting, too, the mediation of information by versatile sensory input from the background. Examples of this include such display media as light, sound and airflow, which exert their impact on the more peripheral senses. Tangible Bits thus copies the rich potential of the division between foreground and background of awareness in regular human activity in the real world. Here one could talk about ambient intelligence, which makes the environment intelligent by extending and augmenting space with digital information and objects. This vision of augmented reality by TUI turns walls and tables into interface surfaces, coupling graspable objects like books with digital information as well as exploiting other senses than vision (e.g. touch by airflow) in communication. With TUI, computing will become "truly ubiquitous" (Ishii and Ullmer, 1997), an integral, although invisible, part of our everyday environment.

The development of context-aware systems and augmented reality gets a boost from sensor technologies. Today we have a rich supply of minuscule, very cheap sensors – so-called sentient objects. Sentient objects interact with the physical environment, making applications "aware" of the physical space they occupy. Sentient objects, which are especially important in mobile environments, extend the possibilities of communication and flow of information between machines and humans further (see e.g. Biegel and Cahill, 2003). As a result, the scope of the semiotic paradigm of knowledge gets wider. The resultant environment is artificial (compared to a natural environment) in the sense that the experiential (e.g. learning) materials can to a greater extent than before be trumped up, arranged and manipulated by the users or by others.

7. CONCLUSION

The train of thought presented in this paper proceeds as follows: ICT-enhanced learning realizes the central ideals of constructivist pedagogy. Abduction goes a long way towards describing and explaining the special epistemological circumstances of ICT-enhanced interaction and learning. ICT cuts out aspects of knowledge and reality, making abduction at some point inoperable. Aura and tacit knowledge, too, help in marking out the limits of discursive means via abduction (i.e., semiotic means). Context-awareness, multisensoriality and vireality (a balanced mixture of the real and the virtual) broaden the potential of abduction (i.e., the semiotic paradigm of knowledge). These three selected, new-paradigm features broaden the scope of abductive reasoning because they bring us (as users) a step closer to kicking tyres and feeling the fabric.

REFERENCES

Abowd, G.D. and E.D. Mynatt (2000), Charting past, present, and future research in ubiquitous computing, ACM Transactions on Computer-Human Interaction, 7(1), 29-58.

Ahtee, M. (1994), The development in teaching of physics, in Ahtee, M. and Pehkonen, E. (eds.), 43-50.

Ahtee, M. and Pehkonen, E. (eds.) (1994), Constructivist Viewpoints for School Teaching and Learning in Mathematics and Science, Research Report 131. Yliopistopaino, Helsinki.

Anckar, B. and N. Eriksson (2003), Mobility: The Basis for Value Creation in Mobile Commerce? Proceedings of the SSGRR 2003s Conference, L'Aquila, Italy.

Aukstakalnis, S. and D. Blatner, S.F. Roth (1992), Silicon Mirage: The Art and Science of Virtual Reality, Peachbit Press.

Bahl, P. and V. N. Padmanabhan (2000), Radar: An in-building rf-based user location and tracking system, Proceedings of the IEEE Infocom, Tel-Aviv, Israel.

Baus, J. and C. Kray, A. Krüger, W. Wahlster (2001), A Resource-Adaptive Mobile Navigation System, online at http://w5.cs.uni-sb.de/~krueger/papers/iui2002.pdf accessed 22.04.2003.

Bellavista, P. and A. Corradi, R. Montanari, C. Stefanelli (2003), Dynamic Binding in Mobile Applications: A Middleware Approach, IEEE Internet Computing. 7(2), 34-42.

Benjamin, W. (1991), Bild och dialektik, Brutus Östlings bokförlag Symposion Ab: Stockholm.

Biegel, G. and V. Cahill (2003), Sentient Objects: Towards Middleware for Mobile, Context-aware Applications, in European Research Consortium for Informatics and Mathematics, ERCIM News No. 54.

Björkqvist, O. (1994), Social constructivism and assessment, in Ahtee, M. and Pehkonen, E. (eds.), 19-26.

Carlsson C., P. Walden (2002), Mobile Commerce: Some Extensions of Core Concepts and Key Issues, Proceedings of the SSGRR International Conference on Advances in Infrastructure for e-Business, e-Education, e-Science and e-Medicine on the Internet, L'Aquila, Italy.

Chen, Y-F.R. and C. Petrie. (2003), Ubiquitous Mobile Computing, IEEE Internet Computing, 7(2), 16-17.

Collins, H. and M. Kusch (1998), The shape of actions: what humans and machines can do, Cambridge (Mass.), MIT Press.

Eales, R. T.J. (2004), Crossing the Border: Comparing Partial and Fully Online Learning, in e-Society 2003, IADIS International Conference, 218-225.

Engeström, Y. (1987), Learning by Expanding, Orienta-Konsultit Oy, Helsinki.

Filman, R.E. (2003), Do You Know How to Get to Carnegie Hall? IEEE Internet Computing, March and April, 4-5.

Floch, J. and S. Hallsteinsen, A. Lie, H.I. Myrhaug (2001), A Reference Model for Context-Aware Mobile Services, online at www.nik.no/2001/06-floch.pdf accessed 29.07.2003.

Ginzburg, C. (1989), Ledtrådar. Essäer om konst, förbjuden kunskap och dold historia, Stockholm: häften för kritiska studier.

Goldin, D., P. Wegner (2004), The Origins of the Turing Thesis Myth, Brown University Technical Report CS-04-13.

Haapasalo, L. (1994), Model for construction and assessment of conceptual and procedural knowledge, in Ahtee, M. and Pehkonen, E. (eds.), 87-92.

Hussain, H. and Embi, Z.C., Hashim, S. (2003), A Conceptualized Framework for Edutainment, Informing Science: InSite – Where Parallels Intersect, 1077-1083.

Ishii, H. and B. Ullmer (1997), Tangible Bits: Towards Seamless Interfaces between People, Bits and Atoms, online at http://www.acm.org/sigchi/chi97/proceedings/paper/hi.htm accessed 24.07.2003.

Järvinen, E-M. (2001), Education about and through Technology. In search of More Appropriate Pedagogical Approaches to Technology Education, Acta Universitates Ouluensis, E 50. Oulun yliopisto, Oulu.

Johansson, K. (1999), Konstruktivism i distansutbildning. Studerandes uppfattning om konstrukivistisk lärande. Umeå universitet, Umeå.

Judge, M. (2004), The Wired for Learning Project in Ireland. A Classic Tale of Technology, School Culture and the Problem of Change, in e-Society 2003, IADIS International Conference, 226-235.

Kakihara, M. and C. Sørensen (2001), Expanding the 'mobility' concept, ACM SIGGROUP Bulletin archive. 22(3), 33-37.

Kakihara, M. and C. Sørensen (2002), Mobility: An Extended Perspective, in Proceedings of the Hawai'i International Conference on System Sciences, Big Island, Hawaii.

Kanet, J.J. and Barut, M. (2003), Problem-Based Learning for Production and Operations Management, Decision Sciences, A Journal of Innovative Education. Volume 1, Number 1, Spring, 99-114.

Keen, P.G.W. and R. Mackintosh (2001), The Freedom Economy: Gaining the MCommerce Edge in the Era of the Wireless Internet, New York: Osborne/McGraw-Hill.

Keil, D. and D. Goldin (2003), Modelling Indirect Interaction in Open Computational Systems, in Proceedings of the Twelfth IEEE International Workshops on Enabling Technologies: Infrastructure for Collaborative Enterprises (WETICE'03), Linz, Austria.

Kleinrock, L. (1996), Nomadicity: Anytime, anywhere in a Disconnected World. Mobile Networks and Applications. 1, 351-357.

Kleinrock, L. (2001), Breaking Loose. Communications of the ACM, 44(9), 41-45.

Kopomaa, T. (2000), The City in Your Pocket. Birth of the mobile Information Society, Gaudeamus: Helsinki.

Kurzel, F. and Slay, J., Hagenus, K. (2003), Personalising the Learning Environment, Informing Science: InSite – Where Parallels Intersect, 589-596.

Langseth, I. (2002), Sense of Identity, Karppinen, S. (ed.),123-128. Neothemi-Cultural Heritage and ICT at a Glance, Studia Pedagogica 28, Helsinki: Hakapaino.

Lehtonen, H. (2002), Oppimisen halu ja opiskelu, Poikela, E. (ed.), Ongelmaperustainen pedagogiikka: Teoriaa ja käytäntöä. Tampere University Press, Tampere, 148-161.

Leino, J. (1994), Theoretical considerations on constructivism, Ahtee, M. and Pehkonen, E. (eds.), 13-18.

Leontjev, A.N. (1977), Toiminta, tietoisuus, persoonallisuus. Kansankulttuuri, Helsinki.

Liljedal, A. (2002), Design Implications for Context Aware Mobile Games, online at www.interactiveinstitute.se/mobility/Files/Master%20Thesis.pdf accessed 18.02.2003.

Lyytinen K., Y. Yoo (2002), Issues and Challenges in Ubiquitous Computing. Communications of the ACM, 45(12), 63-65.

Lyytinen, K., Y.Yoo (2002), Research Commentary: The Next Wave of Nomadic Computing, Information Systems Research. 13(4), 377-388.

O'Hare, G.M.P. (2000), Agents, Mobility and Virtuality: A Necessary Synergy. Proceedings of International ICSC Symposium on Multi-Agents and Mobile Agents in Virtual Organisations and E-Commerce – MAMA.

Omojokun, O. and C.L. Isbell Jr. (2003), User Modeling for Personalized Universal Appliance Interaction. Proceedings of the 2003 Conference on Diversity in Computing, 65-68.

Pehkonen, L. (1994), Project work – a way to learn actively, Ahtee, M. and Pehkonen, E. (eds.), 161-164.

Peirce, C.S. (1996), Collected Papers 1931-58, C. Hartshorne, P. Weiss and A. Burks. (eds.), Cambridge (Mass.): Harvard University Press.

Peirce, C.S. (2001), Johdatus tieteen logiikkaan: ja muita kirjoituksia. Tampere: Vastapaino.

Peltonen, M. (1999), Mikrohistoriasta, Helsinki: Gaudeamus.

Piaget, J. (1982), The Essential Piaget. Routledge, Kegan & Paul, London.

Piaget, J. and Inhälder, B. (1975), Die Entwicklung des räumlichen Denkens beim Kinde. Gesammelte Werke 6. Studienausgabe. Ernst Klett Verlag, Stuttgart.

Pica, D. and M. Kakihara (2003), The Duality of Mobility: Designing Fluid Organizations through Stable Interaction, The 11th European Conference on Information Systems (ECIS 2003), Naples, Italy.

Poikela, E. (ed.) (2002), Ongelmaperustainen pedagogiikka: Teoriaa ja käytäntöä. Tampere University Press, Tampere.

Poikela, E. and Nummenmaa, A.R. (2002), Ongelmaperustainen oppiminen tiedon ja osaamisen tuottamisen strategiana, Poikela, E. (ed.), Ongelmaperustainen pedagogiikka – teoriaa ja käytäntöä. Tampere University Press, Tampere.

Polanyí, M. (1964), Personal knowledge: towards a post-critical philosophy, New York: Harper Torchbooks,.

Polanyí, M. (1967), The tacit dimension. London : Routledge & Kegan Paul.

Priyantha, N.B. and A.K.L., Miu, H Balakrishnan, Teller, S. (2001), The Cricket Compass for Context-Aware Mobile Applications. MIT Laboratory for Computer Science, online at http://nms.lcs.mit.edu/papers/CricketCompass.pdf accessed 18.02.2003.

Puurula, A. (2002), Searching for a pedagogical basis for teaching cultural heritage using virtual environments, Karppinen, S. (ed.), 17-32. Neothemi-Cultural Heritage and ICT at a Glance. Studia Pedagogica 28, Helsinki: Hakapaino.

Rappa, M. (2004), The Utility Business Model and the Future of Computing Services, IBM Systems Journal, 43(1), 32-42.

Schilit, B. and N. Adams, R. Want (1994), Context-aware computing applications, IEEE Workshop on Mobile Computing Systems and Applications, Santa Cruz, CA, US.

Shapin, S. and S. Schaffer (1989), Leviathan and the air-pump: Hobbes, Boyle, and the experimental life, Princeton (NJ): Princeton University Press.

Sørensen, C. (2002), Digital Nomads and Mobile Service, Receiver. Vodafone, online at www.receiver.vodafone.com accessed 11.12.2004.

Sørensen, C. (2003), Research Issues in Mobile Informatics: Classical Concerns, Pragmatic Issues and Emerging Discourses, Workshop on Ubiquitous Working Environment at Weatherhead School of Management, Case Western Reserve University, Cleveland Ohio, USA, K. Lyytinen & Y. Yoo (eds.), online at is.lse.ac.uk/staff/sorensen/downloads/Sorensen2003.pdf accessed 5.1.2005.

Sotillo, S.M. (2003), Pedagogical Advantages of Ubiquitous Computing in a Wireless Environment, Case Studies, May/June 2003, online at: http://ts.mivu.org/default.asp?show=article&id=950 accessed 25.5.2004.

Spriestersbach, A. and H. Vogler (2002), Location-Awareness for Improving the Usability of Mobile Enterprise Applications, SAP AG and SAP Labs, online at http://www.sapdesignguild.org/community/readers/reader_mobile.asp accessed 18.02.2003.

Turoff, M. (1997), Virtuality, Communications of the ACM, September 1997/Vol. 40. No. 9, 38-43.

Tynjälä, P. and L. Helle, K. Lonka, M. Murtonen, J. Mäkinen, Olkinuora, E. (2001), A University Studies Perspectives into the Development of Professional Expertise, in Pantzar, E. and R. Savolainen, P. Tynjälä (eds.), In Search for a Human-Centred Information Society, Tampere University Press, Tampere, 143-170.

Tynjälä. P. (1999), Oppiminen tiedon rakentamisen. Konstruktivistisen oppimiskäsityksen perusteita, Tammer-Paino Oy, Tampere.

Vygotsky, L.S. (1969), Denken und Sprechen, Fischer, Frankfurt am Main.

Wegner, P. (1997), Why Interaction Is More Powerful than Algorithms? Communications of the ACM, 40(5), 81-91.

Wegner, P. and D. Goldin (1999), Interaction, Computability, and Church's Thesis. Draft, online at http://www.cse.uconn.edu/~dqg/papers/ accessed 29.10.2004.

PART 3

SOCIAL ASPECTS

E-CARE CO-ORDINATION: AN INCLUSIVE COMMUNITY-WIDE HOLISTIC APPROACH

M. McKeon Stosuy, B.R.M. Manning, B.R. Layzell
European Federation for Medical Informatics:Working Group on Planning and Modelling in Healthcare

Abstract: Substantial demographic changes, while centred on the number of elderly in the developed world, are forcing a radical re-evaluation of how to deliver care more effectively to all, including those with chronic conditions or disabilities. Optimizing and co-ordinating complete multi-disciplinary, multi-agency end-to-end service processes are seen as key to this. As real-time access to comprehensive care records and relevant knowledge systems is a critical enabler, the paper explores the closer integration of the patient experience as an "expert" knowledge source rather than just an "informed" one. It highlights the dependency on the effective management of change will have on such a major transformation.

Key words: One-stop-shops, customer relationship management [CRM], electronic healthcare/social care records [EHR], knowledge acquisition and management, genomaps, virtual enterprises, end-to-end processes.

1. INTRODUCTION – THE DEMOGRAPHIC IMPERATIVE

Governments across much of the developed world are having to respond to growing impacts of an ageing population. As forecasts all show a steep rise in the percentage of the population who are older than 65 years old doubling to close to 40% by the middle of the century (Commission of the European Communities, 2004) the pattern of service demand is likely alter radically.

In addition to the inevitable increase in acute care episodes there will be substantial growth in the number patients with chronic conditions needing a wide spectrum of care to be delivered within the community. The overall effect will almost certainly be a major shift in the balance of service provision towards chronic care.

Even from these crude estimates it is evident that current models of care are wholly unsustainable on resource grounds alone. This suggests that end-to-end care processes will have to be streamlined to optimize carer input through increasing use of assistive technologies.

This in turn will mean a substantial revision away from the present split separating clinical from "social" interventions to a more "holistic" one. While remaining an essential key component, medicine will need to cede elements of its traditionally care controlling role and concentrate more on maximizing use of its professional expertise.

Early moves in this direction can already be seen in the use of multi-disciplinary team approaches in acute care both in hospitals and the community. Exactly how this will evolve will not only on depend how the various professions adapt and re-balance their responsibilities, but also on how rapidly new enabling technologies emerge and how acceptable they become to those in need.

2.   E-HEALTHCARE

Current initiatives (Commission of the European Communities, 2001, and Braun et al, 2003) in the e-health arena have tended to split between acute care, which is generally centred on shared life-long Electronic Health Records and transfer of clinical information; and "one-stop-shop" community Resource Centres where people can turn for information, advice and action across a wide spectrum of Health and Welfare/Human Services support.

While the emphasis on information requirements and flows differs in detail between them, they share the common need for access to patient history data as well as to relevant knowledge and/or expertise. This paper focuses on the latter area and its development potential.

3.   AGEING AND DISABILITY COMMUNITY RESOURCE CENTRES

Current "one-stop-shop" initiatives tend to follow commercial practice presenting a centralized front office interfacing with the citizen (McKeon Stosuy and Manning, 2005). This is generally designed around a multi-service bureaux split between a direct face-to-face contact facility and a call centre, often using somewhat rudimentary processes and information systems.

Figure 1. Multi-mode, Multi Agency Service Coordination Model

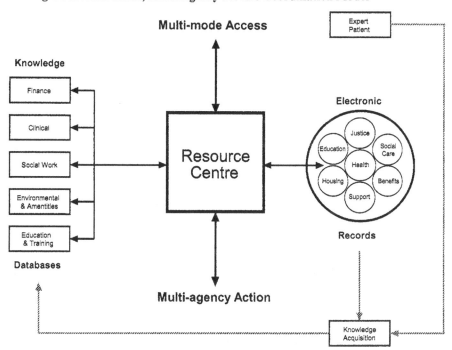

The proposed Resource Centre concept (Manning et al, 2004) is outlined in Figure 1 above. In order to serve the widest possible range of clients/patients, it needs to span the complete spectrum of communications media ranging from direct personal contact through to current and emergent digital technologies. Similarly it will have to resolve and co-ordinate action on anything from the seemingly trivial to immensely complex long-term issues that involve a multiplicity of agencies and professions (Stosuy. and Eaglin, 1999).

An intrinsic aspect of these responses will be the need for rapid access to appropriate multi-agency background historic client/patient data together with the most relevant expertise and supporting knowledge. As currency and accuracy of information from both sources will be vital to ensuring that correct action is taken and right advice and guidance is given, the underlying information systems will need to maintained and validated in real-time[7]. Moreover these systems will need to be fully secure both to protect patient confidentiality and to conform to data protection legislative constraints.

In the longer term the store of appropriate knowledge will need to accommodate the acquisition, validation, indexing and accessible storage of information to be gleaned from "expert patient" groups in addition to that derived from research.

Figure 2. Generic Resource Centre

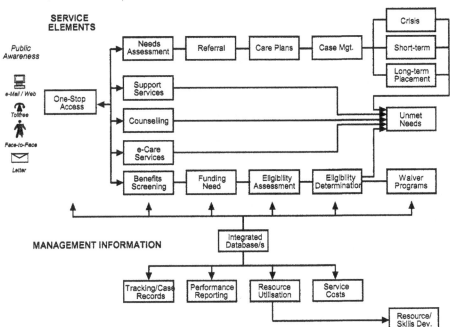

While the scope of the services provided will no doubt continue to evolve steadily with time, some of the more common service features and management information requirements are shown above in Fig 2.

The bulk of the workload will almost inevitably focus on case co-ordination action through the usual sequence of assessment, planning and delivery, frequently together with one or more of the other streams shown. Due to age or disability many cases will involve some measure of financial screening and subsequent securing of necessary support. With many cases involving access to multi-agency records this brings with it the problem of identity validation due to the lack of agreed standards and differing indexing and registration referencing.

From a management perspective the complete set of end-to-end processes will need to be properly underpinned not only with appropriate operational support systems and communications infrastructure, but also with relevant cross-agency service delivery performance information. Within this latter context, shortfalls in terms of unmet needs, resources, efficiency, effectiveness and quality will be a major priority in ensuring that high standards are maintained as the changing demographic situation begins to impact service delivery.

4.   E-CARE IN THE COMMUNITY

As e-Care becomes an increasingly available option that enables patients/clients to maintain an independent lifestyle through the use of a combination of monitoring and assistive technologies, it will introduce an additional "care watch" role within the Resource Centre. This will provide continuous monitoring of its patients/clients for any abnormal or untoward clinical, lifestyle or environmental condition coupled with the ability to call out/deploy resources as necessary in response to their professional assessment of the urgency and type of need.

Figure 3. e-Care Support Service Features (Barlow et al 2003)

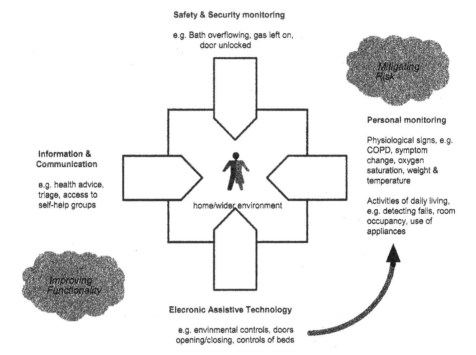

Within the overall aim of maximizing its patient's/client's capacity for continued independent living, e-Care will also provide a two way link to the Resource Centre for advice and help as well as to support groups all targeted to reduce isolation and build "virtual communities" of shared interests.

In addition to the networked support services shown in Fig 3 above, an evolving range of autonomous closed loop and interlinked Assistive Technologies will not only fill gaps left by the shortfall in available carers, but also provide increasing functionality to all concerned. As indicated this will steadily extend to combine elements of the "Smart House" and the "Hospital at Home" into a single pro-active support system that optimizes the living environment to the needs of its users (DTI/PERA, 2004). Besides providing much enhanced functionality beyond existing building services, it will also enhance ambulatory capabilities in a variety of ways including Bluetooth linked wearable monitoring devices, advanced prosthetic devices, mobility aids, and sensory/communication aids.

5. KNOWLEDGE EXTRACTION SYSTEM

For Resource Centres to be fully effective, immediate access to information that is current and correct is critically important. This applies equally to comprehensive case data and to multi-disciplinary domain knowledge, the lack of it will rapidly devalue the system and alienate users.

Leading-edge technology (Audentify, 2003) now offers a way to move towards dynamic service updating with input from users and care service agencies all routed through a single Portal as shown in Fig. 4 below. Face-to-face and phone call audio data can be automatically transcribed in a common text format, together with incoming letters, and merged with all other communications traffic.

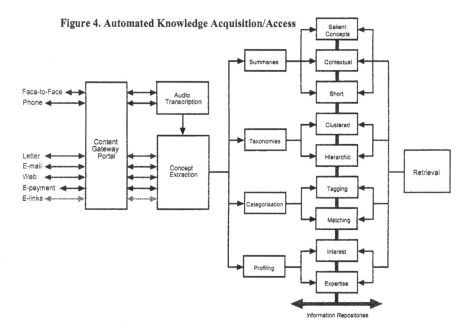

Figure 4. Automated Knowledge Acquisition/Access

In addition to onward transmission of all data to its appropriate destinations, the total content can be filtered through an on-line knowledge extraction process. This analyzes and sorts all throughput into logical concept groups and then classifies the content as required into:

- *Summaries*: compact content down to a more manageable scale that assists rapid assimilation, recognition of recurrent themes and trends, as well as adding valuable cues to hidden key contextual information
- *Taxonomies*: minimize the work involved in organizing content for intuitive navigation and provide a useful aid to recognition of emergent patterns and trends.
- *Categories*: enable hypertext and other linkage mechanisms required to support rapid searches.
- *Profiles:* provide search criteria for interest groups and expertise holders.

6.   THE "EXPERT" PATIENT – CONCEPT AND CONTEXT

The concept of the expert patient is not a new phenomenon, but one that has matured over decades. Latterly it has begun to move out of the shadows as the recognition of the swelling numbers of the aged who already do, or shortly will, present ever more cases with chronic conditions.

While the patient has traditionally been seen as the "subject of care", this also has begun to change from an "arms-length" position to one more directly involved in the care decision process. This is particularly true of some chronic conditions where the role of the "expert patient" is effectively integrated within the care team, as circumstance has often made them the more knowledgeable member in terms of what works for them.

In the UK the concept of the expert patient (UK Department of Health, 2001) recognizes that clinicians often accept that "my patient understands their disease better than I do" and that as such patients have too long been an untapped resource. However their focus is more on developing the "informed" patients as key decision-makers in self-management programmes. rather than as true "experts" adding to the sum of clinical knowledge of their condition.

This can also be particularly true for disabled people, where the nature of their disability may pose problems and even a very real risk of harm of through inappropriate medical, nursing or therapeutic interventions due to the specific characteristics of their physiology. In such circumstances the patient is revealed as the real expert who often has to lead and "teach" unfamiliar health professionals in alternative methods of diagnosis, treatment, therapy and care.

There is evidence that some disabled people who, while not ill, often find that the nature of their disability can be a barrier to getting the proper treatment when they are actually ill. Relatively simple clinical procedures, such as, taking a blood sample, giving an injection, etc., often become exceedingly complicated or even dangerous with such disabilities as e.g. spina bifida; congenital organ or musculo-skeletal or limb deficiencies. Inappropriate medical or nursing intervention through lack of specialist expertise can all too easily worsen matters however well intentioned this is.

In this context there is an evident need to accept differences between the "informed" and the true "expert" and take the concept a stage further by seeking ways to secure and formalize this additional body of knowledge. The evolution of this approach, backed by easily accessible information and assistive technologies may provide a solution to the demographic dilemma as it would allow elderly, disabled people and those suffering with chronic health conditions to maintain an independent lifestyle with less involvement from a waning pool of carers.

This transformation from "self informed" patients into recognisable "experts" will be undoubtedly a move in the right direction. However as their conditions have no definable clinical outcome it is all too easy for them to be referred to various other sources of help, e.g. self help groups or other voluntary agencies, and then, as of old, quietly slipping out of the national health care service ambit, as they do not fit the conventional medical model.

Initial moves to make access to information and services more coherent have led towards a "one-stop-shop" Contact/Advice Centre approach that combines new technology with traditional personal contact procedures. This evolution of e-care provision across the public and associated private and voluntary sectors has begun to lay the foundations for such interactive multi-disciplinary team co-ordination with "expert patients" at its heart.

This would follow the established path of e-business development with the creation of "virtual utilities" linking the multiple agencies that are involved in providing health and welfare/human services into a single seamless entity.

7.   THE EXPERT PATIENT – KNOWLEDGE ACQUISITION, TRANSFER AND INTEGRITY

National health care providers have begun a series of programmes focusing on chronic disease self-management as a way to encourage and enable patients to develop the skills, abilities and coping strategies needed to improve their quality of life. This will also free up care resources needed to cope with increasing demand, as well as accepting that as many patient's "understand their disease better than clinicians" they should become key decision takers in the treatment process.

The knowledge that patients with chronic conditions have can be demonstrated to be far more than that which clinicians usually collect, as it includes considerable in-depth experience of the relative merits or otherwise of treatment practiced on them. Paradoxically little or no attempt has been made to collect, collate and disseminate this information within the clinical community at large.

Much of this probably stems from the traditional position of the patient as the passive "subject of care", rather than as an active contributor of unique practical expertise on optimum outcomes of different treatment processes. This is reinforced by the "womb-to-tomb" longitudinal Electronic Health Record which has no place for direct inclusion of the patient's own observations as an "expert".

The implication of this is that current records are incomplete, since they exclude insight into optimal treatment processes and outcome quality measures from the patient's point of view. However it poses the question of how to "qualify", and hence ensure the validity, quality and level of "expertise" presented by such patients. While traditional methods are obviously impractical and out of place, this is hardly a justifiable reason for rejecting such potentially valuable input.

Two fairly pragmatic options for collecting and analysing this information would seem to be by:

• Selection of suitably perceptive and articulate patients who would be given internet access to record their input to a secure site possibly as a blog.
• Creation of secure condition-specific patient membership only interactive self-help/support websites encouraging exchange of experience.

As all input would be received via a web portal its evolving knowledge content could be extracted, analysed and categorised within metadata architectures (Layzell and Lindsay, 2004) using some of the more sophisticated knowledge acquisition techniques described below. This automatic process would have the advantage that, as the resulting aggregated data will remain anonymised it would not include references to the patient data sources.

In the former case the source data would be lodged either within the EHR along with other clinical input or within a separate record. Although the latter already exist in some countries in terms of chronic condition self-help information exchange websites, their open unregulated nature leaves them open to abuse. However this could be countered by re-creating them within a secure controlled access service, whose conformance to EU recommended codes of conduct and system "seals of approval" (Försstrom et al, 1999) would enhance trust and confidence.

In both cases membership would be clinician approved to ensure patient validity, and would have to conform both to national Data Protection legislation together with prevailing ethical and confidentiality constraints. This does not however remove the need for appropriate professional oversight to double-check and validate this input to obviate perceptual or factual errors creeping in and devaluing its content (Layzell, 2001).

8.   DELIVERING MEASURABLE BENEFITS

However desirable acceptance of change across communities of users and providers may be, it is entirely dependent on gaining sufficient consensus across all the various organizations concerned, not only in terms of economies of scale and cost but also service quality concerns.

However as cost-benefit modelling is a major topic in its own right and the economic implications of this proposed approach have been addressed elsewhere (McKeon Stosuy and Manning, 2005), these issues have been considered beyond the scope of this paper. Instead the focus has been on the more qualitative, yet critical issue of system benefits realization that has all too frequently been the rock on which so many IT-driven initiatives have foundered

This needs to span all parties and individuals involved at every level, so that the potential benefits to be attained outweigh the pain and anguish likely to result. A major move to the proposed radically new e-care coordinated model will need to be tightly focused on delivering significant and easily recognisable measurable benefits to all.

The key issue is how to manage the transition from the current "as is" condition to the desired "to be" situation. This is considerably magnified when it involves creating a multi-agency "Virtual Enterprise", as outlined below in Figure 5.

Figure 5. Benefits realization

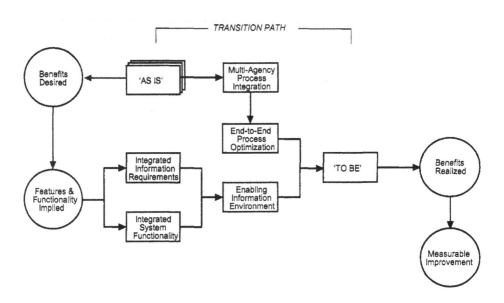

The re-configuration of the set of multiple and disconnected business processes into a single optimized end-to-end one requires the re-design of both business and enabling technology infrastructures to deliver the full "to be" functionality. Its implementation however has to be seen as a business transformation process involving significant change in professional cultures and working practice, which needs very careful management to ensure expectations are met and desired benefits are realized.

9.   CONCLUSION

The proposed approach brings together several strands of development in response to national and international initiatives that can potentially provide a generic model for the necessary sea-change in multi-disciplinary, multi-agency care service provision that will be needed to address the demographic imperatives of this century. As part of this it recommends further evolution and formalisation of the concept of the Expert Patient into a valued source clinical knowledge, together with a better understanding of issues that are central to the success of such changes.

REFERENCES

Audentify. 2003. Audentify: Contact Centre Solutions – White Paper.

Braun, A; Constantelou A, Karounou V, Ligtoet A & Burgelmann J-C., 2003. Prospecting e-health in the context of a Eurpean Ageing Society; Quantifying and qualifying needs. Final report November 2003 IPTS/ESTO: Sevilla, Spain

Commission of the European Communities, 2001. [COM(2001) 723 Final]: The future of healthcare and care for the elderly: guaranteeing accessibility, quality and financial viability. 5/12/2001

Commission of the European Communities, 2004. [COM(2004) 356]: e-Health – making healthcare better for European citizens: An action plan for a European e-Health Area

DTI/PERA, 2004. Technology and Delivery of care for older people – a mission to Japan October 2004.

Försstrom J, et al, "1999. Towards Evaluation and Certification of Telematics Services for Health (TEAC-Health) – Key Recommendations" Commission of the European Union, DG XIII, Health Telematics Application Programme HC4101 Deliverable 8.1. University of Turku, ISBN 951-29-1577-4, Grafia Oy, Turku, Finland, 1999.

Layzell B R and Lindsay J, 2004. "Les informatiques sans frontiers – Health Informatics, Information Literacy, Social/Digital Inclusion, Globalization – and the role of health informaticians in knowledge transfer" "British Journal of Healthcare Computing & Information Management" volume 21, number 6, July 2004

Layzell B R, 2001. "Globalisation and Development (a brief perspective in relation to access to health information)" presentation to IMIA Working Group 9 Workshop, Medinfo 2001, London see http://www.mifound.org/WG9/id18.htm

Manning, B.R.M., Lusted , M.J., Wong, BL.W., Budgen,, Y.M.2004.' E-Community Care: Bridging the Information Access Gaps. Healthcare Digital Libraries Workshop Proceedings University of Bath September 2004

Manning, B.R.M.. 2002   Consumer Relationship Management in the Community. International Consultants Guide. Feb 2002

McKeon Stosuy , M. and Manning, B.R.M., 2005. Joining Up e-Health & e-Care Services: Meeting the Demographic Challenge. Administration on Aging: Aging & Disability Resource Centers . www.aoa.gov/prof/aging_dis/aging_dis.asp

McKeon Stosuy, M and Manning. B.R.M. 2005. e-Health Symposium Proceedings of the 2nd International Council of Medical and Care Compunetics Conference. Den Haag, Netherlands. June 2005.

Stosuy, G.A. and Eaglin, J.P.1999. The Community Services Network: Creating an integrated Service Delivery Network – The Baltimore open systems laboratory model. New Technology in the Human Services Vol 12 1/2 87-98. NTHS 1999

UK Department of Health, 2001. The Expert Patient: A New Approach to Chronic Disease Management for the 21st Century. Crown Copyright 24810 1p 15k AUG 01 (WOO) August 2001 see http://doh.gov.uk/healthinequalities

ONLINE HEALTHCARE: INTERNET PHARMACIES MAY NOT ALWAYS BE GOOD FOR YOUR HEALTH

Carlisle George
Middlesex University, United Kingdom, c.george@mdx.ac.uk

Abstract: Rapid developments in information and communication technologies (ICT) have resulted in the widespread use of the Internet as an important medium for commercial activity. Such activity commonly referred to as electronic commerce, or e-commerce has facilitated new business models in many different commercial endeavours including pharmaceutical and medical practice. This paper investigates the growing phenomenon of drugs sales and medical services over the Internet via Internet Pharmacies. Although Internet Pharmacies have resulted in many benefits to consumers, there are serious health and safety concerns about various aspects of this commercial activity, especially where laws and regulations are not adhered to. Such concerns raise important issues regarding social accountability when using ICT to facilitate the provision of medical services. The paper examines the benefits and problems associated with Internet pharmacies with a view to discussing some of the challenges faced especially by legislators and regulators. It argues that many of these challenges are compounded by the nature of the Internet itself, social and economic realities, different national regulatory structures and the difficulty of enforcing national laws outside of legal jurisdictions. Finally it discusses how some of the present challenges may be addressed.

1. INTRODUCTION

The Internet provides a new and exciting medium for doing business, with many advantages over the traditional physical marketplace. The physical marketplace has become the 'marketspace' which is free from physical restrictions, making commerce available almost everywhere and at all times[1]. This new medium also offers universal technical standards, global reach, interactivity, personalisation and customization, among other capabilities[2].

The many advantages of the Internet, however, are counterbalanced by many problems especially with regard to effective regulation. E-commerce brings new challenges to regulators mainly due to new possibilities with digital technology and its ability to transcend traditional legal jurisdictions. The commercial availability of drugs on the Internet (sold via Internet Pharmacies[3]) has resulted in many benefits to consumers. There are, however, serious health and safety concerns about various aspects of this commercial activity, especially were laws and regulations are adhered to.

This paper first examines the legal classification of drugs which determines how they are sold. It then gives an overview of Internet Pharmacies followed by a discussion of the benefits and problems which they bring. The paper ends by discussing the challenges ahead for regulators and suggests possible ways of addressing these challenges.

2. DRUG SALES ON THE INTERNET

Consumers have legal access to drugs/medications usually by either two or three mechanisms depending on the country of sale. In the UK, three mechanism exists: (i) A consumer needs a prescription issued by a licensed health care professional,[4] to purchase drugs classified as 'prescription-only drugs.[5] These drugs must be dispensed by a pharmacist in licensed premises; (ii) for certain drugs called 'pharmacy-only drugs' a prescription is not required but a pharmacist must be consulted before purchase;[6] (iii) otherwise

---

[1] K, Laudon and C, Traver, *Ecommerce: business, technology, society.* Addison Wesley 2002
[2] Ibid
[3] Pharmacies which offer medicines (or pharmaceutical products) for the sale or supply over the internet or otherwise makes arrangements for the supply of such products over the internet.
[4] In the UK until 1992, only doctors and dentists were allowed to prescribe. However, the Medicinal Products: Prescription by Nurses Act 1992, further allowed certain specially qualified health visitors and nurses to prescribe.
[5] Listed in The Prescription-Only Medicines (Human Use) Order 1997
[6] There is no statutory list of such drugs. Any medicine which is not prescription only or general sales list, is pharmacy only.

a consumer can purchase drugs classified as 'general sales list' drugs which do not require a prescription.[7]

In the US, drugs are classified into two categories namely prescription drugs and over-the-counter drugs. Two mechanisms for buying drugs exists:[8] (i) prescription drugs must be purchased with a valid prescription; and (ii) over-the-counter drugs, do not require a prescription nor a consultation with a pharmacist. In this paper, the term 'prescription drugs' will be used to mean drugs requiring a prescription before sale. This includes the UK classification of 'prescription-only drugs'.

3.   INTERNET PHARMACIES – AN OVERVIEW

The widespread use of the Internet as a medium of information, communication and commercial activity inevitably resulted in the selling of prescription drugs online (since January 1999) by businesses called Internet pharmacies.[9] An Internet pharmacy is also referred to by various other names such as an online pharmacy, cyberpharmacy, ePharmacy and virtual pharmacy/drugstore.[10] For purposes of this paper, the term 'Internet pharmacy' refers to the all the terms above.

Generally, Internet pharmacies sell a variety of products (e.g. for health, beauty) in addition to prescription drugs. They vary significantly in type and mode of operation and have been categorized into various types. One useful categorization focuses on the mechanism for dispensing/selling medications and distinguishes between three types namely: [11] (i) pharmacies which dispense drugs only with a valid prescription; (ii) pharmacies that provided online consultations (in place of a physical examination by a physician) for prescribing and dispensing medicines; and (iii) pharmacies that dispense medications without a prescription.

---

[7] Listed under The Medicines (Products other than Veterinary Drugs)(General Sales List) Order 1984.

[8] E, Brass. *Changing the Status of Drugs from Prescription to Over-the-Counter Availability.* N Engl J Med, Vol. 345, No 11. September 13, 2001.

[9] S. Crawford, *Internet Pharmacy: Issues of Access, Quality, Costs and Regulation.* Journal of Medical Systems, Vol.27, No.1, Feb 2003. Also see Supra 3

[10] Ibid

[11] C. Radatz, *Internet Pharmacies*, Wisconson Briefs, Brief 04-5, March 2004. http://www.legis.state.wi.us/lrb/pubs/wb/04wb5.pdf

3.1   US Internet Pharmacies

The US has had a long history of delivering medical and pharmacy services over long distances and this has continued to develop with technology.[12] Widespread use of the telephone in the 1870's enabled 'pharmacy-based telephone services', whereby pharmacies were able to directly communicate and exchange information with patients' physicians.[13] Also by the mid 20th century, patients used the telephone to obtain medical attention from their physicians.[14]

As early as 1872, Americans began purchasing goods via mail order, after the world's first general merchandise mail-order company was started in the US by Aaron Montgomery Ward.[15] Since then mail-order has been used to purchase almost every consumer product including prescription drugs.[16] Generally mail-order pharmacies have provided drugs at a lower cost (especially for patients on long term prescriptions) than retail pharmacies.

With the advent of the Internet along with its many advantages (e.g. global reach, advertising potential), the traditional 'mail order' drug business model (which still exists) was extended to the online electronic business model. This led to the first major online/Internet pharmacy, 'Soma.com', which began operations in the US in January 1999[17] (it has since been bought by the large US drugstore chain CVS and is now CVS.com). Soma.com was followed by other well known and reputable Internet pharmacies such as PlanetRx.com (which is now closed) and Drugstore.com.[18] Since then numerous Internet Pharmacies sites have surfaced.

In order to purchase prescription drugs, a potential purchaser first opens an account with the pharmacy which involves giving credit and insurance information. The potential purchaser must then submit a valid prescription (via fax, email, or his/her doctor can send it directly to the pharmacy) which is verified (for integrity) before dispensing. After payment and dispensing of the medication it is then sent either via mail, courier or picked up from a

---

[12] S. Kahan, A. Seftel and M. Resnick, *Sildenafil and the Internet.* The Journal of Urology. Vol. 163, 919-923, March 2000.

[13] Ibid

[14] Ibid

[15] http://www.graveyards.com/rosehill/ward.html

[16] Mail-order pharmacies are not legal in all US states, e.g. in Michigan state law prohibits mail-order pharmacies.

[17] Supra 9

[18] Ibid

local drugstore. Usually, the Internet pharmacy enables the purchaser to communicate with the pharmacist (e.g. ask questions about their medication) via email or telephone.

3.2 UK Internet Pharmacies

The first British Internet pharmacy was Pharmacy2u.co.uk which began online operations on November 22, 1999.[19] Pharmacy2u.co.uk was inspired by the Internet pharmacy model existing at that time in the US and was adapted for the UK market.[20] It is operative to date and its services include dispensing and delivering private prescriptions, as well as selling various medical, healthcare, and beauty products among others.

Strict protocols were specially adapted for the sale of medicines over the Internet in the UK. For general pharmacy medicines (i.e. not requiring a prescription) a potential purchaser must choose the desired product(s) then complete an online questionnaire. The pharmacist will then examine the questionnaire and decide either: to allow the sale; or to refer the potential purchaser (via email) to visit a local pharmacy or doctor. To purchase prescriptions-only medicines, first a potential purchaser needs to register in order to submit his/her prescription details so as to receive price quotes via email. Once a price is agreed, the potential purchaser needs to send his/her prescription to the pharmacy, which then dispenses the medicine and delivers it to the purchaser.

4. BENEFITS

Use of the Internet to sell drugs has resulted in many benefits to consumers.[21] In a June 2000 US study conducted by Forrester Research,[22] consumers gave the following motivating factors for buying prescription drugs from online pharmacies: order during off hours (59%); saves time (50%); easier than mail order (50%); cheaper (44%); cuts trip to the drug store (41%); refill reminders (26%); online medication information (23%);

---

[19] *Britian's first Internet pharmacy opens.* The Pharmaceutical Journal, Vol 263, No 7073, p849, Nov, 27, 1999.

[20] Ibid

[21] *Statement of William K. Hubbard, Associate Commissioner for Policy and Planning before The Committee on Government Reform U.S. House of Representatives Hearing on Internet Drug Sales,* March 18, 2004. http://www.fda.gov/ola/2004/internetdrugs0318.html

[22] C. Fung, H.Woo and S. Asch, *Controversies and legal Issues of Prescribing and Dispensing Medicines Using the Internet.* Mayo Clinic Proc. 2004; 79: 188-194

customer service (20%). In 2003, a survey by the UK The National Audit Office, found that consumers were buying prescription medicines online because it was easy to obtain (without a prescription) and cheaper.[23] The following sections further explores some of the benefits of buying drugs online.

4.1   Ease, Convenience and Increased Choice

Prescription drugs are now accessible on a twenty-four hour basis, resulting in shopping convenience especially for the disabled people in remote areas and those who have difficulty travelling to a pharmacy.[24] The Internet also makes available a wide selection of pharmaceutical products giving consumers increased choice, and allowing them to easily compare prices and check availability of medications.

4.2   Increased Consumer Information and Information Exchange

Consumers can access a huge amount of medical information (provided by Internet pharmacies) which may help them better understand issues related to health and treatment. This may have an effect of loosening the grip of the professions and increasing patient autonomy. Consumers can investigate issues such as the effectiveness of different drugs, side/adverse effects of medications, new and alternative treatments among others.[25] In some cases patients are also able to check and verify the advice and treatment they receive from their doctors.[26] One small study comparing Internet and community pharmacies in the US concluded that in general more comprehensive information on drugs were provided by Internet pharmacies, although they were slower to respond.[27] In addition to information on drugs and treatment, Internet pharmacies facilitate the reporting (by patients) of adverse drug effects and reactions[28] and allow

---

[23] NAO. *Safety, quality, efficacy: regulating medicines in the UK*, 16th Kan 2003
http://www.nao.uk/publications/nao_reports/02-03/0203255.pdf

[24] *Consumer advice: buying drugs online*. Harv Health Lett. June 2000; 25: 1-3.

[25] J. Henney. *Cyberpharmacies and the role of the US Food and Drug Administration*. J Med Internet Res. 2001; 3(1):E3

[26] A study reported in the British Medical Journal, 6 March 2004 (p564) concluded that some cancer patients were able to use the Internet verify their treatment and advice, which helped them to better understand their illness.

[27] M, Wagner, J, Alonso and A, Mehlhorn. *Comparison of Internet and community pharmacies*. Ann Pharmacother. 2001; 35; 116-119.

[28] S. Zeman. *Regulation of Online Pharmacies: a case for cooperative federalism*. Ann health Law, 2001; 10:105-137.

pharmacists to easily send reminders to patients to adhere to their medications.[29]

4.3 Privacy and Anonymity

Use of the Internet can afford privacy to consumers who may not want to shop in a public place. Anonymity on the Internet may also allow consumers to ask questions regarding medications and treatments, which they may otherwise be embarrassed to ask in public.[30]

4.4 Generally Cheaper Costs

In many instances online prescription drug sales have resulted in cheaper drugs and medicines for consumers. For example, many US residents re-import drugs into the US from Canada, due to lower prices which can be up to 70% cheaper.[31] This has led to drug sales from Canadian pharmacies (reported in March 2004) at an estimated value of US$1billion.[32] Generally, the cost of drugs are lower in Canada, due to the regulation of drug prices (unlike in the US) and patent laws which make it easier to market generic versions of brand names.[33] Even within the US, due to marketplace competition prescription, drugs are cheaper when bought online.[34] A 2001 US study comparing prices in Internet pharmacies with retail chain drugstores found that drugs for Parkinson's Disease was 7-58% cheaper for brand name drugs and 31-78% cheaper for generic drugs.[35] A few previous surveys, however, have found instances where certain drugs purchased online were not cheaper especially when shipping and handling costs were added to advertised prices.[36]

---

[29] *Drug and biotechnology news: patients to control health with help of Internet pharmacy.* Med Ind Today. January 7 1999.

[30] Supra 22

[31] M. Korcok, *Internet Pharmacy: the tug-of-war intensifies.* JMAC, 16 March, 2004.

[32] Ibid

[33] *Buyinsg Rx Drugs Online*, Financial Awareness Bulletin, Vol. XII, No. 2, October 2003. http://www.neamb.com/memsrvcr/communications/articles/102003_fab.jsp

[34] Supra 27

[35] Ibid

[36] Example see W.Weber, *Austrian survey shows hazards of internet prescription drugs.* The Lancet, Vol 356, No 9236, 30, Sept 2000;

4.5   Availability of Alternative Treatments

The licensing of drugs can a very slow process (due to testing requirements). The Internet, however, can facilitate access to non-licensed drugs which patients with terminal illness (e.g. Cancer, AIDS) may be willing to use on an experimental basis. This may be beneficial in some cases, for example, where a drug has been licensed and used successfully in one country but has not been licensed in another country. Patients who have exhausted other avenues of treatment can gain access to this drug.

5.   PROBLEMS

In many cases Internet pharmacies engage in activities which may expose patients and consumers to risks. Many of these activities also have legal implications. Some of the more important concerns are discussed below.

5.1   Online Prescriptions Without Prior Physical Examination by Doctor

Many online pharmacies operate by giving an online consultation, which requires a customer to fill out a general questionnaire online. This is then evaluated (reportedly by a physician affiliated to the pharmacy) in order to issue a prescription, and dispense drugs. The use of prescription drugs without prior examination in person by a healthcare practitioner can be very dangerous. Also, without further supervision/monitoring (by a healthcare professional) there may be no way of determining whether a particular drug treatment is effective.

Online consultations assume that questionnaires are completed truthfully and therefore run the risk of prescribing medications on false information. The absence of a prior physical examination by a qualified healthcare professional can result in misdiagnosis or drug interaction among other problems.[37,38] Patients also run the risk that a legitimate consulting physician may not exist to evaluate the online questionnaire. Furthermore, use of general questionnaires may not provide the necessary information for the determination of a number of important issues such as whether a particular

---

[37] J, Henny, *Online Pharmacies – Maintaining the Safety Net.* Medscape Pharmacists 1(1), 2000.

[38] Contrary to the generally held opinion, one study reported that Internet prescribing for Viagra was safe and effective. See. M. Jones, *Internet-bases Prescription of Sildenafil: A 2104-Patient Series.* Journal of Medical Internet Research, 2001; 3(1): e2

drug: [39] (i) will work for an individual; (ii) is safe to use; (iii) is more appropriate than another treatment; (iv) may cause adverse reactions if an individual is taking another medication; or (v) may be harmful due to an underlying medical condition such as an allergy.

In some cases, doctors who issue online prescriptions (cyberdoctors) are either not licensed to practice medicine in the consumer's state/country or are not credible. A US study (October 2003) into the background of cyberdoctors, found that most either:[40] had financial problems; were sued for malpractice, had their licence revoked or were recovering from drug addiction. Another 2003 US study reported that many cyberdoctors recruited by Internet Pharmacies were previously unemployed, semi-retired or had declining practice incomes.[41]

The writing of prescriptions via online consultation may raise important legal issues especially related to confidentiality and civil liability for medical malpractice should something go wrong.[42] Confidentiality issues may arise because information given for online consultations may be prone to be seen by people other then the consulting doctor, unless strict security and protocols are in place.[43] Civil liability issues may arise since liability for malpractice may not be clearly established where an online prescription is issued. This is because whereas in a traditional doctor-patient relationship a clear duty of care exists, it is debatable whether a doctor who prescribes medication online (without any direct verbal or physical contact with a patient), forms a doctor-patient relationship and therefore attracts a duty of care.[44]

5.2 Dispensing Prescription Drugs Without a Prescription

A large number of online pharmacies have been found to dispense prescription drugs without a prescription.[45,46] Well documented examples

---

[39] *Offers to Treat Biological Threats: What You Need to Know.* Federal Trade Commission, Consumer Alert. October, 2001. http://www.ftc.gov/bcp/conline/pubs/alerts/bioalrt.htm

[40] *Beau Dietl Conducts Investigation Into Internet Prescription Drug Scams.* October 2003.
http://www.investigations.com/bd_news_10-03.htm

[41] Supra 9

[42] Supra 12

[43] Ibid

[44] Ibid

[45] *Employers urged to monitor access to Internet Pharmacies.* Workplace Subst Abuse Advis. 2002; 16(14).

include the selling of sildenfil (Viagra) and ciprofloxacin (an antidote for anthrax).[47,48] In 1999 a US research study reported up to 19% (9/46) of Internet Pharmacies not requiring a prescription or consultation by a health care professional before dispensing.[49] In 2000 a study by the US General Accounting Office reported up to 13% (25/190) dispensing medications without prescriptions.[50] In 2004 the National Centre on Addiction and Substance Abuse (Columbia University), identified 496 web sites selling controlled prescription drugs: 99% did not require a prescription (41% stated that no prescription was needed and 49% used online consultation with a questionnaire).[51] In the UK, the National Audit Office (2003) reported that 1 in 100 people were buying prescription medicines on the Internet (without a prescription) for various conditions such as obesity, prostate cancer, hair loss, or erectile dysfunction.[52] A study by WHICH ONLINE, published in March 2004, reported that researchers were able to buy various prescription drugs (e.g. Seroxat – antidepressant, Xenical – for fat absorption, Reductil – for weight loss) on UK Internet sites without prescriptions.[53]

The dispensing of drugs without a prescription can have serious implications for consumers such as adverse drug effects, and the various dangers identified in the previous section. Another potential danger of dispensing prescription medicines without a prescription is that such medicines can fall into the wrong hands such as: people addicted to medication; people who have misdiagnosed themselves; people who may not be suitable for a particular medication; and even children. This is illustrated by the following examples given below.

---

[46] For example various prescription-only drugs are offered for sale (August 2004) without a prescription at the 'OffShore Pharmacy'. http://smart-drugs.net/index.html

[47] *Expanded reporting: anthrax: study finds outbreak of cipro web sites followed mail attacks.* Med Lett CDC & FDA. October 9, 2002.
http://www.obgyn.net/newsheadlines/headline_medical_news-Anthrax-20021009-0.asp

[48] E. Gursky, T. Inglesby and T, O'Toole, *Anthrax 2001: Observations on the Medical and Public Health Response.* Biosecurity and Bioterrorism: Biodefence Strategy, Practice and Science, Volume1, Number 2, 2003.

[49] B. Bloom, and R. Iannacone. *Internet availability of prescription pharmaceuticals to the public.* Ann Inter Med. 1999; 131:830-833.

[50] US General Accounting Office. *Internet pharmacies - Adding Disclosure Requirements Would Aid State and Federal Oversight.* Washington, DC: October 2000. Publication GAO-01-69. http://www.gao.gov/new.items/d0169.pdf

[51] National Center on Addiction and Substance Abuse at Columbia University. *You've got drugs! Prescription drug pushers on the Internet.* February 2004. http://www.casacolumbia.org/pdshopprov/files/you_ve_got_drugs.pdf

[52] Supra 23

[53] WHICH ONLINE, *Internet Pharmacies fail our medical as Computing Which? Investigates the sale of prescription only medicines online.* WHICH ONLINE, March 2004. http://sub.which.net/ict/reports/mar2004co6t7/01frontpage.jsp

In 2001, a young UK (London) male drug abuser committed suicide after suffering from a drug addiction.[54] He had bought large amounts of drugs (painkillers, tranquillisers and antipsychotics[55]) over the Internet. An inquest into his death reported that at one point he was receiving 300 anti-depressant tablets in the post every day at his East London home and that he had tried 23 types of prescription drugs.[56,57] In 2002, a 40 year old UK (Birmingham) male (who had an undiscovered heart condition), collapsed and died after taking Viagra purchased from the Internet but not prescribed by his physician.[58] In a 2003 briefing to the US Congress, an investigator reported that his children were able to order prescription drugs online.[59] His 9 year old daughter ordered a prescription weight-loss drug on the US Drug Enforcement Administration (DEA) Controlled Substance list and his 13 year old son ordered and received Prozac (a drug on the US Food and Drug Administration's (FDA) Import Alert list).[60]

The selling of prescription drugs without a prescription is a clear breach of medical ethics and of laws in the UK and US. Such practices also attract potential criminal and civil liability against pharmacies. Product liability issues may also arise since normally when drugs are prescribed by a physician, under the 'Learned Intermediary Doctrine', the prescribing physician and not the drug manufacturer has a duty to give adequate warning to patients[61]. If no prescribing physician is involved in the sale of prescription drugs, then either the pharmacy or manufacturer may be liable for any harm suffered. Some Internet pharmacies have addressed this problem by requiring that purchasers agree to a waiver of liability for any harm caused by products sold. A 2004 UK study found that 41% of Internet pharmacies surveyed issued such waivers[62]. This practice clearly violates unfair contracts legislation.

---

[54] M. Thompson, *Buying medicines one the world wide web: what is legal and what is not?* The Pharmaceutical Journal, Vol 271 No 7262, p202.

[55] Antipsychotics are prescription-only drugs used to symptoms of schizophrenia and other kinds of psychosis.

[56] A. Barnett, *Deadly cost of the trade in online prescription drugs.* The Observer Sunday August 10, 2003. http://observer.guardian.co.uk/drugs/story/0,11908,1015880,00.html

[57] T. Mangold & S. Hann. *Online Pharmacies: the Poisoned Pill. 2002* http://www.readersdigest.co.uk/magazine/pharmacies.htm

[58] Ibid

[59] S. Lueck, *Drug Industry Enlists An Ex-Cop Lobbyist.* The Wall Street Journal. Oct 22, 2003.

[60] Ibid

[61] Supra 12

[62] Supra 53

5.3   Purity and Quality of Drugs

Drugs sold in any country must meet the required quality and safety standards set by the law of that country. A major concern when buying drugs on the Internet is the purity/quality of the drugs purchased. In May 2004, a study which evaluated the risks of importing drugs into the US concluded that many drugs imported through the Internet were:[63] past their expiry date; sub-potent or above potency indicated; contained the wrong dosage; contaminated or counterfeit; and not stored/shipped properly, among other problems.

When purchasing drugs online consumers have no way of knowing the origins of a particular drug, or where it was manufactured and hence it may be impossible to verify the quality of the drug. The May 2004 report also found that many drugs which claimed to be manufactured under FDA guidance or sent from Canadian pharmacies were manufactured in other countries such as China, Pakistan, Thailand, India, the Islamic Republic of Iran and Singapore.[64] Random inspection visits to various mail ports reported evidence such as: [65] 88% (1019/1153) of drugs examined were not FDA approved and were sent from countries such as Thailand, India and the Philippines; 87% (1728/1982) of drugs examined were not FDA approved and were sent from Mexico; antibiotics were two years past their expiration date.

The quality/purity of drugs is an important issue since consumers can be affected either directly by harmful drugs or indirectly by their condition getting worse due to ineffective drugs.[66]

---

[63] *Giuliani Partners LLC, Examination and Assessment of Prescription Drug Importation from Foreign Sources to the United States. Interim Findings*, May 11, 2004. http://www.heartland.org/pdf/14978.pdf

[64] Ibid

[65] Ibid

[66] *Buying Drugs over the Internet.* Its your health. May 2003. http://www.hc-sc.gc.ca/english/pdf/iyh/buying_drugs_internet.pdf

5.4 Counterfeit Drugs

The sale of counterfeit[67] drugs via the internet presents a very worrying prospect. For example in February 2004, The New England Journal of Medicine, reported several web sites selling contraceptive patches (under the brand name "Ortho Eva"), which did not contain any active ingredient.[68] In the US, counterfeiters have mainly targeted expensive drugs such as:[69] injectables (e.g. Procrit, used to help the body make red blood cells and used to treat anemia associated with kidney disease); treatments for HIV and AIDS (e.g. Neupogen, which promotes the growth of white blood cells which help to fight infections); psychiatric medications (e.g. Zyprexa – used to treat schizophrenia) and other popular drugs such as Viagra (which increases the ability for the body to maintain an erection). In 2004 reports of fake versions of drugs imported into the US included Viagra, Accutane acne treatment and OxyContin painkiller.[70] In 2003 the FDA estimated that 10% of the global medicines market were counterfeit and that over US$32 Billion was being earned annually from the sale of counterfeit and substandard medicines.[71]

5.5 Foreign Labels and Different Drug Names

The importation of drugs manufactured or sold in a foreign country may pose problems and risks to consumers. Different countries have different drug labelling requirements.[72] This means that a drug produced/marketed for sale in one country and sold in another may be misbranded (i.e. not meeting the requirements of the second country) and therefore illegal. In addition

---

[67] "Counterfeit medicines are part of the broader phenomenon of substandard pharmaceuticals. The difference is that they are deliberately and fraudulently mislabeled with respect to identity and/or source. Counterfeiting can apply to both branded and generic products and counterfeit medicines may include products with the correct ingredients but fake packaging, with the wrong ingredients, without active ingredients or with insufficient active ingredients". World Health Organisation, Fact Sheet No 275, Nov. 2003. http://www.who.int/mediacentre/factsheets/2003/fs275/en/

[68] P. Rudolf, and I, Bernstein, *Counterfeit Drugs*, N Engl J Med 350; 14, April 1, 2004.

[69] Ibid

[70] K. Dooley, *Online pharmacies shipped fake drugs to U.S., report says.*, Bloomberg News, Thurs 17 June, 2004. http://the.honoluluadvertiser.com/article/2004/Jun/17/bz/bz10a.html

[71] Supra 67

[72] H, Waxman, *Prescription Drugs with foreign labels.* October 11, 2000 http://216.239.59.104/search?q=cache:27OiM3Kw7cMJ:www.house.gov/reform/min/pdfs/pdf_inves/pdf_prescrip_loop_rep.pdf+Prescription+Drugs+with+foreign+labels.&hl=en

foreign labels may result in the following problems:[73] Labels may be in a different (foreign) language which consumers may not understand; drugs may be sold under different names in different countries (e.g. An ulcer medication named Prilosec in the US is sold as Losec in Canada); Label identification numbers may be different according to country (e.g US drug labels have a National Drug Code Number and Canadian drug labels have a different Drug Information Number); Labels may have different indications and instructions according to country (e.g. the US and Canadia have slightly different dosage instructions for the anticonvulsant drug called Dilantin).

5.6 Availability of Unapproved or Illegal Substances & Fraudulent Products

The Internet has been used to promote the use and sale of many unapproved substances (including narcotic[74] and psychotropic[75] drugs, designer drugs[76], banned drugs and fraudulent products).[77] In some cases a drug may be licensed for a particular use, however, some web sites may suggest uses other than what it is licenced for. [78] In other cases a drug may be a prescription drug in one country but can be ordered online without a prescription.[79] Yet in other cases a drug may be banned or unlicensed in one country but is obtainable online.[80] Many sites sell nootropics/'smart drugs'[81] (e.g. Piracetam[82] and Hydergine[83]) which claim to enhance cognitive abilities

---

[73] Ibid

[74] Narcotic drugs are those which produce numbness or stupor. They are often taken for pleasure or to reduce pain, and prolonged use can lead to addiction (e.g. Cocaine).

[75] Psychotropic drugs affect the mind or mood or other mental processes e.g. Diazepam (valium)- a sedative and muscle relaxant; Alprazolam (xanax)- an anti-anxiety agent. These drugs are controlled under The United Nations Convention on Psychotropic Substances, 1971.

[76] Designer drugs are derived from making minor alterations of approved drugs in an effort to circumvent legal restrictions. They are intended for recreational use to give hallucinogenic experiences. (e.g. KAT, Special K, Cloud 9, Sextasy- Viagra combined with Ecstasy).
http://northport.k12.ny.us/~nms/masih/desdrugs.html
http://ncaddoc.org/atod-pages/dsgnr-drugs.htm

[77] M. Childs, L.Ellison and D. Prayle. *Drugs and the Internet. New Law Journal*, Vol 148, No 6868, p 1840, 11 Dec 1998.

[78] Ibid

[79] The International Narcotics Control Board Annual report (released March 2004, stated that in some Internet pharmacies nearly 90% of the orders were for internationally controlled substances such as hydrodone, diazepan and alprazolam.

[80] During a investigation by BBC1 (reported in May 2004) the date-rape- drug Rohypnol was purchased on the Internet at £60 per tablet and shipped from Thailand.
http://www.netdoctor.co.uk/news/index.asp?id=111455&D=14&M=5&Y=2004

[81] For comprehensive coverage of smart drugs see: http://www.damicon.fi/sd/

[82] See: http://www.ceri.com/noot.htm

(e.g. memory boosting[84]). Other sites sell 'wonder drugs' such as growth hormone[85] and melatonin. Yet others sell 'miracle cures' and fraudulent treatments. For example, in 2000 the Federal Trade Commission (FTC) of the US took action against several companies whose web sites offered fraudulent products for sale.[86] Among claims made were: a cure for arthritis with a fatty acid derived from beef tallow; and a treatment for cancer and AIDS with a Peruvian plant derivative.[87]

Cyber trafficking in unapproved substances is highly detrimental to consumers both in terms of the financial costs and the potential danger to their health. These activities are also contrary to international law such as the 1971 United Nations Convention of Psychotropic Substances.[88] In its 2003 Annual Report dated 3rd March 2004, the International Narcotics Control Board (INCB), highlighted the increase in cyber trafficking of pharmaceutical products containing internationally controlled substances (e.g. narcotic or psychotropic substances)[89]. This problem may therefore continue to increase more pharmacies appear online.

5.7 Medical and Financial Privacy Concerns

The US Federal Trade Commission, in its July 2000 report, identified that many US based Internet pharmacies were not adhering to their assurances on privacy and confidentiality[90]. Furthermore many of them did not even post privacy policy statements. This situation continues to be the case in 2004.[91] In July 2004 a US based Privacy Rights Clearinghouse found that only 11 out of 50 US Internet pharmacies surveyed (i.e. 22%) complied with the necessary federal legal requirements to show that they protect

---

[83] See: http://www.antiaging-systems.com/a2z/hydergine.htm

[84] Currently (July 2004) the 'OffShore Pharmacy' sells various smart drugs. http://smart-drugs.net/index.html

[85] Example, Saizen® Human Growth Hormone can be bought at http://smart-drugs.net/index.html

[86] *Buying Drugs Online: It's convenient and private, but beware of 'rogue sites'*. FDA Consumer Magazine. Jan-Feb 2000. http://www.fda.gov/fdac/features/2000/100_online.html

[87] Ibid

[88] For more information see the web site of the International Narcotics Control Board. http://www.incb.org

[89] INCB Annual report for 2003: http://www.incb.org/e/ind_ar.htm

[90] *Online Pharmacies Settle FTC Charges*. FTC Report, July 12, 2000. http://www.ftc.gov/opa/2000/07/iog.htm

[91] M. Hochhauser, *Study Finds No Privacy Rights at Many Online Pharmacies*. July 9th, 2004. http://www.privacyrights.org/ar/PharmacyPrivacy.htm

consumer information.[92] The study also identified that 17 (34%) offered some kind of privacy policy and 22 (44%), had absolutely no privacy policy.[93] While the violations by US based pharmacies are a cause for concern, even more serious are the potential for privacy breaches for Internet sites based in other parts of the world with lax privacy laws. The implications of inadequate privacy protection include the potential misuse of an individual's personal, financial or medical information for illegal activity such as spamming, identity theft and fraud among others.

5.8 Direct to Consumer Advertising of Prescription Drugs

Many online pharmacies advertise prescription medicines directly to consumers. This practice is legal in the US[94] but prohibited in the UK/EU.[95] Due to the global nature of the Internet however, potential purchasers in the UK are exposed to these advertisements. Direct to consumer advertisements may have the effect of stimulating the use of prescription drugs and other inappropriate behaviour.[96] A US study in 2001, examining public information published on 104 global Internet pharmacies found that:[97] 19% promoted prescription medicines; 23% promoted non-prescription medicines; and 23% promoted health and beauty products.

Use of direct-to-consumer advertising can intrude into the doctor-patient relationship and also cause confusion especially where promotional material (driven by commercial motives) is disguised as being educational.[98] Although advertising may improve patient knowledge[99], it may also result in doctors wasting time discussing patients' questions or being pressured into

---

[92] P. Wenske, *Online Pharmacies put Privacy at Risk*. The Kansas City Star. July 18, 2004. http://www.kansascity.com/mld/kansascity/news/consumer_news/9164250.htm

[93] Ibid

[94] The 1st Amendment to the US constitution generally protects the advertising of prescription drugs (directly to the public) as a form of commercial speech. Advertisements are however subject to the *Central Hudson Test*.

[95] The Medicines (Advertising) Regulations 1994 (as amended). UK Statutory Instrument 1994/1932, http://www.legislation.hmso.gov.uk/si/si1994/Uksi_19941932_en_2.htm

[96] T. Bessell et al, *Quality of global e-pharmacies: can we safeguard consumers?* Eur J Clin Pharmacol (2002) 58; 567-572.

[97] Ibid

[98] S. Wolfe, *Direct-to-Consumer Advertising – Education or Emotion Promotion?* N Engl J Med, Vol 346, No. 7, Feb, 14, 2002.

[99] P. Rubin, *Ignorance is Death: The FDA's Advertising Restrictions*, in R.D. Feldman (Ed), American Health Care, 2000.

prescribing drugs that they would not necessary prescribe.[100] This is particularly worrying since some studies have found that many drug advertisements are unbalanced or inaccurate.[101,102]

5.9 Risks of Buying Drugs Online

Some Internet pharmacies do not provide an address, telephone number or details to indicate where they are located.[103] Also, an Internet site may be held on a server located in one country, using a postal address in another country and dispatching drugs from yet another country. This may result in difficulty such as: tracing a particular company if a problem develops; knowing where drugs are from; or what is in the drugs sold.[104] Many of these sites may sell counterfeit drugs, or drugs containing dangerous ingredients/additives or drugs which have expired.[105] As indicated earlier, consumers can be affected either directly by harmful drugs or indirectly by their condition getting worse due to ineffective drugs.[106] Consumers may also suffer financial risks, such as not receiving the drugs paid for through either non-shipment or confiscation by customs authorities.[107,108]

6. CHALLENGES AHEAD

The foregoing demonstrates that many Internet Pharmacies are not socially accountable and may therefore pose a danger to consumers. This is particularly worrying since information and communication technologies provide a global market for commercial activity. While Internet Pharmacies bring some benefits, there are many problems which may arise and by extension bring regulatory challenges to authorities. These challenges, are compounded by the nature of the Internet itself. Enforcement of regulatory rules are mainly possible within a legal jurisdiction and businesses which

---

[100] M. Rosenthal et al, *Promotion of prescription drugs to consumers.* N Engl J Med, Vol. 346, No. 7, Feb 14, 2002.

[101] D. Stryer and L Bero. *Characteristics of materials distributed by drug companies: an evaluation of appropriateness.* J Gen Intern Med 1996; 11:575-83.

[102] M. Wilkes, B. Dobin and M. Shapiro, *Pharmaceutical advertisments in leading medical journals: experts' assessment.* Ann Intern Med 1992; 116:912-9.

[103] Supra 53

[104] Supra 66

[105] Ibid

[106] Ibid

[107] Ibid

[108] A study by the Austrian Federal Ministry of Social Security found that one third of all medicines ordered from 20 inline pharmacies did not arrive. Supra 36

operate outside the scope of that legal jurisdiction present difficult problems to regulators. The nature of the Internet means that residents of one state/country are exposed to all online commerce, except where country-specific filtering software is used to block certain sites. Internet filtering is not in widespread use for commercial Internet activity in the EU/UK and US as seen in other jurisdictions like China and Singapore. It is also unlikely that the democratic ethos of the EU/UK and US will tolerate the censoring of commercial activity on the Internet.

It is difficult or impossible for regulatory bodies to control advertising of prescription drugs from Internet sites beyond their legal jurisdiction. This is especially true for the UK where national rules prohibit the advertising of prescription drugs to the public unlike in the US. It is highly unlikely, however that the advertising of prescription drugs will every be made illegal in the US, due to fact that it is constitutionally protected. This therefore will continue to create a challenge to regulators in the EU/UK.

Tracing website servers which may be mobile or located in certain countries presents a major challenge to regulators. Such web sites will continue to practice regulatory arbitrage[109] and hence evade enforcement action in countries like the UK and US with stricter regulatory standards compared to some other countries.

Economic considerations provide a major reason for the use of Internet pharmacies. In the US unregulated drug prices and strong patent laws have resulted in high drug costs. This has lead to many US citizens seeking cheaper sources of drugs elsewhere especially in Canada. Many US states are in favour of their citizens benefiting from low drug prices in Canada and have facilitated this, in defiance of Federal law.[110] This issue continues to escalate with challenges against the US Federal Government by several states including Vermont[111], Oregon[112], Illinois[113] and Columbia. The above

---

[109] M, Froomkin. *The Internet As A Source Of Regulatory Arbitrage*, 1996
http://www.law.miami.edu/~froomkin/articles/arbitr.htm

[110] C, Rowland , *Vt. sues over importing drugs. State challenges US after waiver of ban is denied*
Globe Staff , August 20, 2004.
http://www.boston.com/business/articles/2004/08/20/vt_sues_over_importing_drugs/

[111] Ibid

[112] S, Tools, *Gov pushes feds on Canadian drug imports Seeks federal waiver for effort to ease drug costs.* August 19, 2004.
http://www.bend.com/news/ar_view%5E3Far_id%5E3D17430.htm

[113] J, Hu, *Illinois Web site to import cheaper drugs.* CNET News.com, August 17, 2004.

indicates that unless countries like the US consider ways of regulating domestic drug prices or changing patent laws to lower production costs, then their citizens will continue to be attracted to cheaper drug sources, especially on the Internet. This may mean that they will be exposed to drugs of poor quality and counterfeit drugs.

National governments will need to cooperate at an international level. This is because differences in national policy can be easily exploited by Internet Pharmacies wishing to engage in regulatory arbitrage. A common international regulatory approach needs to be developed to facilitate better protection for citizens in all countries, since Internet Pharmacies have a global reach.

---

http://news.com.com/Illinois+Web+site+to+import+cheaper+drugs/2100-1038_3-5313670.html

PART 4

POLITICS AND REGULATION

THE IMPACT OF SECURITY CONCERNS ON CYBER LIBERTIES

Julie Cameron and David Vaile
Julie Cameron is with Info.T.EC Solutions Pty Ltd, Sydney, Australia, infotec_solutions@yahoo.com.au and Vaile is with Baker & McKenzie Cyberspace Law & Policy Centre, Faculty of Law, University of NSW, Sydney, Australia, d.vaile@unsw.edu.au

Abstract: Case studies from Australia, Canada, United Kingdom and USA are used to illustrate the impact of the "war on terrorism" on cybercitizens. The authors use relevant Articles of the *Universal Declaration of Human Rights* as a benchmark against which to assess new and changed legislation in democratic societies. It is proposed that "Principles of Cyber Liberty" be articulated within the framework of the *Universal Declaration of Human Rights* by providing adjuncts to the relevant Articles to clarify the application of these liberties and rights in cyberspace, and the potential conflicts between these rights and the new "war on terrorism" initiatives.

1.   INTRODUCTION

The attack on the World Trade Centre in New York on 11 September 2001 was a shocking assault on civilians in a country that was not at war. It has resulted in extraordinary impacts on the lives of citizens throughout the world. Some impacts were a direct response to the events and could reasonably be expected (e.g., increased security around key buildings) but other consequences resulting from government reaction appear only indirectly related to the attack and/or can be described as opportunistic and unjustified.

The declaration of war on terrorism by many nations and United Nations' Security Council Resolution 1373 has resulted internationally in governments demanding increased surveillance of cyberspace[1], global intrusion and claims for jurisdiction outside national territories which threaten the liberties and rights of cybercitizens. The challenge for both citizens and cybercitizens is to understand the consequences of these demands and to limit or reduce any harm, including impacts on their liberties.

This paper which is developed from an extended abstract entitled 'The War on Terrorism versus Cyber Liberties' published in the conference proceedings[2] of the Second International Summer School organized by IFIP-WG9.2 & 9.6/11.7, presents brief case studies that examine legislative reactions to the war on terrorism and outcomes in Australia, Canada, United Kingdom and the USA. The United Nations *Universal Declaration of Human Rights* has been adopted as a benchmark to assess the appropriateness of this legislation because it provides an ethical and legal framework that is generally accepted as a definitive statement of the expectations citizens should have of their government. The authors focus on the consequences of the new legislation for cyber liberties. Currently "Principles of Cyber Liberty" have not been adopted internationally. Increased surveillance of cyberspace, global intrusion and claims for jurisdiction outside national territories threaten the liberties and rights of cybercitizens.

2.   CASE STUDIES

2.1 Australia

The Australian government moved fast. Immediately after the attack the Commonwealth Parliament (comprising the House of Representatives and Senate) passed a raft of Acts related to security and border protection including the:

---

[1] "Cyberspace" is defined as "the electronic environment established by and/or within the information and communications technologies and infrastructure and associated peripheral equipment".

[2] Fischer-Hubner, Simone (editor) August 4-8, 2003, "Risks and Challenges of the Network Society", Proceedings of the Second International Summer School organized by IFIP-WG9.2 & 9.6/11.7 published by Karlstad University. This subsequent paper is published with the permission of the editor and publishers.

- *Migration Legislation Amendment Acts 2001[3]* – changes include authorising an airline operator, shipping operator, travel agent or proscribed organisation to disclose information from their databases about any matter relating to travel by persons to or from a migration zone to an officer, even if information is personal as defined in the *Commonwealth Privacy Act 1998*.
- *Measures to Combat Serious and Organised Crime Act 2001[4]* – changes include exempting law enforcement officers and authorized persons from criminal liability for offences committed in the process of an operation for the purposes of obtaining evidence (including electronic material) that may lead to the prosecution of a person for a serious offence (including threats to national security punishable by imprisonment for 3 years or more).
- *Intelligence Services Act 2001[5]* – changes include expanding the functions and services of the Australian Security and Intelligence Service (ASIS) and Defence Signals Directorate to include intelligence and counter intelligence (in the form of electromagnetic, electric, magnetic or acoustic energy) within and outside Australia.

At the time these laws were passed, Australia was in the midst of both an election campaign and controversy over immigration and "illegal" boat people. There was no time for public debate.

Justified by United Nations Security Council Resolution 1373, the following additional legislation was passed by House of Representatives in March 2002:

- Security Legislation (Terrorism) Act 2002 (No 2) [6]
- Suppression of the Financing of Terrorism Act 2002[7]
- Criminal Code Amendment (Suppression of Terrorist Bombings) Act 2002[8]
- Border Security Legislation Amendment Act 2002[9]
- Telecommunications Interception Legislation Amendment Act 2000[10].

---

[3] http://www.austlii.edu.au/cgi-bin/disp.pl/au/legis/cth/num_act/mlaormsa2001n332001709/

[4] http://www.austlii.edu.au/au/legis/cth/consol_act/mtcsaoca2001436/index.html

[5] http://www.austlii.edu.au/au/legis/cth/consol_act/isa2001216/index.html

[6] http://scaletext.law.gov.au/html/comact/11/6499/top.htm

[7] http://scaletext.law.gov.au/html/pasteact/3/3496/top.htm

[8] http://scaletext.law.gov.au/html/comact/11/6497/top.htm

[9] http://scaletext.law.gov.au/html/comact/11/6498/top.htm

[10] http://scaletext.law.gov.au/html/comact/11/6501/top.htm

Members of the Senate referred the Bills to Senate Legislation Committee (a body of 6 senators from the main political parties represented in Parliament). Despite a short one weeks notice period for the public, 431 public submissions were received in writing by 19 April and/or put verbally to a public hearing in Sydney on 1 May (Senate Consideration, 2002).

Key adverse provisions of Australian bills identified in the submissions that relate to cybercitizens and the online domain [1] were:

- Reversal of the traditional criminal onus of proof from "innocent until proven guilty", and removal of the need of the prosecution to prove "intent" to commit a deed, including for online activities. This reversal combined with broad definitions of "terrorist" and "terrorist acts" including online actions would have also make it easier to use digital evidence.
- Overruling of Information Privacy Principles of *Privacy Act* 1988 (e.g., collection, retention, use of personal data).
- Contravention of *Telecommunications (Interception) Act* 1979 (that provided protections against interception of communications passing over a telecommunications system without the knowledge of the person making the communication – subject to exceptions related to law enforcement).
- Power for one government Minister to "proscribe" an organization, and power to imprison any individual for life for supporting such organizations. This included online communications and accessing websites.
- Immunity for law enforcement officers from civil and criminal liability for breaches of privacy and data protection and other authorized activities provided a warrant has been obtained.
- Additional powers to ASIS (Australian Secret and Intelligence Service[11]) including the power to move and retain things and records (e.g., computers and files).
- Creation of an offence making it illegal to provide information (including emails and electronic documents) related to security and defence, and removal of the need to prove a recipient knew or had grounds to believe information involved a breach of official secrets.
- Permission to refer financial information and personal information to foreign nations.

---

[11] http://www.asis.gov.au/

As a result of arguments from the public, the *Report of the Senate Legal and Constitutional Legislation Committee* May 2002 recommended the Bills [2] be amended to provide:

- Requirements for tighter definitions to restrict offences (e.g., "conduct that assists", "terrorist act") and for an "intention" for an act to cause (not just "involve") serious harm.
- Removal of "absolute liability" for "terrorist acts" and presumption of guilt (reversal of presumption of innocence and onus of proof for criminal offences).
- Limitations to the right of the Attorney-General to "proscribe" organizations with terrorist connections.
- Review of the provisions of the Bills that provide access by agencies to stored communications or delayed message services by "search warrant" or "seizure order" (may be issued administratively) rather than by a "telecommunications interception warrant" (which requires judicial approval).

2.2 Canada

Like Australia, the Canadian Government quickly passed "anti-terrorist" legislation.

Bill C-36 was passed in December 2001 with very broad definitions of 'unlawful activity' and 'groups', which was watered down after protest [3, p139]. In addition to restrictions to civil liberties, this bill as passed in December 2001 provides for:

- The Attorney General of Canada to issue certificates to prohibit disclosure of information related to international relations, defence or security – after a proceeding and subject to review of a judge of the Federal Court of Appeal.
- Restrictions related to computing networks and cyberspace.

Amendments to the Criminal Code place restrictions on content and give power to the court to subpoena copies of electronic material and to a judge to determine whether content can be considered as "hate speech".

Bill C-55, and its replacement the Bill C-17, Public Safety Act 2002, (which lapsed at the end of the Parliamentary session) included controversial provisions like:

- Power to share passenger lists among security agencies and federal departments for restricted purposes (eg transportation security).
- Establishment of "controlled access military zones" on grounds of protection of international relations, defence or security [3, p142].
- Due to strong opposition the government did not proceed to pass the legislation.

Significantly it was reported on CNET News.com, August 27, 2002 that "the Canadian government is considering a proposal that would force Internet providers to rewire their networks for easy surveillance by police and spy agencies. A discussion draft ... contemplates creating a national database of every Canadian with an Internet account, a plan that could sharply curtail the right to be anonymous online. ..." and "compelling Internet providers and telephone companies to reconfigure their networks to facilitate government eavesdropping and data-retention orders. The United States has a similar requirement, called the *Communications Assistance for Law Enforcement Act*, but it applies only to pre-Internet telecommunications companies.[12"]

2.3 United Kingdom

Key terrorism acts in the UK are the:

- Terrorism Act 2000[13].
- Anti-Terrorism, Crime and Security Act 2001[14].
- Regulation of Investigatory Powers Act 2000.

Following the introduction of the *Regulation of Investigatory Powers Act 2000* security and privacy of communications has become a real concern for Internet users in the UK. The monitoring of communications including interception of content data under the *Regulation of Investigatory Powers Act 2000*, and the retention of communications data under the *Anti-Terrorism, Crime, and Security Act* 2001 can constitute an interference with the right to respect for private life and correspondence in breach of Art. 8(2) of the *European Convention on Human Rights* [4]. UK citizens are to be affected by a proposal whereby 'all telecommunications firms including mobile phone operators and Internet Service Providers will have to keep the

---

[12] Declan McCullagh, 'Will Canada's ISP become Spies?' CNET News.com, August 27, 2002 http://www.statewatch.org/news/2002/aug/10can.htmUSA

[13] http://www.hmso.gov.uk/acts/acts2000/20000011.htm

[14] http://www.hmso.gov.uk/acts/acts2001/20010024.htm

number and addresses of all calls and emails made and received by EU citizens' for at least a year[15].

There is alleged involvement of the UK Government, a member of both the European Union and the Council of Europe, with the Echelon interception systems. So far, the UK government's preferred practice in relation to the existence and use of Echelon systems has been not to comment on such allegations. However, in September 2001, the European Parliament in a resolution concluded that "the existence of a global system for intercepting communications, operating by means of cooperation proportionate to their capabilities among the US, the UK, Canada, Australia and New Zealand under the UK-USA Agreement, is no longer in doubt."

2.4 USA

As would be expected, the legislators of the USA acted rapidly to tighten security and surveillance after the events of September 11. Major themes were increased surveillance and monitoring of all forms of electronic communication.

The key legislation is the USA is the *Uniting and Strengthening America by Providing Appropriate Tools Required to Intercept and Obstruct Terrorism (USA PATRIOT ACT) Act* of 2001[16] "The *USA PATRIOT Act* is a synecdoche for the freedom-for-safety swap. Among many other things, it sanctioned roving wiretaps (which allow police to track individuals over different phones and computers) and spying on the Web browsers of people who are not even criminal suspects. It rewrote the definitions of terrorism and money laundering to include all sorts of lesser and wider-ranging offences. More important, as EFF underscored, 'In asking for these broad new powers, the government made no showing that the previous powers of law enforcement and intelligence agencies to spy on U.S. citizens were insufficient to allow them to investigate and prosecute acts of terrorism.'"[17] Not only does it expand the government's power to tap phones, monitor the Internet, conduct 'sneak-and-peak' searches, it even gives the FBI power to force librarians and bookstores to reveal the names of customers.

Michelle Wibisono [5] summarized provisions of the *PATRIOT Act* that contributed to the expansion of surveillance:

---

[15] Richard Norton Taylor and Stuart Miller, 'Privacy Fears over EU plan to store email' The Guardian Weekly, August 22 2002, p1.

[16] http://www.epic.org/privacy/terrorism/hr3162.html

[17] http://www.reason.com/0210/fe.ng.freedom.shtml

- Terrorism is now included in a list of crimes for which authority is given to intercept wire, oral and electronic communications.
- Routing and addressing information, e^mail and electronic communications can be obtained on a appropriate Court order, but not the "contents" of the communications.
- The *Electronic Communications Privacy Act* is amended to expand the classes of records that can be sought without a court order including cables.
- Internet service providers and other telecommunications providers can voluntarily disclose to the government both content and customer records if there is reason to believe the emergency involves danger of death or serious physical injury.
- Foreign intelligence gathering needs only to be a "significant purpose" of surveillance to invoke powers under the *Foreign Intelligence Surveillance Act* 1978 (FISA).
- Increased disclosure of surveillance or intelligence (whether foreign or not) evidence to State agencies involved in intelligence or national defence or security is permitted.

Extraordinary power to utilize biometrics, including fingerprint, voice recognition, face recognition and retinal scanning has been implemented.

"A measure was introduced in the Virginia legislature requiring a judge's approval to use FRT... Then the terrorists attacked, and everything seemed to change. The Virginia legislature dropped the bill requiring judicial approval."[18]

eBusiness has also been affected by security concerns. "Much of the past decade has been spent opening up databases ... through ... data warehouses ... and Internet-enabled B2B (business to business) exchanges. It's already evident that terrorists can buy a plane ticket with a credit card via Internet travel sites; ... the chemical industry is now examining its B2B exchanges to ensure that their security systems and business practices will prevent terrorists from using such 'anonymous' marketplaces to purchase materials for chemical or biological attacks". [6, p81-82]. Reflecting these concerns *Cyber Security Enhancement Act*, US House of Representatives passed July 15 2002 increases penalties for hackers up to life imprisonment. [19]

---

[18] http://www.reason.com/0210/fe.dk.face.shtml
[19] Ira Slager, "CyberSleaze", Australian Financial Review, September 14 p.44

Cyberspace surveillance has been intensified. Yourdon reports significant increase in the use and retention of computer logs and audit trails. "Inevitably the (huge volume of logging data) will lead to greater emphasis on spotting patterns of behaviour in order to spot security threats after they have occurred, or (ideally) before they have occurred. ... We'll see greater efforts to combine public sector and private sector trend analysis efforts." Search engines may become another focus of concern: "Much of the necessary information about the type, location, and vulnerabilities of critical infrastructure systems needed to organize and launch a serious attack is already available on the Internet."[20]

3. BENCHMARK: THE UNIVERSAL DECLARATION OF HUMAN RIGHTS

The case studies show the adverse affects of government reaction to the war of terrorism in societies considered "democratic". We can measure these impacts of legislation presented in the case studies against an internationally ratified set of standards – the UN *Universal Declaration of Human Rights*.[7] The relevant Articles that have been breached are:

Article 11

1. Everyone charged with a penal offence has the right to be presumed innocent until proved guilty according to law in a public trial at which he has had all the guarantees necessary for his defence.
2. No one shall be held guilty of any penal offence on account of any act or omission which did not constitute a penal offence, under national or international law, at the time when it was committed. Nor shall a heavier penalty be imposed than the one that was applicable at the time the penal offence was committed.

Article 12.

No one shall be subjected to arbitrary interference with his privacy, family, home or correspondence, nor to attacks upon his honour and reputation. Everyone has the right to the protection of the law against such interference or attacks.

---

[20] J Hernandez, Sierra and Ribagorda 'Search engines as security threat?', IEEE Computer, Oct. 2001, p.25, in Yourdon p.109.

Article 13

1. Everyone has the right to freedom of movement and residence within the borders of each state.
2. Everyone has the right to leave any country, including his own, and to return to his country.

Article 19

Everyone has the right to freedom of opinion and expression; this right includes freedom to hold opinions without interference and to seek, receive and impart information and ideas through any media and regardless of frontiers.

Article 20

1. Everyone has the right to freedom of peaceful assembly and association.
2. No one may be compelled to belong to an association.

The concern is that, in their response to the recent terrorist events, most governments that have ratified these Articles appear to have ignored or constrained these clearly stated and recognized rights – with apparent impunity.

4.   IMPLICATIONS FOR CYBER CITIZENS

Significantly, the implications for cyber citizens appear to be not fully understood by either the governments concerned or the users of cyberspace. The result is:

- Decreased human rights, civil liberties and cyber liberties[21] including reduced freedom of speech and association and presumption of innocence.
- Significantly increased use of surveillance.
- Increased willingness of citizens to trade civil liberties for security.
- Increased opportunity for security and administrative "function creep" related to government activities including those related to the online domain.
- Increased move to self censorship by citizens and cyber citizens.

[21] Cyber Liberties are defined as "the extension of the rights stated in the Declaration of Human Rights to cyberspace".

The key implications for cyber citizens (not in order of importance) are:

1. Creation of new offences that apply outside the country of citizenship.

The new offences with which cyber citizens may be charged are not necessarily those within the country of citizenship. Major issues relate to what is "connected" in cyberspace and which jurisdiction should apply at any time for example, in relation to:

* Disruption or destruction of ICT systems and infrastructure. How will e-protest and "hacktivism" be viewed by different jurisdictions?
* Possession or creation of documents related to or connected with terrorism or proscribed organizations. Presumably each government will retain its own list of proscribed organizations that will not necessary be known by their own citizens let alone cyber citizens from other countries. Some offences created may relate to:
Receipt of emails (solicited or unsolicited)
Access to "proscribed" websites (knowingly or unknowingly)
Access to "proscribed" chat sites (knowingly or unknowingly)
Membership of, or connection with proscribed "groups"
"Misuse" of services, without knowledge of offence.

2. Incursions into rights to "privacy" for citizens and non-citizens.

These incursions include the transfer of personal data outside national borders. Governments are claiming the right to:

* Access intelligence (including in electronic form) related to capabilities, activities or intentions of organizations and people outside national borders (Australia – *Intelligence Services Act* 2001 Cth; US – *US Patriot Act*)
* Access "required identity information" from airline reservation systems and lists of ships passengers prior to arrival (Australia – *Migration Legislation Amendment Act* 2001 (No 5) Cth[22]; Canada – *Public Safety Act 2002*)
* Additional sharing of personal data from private and public sectors among agencies at all levels of government (Australia, Canada, UK and USA).

[22] http://scaletext.law.gov.au/html/comact/9/4574/top.htm.

3. *Increased powers of defence, security and police organizations to undertake electronic surveillance.*

These increased powers include the use of sophisticated "surveillance" technologies and techniques like:

- Data mining, matching and trawling (regardless of errors, mismatches and wrong identifications that result from using these methods).
- Intelligent agents/bots (i.e., just looking!).
- Intelligent contact mapping (i.e., guilt by association).
- Intelligent "rule based" applications (e.g., "suspicious" transactions, key words).
- Powerful ongoing global surveillance of communications (e.g., use of the Echelon systems by the United States, and to a lesser degree by United Kingdom, Canada, Australia and New Zealand to intercept communications).
- Use of system audit and security tools including transaction history and logs.
- Use of systems capabilities regardless of proven need (e.g., mobile phones and global positioning systems).
- Shift from ad hoc monitoring of communications to continual reporting (to gain additional data – just in case).
- Increase in requirements for retention of records and extension of time the archives must be held and made accessible on demand.
- Loss of anonymous transactions.

In some cases the checks on existing powers of defence, security and police organizations have been reduced (e.g., USA and Australia – security agencies need to obtain only an administrative warrant and not a warrant issued by the Court to detain and question people, remove and retain records and things). Even more serious is the granting of immunity from civil and criminal proceedings for unintended consequences of obtaining intelligence. We must ask, "who guards the guardians"?

4. Risk of detention when travelling without appropriate rights of redress or protection of citizenship.

If cyber citizens have committed offences in another country they may not be aware of the risk of apprehension when they enter the territory of jurisdiction. For some, the fear of contravening terrorist laws may lead to caution and failure to act or protest.

Issues of equal concern, particularly to the growing number of cyber citizens, must be the:

- Impossibility of nations to protecting the cyber liberties of their citizens, due to the extra-territoriality of some of the responses.
- The lack of certainty when the laws of more than one jurisdiction may apply.
- Loss or enclosure of the information "commons" which means that cybercitizens are no longer free to use cyberspace and content in their preferred manner.
- Claim by owners of infrastructure to rights to surveillance of users (to avoid misuse).

5. SOLUTIONS

Although the UN *Universal Declaration of Human Rights* was developed prior to the use of the Internet and predates the period known as the "information age", its Articles are expressed in broad terms and in many cases can be reasonably interpreted to cover the events and circumstances encountered by cybercitizens – individuals that use cyberspace[23]. We can establish Principles[24] of Cyber Liberty within the existing framework of the *Universal Declaration of Human Rights* by clarifying the application of the relevant Articles to clearly specify they protect the rights of cybercitizens.

5.1 Principles of Cyber Liberties – Proposed Statement of Rights Based on the UN *Universal Declaration of Human Rights*

1. Right to freedom from electronic and other forms of surveillance and fear of surveillance unless accused under a legitimate law of the country of citizenship or international law, and surveillance is undertaken with appropriate judicial authority obtained from any country affected (Article 12).
2. Presumption of a right to privacy and anonymity in cyberspace (Article 12).

---

[23] "Cyberspace" is defined as the electronic environment established by and/or within the information and communications technologies and infrastructure and associated peripheral equipment.

[24] Principles are statements that may provide international guidance, or act as a reference document, or provide a basis for the development of legal instruments in particular jurisdictions.

3. Right to free exchange of knowledge, opinion and expression in cyberspace without fear (Article 19).
4. Right of cyber citizens to protest in cyberspace without fear, limited only by proven intent to commit a criminal or terrorist act as defined by a legitimate law of the country of citizenship or international law (Article 19).
5. Right to freedom of association within cyberspace (Article 20).
6. Right to transparency within cyberspace, including the right to know the governing laws of any site (Article 11).
7. Protection from arrest or detention outside the country of citizenship or residency for actions undertaken within cyberspace unless those activities contravene international law (Article 11).
8. Right to trial by country of citizenship or international law and treatment in accordance with the Declaration of Human Rights (Article 11).
9. Right to appropriate representation and knowledge of evidence (Article 11).
10. Right of the data subject to ownership of personal data (Article 17[25]).

6.   CONCLUSIONS

Terrorists aim to disrupt and displace ways of life. Over-reaction by governments can ensure they achieve this goal without further effort. A reality check is required. We need to consider a number of issues:

- "Terrorism" is an emotional concept; one that is often selectively applied and dependent on historical and political context. There is a high risk of previously acceptable online activity and use of information and communications technology being stifled without adequate justification.
- Prevention of terrorism requires the causes of terrorism to be addressed. What triggers terrorism? Why are terrorists targeting particular groups? Attempts to suppress it by hyper-vigilance, implementing technologies of universal surveillance and control, may be ineffective and counterproductive to the extent they distract from efforts to address the causes.
- Proportionality and appropriateness of response to threat is imperative. Terrorism is often not 'high tech', and technical responses are not effective (e.g., SMS message: code word 'suit' was used to refer to the payment of bribes to a local councillor in Sydney, Australia; open email messages that avoid key words that could be used by Echelon and

---

[25] Article 17: (1) Everyone has the right to own property alone as well as in association with others; (2) No one shall be arbitrarily deprived of his property;

surveillance software to trigger 'alerts', were thought to be used by Al Qa'eda; the most successful spy in recent US history used 'dead drops', paper copies of sensitive material in envelopes left for collection by Russian agents!).

- Governments need to consider the lack of success of existing surveillance (e.g., outcomes for the Australian government compared with data collected and scanned under the *Australian Financial Transactions Reporting Act* provisions.) Lack of data is not the key problem in preventing terrorist acts. Recent reviews of security functions in the US and other countries found that bureaucratic and human intervention, and misinterpretation prevented or hindered the use of available information.

Significant intrusions on both civil and cyber liberties have resulted from the war on terrorism. There appears to be growing concern even among the security elite that extreme measures may be counterproductive. "To behave differently [than to always lean towards providing maximum civil liberty] is to let terrorism win its war against democracy before the first shot is fired" writes Stella Rimington, former head of MI5.[26]

The *Universal Declaration of Human Rights* provides a benchmark against which the impacts of reactions of governments on citizens can be assessed but we do not have a similar comparison for cyber liberties. By extending the Articles to specifically address cyber liberties we would at least provoke debate and at best achieve acceptance of the Rights of cybercitizens and the protection of legitimate actions in cyberspace. Cyber liberties are required to facilitate an equitable, democratic global information society.

---

[26] 'Terrorism did not begin on September 11', *Guardian Weekly* September 12, 2002, p22."

WHAT GOVERNANCE AND REGULATIONS FOR THE INTERNET? ETHICAL ISSUES

Jacques Berleur and Yves Poullet[1]
Facultés Universitaires Notre-Dame de la Paix, Namur, Belgium, jberleur@info.fundp.ac.be, yves.poullet@fundp.ac.be

Key words: Technical regulation, IETF, W3C, ICANN, Self-regulation, Legal regulation, Ethics

1.   INTRODUCTION

If Vinton Cerf, one of the fathers of the Internet and the founder of the Internet Society (ISOC) is to be believed, then "As we move into a new century marked by the Internet's ubiquitous presence, we must dedicate ourselves to keeping the network unrestricted, unfettered, and unregulated." [Cerf, 1999] Few still share such radical views. Philippe Quéau, at the time Director of the Information and Informatics Division of UNESCO, specifically hinted at such an intention: "The structural imbalances in the world infrastructure of the Internet, the profound inequalities of access to information, the trans-national oligopolies controlling the planet's info-

---

[1]   A shorter version of this text has been published in a French monthly journal, *ETVDES*, tome 397, Paris, 2002, Assas-Editions http://perso.wanadoo.fr/assas-editions/etudes.htm The text has been updated according to the discussions at the worldwide level, in particular at the occasion of the World Summit on the Information Society (Geneva 2003, Tunis 2005) http://www.itu.int/wsis

structure are equally the area of concern for the regulator. A new form of regulation or of world 'governance' should be conceived, from the perspective of global ethics, for the service of equality and human development." [Quéau, 1999] Others have thought about a *Lex Informatica* of technical Internet regulation, based on the model of the old *Lex Mercatoria* [Reidenberg, 1998]. The question of Internet regulation and governance is without any doubt, technical, political and ethical.

The *Declaration of Principles* of the first phase of the World Summit on the Information Society (Geneva, December 2003) insisted on the fact that "the governance of the Internet should constitute a core issue of the Information Society agenda", and having been unable to reach a consensus before the Summit of 2003, "the Secretary-General of the United Nations was asked to set up a working group on Internet governance, in an open and inclusive process that ensures a mechanism for the full and active participation of governments, the private sector and civil society from both developing and developed countries, involving relevant intergovernmental and international organizations and forums, to investigate and make proposals for action, as appropriate, on the governance of Internet by 2005." [WSIS, 2003] The same *Declaration of Principles* asked for ethical insistence.

We can no longer say today – if ever we could – that we lack regulation because notably the Internet escapes the territorial sovereignty. There is, without doubt, a calling into question of the traditional regulatory framework, but its exact impact remains to be seen. Some stress the prevalence of technical regulation and self-regulation over traditional public regulation. Our intention is to analyse these three sources of regulation – or of governance – and to propose a critical reading of the case for each one to be the only source of regulation of the Internet.

2.   TECHNICAL REGULATIONS

Technical regulations are clearly apparent on the Internet. We refer to three, relating to three organizations: the Internet Engineering Task Force (IETF) and therefore the Internet Society (ISOC), the World Wide Web Consortium (W3C), and the Internet Corporation for Assigned Names and Numbers (ICANN) [Regulating the Internet, 2000], [Brousseau, 2001], [Simonelis, 2005].

2.1   The Internet Engineering Task Force (IETF)

The IETF is an organization that dates back to 1986 and whose essential work is still today to ensure the standards and norms that ensure the full interoperability of the networks. It is an independent organization, that has been supported by the ISOC, and which has had some setbacks with the international standards organizations, such as the International Organization for Standardization (ISO) and the International Telecommunication Union (ITU), both agencies of the UN. The clashes took place notably between 1992 and 1994, at the moment where the ISO was looking to replace TCP/IP (Transmission Control Protocol / Internet Protocol), which was worked out from the beginning of the ARPANET network by the United States Department of Defense (1969) and which ensured the interoperability of today's networks. The ISO and the ITU appeared not to be prepared, in matters of such importance, to allow the practices of an institution with such little institutional organization, working from the grass roots and with ostensibly, although little explained, consensus methods of decision-making. Since then the IETF seems to have continued along its path in relative peace and kept its normative prerogatives, while making it known that it does not see an official delegation close to other organisms of standardization as an adequate solution. [On the Internet, 2001]

The subjects dealt with by the IETF are very technical, among others currently being examined is version 6 of the Internet Protocol (IPv6), which is under construction, but also encoding and transport, of models of impression protocol semantics and so on. Every question relating to the working of the Internet and needing standardization, whether a question of transport, routing, security, service for users, or so on, passes through the IETF. IETF has been often considered as "the protocol engineering and development arm of the Internet." Since the beginning of networks (March – April, 1969) until early July 2005, some 4130 Requests for Comments (RfC: see infra) have been drafted. [RfC, 2005]

The organization remains quite complex; it must be mentioned that it relies on some 2000 volunteers divided into some 130 Working Groups on subjects decided upon by a Steering Committee, the Internet Engineering Steering Group (IESG). We also note the Internet Research Task Force (IRTF) that organizes these research groups and the Internet Architecture Board (IAB), one of the committees nominated by the IETF to assist in its management and to play a formal interfacing role with the Internet Society, the ISOC.

The standardization or normalisation process developed by the IETF is reported in the Requests for comments (RfCs). It has little to do with "requesting comments" as the name suggests, but rather with the notes that report the exchanges on different aspects of communication, the network protocols, the programmes, the underlying concepts; these also include reports about meetings, opinions, and even some humorous notes. More fundamentally, these RfCs, all of which are published on the IEFT site, consist of all the specification protocol documents or Guidelines of the Internet. From 1969 until his death in 1998, this work was scrupulously carried out by one man, Jonathan Postel, the legendary figure to whom the Internet domain names are sometimes attributed. Today (June 2005), the RfCs number more than 4000 and the work of J. Postel is carried on by the person he trained, Joyce Reynolds.

In the final analysis however, what does the IETF consist of? As we have mentioned, it is a *de facto* organization, independent, and without a juridical presence; it is composed of Internet services providers, of users of the Internet, software and hardware vendors, researchers, network operators, academics, and all other interested parties. The volunteers or the people sent by, and at the cost of, their organization meet regularly, even if until three times one week per year. This community has functioned until now with the method of "rough consensus", more than a simple majority, but not unanimity, as *The Economist* noted [Regulating the Internet, 2000]. What does the future hold for it? The same *Economist* called to mind the 'benevolent dictators' that created the consensus doubtless at the expense of more democratic processes where the more societal outcomes of the technical choices could have been discussed. Doubtless it comes down to the "charisma of the pioneers", such as Vint Cerf and Jonathan Postel!

2.2   The World Wide Web Consortium (W3C)

The W3C was also born from the charisma of one person, Tim Berners-Lee. He is the man who created the first server, the first browser; the man who in 1994 created the World Wide Web (WWW).

The W3C was founded in the same year as the WWW at the Massachusetts Institute of Technology (Cambridge USA) in cooperation with CERN (Geneva), and is also a regulatory organ of the web. Until today it has produced some 90 'Recommendations' (technical specifications or set of guidelines) relating to the web's infrastructure, notably in the field of the architecture of the web (and its associated technologies), document formatting (formats and languages for presenting user information), the tools that favour every form of interaction, that develop accessibility for everyone, and every question of social, legal or general political relevance. It is in this way for example that the W3C is progressively transforming the initial web (HTML – the *lingua franca* of the first web -, URLs, HTTP, and so on) into a web for tomorrow, built on the solid foundations provided by XML (Extensible Mark-up Language). As L. Lessig says, technical architecture may correspond to different types of regulation [Lessig, 1999, 30]. Everyone agrees that with the philosophy of the W3C, openness and decentralization, has been incorporated into the technical norms of the WWW to the point that today they are defined as its characteristics. We also note, among the proposals of W3C, the recommendation of the PICS (Platform for Internet Content Selection), standard for filtering notably illicit or harmful content on the Internet [PICS].

The W3C comprises of 500 member organizations, product vendors and technological services, content suppliers, utility companies, research laboratories, standardizing organizations, governmental representatives and so on. Anyone signing the membership agreement may become a member of the W3C, but a 'full member' pays a subscription fee of US$ 1000 to 77000 – on the average 50000 -, while an affiliate member pays only 5000. It is an open organization, without a juridical statute, housed in turn by one of three host research institutions: INRIA (France), the Massachusetts Institute of Technology (USA) and Keio University (Japan).

2.3   The Internet Corporation for Assigned Names and Numbers (ICANN)

Last born of the Internet regulatory organizations that we intend mentioned is the Internet Corporation for Assigned Names and Numbers (ICANN). The birth in 1998 is here not the fruit of any individual charisma, but rather of the liberal ideology of technicians and Internet engineers that brought the American Department of Commerce to get rid of the attribution of TCP/IP addresses and domain names attribution. ICANN is an organization, which, globally and in a centralized way, runs the address system of the web. This centralization brings with it a management system that can differ according to the registration office where the national geographic domain names are attributed. Those that have followed the creation of ICANN know the themes that have progressively appeared. ICANN has been mentioned as an example of the global Internet governance, perhaps reducing it to its technical dimension, and of self-regulation by a "non-profit, private sector corporation", as said on its web site. The capacity of ICANN has been evoked to delete addresses, but without doubt it is more precisely the sign of a new system of governance and Internet regulation that has really been in question: an American federal department gave up one of its prerogatives to transfer it to an organization made by governmental and private representatives at a world level.

The day after the ICANN meeting in Stockholm at the beginning of June 2001, however, some spoilsports broke the beautiful unanimity. The roundtables held during the world ISOC conference (INET 2001) that followed this meeting, where the critics of the electoral procedures, notably that of 'ICANN at large', that is to say ensuring the representation of users flew from all sides: nine seats for 400 million Internet users! Who voted? The users? Those that are affected by the networks? The Internet, a public space, more and more sponsored by private interests! And so on. That which incited Carl Bildt, former Prime Minister of Sweden, given a mission by ICANN, to plead for a different representation than representative democracy! In short, as a number of editorialists have underlined, 'ICANN at large' could well have been restructured, and the ISOC would be approached. Besides the reasons for its representativeness, the efficacy of ICANN was contested, although in fact, it was all about an organization with about twelve people and an annual budget of US\$ 4.3 million.

On February 24, 2002, the ICANN President, Stuart Lynn, published his first annual report: *ICANN – The Case for Reform* – proposing a better balance between private and public, and a better participation of the public, declaring the failure of a pure private structure, and proposing new ways of representation. An "At Large Advisory Committee (ALAC)" was appointed by the ICANN Board, which made proposals of new Bylaws adopted at the Shanghai October 2002 meeting. A totally new ICANN structure has been proposed where the "ICANN At Large" seems to be on the same stand as other Advisory Committees such as the Government Advisory Committee (GAC) [ICANN, 2002].

A new charter of the Board has been designed in 2002, which shows that the majority of representatives comes still from "technical supporting organizations", and "technical advisory committees", whereas, out of the president, 14 voting directors and 6 non voting representatives, the GAC has only one seat and the capacity of being a member of the "nominating committee."

The ICANN saga is still going on, … and recently the *Internet Governance Project* issued some main criticisms, among which the dissatisfaction of the GAC, where governments have only advisory powers, and its legitimacy [Klein & Mueller, 2005]. The ICANN position has been also questioned by the Working Group on the Internet Governance, set up by the Geneva Summit on the Information Society that we mentioned [WGIG, 2005], and it seems today that the US are not to give up to their control of the Net's root to ICANN "The U.S. government will continue to maintain 'oversight' of ICANN and prevent its 'focus' from straying from technical coordination." [McCullagh, 2005]

Some questions regarding ethical aspects arise from this brief description of the technical regulations. What is the degree of transparency and clarity of information about such complex subjects? What is at stake, for example, in the new IPv6 protocol? It should be pointed out in this case that version 4, currently in use, was developed to support 4 billion ($4 \cdot 10^9$) addresses whose two tiers are still today reserved for North America, that is to say 5% of the world population. The new protocol should support $3.4 \cdot 10^{38}$ addresses (340 trillion trillion trillion trillion) and allow the convergence of all communication technologies (current IP addresses, generalization of IP telephony, electronic directories, and so on). Resistances emerge particularly in US Business milieu because of the rather weak support of service providers and networks administrators and because of the transfer costs and of the migration from IPv4 towards IPv6, etc. In summary, a new Y2K could be at the horizon [Lawton, 2001].

Underneath this purely technical character, there are problems of privacy that have not been resolved and which the IETF appears to be currently making proposals on. There are also political decisions about future lifestyles, particularly about more and more intrusive – or ubiquitous as said today – computing, taken outside national and international authorities.

There are only 13 main root servers in the world: 10 in the United States, 2 in Europe (London and Stockholm) and one in Asia. Does this state of affairs contradict the international character of the Internet?

What is the legitimacy of bodies that are given the right of technical regulation apart from all recognized supervision, by the state or by international public bodies? What will happen when China demands that the standards that it developed itself be taken into account by the quasi strictly American standards bodies? And so on.

Those who should not yet been convinced of the technical regulators position, should consult the April 2005 comment of ISOC on the status of the Working Group on Internet Governance (WGIG) work in April 2005:

"The Internet Society believes that the best way to extend the reach of the Internet is to build on those aspects that have worked well – e.g. the long established open, distributed, consensus based processes and many regional forums for the development and administration of the Internet infrastructure. Decision-making about issues such as resource allocation or IP Address Policy has always been in the hands of the Internet community, in order to be as close to those who require and use the resources as possible. It is this participative model, close to the end users, that led to the phenomenal, stable growth of the Internet." (...) "We want to encourage WGIG and WSIS to work with the Internet Community within the already well-established Internet model to improve co-operation between policy makers and the Internet community." [ISOC, 2005] In other words, let ISOC continue its work as before, without taking into account the recommendations of the WSIS for an improved cooperation between the different levels of governance and the multiple stakeholders!

There may be contradictions and surely tensions between the technical regulations and their coordination, and public policy issues [Klein, 2002]. Moreover, as stressed by L. Lessig, the possible architecture of Cyberspace are many: "the values that these architectures embed are different, and one type of difference is *regulability* – a difference in the ability to control behavior within a particular cyberspace. Some architectures make behavior more regulable; other architectures make behavior less regulable. These architectures are displacing architectures of liberty." [Lessig, 1999].

Above all, the point of view of ethics should question the normative character of technical regulation and its limits. It should also question the fact that some 4000 technical norms (RfC, for instance) are decided by only 2000 people and other few organizations without recognized legal status and then become universal norms?

3.   SELF-REGULATION

3.1   What is Self-Regulation?

Pierre Trudel defines self-regulation as "resorting to voluntary norms developed and accepted by those that take part in an activity." [Trudel, 1989, 251] For Pierre Van Ommeslaghe, it is "a legal technique according to which rules of law or behaviour are created by the persons for whom they are destined to be applied, whether these persons design them themselves or whether they are represented to that end." [Van Ommeslaghe, 1995]

The self-regulation documents and the techniques used by it abound. They cover domains as diverse as the general governance of the Internet, the codes of ethics of societies of computer professionals, rules of behaviour and Netiquette of users of the networks, codes of conduct of access and service providers, rules of certification or labelling of websites; they are particularly developed in the electronic commerce sector in general, but also in the private sectors such as health, electronic publishing, software sales, telemarketing, and so on [IFIP-SIG9.2.2, 2000].

The names given to them is also diverse: charter, bills of rights, 10 or 12 commandments, principles, codes of ethics, codes of conduct, codes of practice, guidelines, standards, practices and uses, terms or contractual clauses.

The commitments vary from one to the next and, as we might assume from reading the names above, proposals relevant to pure ethics and codes of ethics are doubtless to be found, but also, more and more, simple commitments of an essentially contractual type defining services offered by companies and their clauses. The Internet users 'click' thus equates to the acceptance of these sorts of 'general contractual conditions'.

3.2   Two Charters

Two interesting French examples appear to us to show this difference: on one hand, the proposal of the French Internet Charter, put together in 1997, following the work of A. Beaussant, who was given the task by the Minister Francois Fillon_[French Internet Charter, 1997]; and on the other hand, the electronic publishing Charter (Le Monde, Libération, ZDNet, La Tribune, Investir, Les Echos, L'Agefi, France), published in 2000 [Electronic Publishing Charter, 2000].

The first one, which was no more than a proposal, was never adopted, in any case no more than the proposal put forward at the time by France at the OECD in the spirit of this Charter. It appeared, in fact, that the associations called to form the 'Internet Council' envisaged by the Charter never arrived at an agreement. The themes that they mentioned and about which signatories confronted each other were of interest to us at that time: protecting new spaces for expression and freedom with respect to everyone and in particular children; referring to the Charter on a site; adding a link to the Internet Council; supplying clear identification, banning all content or action manifestly contrary to public order and principally paedophilia, incitement to racial hatred, denial of crimes against humanity, incitement to murder, procuring, narcotics trafficking and procurement, attacks against national security; supplying parents with means to prevent sensitive material (ex. PICS, and so on); identifying pornographic and violent sites; defending freedoms and fundamental rights (freedom of expression, right to information, mail confidentiality, protection of private life, anonymity, and so on); protecting the intellectual property rights (patents, copyright...); defending the consumer (notably in electronic commerce): clarity of information about products, prices, conditions, the legal status of the vendor; protection against unsolicited advertising by email, honest and fair information; etc.

This charter, whose number of clauses are fairly typical of similar documents of current service providers in Europe [EuroIspa, 2005], might also be compared to the "Practices and uses" of the French Association of Providers of Access and Services (AFA), whose terms appear to us to be a retreat to the proposals of the Internet Charter [AFA, 2002]. They are also mentioned in the ethical dimensions of the Plan of Action of the 2003 WSIS. [WSIS, 2003, C10]

The electronic publishing Charter, another example, reaffirms the habitual rules of the profession and publishing rules that the publisher of a site attempts to respect scrupulously, but goes into the detail of the number of paragraphs that can be reproduced without being accused of plagiarism, defines what a 'short' citation is, gives the exact rules concerning the creation of links (authorized without conditions if the link opens a new browser window), banning, except with prior authorization, reproduction by means such as scanning, digital copying and so on.

This example allows us to appreciate that the word 'Charter' can have different meanings and that self-regulation, on the one hand, tends to define the rights and reciprocal duties of different Internet players, while, on the other, aspects of intellectual property by quickly define self-regulation more from a perspective of self-protection by a sector or company against practices that are harmful to them.

3.3   Documents Related to Electronic Commerce

Without going into too much detail, we should not miss out one of the most important fields in the development of self-regulation, notably electronic commerce. On this subject, we have to cite the efforts made firstly by the Electronic Commerce Platform Nederland (ECP-NL) and the Global Business Dialogue on Electronic Commerce (GBDe), and secondly by the European Commission in its eConfidence program [eCommerce, 2005]. These three initiatives stem from the belief that, if electronic commerce begins with difficulty, it is essentially due to a lack of confidence in the systems themselves and from the lack of legal protection.

ECP-NL is at the third version of what it calls a 'Model Code', which any company wishing to adhere to its principals can base itself, and thereby obtain a 'label of quality'. This code, negotiated with the consumer associations and representatives of companies under the guidance of the Minister of Economic Affairs, underlines the necessity of making commitments vis-à-vis the reliability of information, of systems and vis-à-vis the organization, the transparency in communication, the rights to privacy, confidentiality of information and the rights to intellectual property. It seems to us that the measures of the ECP-NL offer little in addition to the law and do not offer added value to its effectiveness: all by showing the possibility and by supplying some examples of mechanisms in the explanatory notes, the document says that it supplies no clause model of enforcement.

The topics examined by the GBDe related to security, consumer confidence, the content of official communications, market access infrastructures, intellectual property rights, jurisdictions, responsibilities, protection of personal data and questions of taxation and tariffs. After its 2000 and subsequent Summits (Tokyo 2001, Brussels 2002, New York 2003, Kuala Lumpur 2004), these topics have been slightly redefined: consumer confidence, convergence, security, 'digital bridges' versus the 'digital divide', eGovernment, intellectual property rights, taxation, trustmarks, business and the World Trade Organization (WTO),...

In view of the abundance of initiatives of this type and, perhaps also, in view of the will of organizations that support them (GBDe was an initiative of some 60 big company chiefs of the calibre of America Online, Time Warner, Fujitsu, Vivendi Universal, Toshiba, Telekom Malaysia, Seagram, Eastman Kodak, Walt Disney, Hewlett Packard, IBM, MCI Worldcom, Alcatel, ABN AMRO Bank, DaimlerChrysler, and so on), the European Commission has been attempting to develop specific additional demands in its eConfidence program of general principles that would be applicable to all levels of online business, and furthermore, that would not be covered by the European legal clauses, but would be placed in the ensemble of European

legal mechanisms relating to the consumer and to electronic commerce –
here it relates to a compilation of 'best practices', originating from the codes
put together by the Commission working group, and, finally, principles
designed to guide bodies towards official approval (the 'core group' assumes
that the codes will be subject to official approval). The eConfidence Forum
seems to us to be an interesting initiative to pursue, while being conscious
that the current elaboration is being done by the work group.

It is a cause for celebration that the world of electronic commerce cares
about a certain number of questions that otherwise stand a good chance of
not finding a regulatory solution in the near future. The most important thing
in this matter, for us, is to know who defines what and in the name of whom.
It must be recognized that such initiatives are often born with the explicit
concern of opposing governmental interference. The GBDe 'sherpas' call
their annual 'Summit' the 'Davos of eCommerce'. And so be it; it is their
right. We can, however, question the absence of real dialogue and
participation of people who "take part in activities" (we are referring here to
the Pierre Trudel's definition) who define electronic commerce. One cannot
avoid the impression that many current codes, in their present form, hardly
express more than idealistic principles that, too often, are not even
accompanied by sanctions or indictment procedures in the case of disputes.

Without doubt, a number of questions related to our ethical
preoccupation cross our minds that we can merely list here: What forms, or
what techniques does self-regulation cover? Codes? Labelling? What is its
place in the legal pluralism and the normative order? Is it a complement to
the law, its substitute or an anticipation? With regards to democratic order,
what is its legitimacy, how representative is it in its elaboration? What are
the social acceptance places? What is at stake? Are there not any areas that
should escape self-regulation in the name of other principles, for example
democratic or ethical principals? [Berleur, 1999] What protection for
citizens and democracy do we have the right to expect from regulators?
What is the constraining legal force, what are planned sanctions and
procedures to resolve disputes? Is there no place, in the final analysis, to
define a legal framework according to the usual democratic criteria, and
again at the international level – what permits the development of
instruments of self-regulation to genuinely give people confidence, because
they are implicated one way or another?

It is perhaps still too early to give a satisfactory answer to these
questions, but they must surely be kept in mind and worked on. States, as

much as consumer associations, should be more involved in places where such regulatory tools are being prepared.

One thing that has seemed of utmost importance, that we have read on the GBDe site, is that the GBDe, the International Chamber of Commerce (ICC) and the Business and Industry Advisory Committee (BIAC) with the OECD signed an agreement on the problems of electronic commerce on 13th December 2000: "the GBDe, the ICC and the BIAC are working together to further their international cooperation in all areas of general politics linked to the Internet (on the full range of *public policy issues* arising from the Internet; *we highlight*)."

We cannot hide our surprise when looking at the follow up that has been given to the 1997 "Green paper on the protection of minors and human dignity" [Green Paper, 1997]. Measures which have been taken can be read as reinforcing the responsibility of the people on the 'front line' – and that is surely positive, but also as leaving to the 'market' matters which, at least partially, should traditionally depend on the judicial order. Who, for instance, will decide of the 'illegal' or 'harmful' character of the Internet content? Who does the classification? What kind of classification scheme is used? [Resnick, 1999] Self-regulation in this matter is, in our view, a choice allowing the content providers as well as the service providers to establish the minimal rules.

The concept of co-regulation has been advanced by the summit of regulators in 1999, which was convened under that aegis of the Audiovisual High Council (CSA, Conseil Supérieur de l'Audiovisuel), and of UNESCO. Michel Vivant, in his conclusion, preferred the term multi-regulation or 'plural regulation'. It is this movement that we are referring to here. In truth, co-regulation can take different senses according to, as numerous commentators highlighted at the creation of the GBDe, it relates or does not relate to curbing intervention by public authority (Associated Press) and the creation of a sort of 'Net Parliament' (L'Express) or, on the contrary to 'setting up watchdog, dialogue and mobilization authorities', as Madame Falque-Pierrotin, the President of the Internet Rights Forum (Forum des Droits de l'Internet), said. The role of the law will allow us to define our approach more precisely.

Abruptly said: the slogans of self-regulation, 'The least State possible is the best', 'Let us avoid a greater degree of statutory regulation', or 'Let business self-regulate the Net' belong to the "knee-jerk antigovernment rhetoric of our past", and cannot persist without damage for a democratic society [Lessig, 1999]. Does the ubiquity of ICT allow us to leave the choices about the future of our societies and enterprises to the sole forces of market or of lobbies? The State has not to rule everything, sure. But it must define as clearly as possible, and in a transparent manner, the principles and the values that it wants to be respected. Where are the places of dialogue and of early warning?

If self-regulation must reflect ethical concerns, then there would be minimum requirements to be met. IFIP-SIG9.2.2 has expressed its concerns about that and made some recommendations [IFIP-SIG9.2.2, 2004]. A recent initiative of the European Commission aiming at developing a methodology for assisting self-regulatory bodies to implement codes of conduct within/across the various media sectors in Europe goes along the same line.

From a strict ethical point of view, let us make the following comments or raise certain questions: we should request more professionalism from professional bodies, i.e. clearer statements on issues in specialized fields where they develop their competence; anticipate threats and dangers; increase international exchange between professional societies and institutional groups, respecting the cultural, social, and legal differences; reflect on the "shift from deontology for informaticians to a deontology of informatics under the control of the law" (Herbert Maisl); question self-regulation in terms of improvement of commitment and responsibility of organizations – is it not too minimalist? Increase self-regulation legitimacy by promoting large participation of all the concerned parties; refrain from slogans of the past, such as "Let business self-regulate the Net" which are at risk of damaging societal fabric, and which are not favouring the cooperation between private and public; clarify the relationship between deontology, self-regulation, the law, and ethics.

Some last ethical important questions: self-regulation is trying to find its place in the normative order, but doesn't it still remain, from the content point of view, minimal if not minimalist? One of the main questions: the normative role of private actors. What should be the role of the regulators to protect citizen and customers? The signs of real participation of the actors are rare: where is democracy? Is self-regulation making the actors more responsible?

4. LEGAL REGULATIONS

Among Internet regulators, certain authors have, doubtless too quickly, described the legislator as too slow, too unqualified, and too national to frame such a mobile, technical and global reality as cyberspace. They were ill-advised. Some authors have opposed criticisms and proposed alternatives [Trudel 1996, 137], [Lessig, 1999], [Poullet, 2000]. Europe, in particular, issues repeated directives on this subject and, in an area where the United States is refusing to legislate, like data protection, a body as official as the Federal Trade Commission (FTC) pleaded recently for a legislative initiative in the area of protection of privacy on the Internet [FTC, 2000]. How can this phenomenon be explained? A single word: confidence. It is clear that the difficulties that are increasingly resented by the electronic commerce sector for example, can be explained by the absence of confidence by Internet users as much in network security and transactions that build up, as in the possibility, in the case of dispute, to be able to clearly identify the legal frame of reference to bring about a solution and take exact decisions [European Parliament, 2000].

In general, the law undeniably has a reassuring function in this respect. It creates a clear frame of reference, subjugates players to stipulations that guarantee security, fairness and a good outcome. Moreover, it gives the public power teeth for complaints by those who are at risk on the web. Doubtless, its territorial limits are questioned at a time of the global network of networks, but the construction of regional legal spaces like the European Union and the increasingly numerous discussions at the heart of supranational official bodies like the OECD, WIPO, WTO, the Council of Europe, and so on, allow the progressive establishment of adequate regulatory consensus [Trudel, 1995].

That said, it is perhaps useful to consider the areas of intervention by the legislator and to study its goals in the various areas. It is about, they say, building confidence, but in what and in favour of whom?

We will limit our analysis to a comparison of the European and American interventions.

The first area of legal intervention is undeniably that of *intellectual property* and related rights. As the Bangemann report noted, it is about protecting the agreed investments by those that tomorrow will become the service providers of the information society. This political will to protect the investment translates into laws which, very often, neglect to take into consideration the balances written into the heart of traditional legislation on copyright. Whatever happened to exceptions about private copying, copying for educational, research or critical purposes, and so on, that became simply optional according to the recent 2001 European directive on copyright and related rights [European Commission, 2001]? Following the example of the 1998 US Digital Copyright clauses, the law protects technical measures that permit the restriction of access to information, even when this is not entitled to legal protection. Furthermore, they institute – this is at least what the 1996 European directive on databases decided – protection of data compilations, even those that are not protected by copyright by inventing a right *sui generis* to protection [European Commission, 1996].

Protecting investors guarantees the presence of content on the Internet. Then, secondly, transactions still have to be developed, be it transactions between professionals (B to B) or with consumers (B to C). To do this, the issue is one of reassuring about the identity of the partners in a transaction, about the authentication of messages and the assurance of confidentiality. The legislation, adopted as much by one side of the Atlantic as by the other on the subject of *electronic signatures,* granting them the same value as written signatures and granting electronic documents the same value as written ones, answers this first concern [European Commission, 1999]. The failure of electronic B to C commerce has led Europe to answer the Internet users' fears through legislative initiatives. The directive on electronic commerce adopted in June 2000 had two goals. On the one hand, to oblige member states to brush away their legal arsenals by repealing all legal constraints that could deprive electronic transactions (e.g. formal rules based on paper documents) of validity or efficacy. There, it plays a role of promoting electronic commerce. On the other hand, it plans new requirements about transparency of service providers and the sequence of transactions in various stages by way of assuring the complete and conscious consent of the Internet user [European Commission, 2000].

The protection of investments and transactions on the Internet equally demands the possibility of detecting illicit schemes on the Internet and of efficiently punishing their perpetrators. That was the third common legislative measure. The attention drawn to the crime of paedophiles on the Internet and other actions against human dignity, like xenophobic or racist messages, has brought legislators, with the support of public opinion, to largely define *computer crime* (in certain countries, the simple fact of having accessed a site, without even having any fraudulent intent, is punishable), to considerably extend the means of investigating policing authorities by giving them the right to search using the networks, by obliging private providers (i.e. access providers) to keep data about usage of their services and to cooperate with the authorities and finally, by promoting international police cooperation. We could talk about transforming them into genuine representatives of the law. Under American pressure, the Council of Europe adopted an international convention on cybercrime in December 2000 that conveys the whole of these tendencies and allows effective cyber-surveillance of the actions of everyone on the web [Council of Europe, 2000]. In this field, the principles of freedom of expression and the protection of privacy were too quickly forgotten, although these were the principles, which the Council of Europe had previously demanded absolute protection of at its founding convention.

It is precisely with respect to the last topic, the protection of freedom, that legal intervention should be analysed. *Freedom of expression* is certainly one of the founding dogmas of the Internet. Certain people even said that self-regulation would be a compromise to maintain the Internet's spirit of freedom. The question of the abuses of this freedom (illicit or prejudicial messages) has been envisaged, away from the question of punishment of their perpetrators, by a system of exoneration of responsibilities of intermediaries regarding surveillance of information that it gives access to [Montero, 2000]. It is about avoiding every preventative measure that could take these intermediaries who, to avoid being investigated, would censor the content of information that they give access to. For the rest, freedom of expression on the Internet is considered a given considering the low cost of having a network presence and the potential global access of the content of sites. Organizations like UNESCO are frequently reminded that such access was not as straightforward for everyone, so that there is room to encourage not just the pluralism but also the cultural diversity and geographical origin of messages to be seen on the network, and not to be content with a pure and simple application of competition laws [UNESCO, 2000]. Furthermore, the United States more than Europe had defined a legislative policy of *universal access* to infrastructures for all (right to electronic signature, right to email and so on) but equally to certain content judged to be essential in an information society [de Terwangne, 2001]. Is this right of access not effectively the condition of the participation of everyone in the information society and therefore of their freedom of expression?

From the legal regulations point of view, the question of the protection of personal data still appears to be the one that most profoundly divides the United States and Europe. Even considering the greater sensitivity of American Internet users than Europeans, the United States refuses every initiative on this subject, where Europe attempts to sharply adapt its regular demands to answer the challenges set by new technologies. Thus Europe has recently produced a directive [European Commission, 2002] that limits the use of traffic and location data, subjects the sending of emails to consent and reserves the right for the Commission to use technical standards to combat 'privaticides': technologies such as cookies, invisible hyperlinks, and so on [Dinant, 1999]. The demand for adequate protection to be offered by third countries in the case of flows across frontiers has led Europe to get the United States to adopt the 'Safe Harbor Principles', a self-regulatory system that offers certain protection for European personal data, that the Commission deems adequate [Poullet, 2000b]. We know that the new American administration has attempted to change the Commission's decision, but to date unsuccessfully.

5.   CONCLUSION

The hierarchy in the field of protection that is ensured by the law reveals the values of the societies that give rise to those laws. To the American authors denying the need for laws to regulate cyberspace, we retort that the Americans were the first to intensively legislate in the field of intellectual property and new technologies, and that only certain questions like the protection of privacy or limits on freedom of expression are currently left in the realm of self-regulation.

The European legal approach to the other means of regulation deserves to be underlined. If technical regulation and self-regulation are promoted, it is under the control or in any case, within the framework and control – the word is perhaps too strong – of public authorities. Recent European and worldwide interventions in the field of 'governance' of the Internet have demonstrated this tendency well. Through various documents, the European Parliament and the European Commission as well as, now, the World Summit on Information Society through notably its Working Group on Internet Governance have insisted on the need to play a leading role in the functioning and decision making of organizations such as ICANN, the need for a better regional balance in its leadership bodies, and above all of the recognition of the system of domain names as a public resource, in accordance with intellectual property rights, competition and the protection of data and representative of the world's cultural and linguistic diversity [Delmas, 2001], [Froomkin, 2000]. However, it appears that the US Government is not ready to leave to others the control of an organization that it has accepted to be "private under control"! (U.S. Statement of Principles,

http://www.ntia.doc.gov/ntiahome/domainname/USDNSprinciples_0630200
5.htm)

The European Commission's proposal to be able to intervene in the field
of technical standardization with the aim of ensuring the respect of principles
of protection of personal data, during Internet use is equally indicative of the
tendency to more control. It is clear that the public authorities cannot remain
absent from technical debates where the choices made have a profound
impact on the rights and freedoms of users of those technologies.
Accordingly, all self-regulation is subject to certain conditions through the
texts of the European Directives [Poullet, 2000c]. The importance of the
participation of all interested actors has already been insisted upon here, a
point which a number of European texts highlight. Self-regulation, far from
being a substitute for regulation appears more like its complement, offering a
real additional value. Thus, the more or less voluntary systems of official
approval, enforced to give a 'legal' label to self-regulation initiatives, are
multiplying. Lastly, the need for effective self-regulation must be insisted
upon and if it is to be applied by private judges or mediators, then should
respect certain procedural rules through certain guarantees concerning the
judges or mediators. Cybercourts and cyberjudges must be legally founded.

It is beyond doubt that the law has a good future, even in Cyberspace. If,
as everyone delights in saying, information technology increasingly governs
our behaviour, determines the life of our companies, and the future of our
societies, there will be no question of leaving such choices to the discretion
of market forces or lobbies. This indicates the place and the role of the State.
For the State, it is not about regulating but about fixing the principles and
social values that it intends to see respected in a clear and transparent way. It
is about, above all, constructing places for dialogue, watch and observation,
where all interested actors can compare their points of view, analyse the
technical and self-regulatory solutions and suggest up to and including legal
actions if necessary [Reidenberg, 1996]. If the law has no more than a
secondary role, then this role is at the same time fundamental because it
represents the basic consensus from which the other regulatory instruments
could define themselves. Should this basic consensus be sought at the
international level, as the global dimension of the Internet demands? We do
not think so. Even as a 'web citizen', the Internet user remains a citizen
attached to his or her values and to his or her local culture [Rodota, 2000].
The reality of cyberspace doubtless opens itself to other cultures and values
more and more each day and therefore begs the search for consensus that is
no longer local, nor national, but rather at the regional or world level. If such
a direction is to be followed however, it should not be at the expense of a

renunciation of the values nor by defining smaller common denominators or at the cost of solutions imposed by the market.

The role of ethics is to keep open an horizon of universality, or to avoid the appropriation of the norms by anybody, be they technical or self-regulatory. This is a must if there are vested interests which do not respect the balance through appropriate levels of democratic discussion. Regulation is multidimensional and must find its coherence and consistence. Today it is still a "battlefield".

REFERENCES

Abramatic, 2005. Jean-François Abramatic, About the World Wide Web Consortium (W3C), http://www.w3.org/Consortium/

AFA, 2002. Association des Fournisseurs d'Accès et de Services, Pratiques et Usages, Mise à jour septembre 2002, http://www.afa-france.com/deontologie.html

Berleur, 1999. We have proposed a simple rule inspired by the Kantian deontological tradition: "As soon as the interest of the majority are at stake and that people concerned risk to be made more fragile and vulnerable, the public authority must interfere and ensure that an 'horizon of universality' remains open." See: Jacques Berleur, Self-Regulation and Democracy: Choice and Limits?, in: *User Identification & Privacy Protection, Applications in Public Administration & Electronic Commerce*, Simone Fischer-Hübner, G. S., Quirchmayr & Louise Yngström, Eds., Dept of Computer and Systems Sciences, Stockholm University/Royal Institute of Technology, Report Series 99-007, 1999, ISBN 91-7153-909-3, pp. 1-19.

Brousseau, 2001. Eric Brousseau, Régulation de l'Internet : l'autorégulation nécessite-t-elle un cadre institutionnel ?, in : E. Brousseau and N. Curien, (éds.), *Economie de l'Internet, Revue Economique*, Numéro spécial, Septembre 2001.

Cerf, 1999. Vinton Cerf, *On the Internet*, July-August, 1999.

Council of Europe, 2000. The text of the Convention n° 185 on Cybercrime is available on the site of the Council of Europe http://conventions.coe.int/Treaty/FR/cadreprojets.htm

de Terwangne, 2001. Cécile de Terwangne, *La mission publique de l'Etat dans la Société de l'Information*, Brussels – Bruylant, 2001.

Delmas, 2001. Richard Delmas, L'Internet et les chantiers législatifs européens, in : *L'Internet et le droit*, Actes du colloque de l'Université de Paris 1, 25 et 26th September 2000, Legipresse, 2001

Froomkin, 2000. M. Froomkin, Lessons learned from the WIPO domain name process, *Regulating the Global Information Society*, C.T. Marsden (ed.), Routledge, London – New York, 2000, p. 210 et sv.

Dinant, 1999. Jean-Marc Dinant, Les traitements invisibles sur Internet, in: Droit des technologies de l'information – Regards prospectifs, in *Cahiers du CRID*, n°16, Brussels – Bruylant, 1999, p.287 sv.

eCommerce, 2005. http://www.ecp.nl, http://www.gbde.org, http://econfidence.jrc.it

Electronic   Publishing   Charter,   2000.   Charte   d'édition   électronique http://www.liberation.fr/licence/charte.html

EuroIspa, 2005., European Internet Services Providers Association, Pages detailing the Codes of Conduct for members of EuroISPA, http://www.euroispa.org/25.htm

European Commission, 1996. Directive of 11th March 1996 on the legal protection of databases, *O.J.E.C*, 27 March 1996, L077/20.

European Commission, 1999. Directive 1999/93/EC of the European Parliament and of the Council of 13 December 1999 on a Community framework for electronic signatures, *O.J.E.C.*, 19th January 2000, L013/12.

European Commission, 2000. Directive 2000/31/EC of the European Parliament and of the Council of 8 June 2000 on certain legal aspects of information society services, in particular electronic commerce, in the Internal Market Directive on electronic commerce, *O.J.E.C.*, L178, 17/07/2000 pp. 01 -16.

European Commission, 2001. Directive 2001/29/EC of the European Parliament and of the Council of 22 May 2001 on the harmonisation of certain aspects of copyright and related rights in the information society, *O.J.E.C.*, 22nd June 2001, L167/10.

European Commission, 2002. Directive 2002/58/EC of the European Parliament and of the Council of 12 July 2002 concerning the processing of personal data and the protection of privacy in the electronic communications sector – Directive on privacy and electronic communications, *O.J.E.C.*, L201, 31/07/2002, pp. 37 – 47.

European Parliament, 2000. Advice of the Economic and Social Committee of the European Parliament on the 'Effects of electronic commerce on the single market (SMO)' of the 2nd March 2000, *O.J.E.C* on the 25th April 2001, C 123/1.

French Internet Charter, 1997. http://www.planete.net/code-internet/ The access to this site is possible through http://www.archive.org

FTC, 2000. Statement given by the Federal Trade Commission on 25th May 2000 before a Senate committee: Privacy Online: Fair Information Practices in the Electronic Marketplace, http://www.ftc.gov/os/2000/05/testimonyprivacy.htm

Green Paper 1997. European Commission: 'Green paper on the protection of minors and human dignity in audiovisual and information services', COM (97) 570 final, 18.11.1997. This text and its following recommendations, decisions or actions are available at http://europa.eu.int/comm/avpolicy/regul/new_srv/pmhd_en.htm

ICANN, 2002. President's Report: ICANN – The Case for Reform, 24 February 2002, http://www.icann.org/general/lynn-reform-proposal-24feb02.htm See also the discussion: Committee on ICANN Evolution and Reform Seeks Public Submissions, 27 March 2002 ; ICANN Board Accepts Contributions to Facilitate At-Large Organizing Efforts, 24 April 2002 ; Working Paper on ICANN Mission and Core Values, 6 May 2002, http://www.icann.org/committees/evol-reform/working-paper-mission-06may02.htm, ...

Klein & Mueller, 2005. Hans Klein & Milton Mueller, The Internet Governance Project, April 5, 2005: *What to do about ICANN, A proposal for Structural Reform*, http://www.internetgovernance.org/)

IFIP-SIG9.2.2, 2000. Jacques Berleur, Penny Duquenoy, Marie d'Udekem-Gevers, Tanguy Ewbank de Wespin, Matt Jones and Diane Whitehouse, *Self-Regulation Instruments – Classification – A Preliminary Inventory*, (HCC-5, Geneva 1998; SIG9.2.2 January 2000; SIG9.2.2 June 2000; IFIP-WCC-SEC2000), http://www.info.fundp.ac.be/~jbl/IFIP/sig922/selfreg.html Other 'Internet Resources on Self-Regulation and the Internet' can also be found on one of the site of the Law Faculty of the University of Washington at http://www.law.washington.edu/lct/publications.html

IFIP-SIG9.2.2, 2004. *Criteria and Procedures for Developing Codes of Ethics or of Conduct.* To Promote Discussion Inside the IFIP National Societies. On behalf of IFIP-SIG9.2.2: Jacques Berleur, Penny Duquenoy, Jan Holvast, Matt Jones, Kai Kimppa, Richard Sizer, and Diane Whitehouse, Laxenburg, IFIP Press 2004, ISBN 3-901882-19-7 http://www.info.fundp.ac.be/~jbl/IFIP/Criteria_and_procedures.pdf

ISOC, 2005. ISOC Commentary on the status of the work of the Working Group on Internet Governance, April 2005, http://www.isoc.org/isoc/conferences/wsis/

Klein, 2002. Hans Klein, ICANN and Internet Governance: Leveraging Technical Coordination to Realize Global Public Policy , *The Information Society – An International Journal* (Taylor and Francis, ed.), vol. 18, n°3, 2002, pp.193-207.

Lawton, 2001. George Lawton, Is IPv6 Finally Gaining Ground, in: *Computer*, IEEE Computer Society, August 2001, pp. 11-15.

Lessig, 1999. Lawrence Lessig, *Code and Other Laws of Cyberspace*, Basic Books 1999.

McCullagh, 2005. Declan McCullagh, U.S. to retain control of Internet domain names, *New York Times*, July 1, 2005

Montero, 2000. Etienne Montero, La responsabilité des prestataires intermédiaires de l'Internet, Rev. *Ubiquité*, June 2000, n°5.

On the Internet, 2001. *On the Internet*, Spring/Summer 2001, pp. 13, 26.

PICS. There are numerous sites about PICS. First, the official one of W3C : Platform for Internet Content Selection, http://www.w3.org/PICS/ ; the papers of Lorrie Faith Cranor, Paul Resnick, and Danielle Gallo, A Catalog of Tools that Support Parents' Ability to Choose Online Content Appropriate for their Children, http://www.research.att.com/~lorrie/pubs/tech4kids/ ; the web site of 'Computer Professionals for Social Responsibility' and its specific page 'Filtering FAQ' in particular the question on PICS at http://www.cpsr.org/filters/faq.html , etc.

Poullet 2000. Yves Poullet, How to regulate the Internet : New paradigms for Internet Governance, *E-Commerce Law and Practice in Europe*, I. Walden – J. Hörnle (éd.), Woodehead, Cambridge, 2000, Section 1. Chapter 2.

Poullet, 2000b. Yves Poullet, Les Safe Harbor Principles : Une protection adequate ?, published at http://www.droit-technologie.org in the column : Dossiers, 10.07.2000.

Poullet, 2000c. Yves Poullet, Les diverses techniques de réglementation d'Internet: l'autorégulation et le rôle du droit étatique, Rev. *Ubiquité*, n°5, Juin 2000, p. 55 et sv.

Quéau, 1999. Philippe Quéau, Internet : vers une régulation mondiale, Sommet mondial des régulateurs sur Internet, CSA – UNESCO, Paris, 30th November – 1st December 1999, http://www.unesco.org/webworld/news/991201_queau_csa.shtml

Regulating the Internet, 2000. Regulating the Internet – The Consensus Machine, in: *The Economist*, June 10th, 2000, pp. 99 sv.

Reidenberg, 1996. Joël Reidenberg, Governing Networks and Cyberspace Rule Making, *Emory Law Journal*, 1996., p. 911 ff.

Reidenberg, 1998., Joël Reidenberg, Lex Informatica: The Formulation of Information Policy Rules through Technology, in: *76 Texas L. Rev.* 553-584 (1998)

RfC, 2005., IETF, Request for Comments Index, http://www.ietf.org/iesg/1rfc_index.txt

Resnick, 1999. Paul Resnick, PICS, Censorship, and Intellectual Freedom FAQ, http://www.w3.org/PICS/PICS-FAQ-980126.html and the PICS sites we mentioned under PICS.

Rodota, 2000., We owe this reflection to S. Rodota, president of the Group called Article 29, made up of representatives of the data protection authorities who defended this idea in the conclusion of 22nd international symposium of data protection ombudsmen, organised by the Italian Garante in Venice (September 2000)

Simonelis, 2005. Alex Simonelis, A Concise Guide to the Major Internet Bodies, in: *Ubiquity, Views*, Issue 5, February 16-22, 2005, http://www.acm.org

Standards, 2001. The Standards Issue, *On the Internet*, Spring/Summer 2001.

Trudel, 1989. Pierre Trudel, Les effets juridiques de l'autoréglementation, in : *Revue de droit de l'université de Sherbrooke*, 1989, vol. 19, n° 2.

Trudel 1995. Pierre Trudel (ed.), *Le droit du cyberespace*, Thémis, 1995.

Trudel 1996. Pierre Trudel, Le cyberespace, réseaux constituants et réseau de réseaux, in : *Les autoroutes de l'information: enjeux et défis*, Actes du colloque Jacques Cartier, Lyon, 1996

UNESCO, 2000. Conclusions of the 3rd InfoEthics Congress (UNESCO, November 2000).

Van Ommeslaghe, 1995. Pierre Van Ommeslaghe, L'autorégulation. Rapport de synthèse, in: *L'autorégulation*, Bruxelles, Ed. Bruylant, 1995, pp. 233-274.

WGIG, 2005., Working Group on the Internet Governance, http://www.wgig.org

WSIS, 2003. *Declaration of Principles,* World Summit on the Information Society, First Phase, Geneva 2003, see in particular nr. 48 & 50, http://www.itu.int/wsis. See also the *Plan of action* nr. 13b, and C10, nr. 25, as well as the Civil Society Declaration *Shaping Information Societies for Human Needs.*

WHAT ARE WORKERS DOING ABOUT ELECTRONIC SURVEILLANCE IN THE WORKPLACE?
An Examination of Trade Union Agreements in Canada

Vincent Mosco and Simon Kiss
Mosco is Canada Research Chair in Communication and Society, moscov@mac.com and Kiss is a Ph.D. student in Political Studies, at Queen's University, Kingston, Ontario, Canada

Abstract: Information and communication technology has deepened the problem of workplace surveillance by expanding the capacity to measure and monitor worker activity. Partly because of inadequate government attention to privacy protection and partly because the government itself has used security concerns to overturn privacy protections, civil society organizations and movements have increasingly taken an active role to secure the right to privacy. This paper assesses the extent to which trade unions in Canada have made privacy a sufficiently serious concern to see that privacy protections are incorporated into collective agreements. It assesses the progress made since Bryant's 1995 study which found practically no reference to electronic privacy protection in Canadian agreements. The paper concludes by identifying best practice language for unions negotiating to incorporate privacy, surveillance, and monitoring language in their collective agreements.

1. INTRODUCTION

The growth of information and communication technology has deepened the problem of workplace surveillance by expanding the capacity to measure and monitor worker activity (Head, 2003; Parenti, 1999; Wallace, 2004). Although there is some research on the extent of this challenge to privacy in the workplace, there is little research on what workers and particularly their unions are doing about it.

Traditionally, privacy and privacy protection have been deemed to be the proper role of the state and this has been embodied in laws and regulations governing the use of consumer and citizen data (Bennett, 2003). But governments in North America have generally ignored worker concerns and those in Europe have been slow to respond. Specific European privacy laws, supported by Europe's unions and opposed by businesses, are in the works. The European Commission is consulting on a new law on the protection of workers' personal data that will cover data about employees, including email, internet use and health records as well as issues of consent, drug and genetic testing, and monitoring and surveillance. A few jurisdictions have put in place workplace surveillance legislation. A notable example is the Australian state of New South Wales which established a Workplace Surveillance law in 2005 making it illegal for employers to engage in covert surveillance of emails and web sites, or the use of tracking devices without a court order. International bodies like the International Labour Organization have issued guidelines on elements of surveillance in the workplace particularly on the use of worker data and records. (International Labour Organization, 1997)

Partly because of inadequate government attention to this area and partly because governments themselves have used security concerns to overturn privacy protections, civil society organizations and movements have increasingly taken an active role to secure the right to privacy (Shane, 2004) These include established civil rights organizations like the American Civil Liberties Union (ACLU, 1998) and groups specifically organized around information technology issues like the Electronic Privacy Information Centre in the U.S. and Privacy International in the U.K. (EPIC, 2004; Rotenberg and Laurant, 2004).

We are beginning to observe some attention to privacy protection in collective bargaining agreements (Findlay and McKinlay, 2003). But developments in this area are slow. The shadow of 9/11 has darkened efforts to protect worker privacy in the United States (Bloom, Schachter, and Steelman, 2003; King, 2003). The situation is slightly better in Europe. According to a 2003 report on the European situation, "there is generally little reference in collective bargaining to the issue of protecting privacy at the workplace, either in general or in relation to the use of e-mail and the internet. This is especially true of bargaining at multi-employer level, and where joint regulation of this matter exists, it generally occurs at company level, either through agreements or through the exercise of the co-determination rights of works councils or other workplace employee representatives." (European Industrial Relations Observatory, 2003: 23)

Notable exceptions include Belgium where national collective agreements provide protections for workers' private lives in the areas of electronic online communications, data and video monitoring. In Norway, the central 'basic agreement' between the Norwegian Confederation of Trade Unions and the Confederation of Norwegian Business and Industry contains a supplementary agreement stipulating a range of conditions under which monitoring and control measures may be implemented by the employer, focusing on the principles of objectivity, proportionality, and universal applicability. The agreement calls for discussion of such measures prior to implementation but negotiations are not required. Workers are also expected to be notified of new surveillance measures prior to their execution and union representatives are also expected to be involved in consultations on the implementation of new practices that might affect member privacy. Measures may be deemed unlawful by the Labour Court, but it is assumed that the agreement does not apply in cases where there are suspicions of criminal acts such as fraud or theft.

Along the same lines, in 2001 the Confederation of Danish Trade Unions and Danish Employers' Confederation agreed that any new surveillance arrangements in the workplace have to be made public at least two weeks in advance of their implementation. Also in Denmark the Union of Commercial and Clerical Employees signed an agreement with Danish Commerce and Service, an employer's organization that serves as a model for companies seeking to establish a policy on employee use of email. In the Netherlands, the collective agreement covering the public transport sector has an annex containing a model privacy code and several collective agreements in the Netherlands protect workers' privacy when they report absent due to illness. Workers in this country also benefit from a law requiring the establishment of Works Councils in all businesses employing more than 35 workers because electronic surveillance cannot take place without the approval of the local Works Council. Some collective agreements in Italy refer to the need to adhere to data protection legislation and especially to the need to protect sensitive personal information about employee health. The Austrian Union of Salaried Employees reports on numerous local collective agreements dealing with relevant privacy issues in all sectors. In France, "information charters" have been put in place with works councils and other employee organizations. The Renault group's 2001 charter provides a model for the use of information resources in the workplace. Finally, Spain has pioneered in collective agreements, particularly in the banking sector, on trade union use of company computer networks for communicating with members and companies, like Ericsson and Barclays Bank SA have agreed to respect the privacy of such communications. (European Industrial Relations

Observatory, 2003) There is less to report from the UK but the Trade Union Congress and Unison, the largest union in the UK representing public service employees, have been active in promoting greater sensitivity to workplace privacy issues and has proposed model policies. (Hazard's Magazine, 2004)

This paper assesses the extent to which trade unions in Canada have made privacy a sufficiently serious concern to see that privacy protections are incorporated into collective agreements. It does so by drawing on two research projects. The first, The Surveillance Project, is a broad analysis of the global problem of surveillance led by a team of scholars at Queen's University, and the second is a project on Trade Unions and Convergence in the Communications Industry based at Queen's and Carleton Universities.

Specifically, the paper reports on a content analysis of existing Canadian collective agreements to determine the extent to which privacy has been recognized by trade unions, to examine which sectors, industries or individual unions have incorporated surveillance protection into their collective agreements, and to identify specific models of collective agreement clauses. The normative object of the study is to produce a "best-practices" model for Canadian unions facing surveillance in the workplace.

The content analysis grew out of a series of interviews with people involved with these issues and the primary data-set consists of collective agreements stored in the Negotech database, maintained by the Canadian federal department of Human Resources Development. This database contains a stratified random sample of Canadian collective agreements under both provincial and federal labour law. The data set encompasses both English and French language agreements. These searches revealed just 76 collective agreements with clauses dealing with electronic surveillance and monitoring. Following a discussion of why so few collective agreements contain surveillance clauses, the paper presents a breakdown of these agreements by sector and union and a discussion of recurrent patterns.

The paper found that unions situated in the "knowledge worker" sector, particularly those representing higher education and government employees, are most substantially represented among the unions with privacy language. Moreover, they have the strongest and clearest restrictions against electronic monitoring and surveillance. The paper also found a very wide range of clauses, some of which contain outright prohibition of all forms of electronic monitoring and surveillance, others call for adjudication of the issues by workplace committees, while the weakest feature explicit recognition by the union that the employer has all rights to use any forms of electronic monitoring when and where it wishes. Additionally, the paper notes the inclusion of clauses which commit the employer to a level of electronic monitoring in the interests of employee safety. This finding supports the general contention put forward by Lyon (1994, 2001) that surveillance in contemporary society contains both negative features as well as positive ones such as security and convenience. The paper concludes by identifying best practice language for unions negotiating to incorporate privacy, surveillance, and monitoring language in their collective agreements.

2.   THE PROBLEM

Electronic surveillance is becoming a common practice in Canadian workplaces. Three recent examples demonstrate the conflicts that can arise over the introduction of technological surveillance practices. In December 2004, a CN railway employee in Winnipeg discovered surveillance cameras in the workplace, brought them to the attention of the union and management and was subsequently fired. In September 2004, the Federal Privacy Commissioner ruled in that an internet service provider's practice of monitoring employees' behaviour with webcams violated privacy rights. Finally, according to media reports, after a group of financial experts left the Canadian Imperial Bank of Commerce, their former employer launched legal action arguing that they had breached contractual obligations prior to severing their employment ties to the bank. As evidence, they put forward intercepted electronic communications from the employees.

Unions represent an important, but often overlooked, element of workplace surveillance practices. They are often the only recourse workers have to protect their privacy from intrusion. Canadian worker organizations are certainly aware of the problem. In fact, the Canadian Labour Congress, the primary federation of Canadian trade unions, has a policy dating from 1999 that calls for strong protections of worker privacy. But the recommendation is entirely focused on a legislative rather than a collective bargaining strategy: "Herefore be it resolved that the Canadian Labour Congress, in conjunction with our social partners, lead a campaign for federal and provincial privacy legislation applying to all workers and workplaces which includes the principle of meaningful consent, accountability, transparency, security, finality (i.e. use only for the purpose indicated), non-intrusiveness and other protections with respect to all personal data collecting, processing and use during a worker's hiring and course of employment." (http://home.clc-ctc.ca/policies/en/rights/civil%20 liberties_civil%20rights/de14_99_privacy_law.htm)

A number of questions arise: how are unions currently addressing electronic surveillance practices in collective agreements? What is potential "best practices" language for unions to model? What patterns are identifiable in union responses to growing surveillance? This paper seeks to answer these questions starting with the expectation that it would find collective agreements containing surveillance language in the information sector of the economy because it contains more highly educated "knowledge" workers who are more likely to be performing communications and language-related tasks. Moreover, evidence from Europe suggests that where collective agreements contain language protecting workers from employer surveillance and permitting worker use of company computer systems for union business, these are invariably in the communication and information sectors (e.g. Telefonica in Spain, IBM in Italy, and France Telecom). (Aranda, 2002)

3.   LITERATURE REVIEW

Although thee is some literature on what people are doing about electronic surveillance (Marx, 2003), in much of the general literature on surveillance in the workplace, the role that unions can play is overlooked or neglected entirely. In *The Soft Cage,* Michael Parenti (2003) dedicates one chapter to the fact of surveillance practices in contemporary workplaces. He links surveillance practices in the workplace with the principles of Taylorism. Remedies, for Parenti, lie in "regulation, legal limitations and a properly enforced reverse surveillance in which corporations are subjected to the gaze of critics... ." (p.150) These remedies again leave out the role that unions can play in restricting surveillance through collective agreements.

Wallace (2004) writes that companies monitor their workplaces through authentication processes, desktop monitoring, the use of location-aware devices, video technologies, and by using "smart" objects which are equipped to communicate with networks and transmit information. The reasons behind surveillance practices range from issues of legal liability to security concerns over leaks to worries about productivity and "cyberslacking." She also emphasizes growing social acceptance of surveillance practices in the wake of the September 11th terrorist attacks. "The notion that it is better to let ten guilty people go free than to convict one innocent person has given way to a heightened desire for security and for greater protection against the horrible acts that any one of those ten people might do -- even if they have done nothing illegal yet....Now, most people would welcome a highly sophisticated video surveillance system that could spot terrorists in an airport or at the Super Bowl." (p.245)

Bryant (1995) directly addressed electronic surveillance in Canadian workplaces and she is among the few scholars who have emphasized the role that unions could play in protecting employee privacy rights, noting the general weakness of statutory and other constitutional protection for the workplace. The reaction of Canadian unions, however, has been decidedly limited. Bennett (2003) argues that the rise of mobile technologies – enabling the creation of mobile workforces – has challenged existing privacy policy instruments to ensure a level of privacy in the workplace. Bennett notes that there is a range of instruments with which issues of privacy and workplace monitoring can be addressed: policy, regulatory, self-regulatory, technological. Beyond a general recognition of the role that they can play in bargaining for privacy rights, there is little attention paid to the role of unions and collective agreements.

A symposium was recently held on the issue of workplace surveillance and the results were published in the *Journal of Labor Research* Vol. 24 (2). Townsend and Barnett (2003) outlined the excessive levels of intrusion into workplace privacy and emphasized the importance that unions have in ensuring the protection of workers' rights. They cited a survey conducted by the AFL – CIO in which surveyed employees expressed overwhelming support for privacy protection in the workplace. Nolan (2003) contrasts the public reasons (productivity, security, union avoidance) and private reasons (curiosity, morality, voyeurism) why employers engage in workplace surveillance. He notes that most cases of employee dismissal are due to infractions of a lascivious nature, rather than for infractions due to simply wasting time or for personal use of electronic communications.

Corry and Nutz (2003), writing in the same issue, address the matter from management's perspective. They argue that employers might need to rely on surveillance practices because they may be held liable for criminal literature, such as hate or sexually harassing material, spread by employees at their workplace. The authors also delve into questions of the effects of electronic communications on questions of union activity in the workplace and employer interference. One important point they emphasize is that in the absence of specific language, employers have greater rights. "Even where such rules as an Internet/E-mail policy do not form part of the [collective] agreement, it is now generally conceded and was held in the case *Crestbrook Forests Industries Ltd.* (1993) that in the absence of specific language to the contrary in the agreement, the making of such rules or policies lies within the prerogative of management, and arbitrators have held this to be so whether or not an express management's rights clause exists reserving the right of management to direct and "manage" the work force" (p. 243). In general, there exists a significant gap in the literature that emphasizes and describes how Canadian unions are reacting to growing practices of surveillance. This paper seeks to fill that gap.

4.   METHODOLOGY

The federal Department of Human Resources and Skills Development maintains the *Negotech* online database of current and historic collective agreements in Canada. The database is not collected based on a census method, but uses a statistical sampling method to obtain a stratified random sample of collective agreements (Roy, 2001). The initial sample was selected from the universe of bargaining units with more than 100 workers. All bargaining units of 2000 or more workers under provincial jurisdiction and all bargaining units of 200 workers or more under federal jurisdiction are sampled. For bargaining units of smaller sizes, there are different proportions of sampling, ranging from one in three to one in ten. The database includes a total of 5,495 English and French language collective agreements, signed under both federal and provincial jurisdiction.

In order to find collective agreements dealing with electronic surveillance, we searched the English-language collective agreements using the following search string "privacy or monitor or surveillance." We followed this with a search for "observation systems," a term which we knew to be used in some collective agreements. Within this initial sub-sample, we searched each individual collective agreement for clauses related specifically to electronic monitoring and surveillance. Of the several hundred collective agreements returned, 67 included collective agreement language directly related to electronic surveillance or monitoring in the workplace. The search was duplicated for the French-language collective agreements. The French-language database posed certain problems. For example, the verb "surveiller" and related nouns refer not only to issues of surveillance but also to supervision. Therefore, we modified the search to include the terms "surveillance électronique," "surveillance vidéo," "contrôl* électronique," and "contrôl* vidéo." (The asterisk serves as a "wildcard" character.)The French search yielded 9 collective agreements with relevant language.

Because this study was most interested in electronic surveillance in the workplace, we rejected collective agreements that only included language on such issues as drug and alcohol testing, references to protection of privacy legislation or protection of individual records. Two collective agreements which required personal surveillance of workers engaged in cargo loading were rejected because the contract did not specify electronic surveillance.

5. FINDINGS

Out of 5,495 collective agreements, 4008 English and 1487 French, 76 (67 English and 9 French) contain language dealing with electronic surveillance in the workplace. Although this represents an undoubtedly small portion of collective agreements in Canada, it does indicate an improvement over the situation identified by Bryant in her 1995 study. In that study, she found virtually no response by unions to electronic surveillance practices in the workplace. Almost a decade later, some progress is being made. There are a number of reasons that could explain the limited response by Canadian unions. The relative decline of the industrial economy in which unions thrived has challenged the very survival of numerous unions in North America. The growth of a large temporary workforce and of companies like Walmart that are skilled in the use of new technologies to cuts costs have posed serious problems for traditional unions. Like their American counterparts Canadian unions have had to focus on fundamental issues like job security, wages, and organizing. Important as privacy is, and most unions recognize the problem that surveillance poses, unions have chosen to place it lower on the list of policy priorities. Furthermore, although this is changing, electronic surveillance and privacy have historically been applied to women workers such as telephone operators and data entry workers, whose limited power in unions has made it all the more difficult to give surveillance a more prominent place on the trade unions agenda. Electronic surveillance has been a feature of the North American workplace for some time, but its intensity and pervasive nature are relatively new. Yes, telephone operators had calls monitored electronically in the 1980s, but now nearly every detail of a trucker's day is monitored as is nearly every web site an office worker surfs. Like many institutions, including governments, trade unions have just begun to absorb the enormity of the challenges posed by electronic monitoring, and it is little wonder that they have called on governments to shoulder the public policy responsibility of dealing with the problem. But the fact that some unions have decided to bargain the issue indicates a growing frustration with the pace of government attention.

Among the unions that have succeeded in putting the issue into collective bargaining agreements, in both language groups, public sector unions predominated over private sector unions. Not unexpectedly, the overwhelming number of collective agreements with surveillance language were in the tertiary or service sector. This largely stems from the greater use of electronic communications and the greater importance of such to workplace measures.

Table 1. Contracts Containing Surveillance Language by Public/ Private Sector

	French	English
Private Sector	6	29
Public Sector	3	38

The two most represented national unions in the sample were the Canadian Auto Workers, who increasingly include service workers among their members and the Canadian Union of Public Employees. This is not surprising given that these unions are two of the three largest unions in Canada. University faculty unions made up the third largest group of unions with surveillance-related clauses.

Table 2. Contracts Containing Surveillance Language by Work Type

	French	English
Primary		2
Secondary		14
Tertiary	9	51

The hypothesis that the collective agreements would be concentrated in the information sector of the economy is partially supported. The CAW and CUPE were the largest groups of unions with relevant language. The CAW collective agreements were, in large part in the auto and aerospace industries. Five of the ten CUPE collective agreements were concentrated in the post-secondary education sector. Taking those unions together with the seven faculty unions and two media unions, it is clear that information or language-oriented workplaces form a large part of the collective agreements with surveillance-related clauses. Five of the nine French-language collective agreements were in the university and media sectors. It was expected that there would have been a greater representation from the call centre industry. In fact, only two collective agreements covered call centre workplaces, one is a electrical power utility and the other is a telecommunications firm. Two explanations are likely for the predominance of the post-secondary sector. First, universities were among the first workplaces to adopt electronic communications in a widespread manner and so unions and management were likely forced to confront issues of surveillance in the workplace at an early stage. Second, unlike the call centre industry, Canadian universities are also largely unionized workplaces.

We identified four different types of surveillance language clause: low privacy protection, moderate privacy protection, high privacy protection and worker-friendly surveillance. The low protection category included cases where the employer was explicitly empowered to engage in surveillance activities or where the only restriction on surveillance was a matter of informing employees. Cases where surveillance practices were accepted but limits were sought (such as a halt to further expansion of surveillance activities) were assigned to the second category. Cases where surveillance practices were extremely limited, most often only to the prosecution of criminal offences, were assigned to the third category. Finally, surveillance language meant to be in the interest of worker safety and protection of their property were placed in the fourth.

Table 3. Contracts Containing Surveillance Language by Union

	French	English
Steelworkers		3
CAW		11
CUPE	3	10
OPEIU		5
Hotel Workers		1
Transport Unions		3
Media Unions		2
Faculty Unions		7
Independent Unions	3	6
SEIU		1
IAM		3
PSAC		3
CEP	2	7
UFCW		4
Fédération Nationale des Communications	1	
Provincial Public Sector Unions		1

Fifteen agreements were found to have the weakest protection against surveillance practices. The most dramatic case of the first is found in the agreement between Edmonton's Shaw Conference Center and the United

Food and Commercial Workers Union which represents the support and catering staff. In their first collective agreement, awarded after a drawn-out strike, one finds the following clause:

3. Management Rights
3(1) EDE [Economic Development Edmonton] has the right to manage its business as it sees fit, including the right to utilize any surveillance methods without notice

Similarly, the agreement reached between Loomis Courier Services and the Canadian Auto Workers contained a clause which required the company to post warning signs:

Letter of Agreement
Electronic Surveillance Equipment

The following notice will be posted in all work places covered by the Collective Agreement: "Due to the nature of our business and occasional requests from customers, electronic surveillance equipment may be installed from time to time in the workplace."

It is understood that such equipment will not be installed in areas where employees are entitled to expect privacy, such a washrooms and locker rooms.

The United Food and Commercial Workers agreed to the following clause in agreements with both Canada Safeway and Overwaitea Foods:

Within the confines of the law, the Employer may use video cameras in almost any part of the store. The vast majority of employees have no need to be concerned and may be assured that common sense and discretion will prevail in choosing who is allowed access to any monitoring equipment or video tapes.

The reliance on the law is problematic as most provincial privacy legislation deals with the protection of personal information and access to government information as opposed to the protection of any individual space. Similarly labour legislation in Canada is generally silent on privacy issues. In short, at the low end of protection for privacy, unions have explicitly agreed to management use of surveillance practices with the only restrictions being the limits of the law or warnings to affected employees.

Twenty-six collective agreements contained moderate protection against surveillance practices. For example, the United Steelworkers of America and an auto parts firm: "(d) No additional surveillance cameras will be installed in employee occupied areas." Presumably the union consented to the existing surveillance cameras in the workplace but won a halt to their spread. A second example is found in two collective agreements covering public libraries in Saskatoon and the Fraser Valley region. In those cases, the clause states: "The parties recognize that volume measurement may be necessary to obtain an objective evaluation of the level of production of a group, a section or an office. However, there shall be no electronic monitoring of an individual's work output for the purpose of evaluating performance." In this case, the union appears to be consenting to electronic monitoring in general, while attempting to restrict the scope of those practices from monitoring the work pace and productivity of individual workers.

Twenty-two agreements carried high protection against surveillance, most often in a written guarantee that video or electronic surveillance practices would not be used, except in narrowly-defined situations. For example, in a letter of intent explicitly dedicated to surveillance issues and supplementary to a collective agreement between a manufacturer and the Communications, Energy and Paperworkers, the union won the following written assurance: "This will confirm that the Company shall not use video security equipment to monitor employee work performance." The Canadian Union of Postal Workers has particularly strong language as well, which is not surprising, given the strength of the union, its history of militancy, and the close proximity of its members to valuable merchandise. One can understand simultaneously the desire of the employer to exercise strict measures to protect property and also the union's desire to restrict employers.

41.02 Surveillance

The watch and observation systems cannot be used except for the purpose of protecting the mail and the property of the State against criminal acts such as theft, depredation and damage to property. At no time may such systems be used as a means to evaluate the performance of employees and to gather evidence in support of disciplinary measures unless such disciplinary measures result from the commission of a criminal act.

It was noted above how some of the strongest language stems from agreements between unions as employers and the unions which represent their own employees. For example, the two agreements between CUPE, the Canadian Staff Union and the Office and Professional Employees International Union include the following:

25.09 Electronic Monitoring, Surveillance, Employee Confidentiality

1. Electronic monitoring and surveillance shall not be used for the purposes of individual work measurement of employees.
2. Surveillance cameras, any technology or systems capable of monitoring employees or their work and any other related equipment shall not be used in employee occupied areas without the knowledge of employees in the area. At no time shall video taping or any other form of electronic tracking or monitoring of employees, work output or attendance in or at a particular location be allowed for the purpose of random surveillance, audits or assessing discipline. At no time may such systems be used as a means to gather evidence in support of disciplinary measures. The Union shall be advised, in writing, of the location and purpose of all surveillance cameras and the reason for installation of such equipment.

Finally, there were five agreements (all English) that could be deemed to be "worker-friendly." This represents less than ten percent of the total sample and thus reinforces the idea that most surveillance practices tend to be in the interests of employers for productivity, security or disciplinary purposes. The protection of property and of the person were the two major reasons behind worker-friendly surveillance. For example, agreements between the Canadian Union of Public Employees and a casino in Calgary and between the CAW and Lear Corp. specified that the company would provide for electronic surveillance of the parking lot to protect staff vehicles. Similarly, an agreement between Nortel and the telecommunications workers of the CEP included the following: "For reasons of safety, when an employee is assigned to perform work in an isolated area and where it may not be possible for him to request assistance, the Company agrees to set up proper surveillance in order to provide help and/or assistance as may be necessary." Although surveillance practices can be put in place to protect the interests of employees, the overwhelming majority of collective agreement clauses on the matter involved unions attempting to restrict employers' use of electronic surveillance practices.

After studying all the collective agreements, it is apparent that there are several possible directions that collective agreements can take. For example:

- Unions can allow surveillance practices and defer to management
- Unions can insist on signage in the workplace, informing employees and customers of the presence of surveillance technologies
- Unions can require that the employer inform the union about the introduction of surveillance practices
- Surveillance practices can be prohibited or prohibited save for criminal investigations.
- Unions can insist on surveillance technologies be put in place to protect workers health, safety and property
- Unions can prevent data gathered by electronic means from being used in productivity evaluation or criminal proceedings
- Unions can require that information above and beyond what was gathered by electronic means be used in any disciplinary or criminal proceeding
- Unions can require that employees be informed when they will be monitored electronically or unions can require the consent of individuals before surveillance can take place.

6. CONCLUSION

Bryant's article in 1995 sounded a decidedly pessimistic tone in evaluating the role that unions play in protecting worker privacy. Since that time, 76 collective agreements maintained in the federal government's database of Canadian collective agreements have enshrined clauses related to electronic monitoring and surveillance practices in the workplace. Out of the total of 5495 collective agreements maintained in the database, this number is very small. However, it does represent a first step. Clearly, the information sector, especially universities and public sector are most strongly represented in the group of collective agreements that formed our sample. And since this is the fastest growing sector of Canadian trade unionism, there is reason to expect growth in the number of collective agreements covering electronic surveillance. Equally important is that these collective agreements generally contained moderate to high degrees of protection for workers from excessive surveillance practices.

Surveillance practices are found in a wide range of industries and workplaces and, labour legislation is generally silent on privacy and surveillance issues. But, as is shown here, collective bargaining offers unions a wide range of options to structure, limit, influence or control such practices.

7. ACKNOWLEDGEMENTS

We would like to thank The Surveillance Project at Queen's University whose grant from the Social Sciences and Humanities Research Project provided financial assistance for the research. We would also like to acknowledge the research assistance of Laura Glithero, an undergraduate student at Queen's. Thanks also to Professor Catherine McKercher, Carleton University, for her valuable comments and to participants at the June 2005 conference on Landscapes of ICT and Social Accountability in Turku, Finland for their helpful suggestions.

REFERENCES

American Civil Liberties Union (1998), Through the keyhole: privacy in the workplace..

Aranda, J. T. (2002), Information technology and worker's privacy: the role of workers' representatives, Comparative Labour Law Policy Journal, 23 (2), 533-549.

Bennett, C. (2003), Surveillance, employment and location: regulating the privacy of mobile workers in the mobile workplace, paper prepared for a conference on The Ethics of Workplace Privacy, Sigtuna, Sweden, November 10-11, 2003.

Bloom, E. M., Schachter, M., and Steelman, E. H (2003), Competing interests in the post-9-11 workplace: the new line between privacy and safety, William Mitchell Law Review, 29 (3), 897-920.

Bryant, S. (1995), Electronic surveillance in the workplace, Canadian Journal of Communication, Vol. 20 (4), 505-522.

Corry, D. J., and Nutz, K.E. (2003), Employee email and internet use: Canadian legal issues, Journal of Labor Research, 24 (3), 233-256.

Electronic Privacy Information Center (2004), Workplace privacy, online at http://www.epic.org/privacy/workplace/ accessed 31.01.2005

European Industrial Relations Observatory (2003), New technology and respect for privacy at the workplace, European Foundation for the Improvement of Living and Working Conditions.

Finlay, P. and McKinlay, A. (2003), Surveillance, electronic communications technologies and regulation, Industrial Relations Journal, 34 (4), 305-318.

Hazard's Magazine (2004), Stop snooping, online at http://www.hazards.org/privacy/ accessed 31.01.2005

Head, S. (2003), The new ruthless economy: work and power in the digital age. Oxford University Press.

International Labour Organization (1997), Protection of workers personal data. ILO.

King, Nancy J. (2003), Electronic monitoring to promote national security impacts workplace privacy, Employee Responsibilities and Rights Journal, 15, (3), 127-147.

Lyon, D. (1994), The electronic eye: the rise of surveillance society, U. of Minnesota Press.

Lyon, D. (2001), Surveillance society: monitoring everyday life, Open University Press.

Marx, G. (2003), A tack in the shoe: neutralizing and resisting the new surveillance, Journal of Social Issues, 59, 2, 369-390.

Nolan, D. (2003), Privacy and profitability in the technological workplace, Journal of Labor Research, 24 (2), 207-231.

Parenti, C. (2003), The soft cage: surveillance in America from slavery to the war on terror. Basic Books.

Rotenberg, M. and Laurant, C. (2004), Privacy and human rights 2004: an international survey of privacy laws and developments. Electronic Privacy Information Center.

Roy, J. (2001), Information on collective bargaining: moving from a census to a sample approach." Workplace Gazette, 3 (2), 12-20.

Rule, J. (1996), High-tech workplace surveillance: what's really new? in D. Lyon and E. Zureik (eds.), Computers, surveillance and privacy, University of Minnesota Press.

Shane, P. (2004), Democracy Online: The Prospects for Democratic Renewal Through the Internet. Routledge.

Townsend, A.M. & Bennett, J. T. (2003), Privacy, technology, and conflict: emerging issues and action in workplace privacy, Journal of Labor Research, 24 (2), 195-205.

Wallace, P. (2004), The internet in the workplace: how new technology is transforming work, Cambridge University Press.

COPYRIGHT MANAGEMENT SYSTEMS
Accessing the power balance

Carlisle E. George
Middlesex University, UK, c.george@mdx.ac.uk

Abstract: This paper first examines technical and legal issues surrounding Copyright Management Systems (CMS). It then examines the rationale for use of these systems and some accompanying criticisms. It argues that there are compelling economic reasons for controlling access to, and use of copyrighted material, especially in light of digital technology and the Internet. It also argues that CMS have very undesirable qualities which raise concerns about social accountability. They can exert strong control over access to material, invade privacy and deprive the public domain of valuable resources (hence affecting innovation) echoing aspects of eighteenth century Blackstonian ideology. The paper concludes that the present state of affairs in which CMS has increased the power to rights-holders may be detrimental to the development of human society. Technology and the law appear to have colluded to potentially stifle innovation, hence producing no ultimate winners in the future.

1.   INTRODUCTION

The advent of digital technology has meant that digital content can be easily copied without loss of quality and also easily distributed (via the Internet) throughout the world. Famous legal battles such as *A&M Records Inc v Napster*[1], demonstrate the potential threat that copyright holders feel from digital copying, especially their inability to control the dissemination of their work.   Rights-holders, however, have fought back by using technological measures to protect their work. This has posed a dilemma. On one hand rights holders aim to protect their work from unauthorised copying

---

[1] *A&M Records, Inc and others v Napster*, Inc D.C. No. CV-99-05183-MHP. Napster facilitated the worldwide distribution of music via their peer-to-peer file sharing system. They were found guilty of contributory and vicarious infringement of copyright.

and use, on the other hand consumers/users desire greater freedom to use these works.

2.   COPYRIGHT MANAGEMENT SYSTEMS (CMS)

CMS are technological measures which aim to protect copyrighted works. These systems range from digital watermarking and web tracking systems[2] to more sophisticated access-control systems. The former seeks to investigate infringement after the event, while the latter seeks to prevent infringement and control access. This paper will focus on the latter.

2.1 Technical Issues

Access control systems prevent unauthorised access to copyrighted works and allow licensed use of works under certain terms and conditions. Some access-control CMS essentially consist of content and rights identification facilities and a facility for licensing[3]. More advanced systems, for example, trusted systems[4] and Digital Rights Management Systems[5,6,7] use software or a semi-conductor chip in hardware (e.g. computers, audio/video players) which controls access by being able to encrypt and decrypt the copyrighted work. The software or chip usually contains instructions which enables it to permit or deny access to the protected work, impose usage rights (e.g. permission to copy, transfer. loan, play, print), specify cost and other terms/ conditions of use. Hence rights-holders can have total control over any interaction between content seekers and the content. Distribution of protected content may be via client/server technology (Internet), digital audio broadcasting or CD's among others.

---

[2] E.g. see http://www.digimarc.com/   for a review of digital watermarking and tracking techniques

[3] Gervais, D.(1999). *Electronic Rights Management and Digital Identifier Systems*. The Journal of Electronic Publishing March, 1999 Volume 4, Issue 3.

[4]   Stefik,   M.(1997).   *Trusted   Systems*. http://www.hackvan.com/pub/stig/articles/trusted-systems/0397stefik.html

[5] Glass, B. (2003). *What does DRM really mean?* , PC Magazine. April 8, 2003.

[6] Sellers, C. (2003). *Digital Rights Management Systems: Recent European Issues*. Ent. L.R. 2003, 14(1), 5-9

[7] Lui, Q et al (2003). *Digital Rights Management for Content Distribution*. AISA2003, Conferences in Research & Practice in Information technology, Vol 21. C. Johnson, P. Montague & C SteKette (Eds)

2.2 Legal Issues

The debate about whether technological protection systems stifle innovation, results not only from the technology itself (architecture) but also from the strong legal protection given to these systems. Hence content is protect by both law and architecture[8] or a hierarchy/design hybrid.[9] Any discussion relating to the said debate, therefore, necessitates a look at the relevant anti-circumvention legislation in the EU (Directive 2001/29/EC, – "Directive"[10]) and US (The Digital Millennium Copyright Act 1998 – "DMCA"[11]). Both legislative frameworks are largely consistent with the WIPO Copyright Treaty 1996.[12]

Under the DMCA (US Code Title 17 Copyrights), three major acts are prohibited namely: circumventing a technological measure that controls access to "a work protected under this title"[13]; manufacturing or trafficking in any technology, device or service which is primarily designed for the purpose of circumventing[14] a technological measure that (a) controls access to "a work protected under this title"[15] or (b) protects the rights of a copyright owner.[16] The DMCA also states that other rights (e.g. limitations, defences, fair use) are not affected[17] and gives seven specific exemptions to the act of circumventing a technical protection system.[18]

---

[8] Lessig, L. (1999). *Code and other laws of cyberspace.* NY, Basic Boooks.

[9] Murray, A & Scott, C. (2002). *Controlling the New Media: Hybrid Responses to New Forms of Power.* The Modern Law Review 2002, Vol 65, No 4.

[10] Directive 2001/29/EC on the harmonization of certain aspects of copyright and related rights in the information society. See http://www.patent.gov.uk/about/consultations/eccopyright/annexb.htm

[11] DMCA 1998. See: http://www.copyright.gov/legislation/dmca.pdf

[12] WIPO Treaty 1996 See: http://www.gseis.ucla.edu/iclp/wipo1.htm
 The WIPO Copyright Treaty (WCT) 1996 focused on prohibiting the act of circumvention where a technological measure "restrict acts, in respect of their [copyright holder] works, which are not authorised by the authors concerned or permitted by law" (Article 11)

[13] Section 1201(a)(1)

[14] Circumvention means "avoiding , bypassing, removing, deactivating, or otherwise impairing a technological measure". DMCA Section 1201(b)(2)(A).

[15] DMCA Section 1201(a)(2)

[16] DMCA Section 1201(b)

[17] DMCA Section 1201 (c)

[18] DMCA Section 1201(d)–(j) These specific exemptions pertain to: allowing non-profit libraries and education institutions to make a determination (in good faith) whether to acquire a copy of the work; activities of law enforcement and government; reverse engineering to achieve interoperability of a computer program; encryption research to investigate flaws of encryption technologies; preventing access of minors to Internet material; protecting personally identifying information; and testing security flaws and weaknesses.

The EU Directive, requires that Member States "provide adequate protection against the circumvention of any effective technological measures", which prevent or restrict acts not authorized by the rights holder.[19] This includes prohibiting the manufacture, importation or possession of any technological device, product or service whose primary function is to circumvent a technological protection measure. The Directive also requires Member States to take appropriate measures to ensure that beneficiaries of exceptions and limitations[20] provided by national laws[21] are given the means to benefit from these exceptions and limitations.

The effects of the laws above will be discussed later. They prohibit the manufacture or importation of anti-circumvention devices, making it impossible for someone to engage in circumvention, whatever the motive. The DMCA in particular has caused enormous controversy and debate regarding its effect on research and innovation.

3. STRONG PROTECTION VERSUS GREATER FREEDOM OF ACCESS

A major reason for the existence of copyright law is to reward rights holders for their work, and to give an incentive to create works in the future. The advent of digital technologies and the Internet, however, have facilitated easy copying, distribution and sharing of information including copyrighted works. For rights holders, stopping the unauthorised reproduction and distribution of their work have become a major concern especially as this translates to a loss of revenue. The Commercial Piracy Report 2003 of the International Federation of the Phonographic Industry, (representing 1500 record companies in 70 countries) reported global sales of pirated CD's totalling US$4.6 billion in 2002.[22] Estimates of money lost in 2001 from pirated software in India amounted to US$24 million.[23] The *Economist* predicts that "Peer-to-peer file sharing will deprive the [music] industry of

---

[19] Article 6(1)

[20] This would imply exceptions and limitations (Article 5) to the reproduction right (Article 2) and the right of communication to the public (Article 3) (e.g. private use, public libraries, broadcast Organizations) should be allowed. Right holders, however can limit the number of reproductions for private use given under Article 5(2)(b).

[21] Directive 2001/29/EC, Article 6(4).

[22] Commercial Piracy Report 2003. http://www.ifpi.org/site-content/antipiracy/piracy2003-the-key-facts.html

[23] http://www.blonnet.com/2002/08/06/stories/2002080600920700.htm

US$4.7 billion of revenues in 2008".[24] Issues such as the above, provide justification for technological measures to control the dissemination and reproduction of works, allowing the copyright owner to dictate usage and access rights. Further, prohibiting circumvention of such measures has been justified by the economic argument that infringement causes an uplift in the price of copyrighted works, hence preventing infringement allows more public access to works at the lower price.[25]

Opponents of strong protection as afforded by CMS, see these systems as going against the spirit of copyright law, which is meant to facilitate the development of creative works for the public good (or benefit of society[26]), and not to confer absolute protection.[27] CMS, accompanying laws against circumvention and contractual restrictions have fortified works, resulting in even stronger protection (for works) than originally intended by copyright law. This stronger protection is manifested in the extension of: the term of the duration of copyright and the scope of copyright.

3.1   Extension of Duration of Copyright

Use of a CMS may mean that works can be locked away under technological protection for longer than copyright law allows. This violates the intention of copyright law, to offer protection for a limited amount of time, after which the work becomes available for free use by the public (i.e. becomes part of the 'public domain'[28]).

The issue of the public domain and limiting the duration of copyright has been one of historical debate. English theorists of property such as Hobbes and Locke, consistently argued[29] for absolute rights of owners and against

---

[24] The Economist (2003), *Is the threat of online piracy receding?* The Economist ,Oct 2003. http://www.economist.com/business/displayStory.cfm?story_id=2177244

[25] (NII Group) 1995 Intellectual property and National Information Infrastructure: The Report of the Working Group on Intellectual property Rights. ISBN 0-9648716-0-1.

[26] Rice, D. (2002) : *Copyright as Talisman: Expanding 'Property' in Digital Works,* 16(2) International Review of Law, Computers & Technology 113.

[27] Copyright protection is subject to a limitation period, fair use/dealing, first sale & other limitations

[28] " Public domain refers to refers to works and parts of works which a copyright owner does not own... ideas, insubstantial parts of works, works which are too insubstantial to attract copyright protection, substantial parts of works which are works used for the purpose of fair dealing, and works whose copyright has expired". Waelde, C. (2001) Infra note 47

[29] Travis, H.(2000): *Pirates of the Information Infrastructure: Blackstonian Copyright and the First Amendment* 15 Berkeley Technology Law Journal. http://www.law.berkeley.edu/journals/btlj/articles/vol15/travis/travis.html

any rights by the public in common lands (commons[30]). This argument was grounded in 'propertarian ideology' which advocated that private property rights and national wealth, weighted against the public right in the commons.[31] In particular enclosures of commons were justified by arguments that public rights in the commons were not really rights as such, use of the commons was wasteful and that utilitarian and economic benefits would arise from more adequate use of such lands (e.g. by merchant farmers).[32] In shifting 'propertarian ideology' from the physical to intellectual commons, another theorist William Blackstone argued for perpetual common-law copyright giving owners unlimited exclusivity to control their works.[33] In 1710, amidst much opposition from booksellers, the Statute of Anne, granted statutory rights to copyright holders but these rights were limited both in duration and scope. The fight for a perpetual common-law copyright, however, continued, culminating in the House of Lords decision in *Donaldson and Becket (1774)[34]* which rejected the notion of perpetual common-law copyright.

In the US, the founding fathers were against perpetual monopolies and supported the idea of limited copyright. As a result of the English *Donaldson* case, congress enacted a copyright clause in the US Constitution which restricted authors exclusive rights as to "purpose, subject matter, beneficiaries and duration".[35]

Presently, limitations on the duration of copyright continue to be the position in both UK and US copyright law.[36]

3.2   Extension of the Scope of Copyright

The extension of the scope of copyright by CMS is primarily manifested by the restriction on access to a work for "fair use" (US) or "fair dealing" (UK/EU) purposes. The doctrines of "fair use" and "fair dealing" have traditionally allowed use of extracts of copyrighted material under certain circumstances without authorization. UK/EU "fair dealing" is limited to a

---

[30] Lessig describes the commons as "a resource to which anyone within the relevant community has a right without obtaining the permission of anyone else." p19-20, Lessig, L. (2001). *The Future of Ideas: The Fate of the Commons in a Connected World* . NY, Random House

[31] See Travis, H. (2000) supra 29

[32] Ibid

[33] Ibid

[34] 98 Eng. Rep. 257 (H.L.1774).

[35] See Travis, H.(2000) supra 29

[36] UK, Copyright and Patents Act 1988 as amended and US Copyright Act 1976 as amended

list of purposes stipulated by law (research and private study, criticism and review, news reporting).[37] US "fair use"[38] does not entail an exhaustive list of purposes but is determined mainly by reference to four factors namely[39]: the purpose and character of use (e.g., commercial, non-profit educational purposes); the nature of the copyrighted work; the amount and substantiality of the portion used in relation to the protected work as a whole; and the effect of the use upon the potential market.

Most UK "fair dealing" purposes, would qualify as "fair use" under US law. Use of CMS raises fair use/dealing concerns from two perspectives, namely the technology and the law.

Regarding technology, with CMS, protected works are inaccessible unless a fee is paid. Further it is perhaps beyond the state of the art to design a system to adequately allow fair use.[40] Such a system would need knowledge of the circumstances of the use (e.g. domestic vs commercial) and complex artificial intelligence techniques to apply the US four-factor "fair use" test[41] (requiring an economic analysis of markets).[42,43]

With regard to the law, while the DMCA and EU Directive 2001/29/EC attempt to address fair use/dealing concerns, it is argued that these provisions are perhaps not very effective. First it is worthwhile to note, that the DMCA and Directive differ in their approaches to fair use/dealing. The DMCA provides exemptions to circumvention under certain circumstances.[44] This, however, is nullified (to a great extent) by the prohibition on the manufacture or trafficking of anti-circumvention devices. The Directive, differs from the DMCA by tackling the problem at the earlier stage (before

---

[37] Copyright, Design and Patents Act (1988) (CDPA), Sections 29, 30. http://www.jenkins-ip.com/patlaw/cdpa1.htm

[38] For a good discussion of 'fair use' see Landau, M (2002) : *Digital Downloads, Access Codes and US Copyright Law* [2002] 16(2) International Review of Law, Computers & Technology 149.

[39] Title 17 US Code, Ch 1, Section 107, see: http://www.copyright.gov/title17/index.html. Also note that the Berne Convention contains a three-step test for limitations and exceptions which such tests are based on.

[40] Felten, E. (2003). *A Skeptical View of DRM and Fair Use*. Communications of the ACM, Vol 46(4).

[41] Supra note 39

[42] Felten, E (2003) supra 40

[43] Also see Erikson,J. (2003). *Fair Use, DRM and Trusted Computing*. Communications of the ACM, Vol 46(4). Erikson contends that "in the case of fair use, no explicit set of rules can be implemented and automatically evaluated by computing systems" p.38.

[44] DMCA Section 1201(d)-(j) supra note 18

lock-up).[45]   It requires Member States to ensure that rights holders make available to a beneficiary of an exception or limitation (e.g. fair dealing), the means of benefiting from that exception or limitation.[46] Ideally, this would involve allowing for fair dealing principles when designing CMS. As discussed earlier, this may not be adequately functional with the state of the art. Additionally, EU Member States can take measures where rights holders fail to provide for private copying. For example in the UK, an application can be made to the Secretary of State, if requests for copies has been exhausted. This procedure, however, appears to be burdensome for the average member of the public.

A second legal issue regards the legitimacy of contractual restrictions in digital licences of CMS.[47] In many instances they prevent uses of works which may be legitimate under copyright law. This therefore results in further protection via private law.

A third legal issue concerns the restrictions on reverse engineering and decompilation (implicit in the regulatory framework) and the potential effects on software security and privacy. Reverse engineering of software involves decompiling software (i.e. converting it from a low level language to a high level language) to understand how it works.[48] In US, the case of *Sega Enterprises Ltd. v. Accolade Inc.*,[49] established the legality of decompilation (as a fair use) if carried out to gain access to unprotected functional elements of a program, in order to create interoperable systems. Under the DMCA (Section 1201(f)) reverse engineering is allowed as a defence (to circumvention of an access control measure) where it is necessary to enable interoperability of an independently created program with other programs. In the process of reverse engineering, copyright infringement must not occur nor should any other US laws be violated. In the EU while decompilation is not listed as a fair dealing purpose, under Directive 91/250/EEC[50] decompilation of a computer program is allowed by

[45] Duollier, S. (2003). *Fair Use by Design in the European Copyright Directive of 2001.* Communications of the ACM, Vol 46(4).

[46] Directive 2001/29/EC, Article 6(4).

[47] Cohen, J (1997) . *Some Reflections on Copyright Management Systems and Laws Designed to Protect Them* 12 Berkeley Technology Law Journal http://www.law.berkeley.edu/journals/btlj/articles/vol12/Cohen/html/reader.html

[48] http://cse.stanford.edu/class/cs201/projects-99-00/intellectual-property-law/reverse_engineering.htm

[49] Sega Enterprises Ltd. v. Accolade Inc., http://digital-law-online.info/cases/24PQ2D1561.htm

[50] Directive (91/250/EEC) on the legal protection of computer programs See: http://europa.eu.int/ISPO/legal/en/ipr/software/software.html

a lawful user "to obtain the information necessary to achieve the interoperability of an independently created computer program with other programs".[51] Several additional restrictions are given in the Directive including that decompilation should not be used to make a program similar to the decompiled program or to violate any acts restricted by copyright.

The restrictions on reverse engineering and decompilation are important because there are legitimate reasons (other than what is legally allowed) for decompiling CMS. An important reason is to evaluate CMS software security and functionality. Without being permitted to legally decompile CMS software, users may not be able to find software bugs, security flaws or hidden functionality (such as user profiling for advertising purposes or other acts of privacy invasion) which may exist.

4. DISCUSSION

From the previous discussion there appears to be legitimate reasons (e.g. loss of revenue as pointed out earlier) why CMS are employed. The threat of the Internet and digital technologies present a real problem of control for rights holders. CMS, however, do not reflect the spirit of copyright law especially with regard to the limitation period and fair use/dealing. They also allow universal control of copyright works. All access to works must be through the granting of permission and the technology exists in some systems to track and monitor individual users. This raises concerns about privacy and data protection.[52] There appears to be a real concern that the power balance in CMS may be too much in favour of a strong control by authors. This has the potential to deter innovation and discourage potential competitors in various markets.

In addition to controlling access to copyrighted works, CMS can restrict access to works which either do not qualify for copyright protection or have exhausted their period of copyright protection. This therefore, can deprive the public domain of valuable resources. Hence use of CMS may result in some 'public domain' and other creative works inaccessible except to those who are able to pay for them.[53] Public domain (and creative works) are a key

---

[51] Ibid Article 6.

[52] Cohen, J (1997) supra 47

[53] Waelde, C. (2001). *The Quest for Access in the Digital Era: Copyright and the Internet.* The Journal of Information, Law and Technology (JILT), 2001(1). http://elj.warwick.ac.uk/jilt/01-1/waelde.html

to innovation, since new ideas are formed from existing ideas.[54] Also new creative works incorporate and build on existing works, hence any barrier to accessing existing works is a barrier to innovation. The more a creator can borrow from previous works (e.g. exercising fair use/dealing), the lower the cost of creating new works.[55] Conversely, the harder it is to access works (e.g. access & licensing costs), the more expensive it becomes to create new works, potentially resulting in a lower number of new works created[56]. It follows that the longer works are kept from the public domain, the higher the cost of creating new works. This inevitably results in less innovation and by extension less competition in relevant markets. The effect of a tight control on intellectual property on innovation can be seen from many past examples. The US company AT&T's control over the telephone network, and Microsoft's restriction on access to its source code[57] are historical examples where control and lack of access to information stifled innovation and competition. In contrast, many innovative developments (e.g. Linux) have been made through the 'Open Source' software movement.[58]

Responding to the claim that CMS may result in inaccessibility to the public domain, it has been argued that technological protection measures are only applied to copies of works in the public domain and not to the underlying work itself.[59] Hence although there may be restrictions on what can be done with a work by technical means (e.g. making digital copies), this does not prevent use of the work by other means (e.g. quoting, manual copying).[60] Prohibition of circumvention therefore focuses on access to a work, via technological means. While plausible, this argument does not address the fact that it may be difficult or impossible to access 'underlying works' in the first place. Consumers may find it difficult to gain access due to geographical location or simply the inability to locate these works.

---

[54] Lessig, L. (2001). *The Future of Ideas: The Fate of the Commons in a Connected World* . NY, Random House.

[55] This economic analysis is an adaptation of the Landes and Posner's argument regarding the counterproductivity of copyright protection when the level of protection raises the cost of creating new works. See, p. 332, Landes, W. & Posner, R (1989). *An Economic Analysis of Copyright Law.* Journal of Legal Studies, Vol XVIII (June 1989).

[56] Ibid

[57] See Lessig, L (2001) supra note 54

[58] DiBona, C, Ockman S, & Stone, M (1999) (Eds). *Open Sources: Voices from the Open Source Revolution.* O'Reilly & Associates.

[59] See (NII Group) supra note 25

[60] Ibid

The DMCA in particular has stirred much debate[61] and many have voiced concerns regarding its effect on innovation[62]. The ACM's US Public Policy Committee have raised concerns that prohibition on circumvention will "produce a chilling effect on US scientific and research enterprise".[63] Also that researchers may not feel free to publish their research which may affect the academic community as a whole.[64] These issues are underscored by several previous US legal cases. In the *Elcomsoft Case*[65], Dmitry Sklyarov was prosecuted under the DMCA[66] for developing the Advanced eBook Processor software which enabled legitimate owners of Adobe's eBook format to change to the more common Portable Document Format (PDF). In the *DeCSS Case*[67], defendants were found liable under the DMCA[68] after publishing details of a program (DeCSS)[69], developed to decrypt the Content Scrambling System (CSS) for DVD's. In the *Felton Case*[70], professor Edward Felton, a Princeton University computer scientist was prevented from presenting his research findings on how to defeat technology for protecting music files. He was threatened by the recording industry for possible violations under the DMCA.[71] Felton commented that the DMCA outlaws the scientific method, which involves analysing technical claims by others and presenting evidence from these analyses. In effect, the DMCA

[61] For a critique of the DMCA see Samuelson, P. (1999). *Intellectual Property and the Digital Economy: Why the Anti-Circumvention Regulations Need to Be Revised* 14 Berkeley Technology Law Journal. http://www.law.berkeley.edu/journals/btlj/articles/vol14/Samuelson/html/reader.html

[62] For example see Blaze, M (2001). *Matt Blaze's declaration regarding the Felton DMCA case* http://www.pairlist.net/pipermail/ietf-idrm/2001-August/000106.html

[63] Grove, J (2003). *Legal and Technological Efforts to Lock up Content Threaten Innovation.* Communications of the ACM, 2003, 46(4)

[64] Ibid. Many US scientists have sought legal advice on whether their current research violates the DMCA and some scientists have not published their scholarly work for fear of legal action.

[65] U.S. v. ElcomSoft & Sklyarov. See:http://www.eff.org/IP/DMCA/US_v_Elcomsoft Sklyarov helped create the Advanced eBook Processor (AEBPR) software for his employer Elcomsoft.
AEBPR which allowed legitimate eBook owners to translate from Adobe's secure eBook format into the more common Portable Document Format (PDF)..

[66] ElcomSoft & Sklyarov faced four criminal charges of circumvention offenses, and aiding and abetting circumvention offenses, under the DMCA section 1201 and one charge of conspiracy

[67] *Universal City Studios Inc v Shawn Reimerdes (2000)* 111 F. Supp. 2d 294. Also see: http://www.nysd.uscourts.gov/courtweb/pdf/00-01149.PDF

[68] Section 1201(a)(2)

[69] The DeCSS program allowed DVD's to be played on the Linux operating system rather than on Windows/Mac (for which it was developed)

[70] Felton v. RIAA *see: http://www.eff.org/Cases/Felten_v_RIAA/*

[71] See: RIAA/SDMI Legal Threat Letter (April 9, 2001) to Professor Felton http://www.eff.org/Legal/Cases/Felten_v_RIAA/20010409_riaa_sdmi_letter.html

prevents the flow of information thereby blocking insight into what has been done and prevents authoritative dialogue on research issues.[72]

5.   CONCLUSION

There are compelling economic reasons for controlling access to copyright material, especially in light of digital technology and the Internet. However, use of CMS (aided by legislation and contract law) appears to have tipped the balance of control too strongly in favour of copyright holders. The public domain is being deprived of valuable resources, an unfortunate development which echoes some aspects of eighteenth century Blackstonian ideology.   There is therefore the need for some social accountability in the use of CMS, since they appear to go against the original sprit of copyright law, impinge on privacy and adversely affect innovation. The threat to innovation is of particular concern since innovation rarely takes place in a vacuum, therefore, unencumbered access to previous work is critical to developing future work. Criminal penalties under laws like the DMCA and EU Copyright Directive are too great a price for researchers and market competitors to pay. Very few are willing to become martyrs. Innovation in the future may be a thing of the past.

---

[72]   Huang,   D   (2002).   *Felton,   Academic   Freedom,   DMCA*
http://www.duke.edu/~dsh4/cps182/cps182-paper1take2.doc

PART 5

ECONOMICS AND WORK

MANAGING THE KNOWLEDGE OF THE ORGANIZATION

Martin Stenberg
Principal Lecturer, Haaga Polytechnic, Helsinki, Finland; martin.stenberg@mstcons.com

Abstract: One of the most influential areas of research that has emerged in the field of Information Systems in the last decade is that of Knowledge Management. This was a natural development arising from work in disciplines such as organization studies, cognitive science and informatics, which all inspired the concepts of knowledge capture and knowledge-based systems. The purpose of this paper is to map the existing research, to describe what is meant by 'knowledge' and the processes of 'knowing', as well as organizational memory, and the contexts in which they occur.

1. INTRODUCTION

Knowledge management has become widely recognized as one of the most important contemporary research themes. Knowledge has been investigated from the viewpoint of learning (Nonaka and Konno 1998; Crossan et al 1999; Cook and Brown 1999; Kasl et al. 1997; Stenberg 2000; Kim 1993, Kolb 1984), society (Stehr 1994; Castells 1996) and technology (Masuda 1981; Robey et al. 2000; Orlikowsky 2000; Johannessen et al 2001). Peter Drucker (1993) has written about knowledge applied to tools, products and processes (embodied knowledge), knowledge applied to human work (embedded knowledge) and knowledge applied to itself (embrained and encultured knowledge). Reich (1991) noted that knowledge is supporting new forms of organizations based on networks, partnership and contacts (embrained knowledge). Theoretical views about organizations seem also to indicate that there are competitive advantages for a company offered by cooperative social contexts which are conductive to the creation, exploring, acquisition, transferring, integrating and coordinating knowledge distributed among employees, teams, business units and partners (Ghoshal and Moran 1996). It has also been suggested that sources of competitive advantage have been based on economies of expertise that are derived by leveraging knowledge in the organization both in intra- and inter-organizational relationships (Subramani and Venkatraman 2003; Nonaka and Konno 1998; Yli-Renko 1999; Pirttilä 1997). Sambamurthy and Subramani (2005) also discuss knowledge research as comprising problems of knowledge coordination, transfer and reuse. There is also theoretical interest aroused by the many and confusing details of the earlier concepts (such as tacit vs explicit; process and element; individual and organizational).

Thus the subject is partly seen as organizational and operational research when it covers core processes and competitive advantages, but also as educational research because of the principal characteristic of learning, which is to acquire knowledge. Furthermore, in considering knowledge assets and the processes through which knowledge is acquired, used and created, Information Systems (technology and applications) are also seen as having an essential role in providing tools facilitating the use of knowledge and speeding knowledge processes (Robey et al. 2000; Orlikowsky 2000; Johannessen et al 2001).

There are a number of essential and common elements present in the studies. First, several of them focus on the processes employed to acquire, use, benefit and share knowledge (Huber 1990; Crossan et al. 1999; Nonaka and Konno 1998; Kim 1993), or recommend that we speak about the act of knowing rather than about knowledge itself (Blackler 1995; Robey et al. 2000), or of combining knowledge into a tool in knowing processes (Cook and Brown 1999).

Second, when knowledge is used in different situations by several actors, it appears to switch between tacit and explicit knowledge (Nonaka and Konno 1998) and create a Social Learning cycle (Boisot 1998). In this, it moves between the abstract and the concrete, codified and uncodified and diffused and undiffused and also between different kinds of images (Blackler 1995).

There are also a number of studies discussing challenges and roles of IS (information technology, applications and data communication) a technological and intermediating tool in knowledge processes (Robey et al. 2000; Daft and Lengel 1986; Andreu and Ciborra 1996; Johannessen et al. 2001; Zuboff 1988).

Organizational memory is often mentioned as a development stage of organizational learning. Organizational memory consists of information acquisition, retention facilities and information retrieval. (Walsh and Ungson 1991)

The significance of the researching unit is important. In the present author's earlier study, prospective knowledge issues have mainly been covered quite theoretically and from a viewpoint focusing often on information-intensive companies (Stenberg 2000). The organization in which the author is currently conducting research is a large logistics company with a large amount of daily business events that provide an interesting and operational context for knowledge sharing.

The present paper will first review the background and common images of "knowing", collecting elements of knowing from a review of the literature. A case study (single case, multiple units) will then be presented, based on interviews of top and middle managers as well as employees of a Finnish logistics company. This study will provide the elements for a sharing model of information and knowledge issues and processes in the company.

2. ISSUES AND ELEMENTS OF KNOWING

2.1 Knowledge and Knowing Levels

Information has been noted as a broad and somewhat confusing concept (Sweiby 1997, pp 42-43). It has also been described as a separate sub-element of knowledge associated with specific requirements of success, thoroughness and truthfulness, and has been defined as stored knowledge that is usable by those having access to the storage medium (Feinman 1976) or as any physical form of representation or surrogate of knowledge, and in particular thought used for communication (Farrandane 1979). Information can also lose its value, becoming commonplace and obsolete and even meaningless (Sweiby 1977, 40; Chen & Edgington 2005, 287). Thus, information seems to be a part of knowledge.

Knowledge itself is more like an event (Luhmann 1995). Research is an important source of the information used to create new knowledge (Fahey & Prusak 1998, p 727). It is also suggested that information becomes knowledge when it is exploited in decision-making processes, thus being inseparable from thinking and acting (Fahey & Prusak 1998, 269).

Explicit knowledge that has been committed to a medium becomes information (Hildreth and Kimble 2002).

Tacit knowledge is a tool or an aid to action. It is not explicitly known or learned and it becomes realized in the context of the group's work, where performing a specific task requires interaction between (tacit) knowledge and present activity. (Crossan et al. 1999; Cook and Brown 1999.)

According to Robillard (1999), knowledge refers to a permanent structure of information stored in memory. For Nonaka (1994), knowledge is a specific entity formed in the mind of an individual, and is conceptually distinct from material and technologies.

Organizational skills are made up of a complex mix of interpersonal, technological and socio-structural factors (Blackler 1995, 1025). According to Blackler (1995) there are five images of knowledge: embrained, embodied, embedded, encultured and encoded.

Knowledge is a fundamental element of the process of *knowing*. Even though there are conflicting views regarding the definition of knowledge (Nonaka 1994; Cook and Brown 1999; Cook and Brown 1999; Wilson 2002; Hildreth and Kimble 2002), it is possible to extract some common elements regarding information and knowledge; both tacit and explicit. The literature recognizes three levels of knowing: individual, team and organizational.

Generally, the concept of *knowing* has been used to distinguish knowledge (as a tool) from knowing (as a process). *Knowledge* is something that is possessed (rules, concepts, procedures) being abstract, static, necessary and used in action. *Knowing* is an essential part of action or practice (dynamic, concrete or relational). Knowledge gives shape and discipline to knowing. Knowing requires present activity and so is understood as part of concrete and dynamic human action. (Cook and Brown 1999.)

Barney (1991, pp 101-103) defines among a firm's resources all assets and capabilities controlled by itself enhancing and improving its efficiency and effectiveness, including organizational processes, knowledge and information. A resource can become a sustained competitive advantage if it is valuable in exploiting opportunities, rare, strategic, imperfectly imitable and cannot be equivalently substituted.

Holsapple and Joshi (2001) consider the main organizational resources to be financial, material, human and knowledge. According to them, productive use of knowledge resources depends on the application of knowledge manipulation skills such as through a decision support system or by exercising a kind of human resource. (ibid. 43.) Dependencies are based on organization's presence and existence.

Ichijo et al. (1998) identifies five different "knowledge enablers", which are organizational mechanisms for intentionally and consistently developing knowledge in organizations.

Ichijo et al (1998) mentioning that to have a knowledge-intensive culture, it is necessary to establish a sense for knowledge as a competitive resource within the company. To provide a focus for organizational conversations on work, a common language must be established within the company, a language which is commonly shared and understood by the organizational members. The organizational structure needs to be implemented using an organizational design that facilitates knowledge development. e.g. to create an organization that works close to its customers and that has access to a variety of information that can be interpreted differently. This is believed to nurture creativity. (Ichijo et al. 1998.)

Helfat and Raubitschek (2000) have described a product sequencing model that consists of a system of knowledge (core and integrative knowledge) and a system of learning, including incremental learning (by doing and by using) and step-function learning (learning from ongoing feedback). They mention that core knowledge can form the foundation for multiple products and stages within vertical chains. Integrative knowledge is required for coordination of tacit knowledge and also complex and codified knowledge (consisting of several activities) within and across vertical chains of activities (ibid. 963-964).

Andreu and Ciborra (1996) discuss the role of core capabilities and organizational context in integrating knowledge exploration and exploitation into strategy (a strategic loop of core capabilities), capabilities (capabilities learning loop) and work practices (routine learning loop).

Hamel and Prahalad (1990) stress the importance of core corporate competencies as key issues in successful knowledge management.

Active forms of facilitation can be seen as acquiring knowledge embedded in long-term physical resources – this implies experimenting, testing, exercising and simulating as goals towards for example mastering a production process. In processing tacit knowledge embodied in an experienced individual, a key element is shared experience. Acquiring tacit knowledge requires observation, imitation and practice (the step of *socialization*). Converting human-embodied knowledge to explicit knowledge implies narrating and using metaphors (the step of *externalization*). Then, processing an individual's embrained knowledge requires combining different bodies of knowledge held by individuals. The reconfiguring of existing embrained knowledge can be accomplished by sorting and adding, re-categorising, re-contextualizing and guided participation (the step of *combination*). Other ways of facilitating knowledge management could be job rotation, modelling, coaching, guidance, proximal guidance by an expert, and distal guidance. Finally, the acquisition of a community's embedded or encultured knowledge implies team-working, coaching and mentoring (Järvinen 2000; Nonaka 1994).

Knowing is a phenomenon that is manifest in systems of language, technology, collaboration and control (*mediated*). It is also located in time and space and is specific to particular contexts (*situated*). Knowing is constructed and constantly developing (*provisional*). It is also purposive and object-oriented (*pragmatic*). Finally, because of the interrelation of the concepts of knowledge and power, knowledge is also *contested*. Changes in the systems of knowing and doing are important. That is why attention should focus on the systems we are using to acquire information and knowledge. (Blackler 1995, 1039-1040.)

Knowledge creation and sharing are widely described as being based on individual learning (Kolb 1984) and also on team learning (Nonaka 1994; Kasl et al 1997). Kasl et al. (1997) speak about team learning as a five-step process involving *framing* (vision, goal and competence of the team), *reframing* (process to create shared understanding), *experimenting* (testing new frame and evaluation of the its function), *crossing boundaries* (information gathering and sharing with other members and groups) and *integrating perspectives* (combining view and ideas through discussion and conflicts). Crossan et al. (1999) have described the framework of organizational learning as starting from an individual, going on in the group, and ending up finally at the organizational level and creating a commercialized set of functions or issues.

A Community can be an organization, team, group or partnership (some employees in a specific place or in a project or a time) or employees in meetings, or some friends, or any random person of a confrontation (including as well social and informal meetings when and wherever people are confronting each other in the company). The definition was ranked according to the internal closeness and co-operation degree of the unit. The unit itself can be also virtually organized locating anywhere anytime. (Brown and Duguid 1991; Boland and Tenkasi 1995.)

According to Senge (1990) the central issues in a learning organization are team-working, systemic thinking, models which lead thinking and functioning, and culture-supporting learning. The vision and goals, leadership, information management and output are also parts of the learning organization.

Essentially, all knowledge is directly or indirectly based on human resources and intellectual capital. The company must take care to develop and exploit this in order to become more effective and competitive. Knowing processes involve individuals, groups and teams, as well as the organization itself.

Finally, information can be described as being a part of explicit knowledge as a tool (knowing what) used by tacit knowledge (knowing how) in every day practices (knowing processes) in different circumstances (context), and all of these being inseparable from each other in knowledge creating, exploiting and sharing processes.

2.2 Knowledge Sharing Processes

Kolb (1984) describes individual learning in the four processes of *concrete experience* (as the starting point), *active experimentation, abstract conceptualization* and *reflective observation*. Some authors have been critical because of the model doesn't describe deeply enough reflective processes (Järvinen 2000). The model also seems to suppose that learning processes always begin from concrete experience even though it is possible to start learning by using explicit or implicit information as a spark or starting point. The context could also play a more essential role in the learning process of an individual.

Nonaka and Konno 1998 describe team and group learning in the four processes of *socialization* (as the starting point), *externalization, combination* and *internalization* during changes between tacit and explicit knowledge. In the model, the starting point is rather critical. It is also questionable to distinguish knowledge so sharply to explicit and tacit (implicit) parts, because it is necessary to use tacit knowledge to create explicit knowledge (Cook and Brown 1999; Wilson 2002; Hildreth and Kimble 2002).

The team learning model of Kasl et al. (1997) also sounds practical, using five steps: *framing* (starting point), *reframing, experimenting, crossing boundaries* and *integrating perspectives*.

The process of changing between tacit and explicit knowledge seems to be problematic, or even unnecessary to specify in practice (Cook and Brown 1999). Majchrzak et al. (2004) also refer to the importance of knowledge reuse for innovation.

Crossan et al. (1999) have created a framework of organizational learning, describing four processes including *intuiting* (as the starting point), *interpreting, integrating* and *institutionalising and linking* the three levels of individual, group and organization. The interest of the model of Crossan et al. lies in the renewal of the overall enterprise. The underlying and important issue and a principal means they cite is organizational learning. Renewal demands that organization has to investigate and learn new knowledge, exploiting things learned earlier in a similar way. They seem also to suppose that the process passes from intuiting to institutionalising.

All the three models have similarities in the number of processes involved. Even though the models have different levels for action (individual, group and organization) they have common interfaces between the actors. They seem to have an idea of systematic and at least partly continuing and mutual or commutual knowing processes.

Järvinen (2000) has integrated the three models, developing a synthesis of them. Based on these three models she has created a consolidated model with social, reflective, cognitive and working processes integrating individual, group and organizational levels. All these processes also have sub-processes drawn from the models of Kolb (1984), Nonaka and Konno 1998 and Crossan et al. (1999) and combined together.

Kim (1993) has defined and recognized several disconnects in learning processes. These learning disconnects could clarify more the interactions between relations of moving from one stage to another (e.g. institutionalizing of intuition).

While Crossan et al. (1999) describe feed-forward and feedback processes, Kim focuses on single-loop and double-loop learning. A central issue in Kim's model seems to be the responses of the individual to environmental actions creating new learning.

Both models are based on experimental (individual) learning and adaptation and also assimilating of mental maps (individual and shared).

2.3   Mental Maps of Knowing

It should be noted that, while exploiting knowledge, there are cognitive maps in the background and these either impede or support the knowledge sharing processes in the organization (Kim 1993; Choo 1998). Employees have different mindsets, because of different motivation and commitment. An organizational mental map is created from its members' shared understanding about the organization's goals and ways to work (Robey et al. 2000). It therefore seems to be based on a common negotiated and accepted belief structure that has to be created in cooperation with employees and managers.

According to Kim (1993) a knowledge cycle occurs between individual actions and organizational routines as they influence the mental model of an individual – the organizational shared map also has an environmental response.

Robey et al. (2000) also describe organizational learning as cognitive entities capable of observing actions in order to improve performance. According to the authors, organizational improvement has much to do with organizational memory – defining it as a shared understanding of the members of an organization, the cognitive maps – connecting organizational actions to outcomes.

Brown and Duguid (1991) speak about canonical (*formal*) and non-canonical (*informal*) work practices based on a misunderstanding about what working, learning and innovation at work really are in practice. Narratives and story-telling have been used as a way to develop a causal map to bridge the gap between canonical and non-canonical – for example between what the company supplies and what a particular community actually needs. Shared narratives also point out collaborative aspects of work. It is also evident that, as a social construct, employees are strengthening their professional identities and becoming members of the image of professionalism. (ibid. 46-47.) Enacting and innovating can be conceived of as a fundamental sense-making and identity-building process (ibid. 53). To foster the whole development process, an organization must recognize itself as a community of communities. Conceptual reorganization to accommodate learning-while-working and innovation must stretch from the individual level to communities of practice and the technology to the level of the overarching organizational architecture, the community-of-communities (ibid. 55).

Crossan et al. (1999) also consider that what they call a mental map is the same as Kim's individual (and also organizational) mental models.

At the most basic level the relevant knowledge that permits effective communication both within and across subunits consists of shared language and symbols (Barney 1999).

2.4   The Environment

Learning and knowing processes seem to happen in special places. Nonaka and Konno (2000) use the term "Ba" to designate a suitable place to create and share knowledge in SECI–processes. These places can be face-to-face or even virtual, where individuals share experiences, feelings, emotions and mental models.

Some offices use an architecture based on the concept of 'Ba' – for example by placing the work stations of the employees around the recreation area. When employees have the time for recreation, they collect together. Information sharing processes start naturally. The bosses are placed among the employees, so that they can easily contact and communicate with each other when walking around. Thus the architecture of the workplace supports many opportunities for information sharing.

Virkkunen and Kuutti (2000) consider organizational learning as involving changes in management's assumptions. The main idea is that a practical and productive interaction can be developed through psychological processes. Individuals' actions are always an active system with a collective praxis. The activity system is internally heterogeneous and multi-voiced, including competing and conflicting things. The authors thus summarize organizational learning as a contextual, situational and historical process. To the present author, this all suggests an extended environment where places and their history constantly increase in significance for the future.

2.5 Tools Supporting the Acquisition, Creation, Use and Sharing of Knowledge

It is important to look at the tools used for acquiring, using and maintaining information and knowledge (Huber 1990; Daft and Engel 1986). According to Johannessen et al. (2001), the mismanagement of IT and of tacit knowledge can lead to a company completely failing to benefit from the competitive advantages of IT. They argue that emphasizing IT by unilateral investments can lead to an underestimation of the tacit knowledge of the company. They point out that the relationship between tacit knowledge and IT is crucial. They discuss the management of the total knowledge base of the company (i.e., explicit and tacit knowledge) internally and externally. The role of IT is, according to them, improving and speeding accessibility to external (explicit) knowledge (ibid. 13).

According to Lee (1994, p 13) communication through electronic mail hides some essential information cues (body language, tones of voice) and does not support immediate feedback. This can be said about most information systems, because of the routine way in which they save information.

Robey et al. (2000) discuss the meaning and measurement of organizational learning, and focus on studying how to apply concepts to use and implement IT in organizations, as well as IT applications that support organizational learning. These themes are independent of each other although they have close conceptual and practical links. According to the authors, organizational learning stresses managerial vision, leadership, communication and teamwork. They also differentiate between organizational learning used as a mean to resolve and explain the problems of benefiting from new IT tools in organizations, and research that develops applications of IT to support the process of organizational learning and knowledge management. The capacity for organizational learning facilitates the adoption of IT that in turn increases the learning capacity of the organization.

Barney (1991, 114) mentions that information technology itself can be purchased easily whereas information processing systems are deeply embedded informal and formal processes of an organization – such systems store potential and are difficult to imitate.

2.6   Organizational Memory

Cross and Baird (2000) studied learning in 22 projects covering different fields. Carrying out interviews across several hierarchical levels, they asked what had been learned and where knowledge was located within the organizations. They found out that an organization's memory (OM) resides in the minds of its employees (who were thus an important part of OM and thus a risk to lose), in the relationships between employees carrying out their work (the social network: who you know affects what you know), in databases and file cabinets (complementing personal networks supported by colleagues), embedded in work processes (methods embedded in recurring processes) and in product and service offering (developing experimental knowledge on the job; may also influence blind spots when changing).

Considering the steps involved in transforming experience into working knowledge the authors mention the need to determine which experiences are worth learning from (strategically important). Important learning events are often critical and most difficult to learn. The next step is to maximize learning potential – this includes providing a structure that encourages individuals and groups to reflect upon and share what they have learned. The final step is to embed into the organization the knowledge gained from enhanced experiences and building organizational memory. Thus, when individual learning occurs, the knowledge should be aggregated, validated and synthesized for organizational learning.

The authors point out that an important part of the organizational learning process is to learn about the backgrounds of individuals in groups and teams and also to develop knowledge about each other by focusing on task-based activities building harmony and providing opportunities for group members to demonstrate their skills and abilities. Communities of practices – informal groups of individuals integrating regularly around work-related issues and challenges – facilitate collaboration and learning from each other. In any case, what is most important is social bonding among the group's members. The authors mention that one of the greatest points of leverage in promoting organizational learning exists at the executive level. Again, it is important for the organization to ensure that learning is not forgotten when it occurs, but rather to fit and store it in the organizational memory.

Walsh and Ungson (1991) state that information is reducing equivocality. They distinguish decision-making information from stored information, called memory. Generally organizational memory is independent of particular individuals although individuals themselves acquire information as actors in the active construction of the memory. They exploit information based on decision-making process cumulating in an organizational memory of encoded and interpreted events with consequences. (ibid. 61-62).

The authors split organizational memory into *information acquisition* (decision making, problem-solving and their consequences), *retention facilities* (varying in their capacity to retain information) and *information retrieval* (varying from automated to controlled) and also refer to external archives.

According to Walsh and Ungson (1991) the retention facility of an organizational memory consists of five internal bins distributed across the organization. The first internal bin of organizational memory is *individuals* with articulated belief structure and cause maps, assumptions and their values.

A second bin is *culture*, which includes language, learned and transmitted feelings and even thinking, shared frameworks and stories, sagas and symbols.

Again, *structure* constructs the concept of a role as a link between individuals and organizational memories and also establishes links with environment. This includes implications for individual role behaviour and the reflection of the institutionalized myths of society as justified by members of an organization. Finally, *ecology* refers to the actual physical structure of the organization or of the workplace: the ecology encodes and retains information about the organization and its membership. (ibid. 63-66.)

An organizational memory plays important roles within organizations: it can be informational, it can fulfil a controlling function, and also play a political role (ibid. 73).

Regarding the misuses of organizational memory, the authors note that the automatic retrieval of information may support a routine response, even in cases where a non-routine response might have been better. (ibid. 75-77). The authors mention that individuals are a key in developing organizational memory because of they are a source of retained information and also determine the acquired and retrieved information in the organization.

It appears, thus, that there remains an open and very interesting question about the length, position and service role of the individual in the organization. The authors also note that there can be cases where there is a synthesis of organizational memory and organizational design in clans (a specific governance structure of members arising under conditions of bureaucratic failure) and in a network (a purposeful and conscious relationship between and among distinct organizations) facilitating the sharing of information (ibid. 80).

Organizational memory is widely known as an instrumental issue, but the extent to which non-routine information is deliberately stored to be used as a basis for future decision making is not well understood.

2.7   Culture and Values

Organizational culture can consist of belief-structures, values, ideals, norms and principles and also common ways of functioning. Organizational culture is created over long periods of time. It is typically hidden knowledge that is mostly tacit. It "learns" from the behaviour and genres of other employees. Culture can also change over time (Inglehart 1990.)

Taking care of relationships implies managing relationships between organizational members and fostering a culture that emphasizes patience and tolerance. Knowledge managers stimulate other managers to actively collect information, and to share information that penetrates different contexts for knowledge creation (e.g. new markets). (Ichijo et al. 1998.)

Functional and open organizational culture seems to support information and knowledge sharing by encouraging members to be active and to trust each others. This is an important issue of organizational knowledge structure.

2.8   Framework of the Knowing Organization

Thus, organizational learning occurs in the form of knowing processes (individual and collective, communities of practices). Furthermore, it needs to be managed and supported by tools and environmental factors. Finally, the learning process is going to create and develop an organizational memory that consists of common learning elements and tools, information acquisition, storing and distribution, individual and organizational relationships, products and services, mental maps, functional models and stories, which are enabled and supported by organizational culture and values.

3. CASE STUDY

3.1 Background

Logistic Company is one of the most biggest logistics companies in Finland, with a turnover in 2003 of 1597 Me and about 1700 employees. The company deals with the logistics of the delivery of products to customers throughout Finland, who buy them through its chain stores. The business idea is to use the logistics chain to deliver products from all over the world to its customers, with economies of scale producing the best price. Knowledgeable logistics employees are important assets in a successful business.

The work and duties in the logistics centre vary from gathering products by truck to work on computers. The logistics centre consists of two very big halls (with a size of about 13 football fields) and a dispatch department. In the logistics centre, fresh and dry products lines are received, gathered and combined for shops all over Finland. The stock in the logistics centre is huge and there is a busy stream of products. Work proceeds to implementation in three shifts in a complex and busy rhythm, demanding accuracy and cooperation. Certain perishable products are also dealt with in an unbroken cold chain to maintain quality. More than 600 trailer trucks visit the logistics centre every day (including weekends), unloading and loading cargo.

The most important function of the company is the core process of ordering and delivery. This starts with receiving and checking the products, moving them to the trucks (loading and unloading the shelves and moving products between different levels of shelves), providing the orders for gathering, gathering the products ordered, and finally transferring them to the dispatch department. The employees doing the gathering can plan and choose their own optimal gathering path. They also have to check and report about missing or understocked products by computer and order more for the shelves.

Similar processes apply in both product lines (fresh and dry goods). Clients can purchase products from both lines, and so both lines must work equally effectively for total success.

Although the employees work in groups, gathering and shelf work is mainly done individually. However, during gathering there are many occasions for a single employee to make the operation more effective by bearing in mind the needs of other gathering employees. She or he can provide information for other employees coming along later, which could help to speed up their work and the whole process. Reception and checking work also involve group work, where the benefits of information sharing can often be seen immediately.

3.2   Some Findings

Knowledgeable logistics employees are important in successful business possessing intellectual capital. Knowledge is situated in routines and processes (core and sub processes) and also in function models (concepts) that have been developed over long periods of time into working methods (Best Practices) and brought into information systems by staff. Of course products and services maintenance are important, but most products come from suppliers and so added value comes from managing logistic processes effectively. The employees tend to think that values and culture are not significant because they believe that values are only created for marketing purposes by managers.

Meanwhile "knowledge paths" have appeared among employees in the work processes and routines on the corridor, middle management (group/team knowledge) taking a stroll and walking among the employees. Top management staff have their own meetings and negotiating situations in which they consider the future facing the company as a whole and try to lead and fight for it as an entity. This creates the additional characteristic of knowledge in that it functions as a way of recognizing and empowering environmental issues for employees (empowered knowledge).

The present author considers that each level uses a different kind of knowledge that is not easy to integrate or exploit. The risk exists that the parties that are involved in knowledge sharing could be misunderstanding each other and losing information as it goes through organizational levels.

There are many places to share information and knowledge in the company. Meetings and negotiations are the most formal ways to gather, create, use and share knowledge. More informal places include discussions in the corridor and at refreshment points, coffee machines and restaurants. First impressions and feelings were often changed in working rooms. On the other hand, hobbies and friends circles were not so deeply or significant used. What is most important is connected with the practical information flows of the company. Gathering information by walking and meeting in the corridors and during working processes (e.g. the place where order lists are collected) also play a practical role.

Motivation and commitment are essential before anybody will want to share information and knowledge that she or he has. Some reasons for sharing are giving benefit to others, appreciating and exploiting information from others, resourcing and participating with others, natural idleness (with less activity leading to more sharing), learning through good experiences and to have more insight. Participating in common sharing processes can become activities which can motivate employees to share information among colleagues. This gives employees opportunities to bring up their own ideas and to participate in others' ideas. This starts the game of playing 'idea ball' with colleagues. Those who are passive won't be motivated to play, unless they participate officially. Some are more inclined to innovate than others, but they need to be encouraged to test themselves.

Equally, some employees are more inclined to follow routines, and to operate in unchanging and fixed styles, seeking internal satisfaction in other ways. It is also possible to derive personal benefit, and even financial profit, and at least to save time and trouble implementing one's own ideas and perceptions. Some employees may become inspired by their own ideas, but then guard them jealously. Others have no interest in developing ideas, reasoning that if an idea is not theirs, it is not worth implementing, and these employees can impede innovations. Finally, it is not enough to be successful oneself, if others are going to be unsuccessful. In such a situation, it is essential to be proactive.

Overall, the following methods have been used to share information and knowledge:

- intuiting, innovating, interpreting, integrating
- discussions
- recommendation
- persuading
- sharing ideas actively
- earlier experience
- participating
- introduction
- job rotation
- development discussions
- training
- support of colleagues.

3.3   Conclusions

Most of the knowledge issues found in the literature can be seen functioning in the practices of the case study company. In addition, the present author would note the concept of physical "knowledge paths", and the issue of recognizing and integrating knowledge images at different hierarchical levels of the organization.

Each level of the organization uses different kinds of knowledge that are not easy to integrate or exploit. The real challenge is to integrate different kinds of knowledge modes and to understand, develop and exploit the integrated knowledge base.

Another problem that appeared was the poor resources of middle managers, some of whom were responsible for 30-40 employees. This leads to the situation where there is little time available to the manager and consequently few contacts between employees and managers. This is one of the important and critical issues. Some of the middle managers have solved the problem having 'daily walks' among employees. It is clear that initiative needs to be fostered among employees and a more flexible and systematic feedback system needs to be developed. At present, some of suggestions of the employees are not even replied to any way, decreasing motivation and activities.

Furthermore, an important question is who is leading and coordinating the whole process of developing the knowing environment. Human resources management (HRM) has been in the background, while operational managers implement what they can but only according their local goals. Thus HRM should play a more active role in knowledge management, creating HR processes and using HR tools (recruiting, familiarizing and mentoring, developing, teaching and compensating) with the cooperation of managers.

Information and knowledge sharing could be a part of everyone's duties. This would need to be supported by the values and culture of the company. It could be a challenge to increase resources for this purpose, and to recognize that it is important to place increased value on experience accumulated in the accumulating tacit knowledge of experienced and often ageing people.

The analysis of this case study is continuing, and future work will focus on the structure of communities of practice and the sharing of knowledge among them.

REFERENCES

Andreu, Rafael and Ciborra, Claudio (1996) Organizational learning and core capabilities development: the role of IT. Journal of Strategic Information Systems Vol. 5, 111-127.

Barnley Jay B. (1991) Firm Resources and Sustained Competitive Advantage. Journal of Management Vol. 17 No. 1, 99-120.

Bonabeau,Eric and Theraulaz, Guy and Dorigo, Marco (1999) Swarm Intelligence – From Natural to Artifial Systems. Oxford University Press 1999. ISBN 0-19-513159-2.

Blackler, Frank (1995) Knowledge, knowledge work and organizations: An overview and interpretation. Organization studies 16.6. 1995, 1021-1046.

Boland R.J. and R.V. Tenkasi (1995), Perspective making and perspective taking in communities of knowing, Organization Science 6, No 4, 350-372.

Brown J.S. and P. Duguid (1991), Organizational learning and communities-of-practice: Toward a unified view of working, learning, and innovation, Organization Science 2, No 1, 40-57.

Castells, Manuel (1996) The Rise of the Networking Society. T.J. International Limited, Padstow, Cornwall. ISBN 1-55786-616-3.

Choo, Chun Wei (1998) Knowing organization. Oxford university press, 1998.

Cook. D. N and Brown John S. (1999) Bridging epistemologies: The GenerativeDance Between Organizational Knowledge and Organizational Knowing. Organization Science Vol. 10 No. 4 July - August 1999, pp. 381-400.

Cross Rob and Baird Lloyd (2000) Technology is not enough: Improving performance by building organizational memory. Sloan Management Review, Vol 41. Cambridge Spring 2000.

Crossan, Mary and Lane, Henry and White Roderick (1999) An organizational learning Framework: from intuition to institution. Academy of Management Review 1999, Vol. 24 No 3 522-537.

Daft R.L. and R.H. Lengel (1986), Organizational information requirements, media richness and structural design, Management Science 32, No. 5, 554-571.

Drucker, Peter E (1999) Knowledge-worker productivity: The biggest challenge. California Management Review, Vol. 41 No. 2, 1999, pp. 79-94.

Hamel and Prahalad (1990) The Core Competence of Corporation. Harward Business Review 68/1990.

Hildreth, Paul and Kimble, Chris (2002) The Duality of Knowledge. Information Research, Vol. 8 No. 1, October 2002.

Holsapple, C.W and Joshi, K.D (2001) Organizational Knowledge Resources. Decision Support Systems 2001, Vol. 31 No. 1, 39-54.

Huber, George P. (1990) Organizational learning: The contributing processes and the literature. Organizational science February 1991 Vol. 2 No. 1, pp. 88-115.

Helfat, Constance E. and Raubitschek, Ruth S. (2000) Product sequencing: Co-evolution of knowledge, capabilities and products. Strategic Management Journal (2000), 21: 961-979.

Ichijo K., G. von Krogh and I. Nonaka (1998), Knowledge enablers, In von Krogh, Roos and Kleine (Eds), Knowing in firms – Understanding, managing and measuring knowledge, Sage, London, 173-203.

Inglehart, Ronald (1990) Culture shift in advanced industrial society. ISBN 0-691-02296-8.

Johannessen, Jon-Arild and Olaisen, Johan and Olsen Bjørn (2001) Mismanagement of tacit knowledge: the importance of tacit knowledge, the danger of information technology, and what to do about it. International Journal of Information Management (2001) No. 1, 21: 3-20.

Järvinen, Annikki (2000) Facilitating knowledge processing in a workplace setting. Presented in the 1st international conference on Researching Work and Learning, 10.-12. September 1999, Leeds.

Kasl E., V.J. Marsick and K. Dechant (1997), Teams as learners - A research- based model of team learning, Journal of Applied Behavioral Science 33, No 2, 227-246.

Kim, Daniel. H (1993) The link between Individual and Organizational Learning. Sloan Management Review 1993, 37-50.

Kolb, David (1984) Experiential Learning. Experience as The Source of Learning and Development. Englewood Cliffs, N.J., Prentice-Hall 1984.

Lee, A.S (1994) Electronic mail as a medium for rich communication: an empirical investigation using hermeneutic interpretation. MIS Quarterly, 1994, 143-147.

Majchrzak, Ann and Cooper Lynne and Neece, Olivia, E. (2004) Knowledge Reuse for Innovation. Management Science Vol 50, No.2 February 2004, 174-188.

Masuda, Yoneji (1980) The Information Society as Post-Industrial Society. Betesda, USA 1980.

Nonaka, I (1994) A dynamic theory of organizational knowledge creation. Organization Sciences 5, No 1, 14-37.

Nonaka, I and Konno, N (1998) The Concept of 'BA'. Building a foundation for knowledge creation. California Management Review , Vol. 40 No. 3, 40-53.

Orlikowski, W (2000) Using technology and constituting structures: A practice lens for studying technology in organizations. Organization Science 11, No 4, 404 – 428.

Otala, Leenamaija (1997) Oppimisen etu-kilpailukykyä muutoksessa. Wsoy , Porvoo.

Robillard P.N (1999) The Role of Knowledge in software development. Comm. ACM 42 No. 1, 87-92.

Robey Daniel and Boudreau Marie-Claude and Rose Gregory M (2000) Information technology and organizational learning: a review and assessment of research. Accounting, Management and information Technology no. 10/2000 pp. 125-155.

Reich, Robert (1991) The Work of Nations.

Stehr, Nico (1994) Knowledge Societies. Sage publications Ltd 1994, London.

Stenberg, Martti (2000) From information into knowing – evaluating knowing of ageing employee. Helsingin yliopiston lahden tutkimus- ja koulutuskeskuksen raportteja ja selvityksiä 34/2000. Gummerus, Saarijärvi 2000. ISBN 951-45-8769-3.

Swanson, E.B (1994) Information Systems innovation among organizations. Management Science 40, No. 9 1069-1092.

Teece, David J (1998) Capturing Value from Knowledge Assets: The new Economy, Markets for Know-How, and Intangible Assets. California Management Review, Vol. 40 No.3, 1998.

Virkkunen J. and K. Kuutti (2000), Understanding organizational learning by focusing on "activity systems", Accounting, Management and Information Technology 10, No 4, 291-319.

Walsh, James. J and Ungson, Gerado R. (1991) Organizational memory. Academy of management Review 1991, Vol. 16 No. 1, 57-91.

Wilson, T.D (2002) The Nonsense of knowledge management'. Information Research, Vol. 8 No. 1, October 2002.

Zuboff, S (1988) In the age of the smart machine: The future of the work and power. New York: Basic books.

FUTURE SKILLS IN THE ICT INDUSTRY: QUALITATIVE AND QUANTITATIVE EXAMINATION

Sami Leppimäki and Tarja Meristö
Institute for Advanced Management Systems Research (IAMSR), Åbo Akademi University, Finland

Abstract: The operational environment of the Information and Communication Technology (ICT) industry is in continuous change due to factors like rapid technological development, uncertain economic development and unpredictable consumer behaviour. Consequently, also the skills needed in the ICT industry are changing. Therefore, the quantitative and qualitative demand of ICT professionals in the future is difficult to forecast. However, anticipation and forecasting of the future ICT skills is very important. Issues related to the ICT skills are crucial for the positive development of the ICT industry as it is an extremely information and knowledge intensive industry. In this paper some of the change factors affecting the ICT industry are presented. In addition, quality and quantity of ICT professionals needed in the future is examined based on ICT company surveys and expert interviews. The future of the Finnish ICT industry is also outlined by using scenarios.

1.   INTRODUCTION

The aim of this paper is to examine what kind of skills the ICT companies need in the future. The examination is based on the ICT company surveys and interviews. The scenario approach is used to examine the alternative future developments of the ICT industry during the next 5-10 years.

This paper is based on recent research, in which the authors of this paper participated. Research projects like the Muunto project (2001, funded by

Ministry of Education), the TIDE project (2000-2002, funded by European Social Fund and coordinated by Technology Industries Finland), EU ICT Foresight project (2001, funded by Technology Industries Finland), ICT Careers project (2003-2004, coordinated by Technology Industries Finland) form the basis for this examination.

In this paper, we will first present general background information of the ICT industry and main change factors affecting it in the future. Then we examine the results of the ICT company surveys and interviews conducted during the years 2001-2004. Finally we present the scenarios used to map the future of the ICT industry.

2. THE DEVELOPMENT OF THE FINNISH ICT INDUSTRY

The Finnish ICT industry has developed very positively over the past decade. The ICT industry is defined here according the OECD's definition in which the ICT industry consist of ICT manufacturing, – services, digital media and telecommunications (OECD 2000; OECD 2002). The number of personnel in the Finnish ICT industry has grown from 100 170 in year 1990 to 154 000 in year 2002. The economic recession in the early 1990s did not affect the ICT industry as severely as it did the economy as a whole (Paija, 2001).

Table 1. Turnover and personnel of the Finnish ICT industry in year 2002. (Statistics Finland 2004)

	Turnover (billion €)	Personnel
ICT manufacturing	26.2	44 300
ICT services (excluding telecommunication)	9.4	47 800
Telecommunications	6.3	19 800
Content production*	6.15	41 800
Total ICT sector	48.1	154 000
The adaptors which use ICT include companies in the service and production sectors, public sector organizations, consumers, various electronic and mobile businesses etc.		

* figures include also so-called traditional content production

The Finnish ICT industry is characterized by the very important role of manufacturing. Its share of turnover exceeds its share of employment. The value added of the whole ICT industry has grown significantly, again especially in manufacturing. (Nordic Council of Ministers 2002.)

Figure 1. Value added in Finnish ICT industry in years 1990-2000

Value added (millions €)

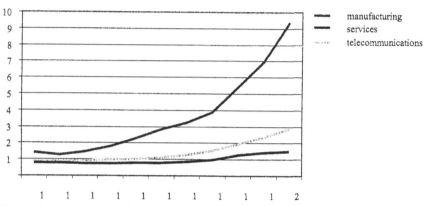

Source: data acquired from Statistics Finland in 3/2002.

3.   FUTURE CHANGE FACTORS AND TRENDS IN FINNISH ICT INDUSTRY

Based on executive and expert interviews of the ICT companies (Manninen and Meristö 2004; Meristö, Leppimäki and Tammi 2002) the main future change factors and trends in the ICT industry are:

- Convergence of technologies, which among the interviewed was considered to be the most important technological change factor.
- Convergence of the sub-branches of the ICT industry. The convergence is taking place partly as a result of the technological convergence and partly as a normal evolution of the industry.
- Outsourcing of non-core business functions: By outsourcing their less important functions the ICT companies seek cost savings, effectiveness and flexibility. Outsourcing also allows companies to concentrate on their core business. Outsourcing is basically a strategic choice made by the companies.

- Importance of software is increasing.
- E-commerce and mobility are seen as new possibilities.
- Public investments as a driver for growth of demand: The public administrations in many countries are planning to provide more and more of their services via the Internet and through other communication systems. Therefore, they are building infrastructure and systems for this purpose.
- Specialization into narrower markets and product segments, which is true especially in the small and medium sized companies.
- The increasing importance of ICT in non-ICT products – ICT everywhere.
- Service and customer orientation, which could generate a need for new skill profiles in the ICT industry.
- Strong R&D investments and quest for new innovations.
- Increase in networking and cooperation.
- Focus on cost efficiency and overall efficiency
- Other factors like the relationship between the ICT sector and other sectors of the economy, the increased weight of the consumer markets (B-to-C) etc.

4.   SKILLS – QUALITATIVE AND QUANTITATIVE EXAMINATION

In the TIDE-project (2000-2002) the qualitative and quantitative demand of ICT professionals in Finland was explored with an ICT company surveys. The survey questionnaire was sent to 450 ICT companies of which 114 companies replied. The aim of the survey was to examine what kind of skills the companies need in the future. No specific job titles, like 'system specialist' or 'programmer', were used. Instead, the survey focused on the more general characteristics of the employees. The steering group of the TIDE-project selected this approach, because the job titles were often considered to be misleading. It was argued, that in the labor markets the same job titles are used to describe many jobs, which in fact have very different duties and requirements.

Based on the survey's results, the new skills required by the ICT companies, additionally to the certain educational degree, are often qualities of personal nature. Factors like attitudes, world-view, personal communication skills, co-operation skills and project management skills are more important than before when companies are recruiting new staff. Also willingness and ability to learn new things and commitment to goals are important.   Skills, which were considered to be less important or less desirable, are for example production-line type of skills, multiple degrees and competitiveness. (Meristö, Leppimäki and Tammi 2002.) No significant differences in the desired skills were found between different sub-branches or different sized companies.

Besides new skills, the ICT professionals of the future also have to possess new skill combinations. For example ICT skills combined with business knowledge is one of the desired combinations. Especially in the Finnish digital media companies the lack of business knowledge was considered to be a major problem. Based on the comments of the survey respondents and interviews, it could be argued that the educational structure of the workforce in the ICT industry is changing and the level of education rising. The new needs of the ICT companies are reflecting the changes taking place inside the ICT industry, but also in the relationship between the ICT and other sectors of the economy and society. The ICT and its integration into strategic thinking and business models has become a necessity in sectors like banking, manufacturing and retail. The other sectors would also like their ICT professionals to have some basic knowledge and skills related to their specific industry and business. In other words, ICT has entered into the core of these businesses (Meristö, Leppimäki and Tammi 2002). Also the core of the ICT industry itself is changing since one of the main development trends listed earlier in this paper is the increased use of outsourcing.

Besides information concerning the skills needed in the ICT industry, the survey also produced estimates concerning the number of employees in the ICT industry in the future. The ICT service companies estimated the highest growth in the number of employees. ICT manufacturing companies estimated more modest growth and telecommunication companies estimated that their number of employees will stay approximately unchanged (see Figure 2 on the next page).

**Figure 2. The employment of the Finnish ICT industry, forecast from
year 2000 to 2010.** (Forecast based on growth estimates indicated by
respondents in the ICT company survey. These estimates were then
extrapolated to cover the ICT industry as a whole. Starting values were from
Statistics Finland 2001)

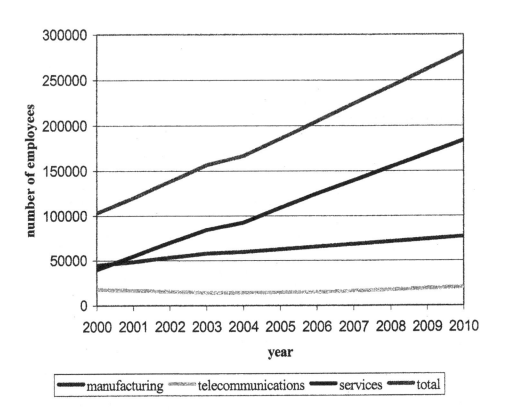

5.   SCENARIOS

In the TIDE project the future developments of the ICT industry and the
Information Society was explored by constructing alternative future
scenarios. The scenarios were constructed from the view point of the ICT
industry. The time span of the scenarios was till year 2010. The scenarios
were based on selected driving forces i.e. powerful change factors capable of
changing the course of development. The driving forces were derived from
the background research, survey data and expert interviews. Thus, the
scenarios are not derived straight from the change factors listed earlier.
Although, some change factors are clearly the main driving forces behind
certain scenarios. For example, 'strong R&D investments and quest for new

innovations' is the main driving force behind scenario II. In addition some scenarios are constructed to challenge the basic beliefs of the ICT-industry or to illustrate threats which could jeopardize the positive development of the ICT industry. Many of the change factors listed earlier indicated that the future of the ICT industry would be distinctively technology and market led. Therefore also the strengthened role of society was deliberately illustrated in one scenario. The resulting scenarios are logical stories illustrating the developments that these driving forces could set off.

The four scenarios constructed are:

I Sustainable development and Information Society. In this society led scenario the positive development of the Information Society is combined with the principles of the sustainable development. Although the scenario is strongly promoted by the political and societal elite, it also has the support of the general public. In this scenario the Finnish model of Information Society (Castells and Himanen 2001) is a success story.

II Innovation Boom of the ICT sector. This technology led scenario could be characterized to be a continuation of the past development of the ICT industry. In this "business as usual" scenario the development of the industry is technology oriented. The society supports the development, but does not steer it. This is clearly a technology push type of scenario, where the needs of the people and consumer are not always sufficiently taken into account.

III U.S. Recession. This market driven scenario describes a development were the global economy plunges into a deep recession and the outlook of the ICT industry is very negative due to the diminishing demand of ICT products and services. Although the world economy eventually recovers from the recession, the ICT industry remains permanently on a more negative development path.

IV Security Risks Materialize. This is a threat-scenario, which is included and shared by the scenarios I, II and III. The scenario illustrates a development where the risks associated to the rapid development and implementation of the ICT come true. The possible risks include for example computerized crime, insecurity of the payment transactions in e & m-commerce, privacy issues, sabotage, virtual terrorism and infrastructure vulnerabilities.

The views of the ICT companies presented in the survey answers were examined once more by cluster analysis. The companies were clustered in terms of how they saw their own and the whole ICT industry's future prospects, markets, threats, effects of the technological development, opportunities etc. As a result of this analysis the companies were divided into four groups according to what scenario they believed in. From the basis of cluster analysis the fourth scenario, i.e. Security Risks Materialize, did not appear to be feasible enough to be treated as an independent scenario. Therefore, it was considered as a threat scenario shared by the other three scenarios. Finally the companies were divided into three groups according to what scenario (I, II or III) they seem to believe.

Figure 4. What scenario does the Finnish ICT industry believe in? (% of the respondents) (scenario IV omitted) (Meristö, Leppimäki and Tammi 2002)

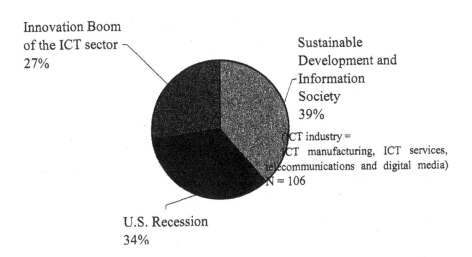

Innovation Boom
of the ICT sector
27%

Sustainable
Development and
Information
Society
39%

CT industry =
CT manufacturing, ICT services,
telecommunications and digital media)
N = 106

U.S. Recession
34%

Figure 4 shows that the Finnish ICT industry sees the sustainable development combined to Information Society development as a very feasible future scenario. It could be said, that the ICT industry strongly is supporting this kind of development. At the same time, there is also a strong belief in technology driven development. In addition, one third of the companies see global recession as the most possible future scenario.

6. CONCLUSIONS

The current trends of the ICT industry suggest that the strategic choice of the industry has been to move closer to the customers and into products with higher value added. In addition, the companies have transformed themselves from pure manufacturers to service providers, consultants and eventually to solution providers. (Manninen and Meristö 2004) These strategic choices have their influence on the skills of the employees needed in the ICT industry.

Over time the ICT has entered into the core of many sectors of the economy. More and more ICT is embedded into various every day products not forgetting the production and distribution of these products. Consequently, also the ICT skills and skill profiles are in continuous change. It is for example becoming almost obligatory for ICT professionals to have some business or marketing skills. Also the ICT industry itself will need new employees with new skills in the future. The qualitative skills gap is among the Finnish ICT companies often considered to be a more serious problem than the quantitative skill shortage. The educational system has been able to meet the quantitative demands, but not the qualitative ones. (Meristö, Leppimäki and Tammi 2002.) All things considered, the rapid development of the ICT creates new challenges to the educational system and the curricula of the educational institutes. Therefore, it is very important to update the curricula.

The Finnish government has actively pursuit development which would lead into a real Information Society. As the results of this research show, also the ICT industry sees the Information Society development as a desirable future scenario.

REFERENCES

Castells, M. and Himanen, P. 2001, *Suomen tietoyhteiskuntamalli*, SITRA and WSOY, ISBN

Koski, H. et al. 2001. *Uuden talouden loppu? ETLA B 184.* The Research Institute of Finnish Economy (in Finnish, English abstract included)

Manninen A, Meristö, T. 2004. *Tulevaisuuden ICT-osaaminen – Yritysten ja yksilöiden strateginen haaste.* IAMSR, Åbo Akademi, April 2004. (in Finnish, English abstract included)

Meristö, T, Leppimäki, S. and Tammi, M. (2002), *ICT Osaaminen 2010, Tietoteollisuuden ja digitaalisen viestinnän osaamisen ennakointi.* Åbo Akademi, ISBN 952-12-1000-1 (in Finnish, English abstract included)

OECD 2000. *Information Technology Outlook.* OECD.

OECD   2002,   *Measuring   the   Information   Economy*,   on   line   at
    http://www.oecd.org/document/5/0,2340,en_2649_37441_2765701_1_1_1_37441,00.html
    accessed 18th of Feb. 2005
Paija, L. (ed.) 2001. *Finnish ICT Cluster in the Digital Economy*. ETLA B 176. The Research
    Institute of Finnish Economy
Nordic Council of Ministers 2002. *Nordic Information Society Statistics 2002. Statistics
    Denmark, Statistics Finland, Statistics Iceland, Statistics Norway,* Statistics Sweden ISBN
    952-467-109-3, Yliopistopaino, Helsinki 2002.
Statistics Finland 2001, *Tiedolla tietoyhteiskuntaan III*. (in Finnish)
Statistics Finland 2004, *Informaatiosektori toimialoittain* 2002. (in Finnish)

ICT FROM THE BOTTOM OF THE PYRAMID: DESIGN AND/OR DE-CONSTRUCTION?

Rocío Rueda Ortiz, Henrik Herlau and Leif Bloch Rasmussen
Rueda Ortiz is with the University of Colombia, Bogota, and Herlau and Rasmussen are with the Copenhagen Business School, Denmark

Abstract: This paper reflects and calls for action on the possibility of using Information and Communication Technologies at the Bottom of the Pyramid by turning the pyramid into a diamond of knowledge creation and knowledge sharing. It tries to show what is at the heart of the challenges that C.K. Prahalad suggests in his vision of the Fortune from the Bottom of the Pyramid. Then it searches a theoretical basis of his claims in Transaction Cost Theory. However Transaction Cost Theory may itself be challenged using the theory of Max Boisot on Information Space and Social Learning, where data is taken to be a productive force along with labor and capital. The potential in the development of a better theory may then be formulated based on economizing on data. Knowledge creation and knowledge sharing at the bottom of the pyramid turns out to be the essence of what the design of ICT may contribute to a landscape of fair globalization. The role of ICT is taking to be support and enhancement of a balance between three forces Information Space and Social Learning: power, culture and knowledge. Finally it suggests a further meandering by a reflection on the need for the de-construction of Western thinking on economy, technology and knowledge.

1. INTRODUCTION

Through the history of mankind we have seen transitions from agricultural and industrial époques taking place in different cultures at different times. At the present day there are signs of a transition into a new époque, which in Western Cultures are labelled under different headings like: information society, bio-society, knowledge society, global society. In other cultures the headings might be – and maybe should be – different.

In a paper with Stu Hart from 2002 and a book from 2005 C.K. Prahalad (Hart and Prahalad, 2002; Prahalad, 2005) asks the question: "What are we doing about the poorest people around the world? Why is it that with all our technology, managerial know-how, and investment capacity, we are unable to make even a minor contribution to the problem of pervasive global poverty and disenfranchisement? Why can't we create inclusive capitalism?"

These questions are not new at all, of course. They also are fundamental to questions of a similar kind in other areas as described in the 1970'ties by Hasan Ozbekhan (1976) as "La problématique"; i.e. "population explosion", "urban spread, or blight", "illiteracy", "hunger", "environmental deterioration", "energy shortage", "inflation", "pollution", "alienation", "dehumanization". Of course we may safely say: We do KNOW!

Thus in order to do something about it Stuart Hart and C.K. Prahalad wrote their paper on Strategies for the Bottom of the Pyramid. Their main point was – and is – that doing more of the same from the past would not help – history has shown that. In stead they suggested "… new and creative approaches are needed to convert poverty into an opportunity for all concerned. That is the challenge." (Hart & Prahalad, 2002)

However, Prahalad writes in 2005: "Needless to say, not a single journal would accept the article for publication. It was too radical. Reviewers thought that it did not follow the work of developmental economics."

Leaders and MBA students took up the challenges raised in the paper when Hart & Prahalad "published" the article on the WEB. Someone was listening in information space.

In another field of "La problématique" other people are working. Fair Globalization has turned out to be the term developed by ILO/UN as a way of handling questions on globalization through labor markets. In a third field of "La problématique" the idea of Fair Trade seems to transform itself into a movement where consumers and producers create alliances based on "commercial" community interests.

Other themes, other networks are created, and they all aim at a kind of community based self-organizing world of heterarchies challenging the well established "wisdom" of economics.

This paper takes the challenges of "La problématique" and the relevance of Hart & Prahalad's challenges for granted and the need for radical new and creative approaches to convert "La problématique" into an opportunity for all concerned individuals and communities.

The paper is by nature created as a bricolage. This means that the ideas in the paper are taken from many different sources not necessarily compatible with each other – but they are taken to be able to expand each other's mental horizon.

First we try to show what is at the heart of the challenges that Hart & Prahalad suggest as expressed by Prahalad in The Fortune from the Bottom of the Pyramid (2005). Then we search for a theoretical basis for his claims in Transaction Cost Theory (TCT). However TCT may itself be challenged which we show by using the theory of Max Boisot on Information Space using data as a productive force along with labour and capital. The potential development of a better theory may then be formulated based on a political theory of economizing on data in which ICT may play a crucial role. Finally we suggest a further meandering by inquiring into the need for a de-construction of Western historical thinking and theories in economics and technology.

2. THE VISION OF PRAHALAD: THE FORTUNE FROM THE BOTTOM OF THE PYRAMID

Prahalad starts with an expression of a dominant cultural logic of the West and a potential manifest for development through social transformations. He writes (Prahalad, 2005, p. xi, p. xiii and p. 2):

"We have to learn from the successes and failures of the past; the promises made and not fulfilled. Doing more of the same, by refining the solutions of the past – development aid, subsidies, governmental support, localized nongovernmental organizations (NGO)-based solutions, exclusive reliance on deregulation and privatization of public assets – is important and has a role to play, but has not redressed the problem of poverty.

The problem of poverty must force us to innovate, not claim "rights to impose our solutions" as the language we use may not be adequate.

The vision that is presented is the co-creation of a solution to the problem of poverty. The opportunities at the Bottom of the Pyramid (BOP) cannot be unlocked if large and small firms, governments, civil society, organizations, development agencies, and the poor themselves do not work together with a shared agenda. Entrepreneurship on a massive scale is the key. This approach will challenge the prejudices about the "role and value added" of each group and its role in the economic development at the BOP."

Though Prahalad's focus is on the role of the private sector it is obvious that the collaboration across various groups will be at the heart of the approach. This seems fine enough and the evidence from cases told by Prahalad are convincing, but we want none the less to inquire whether the hypothesis and suggestions for action are valid theoretically in order to avoid embarking in experiments and/or use of resources in creating empirical evidence. In short we search for a possible theoretical basis of the hypothesis.

2.1   Dominant Logic of Western Thinking

Prahalad tells us that the nature of the BOP market has characteristics that are distinct. And he tells us that some market development imperative must be followed. He lists the following distinct characteristics of the nature of the BOP market:

There Is Money at the BOP: The dominant assumption is that the poor have no purchasing power and therefore do not represent a viable market.

Access to BOP Markets: The dominant assumption is that distribution access to the BOP markets is very difficult and therefore represents a major impediment for the participation of large firms and MNCs.

The BOP Markets Are Brand-Conscious: The dominant assumption is that the poor are not brand-conscious. On the contrary, the poor are very brand-conscious. They are extremely value-conscious by necessity.

The BOP Market is Connected: Contrary to the popular view, BOP consumers are getting connected and networked. They are rapidly exploiting the benefits of information networks

BOP Consumers Accept Advanced Technology Readily: Contrary to popular belief, the BOP consumers accept advanced technology readily.

Then he lists the following imperative for the BOP market:

Create the capacity to Consume: To convert the BOP into a consumer market, we have to create the capacity to consume. Cash-poor and with a low level income, the BOP consumer has to be accessed differently.

The Need for New Goods and Services: The involvement of the private sector at the BOP can provide opportunities for the development of new products and services.

Dignity and Choice: When the poor are converted into consumers, they get more than access to products and services. They acquire the dignity of attention and choices from the private sector that were previously reserved for the middle class and rich.

Trust Is a Prerequisite: Both sides – the large firm and the BOP consumer – have traditionally not trusted each other. The mistrust runs deep. However, private-sector firms approaching the BOP markets must focus on building trust between themselves and the consumers.

The dominant cultural logic then can be told like this (Hart and Prahalad, 2002):

Assumption	Implication
The poor are not target customers; they cannot afford our products or services	Our cost structure is a given; with our cost structure, we cannot serve the BOP market
The poor do not have use for products sold in developed countries	We are committed to a form over functionality. The poor might need sanitation, but can't afford detergents in formats we offer. Therefore, there is no market in BOP.
Only developed countries appreciate and pay for technological innovations	The BOP does not need advanced technology solutions; they will not pay for them. Therefore, the BOP cannot be a source of innovations.
The BOP market is not critical for long-term growth and vitality of MNCs	BOP markets are at best an attractive distraction.
Intellectual excitements is in developed markets; it is very hard to recruit managers for BOP markets.	We cannot assign our best people to work on market development in BOP markets

Finally Prahalad suggests that another cultural logic could be told by changing the Pyramid into a Diamond through "development as social transformation" using the following ideas:

- Breaking down barriers to Communication
- BOP Consumers Upgrade
- Gaining Access to Knowledge
- Identity for the Individual
- Women Are Critical for Development
- Evolving Checks and Balances

The real test, he says, would be to show that the Pyramid could be the changed into a Diamond like the illustration on page 110:

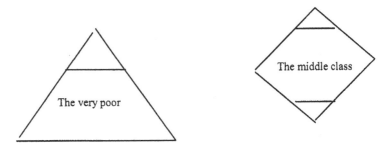

3.   IN SEARCH OF THEORETICAL BASIS
TRANSACTION COST THEORY (TCT)

In order to have a better understanding of the suggestions of Prahalad and thus suggestions for ICT as enabler of the Fortune from the BOP we need to dig a little deeper than done by Prahalad. Maybe and maybe not we are right, but it is our hypothesis that Prahalad bases his calling for the BOP market on a way of using the transaction cost theory. At least his heavy reliance on economic and cultural measures like Self Helping Groups (SHGs), local public e-service shops and Transaction Governance Capacity (TGC) in combination with innovative use of ICT points in that direction.

We suggest that this challenge is based on the theories of – among others – the Nobel Laureates Ronald Coase, John Nash, Douglas North and Joseph Stiglitz:

Either to minimize transaction costs in business by externalizing and sharing these costs through cooperative networks based on mutual trust, or to minimize transaction costs by internalizing these costs through hierarchies based on competition.

Some definitions

Transaction: A transaction is an economic exchange, the transfer of some good or service between *technologically separable* activities. The transaction is regarded by transaction cost economics as the fundamental unit of investigation. The rules and institutions governing a particular transaction constitute its *governance structure*, and the task of transaction cost economics is to determine, for a particular transaction, the most efficient (production and transaction cost minimizing) governance structure from a list of those available.

Transaction costs: Transaction costs are the costs of administering an exchange relationship. These include the costs of negotiating, drafting, and monitoring contracts; the costs of settling disputes and enforcing settlements; and the opportunity costs associated with administering a contract inefficiently until a new agreement is recognized as necessary and then reached.

New Institutional Economics: applying economic theory and quantitative methods in order to explain economic and institutional change.

Prahalad seems to believe that the "market" can take care of the poor (however defined), supported by Transaction Cost Governance, i.e. by some kind of bureaucracy. But in what way does he define market? Is it a market of capital, labour, goods and services or a market of information/knowledge? Are the rules of the game the same in economizing on labour and capital as in economizing on information/data? And is it a necessity to use the rules of the market (the invisible hand, free market, protectionism, fair trade) by Developing Countries in order to follow the same historical track of growing BNP as suggested by neo-liberal economics? Protected or secured by a sort of benevolent bureaucracy in the words of Prahalad: Transaction Cost Governance?

However Coase – the founder of the theory in his Nobel Prize speech in 1991 expresses the need for much more work on the theory and the experimental evidence needed. Coase tells it this way in his Nobel lecture (Coase, 1991):

"Oliver Williamson has ascribed the non-use or limited use of my thesis in *The Nature of the Firm* to the fact that it has not been made "operational", by which he means that the concept of transaction costs has not been incorporated into a general theory. I think this is correct. There have been two reasons for this. First, incorporating transaction costs into standard economic theory which has been based on the assumption that they are zero, would be very difficult and economists who, like most scientists, as Thomas Kuhn has told us, are extremely conservative in their methods, have not been inclined to attempt it. Second, Williamson has also pointed out that although I was correct in making the choice between organization within the firm or through the market the center piece of my analysis, I did not indicate what the factors were that determined the outcome of this choice and thus made it difficult for others to build on what is often described as a "fundamental insight". This also is true. But the interrelationships which govern the mix of market and hierarchy, to use Williamson's terms, are extremely complex and in our present state of ignorance it will not be easy to discover what these factors are. What we need is more empirical work. In a paper written for a conference of the National Bureau of Economic Research. I explained why I thought this was so. This is what I said: "An inspired theoretician might do as well without such empirical work, but my own feeling is that the inspiration is most likely to come through the stimulus provided by the patterns, puzzles and anomalies revealed by the systematic gathering of data, particularly when the prime need is to break our existing habits of thought". This statement was made in 1970. I still think that in essentials it is true today. Although much interesting and important research was done in the seventies and eighties and we certainly know much more than we did in 1970, there is little doubt that a great deal more empirical work is needed. However, I have come to the conclusion that the main obstacle faced by researchers in industrial organization is the lack of available data on contracts and the activities of firms. I have therefore decided to do something about it.

My remarks have sometimes been interpreted as implying that I am hostile to the mathematization of economic theory. This is untrue. Indeed, once we begin to uncover the real factors affecting the performance of the economic system, the complicated interrelations between them will clearly necessitate a mathematical treatment, as in the natural sciences, and economists like myself, who write in prose, will take their bow. May be this period soon come.

I am very much aware that many economists whom I respect and admire will not agree with the opinions I have expressed and some may even be offended by them. But a scholar must be content with the knowledge that what is false in what he says will soon be exposed and, as for what is true, he can count on ultimately seeing it accepted, if only he lives long enough."

Thus Coase himself finds reason for being careful in applying TCT. It is our suggestion that that caring may be taken from a theory developed by Max Boisot, i.e. economizing on data, information and knowledge as a way of minimizing transaction costs.

4.   BOISOT'S VISION ON ECONOMIZING ON LABOUR, CAPITAL AND DATA

Boisot (1995, 1998) uses an approach starting by viewing data as part of an evolutionary production function. Then he shows how data may be turned into knowledge using social learning supported and enhanced by culture (institutions), competencies development and technology, especially ITC. In order to do that he suggests a radical development of the TCT as that theory is taken to be too one-dimensional in its choice on internalizing or externalizing transaction costs.

4.1   Data as a Production Force

In Information Space (1995) Max Boisot suggested that data may be taken to be like labor and capital in a production function. This means that the traditional production function in a two-dimensional space must be expanded to a three-dimensional space, where the level of production (the isoquant) is taken to be a function of labor, capital and data. Using ordinary thinking on minimizing effort in production we then have three factors to minimize. Then the hypothesis is that the neo-classical theory of economics is economizing on labour and capital in two ways:

- Substitution of labour for capital and vice versa
- Jumps towards zero effort (presumably through knowledge and technology)

Boisot suggests that these ways must be supplemented by ways of economizing on data. He does this by joining Capital and Labour into Physical Resources and combine them with data. Then the production function may be shown like this.

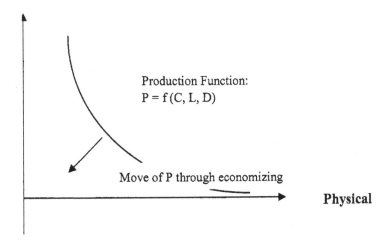

(Naturally this image of the production function should be three-dimensional, but we keep it in two-dimensions for simplicity).

But the question then is: What are the content of the "data" dimension? Boisot suggests that there are three dimensions in economizing on data (which must be seen along with the more traditional economizing on capital and labour):

Coding – naming reality
Abstraction – making models of the world
Diffusion – distributing data/information/knowledge

Together these three dimensions creates an Information Space (I-Space) and can be shown like this:

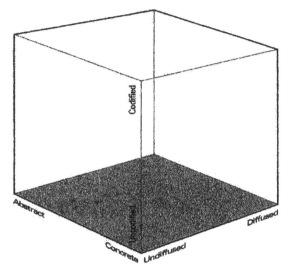

The Information Space

The content of the I-space can be interpreted in three interacting spaces:

Epistemological Space:

Coding

Technical knowledge	Scientific knowledge
Aesthetical knowledge	Craft knowledge

Abstraction

Cultural Space:

Coding

Property knowledge	Public knowledge
Personal knowledge	Common-sense knowledge

Diffusion

Utility Space:

Abstraction	Esoteric knowledge	Global knowledge
	Local knowledge	Topical knowledge

Diffusion

Then value – the creation, sharing and using of knowledge in the production function – is created by movement in the I-Space through six phases by effectively activating all parts of the I-Space. This curve is called the Social Learning Curve (SLC).

The six phases in SLC are as follows:

Scanning: Identifying threats and opportunities; patterns and insights.

Problem-solving: creating structure out of the identified elements of data/information. Reduces uncertainty and challenges existing knowledge.

Abstraction: Generalization of obtained structure of data/information.

Diffusion: Sharing obtained knowledge with target groups.

Absorption: New knowledge being absorbed and made tacit, bodily. Learning-by-doing.

Impacting: Embedding knowledge in praxis, in products, techniques, behaviour.

The model shown here are the ideal as seen by Boisot. In reality, of course, it may take many forms.

The Information Space

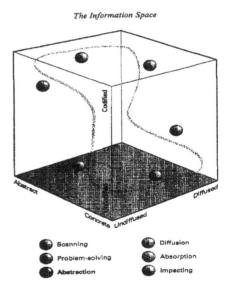

● Scanning	● Diffusion
● Problem-solving	● Absorption
● Abstraction	● Impacting

The Social Learning Cycle (SLC)

Boisot uses the metaphor of data being scattered (centripetal force) or gathered (centrifugal force) in an electro-magnetic field and then turned into information and knowledge according to social learning, culture, institution building, competencies and technology.

4.2   Transaction Costs and Information Space

Boisot interprets the concept of transaction as follows (Knowledge Assets, 1998, p. 124):

"Following the lead given by new institutional economics, we shall take the transaction as our unit of analysis. For our purposes, a transaction can be thought of as any act of social exchange that depends on information flows for its accomplishment. Transactions can be as simple and brief as the purchase of a packet of cigarettes, or as complex as and extended as those which bind a Zen master to his disciples. Like institutional economists, we are interested in the relationship that can be established between different transactional characteristics and the phenomenon of institutionalization. Our use of the term transaction, however, will extend beyond that of institutional economics where the focus has tended to be primarily on transaction costs and efficiency considerations. These, to be sure, are relevant. But, as we shall see, they are not the whole story."

In this critique of the use of transaction cost theory and new institutional economics Boisot tries to keep both the cake and the penny (Boisot, 1995, p. 235):

"To summarize, the production of information and its use in transactions both incur costs and are thus subject to economizing. In the 1970s, there occurred a revival of interest among economists in the economics of transaction, and Oliver Williamson in particular, building on the earlier work of Ronald Coase and John Commons, has explored the different institutional arrangements that govern transactional choices. ... we shall also concern ourselves with the institutional order built up from transactions, but our focus will be less narrowly economic than the one adopted by Williamson. Like him, we shall argue that institutional structures aim partly at achieving transactional efficiencies and that where such efficiencies are effectively achieved they act somewhat like a magnetic field – a mathematician would call them 'attractors' – drawing the uncommitted transaction into a given institutional orbit. Yet in contrast to Williamson's, our concept of transactions is underpinned by an explicit rather than an implicit theory of information production and exchange which yields a different way of classifying them as well as a distinctive approach to their governance. We find ourselves in consequence in the realm of political economy rather than of economics *tout court*."

The first step in doing so is to establish a link between institutional economics and cultural analysis as institutions may be taken to be crystallized out of transactional structures mediating a cultural order or mediated by culture.

The problems ahead of us must be a discussion on the differences between the approach to transactions outlined in the Information Space theory and that adopted by the new institutional economists such as Oliver Williamson. The differences are numerous but the most important according to Boisot are (Information Space, 1995, p. 288-290):

1. Only information diffusion is brought into focus in NIE [New Institutional Economy], not coding and abstraction ... for which NIE uses terms like 'uncertainty' and 'atmosphere'. Much transactional richness relates to codification and abstraction and escapes such formulations/terms.
2. The markets and hierarchies paradigm implies, but does not develop a dynamic theory of information flows ... NIE uses terms like "information impacting', 'opportunism' and 'strategic behaviour' in service of a static theory of transactional assignment.
3. In the absence of a conceptual scheme that could factor out governance issues from transactional ones, the new institutional economists have tended to conflate the two: hierarchies are treated as a matter of course as internal to firms, and markets as institutions that are external to firms. Hybrid forms, to be sure, exist between these polar alternatives, and in such cases one talks of bilateral governance.

Institutional economics thus is part of the way forward, but not the only way (Boisot, 1995, p.290-1):

"In spite of such limitations, the New Institutional Economics research programme, given its willingness to acknowledge the central role played by information in the economic process, constitutes a marked advance over what is on offer from the neoclassical orthodoxy. There, information retains the status of the luminiferous ether of classical physics before Einstein: a ubiquitous medium that admitted of a mechanical account of action at a distance and kept the world conveniently Newtonian.

Institutional economics, however, needs a more explicit and dynamic theory of information flows if it is to make more than a dent in the neoclassical defences. Having established that there exists credible institutional alternatives to markets, it needs to show how information production and exchange underpins them all, shaping their internal evolution as well as how they collaborate and compete. In effect, what is needed is a theory of social learning that extends beyond the individual or the organization to encompass more complex institutional settings. Such as theory, I believe, is foreshadowed in Douglas North's historical studies of institutions. It now needs further development."

Thus we may join forces with Boisot and start inquiring into the ways of using this new theory at the Bottom of the Pyramid. Economizing information costs in its own terms in creation, sharing, using and destroying knowledge through the Social Learning Curve is not the only way of economizing. Culture, individual and collective competencies development and ICT may be designed to take part in that economizing.

4.3   Culture as economizing

Transactions floating around in the I-Space may then be hypothesized as being attracted to each other under the influence of the culture, that so to speak create an electro-magnetic field of attraction in and around the I-Space. Accordingly institutions are built in order to facilitate particular kinds of transactions – in order to minimize costs. In the upper left corner transactions will be build around highly coded and abstract data, where bureaucracies are able to handle the data as they involve explicit information like copyrights, contracts, patents, rule, laws, regulations and procedures. In the upper right corner such data can be distributed more easily to many people along the diffusion scale, as explicit knowledge are more easily distributed using media than implicit, tacit knowledge.

In the lower regions of the I-Space institutions take the form of fiefs (in the lower left region) and clans (in the lower right region) depending on how many people are involved and whether the transactions functions in hierarchies or non-hierarchies. In these regions the transactions are based on personal contacts and shared values and beliefs.

There is strong evidence that national cultures and institutions play a part in predisposing firms to transact from a given region of the I-Space. Boisot suggests that

- The Anglo-Saxon culture with its strong preference for competitively determined contractual relations will prefer market based transaction
- The Latin-American culture are more committed to the role of the state and bureaucracies
- Chinese and Japanese culture will be much more personalized and committed to informal and tacit forms of exchange of data/information, the difference being that Japanese culture are less centralized than Chinese culture.

Different patterns of data may arise bringing all possibilities into play as culture shapes institutions as strong attractors for data. Again using the metaphor of an electro-magnetic field: Quite distinctive cultures manage to

"... confine the larger part of their transacting to a particular region in the space. If the institutions of Marxism-Leninism, for example, tried to restrict the economic and social transactions of the planned economy to the bureaucratic region of the I-Space those of Thatcherism, by contracts attempted to channel what many would consider to be non-economic transactions towards the market region of the space. In each case a distinctive culture was aimed for, one in which ideology was in the drivers seat. Ideology, by legitimating transactional assignments on other grounds than their own merit, can render a given region of the I-Space – at least temporarily – almost impervious to transactional competition from other regions." (Boisot, 1998, p. 143)

Boisot (1998, p. 151) then concludes on economizing by culture:

"At the level of firms, therefore, only those whose cultural repertoire gives them transactional capacity throughout the I-Space can summon and adequate learning response to any emerging gaps between technology and culture. Those operating from too narrow a cultural base in the space, however, must of necessity lose control of the SLC unless they can complement their limited cultural repertoire through carefully selected interfirm and intercultural collaborations – i.e. through an externalization of transactions that link them with agents located elsewhere in the space. However, they will then confront the same problems of integration that more culturally diverse firms encounter inside their organization when trying to coordinate the activities of different functions or businesses. There is no cheap grace."

Related to the issue of ICT we may safely say that ICT should be used for enhancing diversity of cultures and their joint cooperation.

4.4 Competencies and Economizing

The main idea behind bringing competencies into play in the I-Space and the SLC is related to a question of creating and maintaining core-competencies as a strategic competitive (or shouldn't we say cooperative) advantage for a nation, a region or a company.

Boisot is rather critical towards the concept of core competence as it is described by Hamel and Prahalad (1989). They see a core competence to be unique to a firm and largely tacit and hard to imitate. In their view the only strategic relevance of a core competence is the possibility to exploit it in value adding. That can only take place in the upper part of the I-Space. But core competencies need to be coded and abstracted and then put into patents, contracts, property rights etc. In short made scarce, a process Boisot calls knowledge hoarding in contrast to what he takes to be a better road: knowledge sharing.

Boisot sees this other way of development and use of core competencies as a way of handling complexity. He explains (Boisot, 1998, p. 205):

"... it makes sense to describe a core competence as a complex adaptive system, located in the lower regions of the I-Space between an ordered regime in which knowledge assets get frozen into technologies and a chaotic regime in which the stability necessary for effective organizational coordination and integration remains absent. Core competences, then, have their being in a region of the I-Space sandwiched between an excess of usable structure and a total lack of it.

We hypothesize that the possession of a core competence is one measure of a firm's ability to deal with complexity."

It is difficult to keep a balance *between* drifting to the bureaucracy part of the I-space trying to make the core competence explicit in order to get organized *and* re-engineer efforts for competitiveness and letting the entrepreneurial spirit flourish.

However we might conclude with Boisot (Boisot, 1998, p. 205):

"Only firms that can handle a full SLC, together with the multiple cultures required to drive it, will be able to cope with the many and conflicting demands of a complex regime.

We know from section 1.4 that complex structures operate at a higher level of entropy than more traditional and ordered structures, and that their effective management requires greater data-processing capacities. It follows that firms which operate in the complex regime in the I-Space will need different data-processing strategies than firms that do not."

Thus it is of the greatest interest too inquire into what way ICT may affect a firm's, a region's and a nations – a culture's – choice of data-processing strategies, which is the same as asking for ways of handling knowledge assets.

4.5 ICT and Transactions in I-Space.

The overall idea of working on strategies for ICT will then be at least three-fold:

1. In order to be innovative and develop new core competences ICT may be strategically used to move the SLC towards the right and to the bottom of the I-Space
2. In order to handle diversity in SLC's, competencies, cultures and institutions ICT may be strategically used to link and support this diversity.
3. In order to support a variety of cultural logics other means of economizing on data than ICT should be in focus of our social and spiritual awareness, especially inquiring relations among social partners.

5. SOCIAL DIALOGUE AND INFORMATION SPACE

Putting these ways of economizing on data together must call for the participation of the Bottom of the Pyramid, as it is there uncoded and concrete data exist. This call is radical in two ways: (1) it calls for ways of getting the BOP to take part in the knowledge based economy (that is the radicality of Prahalad), and (2) it calls for a political information economy in which the potential wealth created by knowledge sharing are also shared.

As Boisot explains in Information Space (Boisot, 1995, p. 330):

"A cultural pattern in the I-space becomes internally consistent and stable when its constituent institutional linkages and related transactional investments are mutually reinforcing and any antagonist linkages that might emerge are suppressed. Drawing on the connectionist perspective developed in Chapter 2 with its emphasis on excitatory and inhibitory linkages in neural activation patterns, one might even in such a case speak of a *cultural logic* in which different parts of the transactional structure are either jointly activated or mutually exclusive. Where such a logic consistently favours the activation of a particular pattern, whether centripetal or centrifugal, one might then speak of a *cultural order*. The pattern thus favoured may act as an attractor for a particular region of the I-space. For example, a capitalist order is generally thought of as a cultural pattern of transactions that is centrifugally spread out throughout the I-space but whose overall logic is designed to protect and enhance the transactional viability of the market region; a feudal order generates a cultural logic that aims to achieve the same for the fief region, and so on.

A cultural logic may survive the generative or destructive effects of the SLC by shifting to new institutions as they emerge in the I-space, selecting these on the basis of their pattern-preserving properties. It may thus exhibit what Ross Ashby calls ultra-stability."

In the two books of Boisot on which we have based our arguments a conclusion on the design of ICT-systems may be drawn:

Boisot concludes in Knowledge Assets (Boisot, 1998, p. 270-1):

"Putting a political economy of information on the agenda will require academics, managers, and policy-makers to address issues such as the following:

Institutional issues: How does the assumption that the world is for the most part nonlinear modify the nature of institution building?

Organizational issues: How does the 'virtuality' of organizations affect their governance?

Accounting issues: What impact will the shift form energy-based assets to knowledge assets have on accounting practices?

Educational issues: What educational practices best equip agents successfully to manage the six steps of an SLC on a lifetime basis?

Employment issues: what kind of employment policies would make creative destruction less threatening and yet productive.

Political issues: How will nation-states maintain sovereign control over knowledge-based economic activities that have no identifiable spatio-temporal location?

The conclusion of Boisot in Information Space, (Boisot, 1995, p. 356):

"The real contest, from the perspective we have adapted, is not between the ideology of markets and that of hierarchies as alternative ordering principles for economic action but between a centripetal and a centrifugal cultural – and hence economic – order. And since, according to our analysis, only the first can properly be called ideological, this contest cannot be framed as one between competing ideologies. Rather it has to be seen as one between an ideological and evolutionary order. It effectively reaffirms the distinction that Popper has already made between a closed and an open society, but it does so this time on information grounds."

And there of course we start again with new hopes – as is always the case – in an inquiring mood:

1. Since theory building and testing is ultimately a collective enterprise, the hope is that those who have found the ideas presented in these pages of interest – practitioners as well as theoreticians – will help to address the above issues and place the evolving theory on a sounder footing. They can do this either by challenging what has been presented, or by building on it. In either case, doubtless, some rebuilding will be called for. Hopefully, however, the concepts presented in these pages will prove to be robust. This last paragraph is also a citation from Boisot (1998, p. 271)
2. The diamond may not only be found in a fair distribution of economic wealth. The diamond must also be found in a balancing of forces in autonomous, intensive and meaningful creation and sharing of knowledge.
3. That this calling may be put to the most severe test of falsification.

We strongly believe that Boisot has provided for the first of these three hopes. Using his theories on the vision of Prahalad we try (in chapter 6) to provide some guideline for the second hope. For the third hope we try (in chapter 7) to reflect on a possible de-construction of the language used thus far.

6.   THE REAL TEST REVISITED: A DIAMOND IN I-SPACE

The social learning curve may be seen – however its form – as a way of bringing forces in minimizing information costs into play. This is done by bringing all types of transactions into play. That would be an ideal in a world where knowledge creation, knowledge sharing joins forces with a sustainable way of handling labor and capital, physical resources as they are summarized by Boisot.

Thus the diamond called for by Prahalad is only two-dimensional in the I-Space. This means that e-Governance for the poor in a knowledge based economy by necessity will be controlled by either the hierarchy/bureaucracy or the market. That is by those who are able to handle and control explicit knowing, in short cultures and institutions in the upper parts of the I-Space.

It will not be possible to include cultures and institutions in the lower parts of the I-Space. This means that the dichotomy implicit in Transaction Cost Theory between competitiveness and trust is false as it only takes place in the upper part of the I-Space where the rules of the game is power. Getting other parts of the I-Space included in minimizing information costs must include the lower parts, i.e. the dichotomy – or rather the dilemmas – in choosing between power and trust!

One may say then – and act accordingly – that the new hypothesis for a theory on ICT from the Bottom of the Pyramid might be shown as a diamond inside the I-Space, where forces are kept in balance in three dimensions.

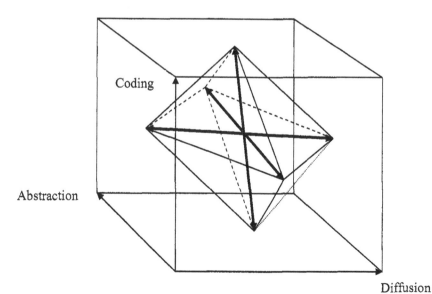

Economize in the utility space (coding-diffusion): that would be a choice on internalizing or externalizing transaction costs based on political power, i.e. hoarding vs. sharing knowledge

Economize in the cultural space (abstraction-diffusion): that would be a choice on cultural diversified knowledge or cultural dominant knowledge, i.e. individualizing vs. socializing

Economize in the epistemological space (coding-abstraction): that would be a choice of generalized interdisciplinary knowledge or disciplinary knowledge; i.e. particularity vs. sensus communis

The three forces in I-space along with their relation to the three-dimensional production function puts our ways of economizing on data to the real test:

How can we design ICT-landscapes in such a way that they support checks and balances of forces in I-Space?
How can we design ICT-systems that support and enhance the three-dimensional production function for sustainability and fair globalization?

Having a map at one's disposal, however, does not necessarily make it safe and secure to choose a journey. It might depend on whether the map is taken to be showing a real or a virtual landscape worthwhile for designing our travel. So we need at least to reflect on a possible de-construction of the language in which the map has been created before we use it for the design of ICT-systems from the Bottom of the Pyramid.

7. REFLECTIONS ON CONCEPTS OF MARKET, CONSUMERS AND POVERTY

Jacques Derrida, in *Specters of Marx* (1998), claims "...that we are all in debt to Marxism as the New World Disorder crumbles.' A Spectre is haunting Europe the spectre of communism'. Challenge or invitation, "encouragement," seduction countering seduction, desire or war, love or hate, provocation of other ghosts: Marx insists on this a lot for there is *a multiple* of this sociality. For if no use-value can *in itself produce* this mysticality or this spectral effect of the commodity, and if the secret is at the same time profound and superficial, opaque and transparent, a secret that is all the more secret in that no substantial essence hides behind it, it is because the effect is born of a *relation* (*ferance,* difference, reference, and diff*a*rence), as double relation, one should say as double social bond.

This double *socius* binds *on the one hand men* to each other. It associates them insofar as they have been for all times interested in time, Marx notes right away, the time or the duration of labour, and this in all cultures and at all stages of techno-economic development. This *socius,* then, binds "men" who are first of all experiences of time, existences determined by this relation to time which itself would not be possible without surviving and returning, without that living present and being "out of joint" that dislocates the self-presence of the living present and installs thereby the relation to the other. The same socius, the same "social form" of the relation binds, on the other hand, commodity-things to each other. *On the other band* how? And how is what takes place *on the one band* among men, in their apprehension of time, explained by what takes place *on the other hand* among those spectres that are commodities? How do those whom one calls "men," living men, temporal and finite existences, become subjected, in their social relations, to these spectres that are relations, *equally social rela*tions among commodities?

If capitalization has no rigorous limit, it is also because it comes itself to be exceeded. But once the limits of phantasmagorization can no longer be controlled or fixed by the simple opposition of presence and absence, actuality and inactuality, sensuous and supersensible, another approach to differences must structure ("conceptually" and "really") the field that has thus been re-opened. Far from effacing differences and analytic determinations, this other logic calls for other concepts. One may hope it will allow for a more refined and more rigorous restructuring. It alone in any case can call for this constant restructuring, as elsewhere for the very progress of the critique.

But also at stake, indissociably, is the differential deployment of *tekkne-, of* techno-science or tele-technology. It obliges us more than ever to think the virtualisation of space and time, the possibility of virtual events whose movement and speed prohibit us more than ever (more and otherwise than ever, for this is not absolutely and thoroughly new) from opposing presence to its representation, "real time" to "deferred time," effectivity to its simulacrum, the living to the non-living, in short, the living to the living-dead of its ghosts. It obliges us to think, from there, another space for democracy. For democracy-to-come and thus for justice. We have suggested that the event we are prowling around here hesitates between the singular "who" of the ghost and the general "what" of the simulacrum. In the virtual space of all the teletechnosciences, in the general dis-location to which our time is destined — as are from now on the places of lovers, families, nations — the messianic trembles on the edge of this event itself. It is this hesitation, it has no other vibration, it does not "live" otherwise, but it would no longer be messianic if it stopped hesitating: how to give rise and to give place, still, to render it, this place, to render it habitable, but without killing the future in the name of old frontiers? Like those of the blood, nationalisms of native soil not only sow hatred, not only commit crimes, they have no future, they promise nothing even if, like stupidity or the unconscious, they hold fast to life. This messianic hesitation does not paralyse any decision, any affirmation, any responsibility. On the contrary, it grants them their elementary condition. It is their very experience.

The question deserves perhaps to be put the other way: Could one *address oneself in general* if already some ghost did not come back? If he loves justice at least, the "scholar" of the future, the "Intellectual" of tomorrow should learn it and from the ghost. He should learn to live by learning not how to make conversation with the ghost but how to talk with him, with her, how to let thus speak or how to give them back speech, even if it is in oneself, in the other, in the other in oneself: they are always *there*, spectres, even if they do not exist, even if they are no longer, even if they are not yet".

What does it mean to come back to the ghost of Marxism? Even accepting the distance and the critique of Marxism (by Marx) there is one basic idea left: social justice and communitarism. A debt from all the ghosts of our history and our past that we cannot forget. We need to live with them, learn from them and dream of other possible worlds.

But deconstruction means that we have to accept paradoxes. For instance, the paradox between the market as institution and the alternative forms of market (individuals or communitarian) that tries to do resistance to the global market and on consequence develop bottom-up processes. On the one hand we need to create institutional alternatives to markets that show how information production and exchange can be done by collaboration, but accepting conflict and antagonism as potential of the social relationships between global and local markets. On the other hand, we need a politics of trust or confidence in the market that encourage us to extend possibilities of action and experience. So the idea of one market, as institution, should leave part of initiative to an "other", should accept that the future can come from the action of an "other", implying the acceptance of the risk of renouncing partially to power and control, accepting a space of freedom where "the other" can be a singular subject or a singular community of subjects.

What does it mean try to change the pyramid? We can see some differances: as exclusion, and as inclusion. What is settled is that the global market in information society is creating a big difference between the regions which are subordinated, e.g., Africa, Latin America which are being excluded from the capital fluxes transported by ICT. That subordination is bound to the poverty conditions of regions and countries. In this case, inverting the pyramid has to be done through the incorporation of ICT to the production, as a way to inclusion. But differance also means postponement, delay, deferment. It is what Derrida called the differential deployment of *tekkne*. How are developing or subordinated counties deploying technologies? Which kind of technologies are being adopted by them? How are those technologies being involved in the social and productive world? And how are they changing societies and cultures?

Let us go one step ahead and then we will come back to Derrida, Marx and his ghosts. Negri (2003) shows that there are three kinds of tasks that lead the post-modern global economy:

- incorporated ICT in transforming the process of industrial production itself
- the "immaterial" work of creative and intelligent manipulation of symbols
- the "immaterial" work bounded to production and manipulation of affects and human contact (virtual or real), or corporal work

What we want to emphasize is that new ways of production (immaterial, computerized, ICT) has cooperation as its main characteristic. The immaterial work includes interactions and social cooperation. The difference with Marxist view of the economy is that the cooperative work is not imposed from the exterior, as it occurred in past forms of labour: no cooperation is completely immanent to the labour activity. This means that we can imagine that productivity and wealth can be acquired through a form of cooperative interactivity through linguistic, communicative and affective nets. In other words we can think (we can dream) that the new "immaterial work" could provide a potential for a kind of spontaneous and basic communism. Now the ghost of Marx has come again.

What cultural changes does this imply? If we accept the cooperative model of production, we have to see the possibility of creating markets organized in a horizontal net, challenging the power structures between regions (developed to developing countries) and even inside of each local or communitarian market. But we have to be alert because along with the global process of the information society there is also decentralization and dispersion that is provoking new ways of centralization and control of the production (as many mega corporations has shown us). So, the paradox is that we need a new model of production that can allow us to create flexible and cooperative nets, but the nets also are being designed and fixed for control. In political terms that mean that the global infrastructure of information has two main mechanisms of power: democracy and oligopoly. The democratic net is a model horizontal and without frontiers, without centre. The oligopoly model is a model where the production is centralized, the distribution is massive and the communication is only in one direction. This is a model in which most of the transnational corporations are interested, a model by which they want to establish and consolidate their monopolies in the new informational infrastructure.

But of course, we believe that the net is not just white or black. The information society is a hybrid of both models: democracy/oligopoly, horizontal/vertical relationships. And there are also portions of resistance but they have to fight without rest to keep their spaces of freedom and cooperation. We do know that ICT and information or knowledge society had promised a new democracy and a new social equality. But, in fact, they created new ways of inequality and exclusion, inside the dominant (developed) countries but also, especially, in developing (subordinated) countries.

Capitalism is always trying to take the public goods as private goods and services, in other words, has tried an expropriation of what is "common". What we need to do from the BOP is to invent or create a new way to think "the common" in our information (post-modern) societies, where to produce means to build in cooperation in cooperative communities. In this sense, the question of the access to goods and services for poor people is not only the main point. Instead we have to think whether we really do need everything to consume, and if every thing (goods or services) require producing, posing and using exclusively. We need a community that produce, reproduce and define itself. Again the ghost of Marx, through Derrida debts is here.

8.   CONCLUSION WITHOUT CLOSING

Overall economizing vs. de-construction of the language of economizing? That is the strategic question for the ICT people. The "conclusion" from our search for a justified cause for ICT in a landscape of economics and culture – of course – would take the form of dilemmas that calls for choices to be made.

- The fact that the contemporary capitalism promote inequalities and exclusions, it seems eternal through control. We suggest a political information economy that surpasses the incapacity of rational and instrumental policies and avoid putting communication in every day life in opposition to the economy and the material development of societies, i.e. as a kind of opposition between public life and private life. The social learning cycle then will have to recognize both levels in each one of its six phases.
- We have suggested ways of de-constructing the language (market, consumer, ICT) and de-sign for innovation working from the Bottom of the Pyramid: It forces us to innovate, not claim rights to impose our solutions upon other's cultural logic. We need to build a new confidence, spreading the possibilities of praxis and experience. But trust insists on leaving part of the initiative to an "other", it means to accept that the future can be in the action of an "other" (in the bottom, on the top, in one side of the pyramid or diamond). It implies a risk, a risk to renounce power and build spaces where "others" can be subjects of decisions and praxis.
- An important part of this de-construction works through the ICT. If we decide that what produces the affective work are social networks, community forms, then we can imagine that the instrumental action of the economic production could be united to the communicative action of the human relations. In this case the communication has not become impoverished, but the production has become enriched with the level of the human complexity. There is a possibility created by ICT and cyberspace which promote the creation of networked cultures without the fixed and homogenized identities assumed by the mass media; they also foster new routes for the circulation of ideas (not subject to centralized controls), the irruption of sub-cultures aware of the need to re-invent social and political orders, and a space for inter-cultural exchange and for the construction of shared artistic and political strategies. Then we are talking about micropolitics for the production of local knowledge made possible by the "fluid architecture" of cyberspace, emphasizing the "molecular" (as opposed to molar or characterized by large,

homogeneous aggregates) nature of cyberspace. These micropolitics consist of practices of mixing, reusing, and recombination of knowledge and information.

- After de-constructing the pyramid and revising the diamond into the I-Space, we need to de-sign concepts, experiences and actions as diamonds of our time, given quality, time and space to the new epistemology and ontology that offered ICT to us. It would have to unite our cooperative work translated into community projects, using the social dialogue.

We must be asked what world we are de-signing; and we must be asked in what kind of world we want to live. We must look for answers that allow the incarnation of the voice of people (not the voice of others), the production and distribution of value for all (in a creative and cooperative action) and the liberation of the societies (in power-free communication).

REFERENCES

Boisot, Max (1995), *Information Space*, Routledge, London

Boisot, Max (1998), *Knowledge Assets*, Oxford University Press, New York

Coase, Ronald (1937): The Nature of the Firm, *Economica*, NS, 4

Coase, Ronald, (1991) *The Institutional Structure of Production*, Nobel Prize Lecture, Stockholm

Derrida, Jacques (1986), *De la gramatología*. México: Ed. Siglo XXI, 4ª. Ed.

Derrida, Jacques (1998), Espectros de Marx. El estado de la deuda, el trabajo del duelo y la nueva internacional. Madrid: Ed. Trotta. English version in: http://www.marxists.org/reference/subject/philosophy/works/fr/derrida2.htm Original source: *Specters of Marx, the state of the debt, the Work of Mourning, & the New International*, translated by Peggy Kamuf, Routledge 1994

Fischer, Edward F. (2001), *Cultural Logics & Global Economics*, University of Texas Press

Hammel, G.; Prahalad, C.K. (1989), *Strategic Intent, Harvard Business Review*, Boston, May-June

Hardt Michael; Negri Antoni (2003), *Imperio*, Buenos Aires: Paidós.

Negri, Antonio (2003), *time for revolution, Continuum*, London

Ozbekhan, Hazan (1976), *The predicament of mankind in C.W.Churchman & R. Mason (eds.)*: World Modelling: A Dialogue, North-Holland American Elsevier, 1976

C.K.Prahalad, C.K.; Stuart Hart: *The Fortune at the Bottom of the Pyramid*, Strategy + Business, Issue 26

Prahalad, C.K. (2005), T*he Fortune from the Bottom of the Pyramid, Wharton School Publishing*, Wupper Saddle River, NJ

Williamson, O.E. (1991), *The Economic Institutions of Capitalism: Frims, Markets and Rational Contracting*, The Free Press, New York

Williamson, O.E. (1991), *The Logic of Economic Organization, in O.E.Williamson and S. Winter (eds.)* The Nature of the Firm: Origins, Evolution and Development, Oxford University Press, New York

WORK ETHICS AND EFFECTIVENESS IN HOME CARE: RATIONALIZATION THROUGH TECHNOLOGICAL INNOVATION

Riikka Vuokko
University of Turku, Lemminkäisenkatu 14 A, FIN20520 Turku, Finland

Abstract: In social home care, the perceived outcomes of implementation of mobile informatics were effectiveness and quality of services. To make the planning of work easier, mobile technology was introduced. In reality, the views on managerial accountability and local accountabilities among care workers have been somewhat contrasting, and it seems that the new information system cannot fulfill all of the information needs of the workers. Thus, longitudinal ethnographic study of changing work has also raised questions about work-related and professional ethics.

1. INTRODUCTION

In Turku, in South-western Finland, social home care offers help to vulnerable clients coping with their everyday life in order to promote independent living. The largest client group nowadays consists of elderly people. It has been estimated that the percentage of people over 65 years old will grow – even double – during the next 30 years. In this context, mobile technology was introduced in the hope of upgrading the services more efficient and better balanced. The original managerial vision was that better planning of working hours would lead to increased efficiency at care work. Before mobile technology, home care workers were rather independent when visiting the clients' homes during service calls. They were in charge of planning by themselves how and in which order to conduct their daily work. No official accounts were given of the service calls. All this made managerial planning a time-consuming work. Mobile technology was implemented in order to gather information about the service calls. At the time, this was seen as an innovative change to the work, but the care workers were rather unprepared to this change. Implementation of new information technology is sometimes seen as a solution, which will automatically exchange existing working practices for more modern ones (Berg 2000, McGrath 2003). In reality, implementation of new technology may bring about unexpected changes, which make the situation even more complex.

From the beginning of the implementation in home care, the rather stereotypical opinions of the workers have been that values embedded in care and in technology cannot be aligned. Negotiations or discourses with co-workers, clients and managers have been taking place as the workers have been trying to construct new technology to suit their professional identity and working practices. According to Suchman (2002), instead of viewing technical artefacts as constituting of objective knowledge, technology is debated in multiple, located and partial perspectives. Also, social home care as an organization compromises both multiple professional identities and views of others, as well as multiple representations of the work and the work of the others.

Banks (2004) debates the professional identity of a social worker and sees its origin in philanthropy and moral education of the late 19th century. In social work, professional identity and professional ethics are closely aligned: care is the core activity, and also the justification of the whole profession. In this research context, professional identity and the values it implies has been defined as a resource, which makes it possible for the workers to act skilfully in unplanned situations during a working day. In a post-modern sense, a person cannot have a definitive identity (Hall and du Gay 1996, Lamb and Davison 2002) and, as such, professional identity is also being reconstructed or negotiated in the interaction between different actors in home care. In other words, professional identity is constructed in constant discourses (Foucault 1980) and thus liable towards change. Banks (2004) argues that "the new accountability" or the rise of managerialism has in practice meant increasing levels of regulation at professional work and also a threat to professional ethics. In this implementation, technological rationalization was viewed firstly as a threat to professional independency and secondly as a threat to professional ethics as the norms and standards of behaviour of the care workers. The need for efficiency was especially found problematic in the caring profession. Quality of care would also mean investing time for each service call in order to socially interact with a client, not just taking care of his or her basic needs.

2. TECHNOLOGICAL EFFECTIVENESS

To modernize work, new technological implementations are often promoted. The manager or the designer of a new technological solution can have a view that technology will automatically have an impact on organizational culture (McGrath 2003) and will promote more efficient working practices. McGrath (2003) describes the situation as one where the attempts to implement technology in order to create organizational effectiveness may cause unintended consequences. This may in turn challenge the original objectives of the implementation project. This situation may partly be caused by what Sachs (1995) calls organizational perspective of work: seeing work consisting of sets of defined tasks and operations that can be efficiently "programmed". Sachs suggests that the work actually consists of a range of activities, communication practices, relationships and coordination, continually mediated by different actors such as workers and managers. Schoech (2002) has the opinion that in social work in particular the implementation of information and communications technology has been slower because of the complexity of human service practices in this work sector. Besides visions of future effectiveness and quality, the existing practices and organization of work, as well as the rediscovery of meaning of social services, should all be taken into consideration during designing and implementation. Scherlis and Eisenberg (2003) argue that government service providers do not necessarily want to face the risks of early adopters, and that this attitude slows implementing new technology.

According to Moon and Welch (2004), proponents of e-government believe that through technological implementations it is possible to advance in managerial efficiency and in effectiveness of the whole public sector. Opposing or more cautious views stress the potential barriers caused by technology, as well as privacy and security concerns. Turisco (2000) also views that new technological solutions have the potential to save time in routine administration and thus lead to improvement in workflow and efficiency. Scherlis and Eisenberg (2003) remind of challenges in designing e-government services. These include ubiquity of service, trustworthiness, information access, and confidentiality. Besides questions of trust and equity, Mullen and Horner (2004) arise questions of new and specific ethical issues while implementing e-Government, partly caused by a lack of well-understood rules. At the moment, evaluation of the case area – namely home care work – consists, besides of the technical implementation, of otherwise upgrading the whole social work sector to a more professional direction by defining service processes anew. Technical implementation seems to better fit to the managerial side of evaluating the work practices. The care workers, however, feel that the changes at work are constant and stressful, making them feel insecure about the future of their work. Star and Strauss (1999) discuss the vulnerable situation of workers when invisible, often so-called unskilled work is made visible. Positive outcomes are increase of legitimacy and rescue from obscurity or exploitation. More questionable outcomes are reification of work or surveillance of the workers and even increase in-group communication and process burdens. Beck (1997), for example, describes the process of changing care (often viewed as women's domestic work of little importance) into "real work" with the help of information technology, and discusses the different rationalities of care and technology. In the case of home care, especially the care workers and the clients have had problems of interpreting what was the actual purpose of the implementation project.

The rather stereotypical opinions of the workers have been that values embedded in care and in technology cannot be aligned. Banks (2004) describes the rise of managerialism in social work, which has in practice meant increasing levels of regulation at professional work and also, as such, a threat to professional ethics. In this context, especially the need for efficiency was found problematic while caring for elderly clients. In a report about developing care and services for older people, effectiveness was defined to consist of efficiency, economy, efficacy and fairness: "On an individual level, effective activities have the maximum positive impact on well-being as economically as possible. On a system level, an effective service system produces the right services by using recourses as efficiently and economically as possible." (Vaarama et al. 2001, p. 59) The new system in home care automates lot of the routine office tasks, such as making different kinds of lists and reports. It is hoped that through this "automation" more time will be saved to actual care work. This would also mean a better quality of care services on the individual level. Seeing the concept of efficiency in this view raises the question of whether the managers and workers are speaking of the same thing when discussing efficiency. During the implementation phase, the workers interpreted efficiency as meaning more service calls to handle per day or even a decrease in the number of care workers, while neither was aimed at. Care of the client can never be automated, and it was not a purpose of the implementation. Fluent interaction and creating an understanding between the different parties in an implementation project is a complex matter. In this implementation project, discussing core concepts with different groups of actors in home care might have lessened the initial resistance. For service workers, quality of care means investing time for each service call in order to socially interact with a client, not just taking care of his or her basic needs.

Appropriation of mobile technology has progressed slowly in home care. From initial resistance and doubt, the workers have progressed to a stage where they are now trying to utilize mobile technology for their own benefit. The new technology may have shaped emerging "efficient" working practices, but the workers are also shaping the technology (Orlikowski 1992) to suit their needs better by, for example, suggesting slight changes in the interface. Chance of attitudes and a growing trust in their own skills with technology has actually made the care workers more independent in their work. This also reflects to the interaction with the clients and with the care managers. In complex situations – for example when the service call does not go as previously planned – the care workers support their own views and decision-making with the information in their palm-based computers, as they can now also access the client database during service calls. The role of information is increasingly important in complex, temporally and spatially distributed work environments (Pica et al. 2004) such as in home care, where the workers are working all around the town, as well as outside normal office hours. In relationships with managers this has meant empowering the care workers.

3. ABOUT THE CASE

The implementation of mobile computers in home care began during the winter 2001. The appropriation process of new technology is still ongoing in 2005 and appears to be continuing slowly, as the care workers and their managers negotiate in interaction about the best practices of using the palm-based computers. In every team there are about 20 care workers and one manager. The city is divided between 38 care teams. Altogether, there are about 750 service workers and about 4000 clients. At the moment, the implementation has been carried out throughout the care area, and every care worker is using a palm-based computer daily. In this study, the organizational implementation was planned to be observed for several years, until the use of the new technology had been fully merged with the working practices, and some of the benefits of its use could be observed. The first aim of this study was to describe changes at work. Negotiations with the management, the designers of the new system, co-workers and with the clients take place while the workers are constructing their interpretations of the situation as intentional actors (Giddens 1984). Giddens argues that human agency has the capacity to make a difference. In this view, the actual impact of technical implementation depends upon the power or powerlessness of the perceived users, who have the capacity to transform their working practices or to resist the change.

This home care case is a research in progress, which aims for a qualitative interpretation of the change process through a longitudinal ethnographic study (Agar 1980, Geertz 1973). The main subjects of the study are the care workers, while the aim is to describe the work practices and possible changes in them as a part of every-day life. The first part of the study was carried out in two care teams that took part in the pilot phase of the implementation during the winter 2001-2002. The methods applied to the study include participant observation, interviews and group interviews. Especially at first, observation of work practices was seen not only as the most important way of getting qualitative data about the daily work, but also as a way of grounding good interactive connections between the subjects and me as a researcher. In order to find out about the internal dynamics of a care team, group sessions were also arranged. According to Orlikowski and Gash (1994), understanding the sense-making process during a technical implementation, i.e. how the workers are interpreting technology, makes it possible to understand how they interact with technology. In the second part of the study, 20 of the care managers were interviewed, and both observing and interviewing the care teams were continued. In this latter part of field work, which was started during the year 2004 and which is still continuing, one of two care teams which were visited already during the pilot phase, and a new one, taken along during the latter part of the implementation, were chosen to be the teams to be observed. The analysis of the two sets of data support each other: more informal observations give fuller understanding of the situation in the work field and, on the other hand, interviews make it possible to explore more in-depth interpretations for interesting phenomena. For the analysis, the data was classified or grouped according to the phenomena that I found interesting and relevant for the study.

Home care is a sensitive area for work and for study. Care workers visit their clients' homes to perform different tasks. To efficiently ensure the wholesome well being of a client, the worker has to have commitment for care work, as well as at least some human interaction skills. These aspects make care a meaningful activity for home care workers:

"You see the work carried out by your own hands. You feel satisfied when you know that you can leave the client alone with a good conscience – you have taken care of the client's needs and you know that he or she will manage at home."

This case has shown that, in social home care, a lot of daily decisions are based on tacit or unmentioned knowledge about the clients, as well as knowledge about the right ways to provide care. The mobile system may raise some of the unmentioned agreements between the workers to the consciousness of the whole staff.

4. WORK ETHICS IN SOCIAL CARE

One aspect of making work visible is constructing organizational reality (Foucault 1980, Harvey 1998). By raising the transparency of actions, it is possible to create open discussion about previously hidden or otherwise unmentioned aspects at work. In the contexts of this implementation, the case is as much about making mobile informatics a meaningful part of work in a care setting as breaking some of the taboos of organizational culture. Suchman (2002, p. 95) calls such cognitive, political and practical structures a "fake collectivity" while describing common assumptions "of a kind of shared reality that provides the self-evidence, for anyone within the community, of the logic of individual actions". One of these unquestioned attributes of home care has been the constant haste at work. Now the reality or possibility of the lack of constant haste has been taken into discussion as care situations and power plays at clients' homes have become more transparent.

"Yesterday I looked through the lists. I was rather surprised that there were such short service calls; many of them were only 30 or 40 minutes. But there were also longer calls, for example lasting 80 minutes; I can't think why they needed such a long call... But surprisingly lot of the service calls are short. Care workers tell me that there is nothing else to do but to chat with the client. And so I said, well, then you chat. Well, it depends on the worker; some are quicker workers, and others are no talkers."

"It depends on the people so much, some only do what's necessary, or are already planning the next service call, or are waiting for a break. It's like, some workers do it 'by the book' – only do what's necessary, but you should also ask around a little, at least if you're not in a hurry. [...] Of course, if you have a new client, you wouldn't probably look for something extra right away, but, still – when you go to a client that you have been taking care of for a long time, looking and asking around at the client's home a little – that is what makes it good care."

Bringing the sufficiency of daily working time to the open discussion helps care workers to cope with their stressful work. Moreover, the fact that some clients are more troublesome than others and, thus, can receive shorter durations of care, has in the past been a silenced or a denied discourse. There have been incidents where a worker has given her mobile computer an active role in a client relationship by telling the client that "the system" does not allow extra service tasks. One manager, for example, noticed how some of the service calls were especially short in duration. In a team meeting, it was found out that the cause for the phenomenon was an especially troublesome client, whom not all of the care workers wanted to visit for long. Now, discussions between the care workers and team managers have been taking place, and ways to cope with "problem-clients" and ways to share the load have been talked openly along with more ethical themes of care-receiver – care-giver -relationship.

In this sense, visibility of work has meant a better situation for both the care workers and the clients. Following Mullen and Horner (2004), information technology is a democratic means promoting transparency and openness, and as a consequence, a means for limiting corruption and fraud. In the future, more transparent care work would really mean more quality in the care work. According to Butler (2002, p. 240) code of ethics in social work is based on self-interest of the actors, and thus, like moral principles on which it rests, a code of ethics needs to be contextualised and situated. Such codes are not morally and ethically neutral but also, insofar, they are social artefacts themselves, and inevitably articulate the occupational, ideological and moral aspirations of their creators.

Most of the care workers have the opinion that the mobile system benefits the managers and their interpretations of efficacy more than the actual field workers, as the original aims of the mobile system was to make planning of working hours easier and to lessen the need of managerial accounting work. The managers justified the implementation by stating that less manual accounting would mean more working time saved for the care of the clients. But the care workers did not actually have a lot of manual paper work to accomplish during their working day to begin with because in the past no accounts were made. Especially during the trial phase of the implementation when problems with the updating were constant, the workers felt that the mobile system promoted a growth of "paperwork". This attitude was perfectly understandable as the workers had to fill in correction reports for unsuccessful updates manually. Furthermore, in the past when care workers were carrying out the paper work together, it was not only about documenting mandatory data. The care workers described the time together at their field office as meaningful interaction, where knowledge concerning the clients and their care was shared. Besides giving resources for problem solving, the interaction provided an important contrast to the demanding, lonely work on field, and, as such, was a way to diminish stress.

Traditionally, accountability has been understood as relations of accountability between employees and managers, but an important form of relations consists of local accountabilities (Randell 2004, Suchman 2002) i.e. of the accountabilities felt to colleagues, friends, or other communities of practice (Wenger 1998). According to Wenger (1998) informal mutual accountability between members in communities of practice is what makes interaction meaningful and creates both local understanding and awareness. Mobile computers can aid the care workers in handling unexpected situations, but even in the future, awareness about the other team members and sharing knowledge about the clients will constitute an important aspect in coping with the work and coordinating actions between different care workers.

Home care has a strong notion of situated action (Suchman 1999) despite of all the planning attached. Awareness of other workers and transparency of work that has been done already supports cooperation in mobile work (Bellotti and Bly 1996, Luff and Heath 1998). Awareness can be achieved through use of mobile technology, but mobile technology can as well mean a lack of awareness and communication problems when the created system is not working accordingly. In home care context, the system supports explicit communication, but does not make implicit communication available. In this context explicit communication consists of information such as who has visited clients, and for how long. The system does not support colloquial information such as what was the present condition and spirits of the client, or what actual care tasks were carried out. Cooperation of a care team relies on the exchange of this kind of informal information, so, in a sense, the new technology does not necessarily enhance cooperation between care workers.

5. CONCLUSIONS

Technological appropriation and learning may be progressing among care workers, but changes in client relationships are somewhat alarming. In home care, professional identity and the values it implies have meant altruism as an overall orientating philosophy to caring and to other attributes that are linked to the preservation of human dignity. But the caring profession also means exercising social control over the clients. Expert knowledge or experience is not only used to meet the needs of the clients but to also monitor them. It is understandable that besides work ethics, a municipal care worker has to remember the need for keeping records and reports, following standard procedures, coordinating work and balancing resources. But in reality, the complexity of human services and the ethics of work are viewed as somewhat contradictory to the technological rationalization of work.

Workers are stressed by the balancing of the demands of the managers and the wishes of the clients. Sometimes "going by the book" might mean overstepping the client's rights for self-determination in their own homes. In this case the backup of new technology gave the care workers a louder voice than, for example, the elderly clients. Now a service call has three actors: a client, a worker and technology. The workers seem to use palm-based computers to back up their own opinions and decisions against the possible wishes of the client. In this sense, upgrading the effectiveness of home care has meant questioning work ethics of the workers, and diminishing the possibilities of clients to decide on the arrangements of his or her daily life.

REFERENCES

Agar, M.H. (1980). *The Professional Stranger*. An Informal Introduction to Ethnography. Academic Press, Inc., San Diego, CA.

Banks S. (2004). *Ethics, Accountability and the social Professions*. Palgrave Macmillan, Bristol.

Beck, E.E. (1997). Managing Diffracted Rationalities: IT in a Home Assistance Service. In: Moser, I. & Aas G.H. (eds.): *Technology and Democracy: Gender, Technology and Politics in Transition?* Proceedings from workshop 4 of Conference "Technology and Democracy – Comparative Perspectives". University of Oslo, Centre for Technology, Innovation and Culture. TMV Skriftserie 29, 109-132.

Bellotti, V. & Bly, S. (1996). Walking away from the Desktop Computer: Distributed Collaboration and Mobility in a Product Design Team. *Proceedings of CSCW 1996*, November 16 – 20, Boston, MA, 209-218.

Berg M. (2000). Lessons from a Dinosaur: Mediating IS Research through an Analysis of the Medical Record. In: Baskerville R., Stage J. & DeGross J.I. (eds.): *Organizational and Social Perspectives on Information Technology*. IFIP WG 8.2 International Working Conference on the Social and Organizational Perspective on Research and Practice in Information Technology, June 9-11, 2000, Aalborg, Denmark. 487-504.

Butler, I. (2002). Critical Commentary. A Code of Ethics fr Social Work and Social Care Research. *British Journal of Social Work* 32, 239-248.

Foucault M. (1980). *Power/Knowledge*. Harwester, Brighter.

Geertz, C. (1973). *The Interpretation of Cultures*. Basic Books, New York.

Giddens, A. (1984). *The Constitution of Society*. Polity Press, Cambridge.

Hall S. and du Gay P. (1996). *Questions of Cultural Identity*. Sage, London.

Harvey, L. (1998). Visibility, Silencing, and Surveillance in an IT Needs Analysis Project. *Proceedings of IFIP Conference on Information systems: Current Issues and Future Changes.* Helsinki, December 10-13, 131-147.

Heath, C. & Luff, P. (1991). Collaborative activity and technological design: task coordination in London Underground control rooms. *ECSCW'91*, The Second European Conference on Computer-Supported Cooperative Work, Kluwer.

Lamb R. & Davidson E. (2002). Social Scientists: Managing Identity in Socio-Technical Networks. *Proceedings of the 35th HICSS*, Jan 7–10, Big Island, Hawaii.

McGrath K. (2003). ICTs Supporting Targetmania. How the UK Health Sector is Trying to Modernise. In: Korpela M. et al. (eds.): *Organizational Information Systems in the Context of Globalization.* IFIP WG8.2 & WG9.4 Working Conference on Information Systems Perspectives and Challenges in the Context of Globalization. June 15-17, 2003, Athens, Greece, 19-33.

Moon, M.J. & Welch, E.W. (2004). Same Bed, Different Dreams?: A Comparative Analysis of Citizen and Bureaucrat Perspectives on E-Government. *Proceedings of the 37th HICSS*, Jan 5-8, Big Island Hawaii.

Mullen, H. & Horner, S.H. (2004). Ethical Problems for e-Government: An Evaluative Framework. Electronic Journal of e-Government 2(3), 187-196. Retrieved February 20, 2005, from http://www.ejeg.com.

Orlikowski W.J. (1992). The Duality of Technology: Rethinking the concept of technology in organizations. *Organization Science* 3(3), 398–428.

Orlikowski, W.J. & Gash, D.C. (1994). Technological Frames: Making Sense of Information Technology in Organizations. *ACM Transactions on Information Systems* 12(2), 174-207.

Pica, D., Sørensen, C. & Allen D. (2004) On Mobility and context of Work: Exploring Mobile Police Work. *Proceedings of the 37th HICSS*, Jan 5-8, Big Island Hawaii.

Randell, R. (2004). Accountable technology appropriation and use. *Proceedings of the 3rd Nordic Conference on Human-Computer Interaction*, October 23-27, Tampere, Finland, 161-270.

Sachs, P. (1995). Transforming Work: Collaboration, Learning and Design. *Communications of the ACM* 38(9), 36-44.

Scherlis, W.L. & Eisenberg, J. (2003). IT Research, Innovation, and E-Government. *Communications of the ACM* 46(1), 67-68.

Star, S. L. & Strauss, A. (1999). Layers of Silence, Arenas of Voice: The Ecology of Visible and Invisible Work. *CSCW* 8, 9-30.

Suchman, L. (1999). *Plans and situated action.* The problem of human-machine

Suchman, L. (2002). Located accountabilities in technology production. *Scandinavian Journal of Information Systems*, 14(2), 91-105.

Turisco, F. (2000). Mobile Computing Is Next Technology for Healthcare Providers. *Healthcare Financial Management* 54(11), 78-81.

Vaarama, M., Luomahaara, J., Peiponen, A. & Voutilainen, P. (2001). *The Whole Municipality Working Together for Older People.* Perspectives on the Development of Elderly People's Independent Living, Care and Services. STAKES, Helsinki.

Wenger, E. (1998). *Communities of Practice: Learning, meaning, and identity.* Cambridge University Press, Cambridge.

PART 6

TECHNOLOGY, VIRTUAL REALITY AND EMERGING TECHNOLOGIES

A 21ST CENTURY ETHICAL DEBATE: PURSUING PERSPECTIVES ON AMBIENT INTELLIGENCE

Penny Duquenoy and Diane Whitehouse
Duquenoy is with the School of Computing Science, Middlesex University, London, England and Whitehouse is with ICT for Health, DG Information Society and Media, European Commission, Brussels, Belgium. The views presented are those of the authors and do not necessarily represent the official view of the European Commission on the subject

Abstract: This paper takes a broad perspective on ambient, intelligent technologies in the context of contemporary European society at the turn of the 21st century. The underlying ideas and expectations of ambient intelligence in a period when Europe focuses progressively on the various social, economic, and ethical challenges facing the Information Society are discussed. The use of information and communication technologies in different organizational and economic settings are explored, with an illustrative focus on eHealth. It is particularly argued that more space, effort and facilities need to be created for a public social and ethical debate among European's citizens with regard to information and communication technologies development.

1.   INTRODUCTION

Ambient intelligence is a concept that combines the notions of intelligent, pervasive and ubiquitous computing. Pervasive and ubiquitous computing are terms that are often used together, but describe different situations. Pervasive is used in the sense of information and communication technologies that are "everywhere, for everyone, at all times"[1], whereas

---

[1] Centre for Pervasive Computing http://www.pervasive.dk/index.html

ubiquitous refers to computers that are disappearing and becoming invisible[2]. The view of one of the major European industrial contributors to advances in the field of ambient intelligence is that it "refers to the presence of a digital environment that is sensitive, adaptive, and responsive to the presence of people. Within a home environment, ambient intelligence will improve the quality of life of people by creating the desired atmosphere and functionality via intelligent, personalized inter-connected systems and services. Ambient intelligence can be characterized by the following basic elements: ubiquity, transparency, and intelligence. Ubiquity refers to a situation in which we are surrounded by a multitude of interconnected embedded systems."[3]

In this paper, three perspectives on an intelligent environment are pursued. The aim in taking this multi-perspective approach is to deconstruct the interactions between intelligent technologies and their social application, in order to understand better the ethical issues that are contained within such a complex techno-social setting. The perspectives taken are those of the technical level, the regulatory level, and the user level.

To set the context for the discussion, an overview of ambient intelligence and its development is laid out. A defence of a multi-perspective approach follows, both as a methodology for identifying relevant issues and for examining those issues in greater detail. The discussion is then taken beyond the more general picture of ambient intelligence by focusing on a particular European application domain that has been at the forefront of information and communication technologies developments – the domain of eHealth.

Having illustrated the type of environment constructed by ambient technologies, an outline of the current situation regarding the consideration of ethics and information and communication technologies is provided. It points to a new view of the place of ethics in the immediate future.

Finally, the discussion is drawn together. It is argued that, using a multi-perspective approach is not only useful as an aid to understanding the interactions and ethical considerations in a complex domain but also provides a basis for discussion among the diverse stakeholder communities. Implicit in this argument is the belief that discussion is necessary, and that space, effort and facilities need to be created for a public social and ethical

---

[2] UbiComp conference 2001: "a new paradigm of computing off-the-desktop that moves towards the notion of a disappearing or invisible computer".

[3] Definition of ambient intelligence from www.research.philips.com/ technologies/syst_softw/ami/vision.html [accessed 24 April 05]

debate within Europe with regard to information and communication technologies development.

2. AMBIENT INTELLIGENCE AND ITS DEVELOPMENT: THE WIDER CONTEXT

Although the 'intelligent environment' is in its early days of development, the notions it captures are not confined to research institutions. In 2005, even taxi drivers talk knowledgeably about the concept of the intelligent fridge and its ordering of the week's grocery shopping from the local supermarket – concepts formulated in the mid-1990s (Buxton, 1996) and operationalized by a number of software developers and appliance manufacturers *circa* 2000[4].

Ambient intelligence is a concept developed over the past decade as a vision for the future, and which is backed in Europe today by a considerable amount of research both academic and applied. These types of applications are at different stages of development: either, currently at the research stage; even early development; and – in some cases – at the stage of application and deployment. However, they are generally based on existing computing technologies integrated with concepts from artificial intelligence, where the technological foundations already exist.

Ambient intelligence combines developments in information and communication technologies with notions of 'pervasive' and 'ubiquitous' computing, and describes an intelligent environment operating in the background in an invisible and non-intrusive way. The vision of ambient intelligence is of an environment where computer intelligence is used to enhance the operation of daily activities, and to assist individuals and organizations in the management of their lives.

In the home, ambient intelligence can respond to individual preferences and requirements in lighting, heating, entertainment – adjusting room conditions as appropriate[5]. In the office, among the many possible applications, it can be used to encourage working relationships by enhancing

---

[4] 'The Smart Home Revisited' (March 2000) http://www.throughtheloop.com/ [accessed 17 April 2005] and 'Recipe for success – the kitchen of the future' http://www.vnunet.com/features/601712 (5 April 2000) [accessed 17 April 2005]

[5] For example, "A Pervasive Identification and Adaptation System for the Smart House" (Rosa *et al*, 2004) and "Interaction in sensitive house – future room that sense human mood and responds to it" (Thomas 2004).

and emphasizing group discussions around the coffee machine. In the domain of handheld and mobile devices it will provide context-sensitive information to users, based on location and user profile[6]. Ambient intelligence will also play an important role in healthcare, coordinating information between medical implants and diagnostic databases, and making that information available to health carers[7].

Communicating intelligent devices are foreseen as being embedded in such diverse locations as the environment at large, homes, vehicles, mobile devices, fabrics, wearable devices, and the body – in other words, almost everywhere. Not all intelligent devices – smart clothing for example – are yet intended for network-to-network communications use. Nevertheless, it is a short step from smart clothing that can not only inform the user of low blood sugar levels but that can also contact local medical aid centres.

Such developments in information and communication technologies have raised public concern regarding ethical issues. On the one hand, the incorporation of information technologies within the social sphere is as yet at a comparatively early stage. Many of the effects and impacts are unfamiliar to users within this new context of use. Thus, legislation and appropriate ethical principles have not yet been implicitly incorporated into the general application areas under development. On the other hand, although the medical informatics domain is well served as far as ethical principles and legislation are concerned – since this is a field in which such issues have traditionally been extremely adequately covered – a number of inter-disciplinary areas of research, such as biological, genomic, and proteonomic research are now coming together. In this innovative merging of cross-scientific disciplines, they may pose new social and ethical considerations.

Because such technologies form part of a complex system of devices that directly inform interactions between the personal/private and the public/social domain, it is argued that a broader perspective is needed in order to fully appreciate the dynamics of the interactions, and their impacts in a wider setting. This multi-perspective and holistic notion of ambient intelligence – a view that all the issues raised are more than the sum of their

---

[6] For example EurEauWeb (EURopEAn WatErways networked information system) funded under the Fifth Framework Programme – see http://www.ipsi.fraunhofer.de/oasys/projects/eureauweb/index_e.html [accessed 24 April 05],
and a software agent funded by consumer electronic companies (such as Nokia, Sony and Vodaphone). (Graham-Rowe, 2003).

[7] IST-2001-36006 Mobihealth http://www.mobihealth.org/

individual parts – is now explored. It brings to the fore a social and ethical analysis of the considerations of the domain.

3.   A HOLISTIC AND MULTI-PERSPECTIVE VIEW OF AMBIENT INTELLIGENCE

While current research initiatives in this field aim individually and even collectively at bringing benefits, it is not enough to focus simply on technical feasibility or achievement. Technology is situated in a specific context (Suchman, 1987). The context of ambient intelligent systems is diverse and, in some cases, far-reaching; for example, if used within the context of a global network.

The intelligent fridge is a recognisable example of the type of 'intelligent, personalized inter-connected systems and services' that have captured the public imagination. However, this example, while familiar and seemingly simple, does not convey either the complexity within the information system itself or, indeed, the increased integration and interrelationships of the 'multitude of interconnected embedded systems'. There are particular challenges raised by the sophistication of these systems in an ambient intelligent environment. This is not only because the operations are invisible, but also because the exchange of information between diverse systems and stakeholders is likely to be made based on decisions of intelligent agents.

By viewing a system from different perspectives, it is possible to become aware of the diverse interactions and relationships of the system. From that foundation, one can see the challenges that need to be considered from the broader whole-system view.

Allen's (2004) work on a social analysis of ubiquitous information systems describes how a range of perspectives bring out differing properties of a system. It further identifies how the various technical communities have diverse views on the wider implications of their products. Allen uses this bottom-up approach to bring out the assumptions of the different communities, and to clarify the value conflicts and social choices in the development process.

To begin with, Allen distinguishes between the material aspect of technology, and its symbolic vision. He notes that at the *material* level the technological community has a vision of the exemplary artefact described by its physical form, and how it should be built. The *symbolic* level describes the problems the artefact will solve, together with the key performance criteria (those aspects that need to be present to produce a successful solution). Table 1 below summarizes these points.

Table 1: Multi-perspective approach, following Allen (2004)

The material level (the artefact)	• Description of physical form and how it should be built
The symbolic level	• The problems to be solved • Key performance criteria (aspects to be satisfied to produce a successful solution)

Allen applies this framework to clarify the scope of the different technological communities within the domain of ambient intelligence. These communities are the embedded computing community, the pervasive computing community, and the ubiquitous computing community. He then examines the assumptions made by each community with regard to the social relationships surrounding their creations. Table 2 below details the key points of Allen's findings.

Table 2: Multi-perspective approach to research communities, following Allen (2004)

Embedded computing community	• Focuses on interactions between individuals, but fails to examine the broader social context.
Pervasive computing community	• Is sensitive to local conditions • Places emphasis on cooperation and egalitarianism
Ubiquitous computing community	• Considers user control as central[8] • Concentrates on the system level

This paper takes a similarly structured approach, but adopts the various perspectives relevant to a system of ambient intelligence embedded in the social infrastructure. It contrasts with Allen's work, however, in so far as it is a top-down approach: it begins with the whole system and then

---

[8] Allen notes the dilemma of attempting to maintain user control of a technology that is seamless and unobtrusive (2004: 15).

deconstructs it, by taking three separate perspectives. These three approaches are: the technical infrastructure, regulation, and the individual user experience. These concepts are outlined in Table 3 below, and are explored in more detail in the three sections that follow.

Table 3: Multi-perspective approach to ambient intelligence

Technical infrastructure **(the architectural level)**	• Compatibility • Availability of resources • Reliability • Dependability
Regulation **(the legal and regulatory level)**	• Informal self-regulation • Formal legislation • Local compliance • International enforcement • Conflict of governmental and/or commercial interests with private/ individual interests
The user experience **(the level of the individual user)**	• Information overload • Information management • Personal control • Choice of use

3.1 Technical Infrastructure

At the architectural level, four areas of importance are identified with regard to the technical infrastructure: compatibility, availability of resources, reliability, and dependability. These reflections could also be extended to aspects of software applications.

Assuming that many applications will be operating in a wider networked environment, a key consideration must be *compatibility* across platforms and with other relevant applications. In itself, achieving compatibility is not a trivial task and, even at the level of applications available today, it is a considerable preoccupation of the computing science community. Consider, for example, the integration of intelligent systems as everyday appliances in the home, at work and in the environment. In order for such systems to work 'seamlessly' – which is considered to be one of the essential requirements of future technologies – all systems must be compatible. This compatibility clearly does not exist at present – rather, the rapid advances in applications result in a constant 'catch-up' process and variances between applications and versions.

A second consideration is the *availability of technical resources*, or the lack of them, in terms of bandwidth, storage, and processing power. Users have been assured by reports in the media over the years that these resources are increasing and are becoming less costly. While this is true to a certain extent, in practice there appears to be a constant need to upgrade equipment and services in order to gain the full benefit of what available systems can offer. It is never long before the systems are struggling to cope with the demands of new applications. How often at work, for instance, are we constrained by the limits of computer memory and storage? If the role of intelligent technologies is to underpin daily life, it will not be good enough for users to exist at a level of 'barely coping'.

Finally in this context, the issues of *reliability* and *dependability* are raised. These are key concerns within the computing community not only where systems are safety critical, but also when a loss of confidence by users would have a serious impact on uptake. Some of the specific issues that have been identified within this area are: loss of use; data vulnerability during transmission –for example, from a malicious attack; and safety aspects – where the technology is deployed within societal infrastructures such as traffic management systems (Simoncini *et al*, 2004). These same authors remark on the difficulties of predicting the effects within complex systems:

> "[t]he propagation and cascading effects that can derive from the failure of single elements might cause effects that are unforeseeable at first sight", and further note that it is "misleading to understand each dependability attribute in isolation" (Ibid: 303)

3.2   Regulation

The legal and regulatory circumstances surrounding ambient intelligence are of considerable importance. As well as the multi-tiered levels of types of regulation (informal self regulation through to formal legislation) systems need to be compliant with legislation both locally and, where appropriate, globally[9]. There are a number of challenges that are causing concern at the present time – privacy, intellectual property, and other types of computer misuse common to the Internet – that are extremely difficult to address technologically and enforce internationally.

---

[9] See, for example, the chapter by Berleur and Poullet in this volume on ethical aspects of the Internet.

At an ethical level, consideration must be given to how cultural diversity in social norms and practices can be reconciled in the use of intelligent technologies and, at the political level, it is necessary to consider the power balance between government (and commercial) interests with private (individual) interests. This dilemma is particularly important at the early stages of development when funding comes from government and industry (e.g., Gallant, 2004).

3.3   The Individual User Experience

For individual users, challenges arise from information overload, information management, personal control and choice of use. The introduction of today's technologies has resulted in a considerable cognitive load for users. Proponents of ambient intelligence would no doubt argue that the cognitive load will be reduced by virtue of the 'invisible' and 'seamless' characteristics of technology. The trade-off, however, for the user, could be loss of personal control in a number of areas: the validity and integrity of the information being processed; user orientations, such as cultural[10] preferences; personal control of the use of information (for example, third party use of personal information); and personal choice in taking advantage of the technologies especially where the technologies are used in places which were previously recognized as 'private' – such as, in the home, in clothing, and in the body.

3.4   Ethical Issues Arising from Taking a Holistic, Multi-Perspective View

Thus, the ambient environment has been deconstructed into the three perspectives of technical infrastructure, regulation, and individual user experience. The analysis developed has been used to identify the main ethical challenges apparent in these fields. Thus, the analysis can be used to present more clearly the ethical issues within the system.

The technical aspects have potential ethical impacts on users in several areas:

* Compatibility: a user may be tied in to a particular set of system applications or may be forced to upgrade to maintain compatibility. This, in turn, raises issues of affordability and opportunity for equal access.

---

[10] Cultural is used here in a broader sense – not necessarily national culture.

- Availability of resources: If bandwidth, storage, or download time are scarce resources, the question of prioritizing use becomes an issue. In the ambient environment scenario, some communications are likely to be more important than others. The challenge becomes: Important to whom? Who decides the priorities of use? Is the prime decision-maker the user, the marketplace, the government, or individual members of the design team?
- Reliability and dependability: For the user, there are likely to be circumstances where ambient systems are life-critical (in the eHealth domain, for example). However, even in less critical circumstances, users need to know how reliable they can expect the systems to be or whether an alert will be given when any problems arise.

As far as regulation is concerned, the main ethical concerns will occur where regulation is applied globally to diverse cultural groups. One nation's law does not necessarily fit together with the cultural or religious beliefs of another. Where compliance with legislation is written into the software applications used, an additional dilemma is raised. Users could be forced to submit to legislation that may not be applicable to their own country or culture. This is a complex situation which certainly involves different layers of regulation, many of which are not legislatively-based or mandatory, and may even be relatively informal in their character. A certain flexibility in approach towards localization of approaches, and openness to national, regional, and domestic adaptation may therefore be necessary.

At the level of the individual user, a raft of ethical issues may need consideration. These are mainly due to the lack of knowledge and control that a user may have of the system (particularly where systems are invisible). If it is accepted that informed consent is a key principle of ethical interactions, one should ask to what extent and in what way, using what methods, the particular user is "informed". An additional issue that should be taken into consideration in any design of these systems is user privacy. With the increased use of information systems in society, this is becoming an issue of major social concern. With the growing invisibility of technologies, the potential opportunity for abuse of privacy requirements increases. A more obvious issue as far as privacy is concerned, is the collection and storage of personal information that is necessary for user-profiling. Such data collection needs careful management (such as security in storage, transmission and third party use), with regard to the personal information that is likely to be collected in the home, in clothing, through vital signs measured close to or within the body. This is to ensure that the system provides the precise service that the system has been designed and specified to provide. In addition to these information management, control, and choice of use issues, the user may experience information overload. However, this is a concern which perhaps poses fewer ethical than psychological or occupational and health and safety concerns. The degree and intensity of such concerns may well differ according to the social and cultural background of the particular user environment into which such invisible technologies are introduced.

To conclude, each of these three levels – the technical, the regulatory and, ultimately, the user – are linked and each poses at least one ethical consideration. For example, reliability may affect privacy; compatibility extends to regulation – particularly in a global context; and the invisibility of the system, while bringing benefits to the user, also raises a certain number of concerns.

4. WHERE ARE WE TODAY? E-HEALTH AS A SPECIFIC EXAMPLE

Healthcare systems around the globe are currently facing major challenges[11]. For the Member States of the European Union, these challenges include – but are not limited to:

- a rising demand for health and social services, due to an ageing population and higher income and educational levels.
- the increasing expectations of citizens who want the best care available, and at the same time to experience a reduction in inequalities in access to good health care;
- increasing mobility of patients[12] and health professionals including the opening of the internal markets in services – that are likely to result in a higher demand for reimbursable cross-border healthcare products and services[13];

---

[11]COM (2001)723 final The future of health care and care for the elderly: guaranteeing accessibility, quality and financial viability

[12] COM(2004) 301 Follow-up to the high level reflection process on patient mobility and healthcare developments in the European Union

[13] Regulation 1408/71 that co-ordinates social security legal schemes was amended in 2004 to streamline and modernise access to health care across borders, particularly when undue delays occur in the patient's home Member State. In January 2004, the Commission tabled a proposal for a directive on freedom of provision of services which laid down a framework for the provision of health care services in the internal market and for their reimbursement by the relevant health insurance institutions.

- the need to reduce the so-called 'disease burden'[14], and to respond to emerging disease risks;
- the difficulties experienced by public authorities in matching investment in technology with investment in the complex organizational changes needed to exploit its potential;
- management of huge amounts of health information that need to be available securely, accessibly, and in a timely manner at the point of need, processed efficiently for administrative purposes, and
- the need to provide the best possible health care under limited budgetary conditions.

The recognition of these challenges to the field of healthcare provision has culminated in the publication of a Commission Communication[15] which advocates concentration on the concept of a European eHealth Area. It has been determined that this Area will be implemented throughout the next five-year period until 2010, focusing in particular on the need for interoperability of systems while continuing to bear in mind the important consideration of subsidiarity and the principle of Member State's domestic responsibility for healthcare provision.

The challenges outlined in this eHealth Communication are principally political, social, organizational, and economic. Relatively few are legal and regulatory, and even fewer are ethical in orientation. This is because such challenges are based on tried and tested eHealth technologies, developed over a 30-year period of research and development (Wilson, Leitner, & Moussalli, 2004; Wilson, 2005), and are relatively close to deployment and implementation.

Any treatment of legal and regulatory issues in eHealth is, however, likely to cover issues such as the collection and sharing of health-related data, use or sale of health-related products, privacy and data protection, use of electronic signatures, delivery of eHealthcare, eCommerce in health, ePharmacies, and cross-border access to healthcare provided electronically.

Nevertheless, there are on the horizon a number of potentially more challenging eHealth developments. As technologies and sciences converge, exciting new disciplines and domains are emerging. One example is that of

---

[14] The disease burden is a measure of the health of a population and quantifies the total impact of disease in terms of incidence, mortality, disability, and the cost of illness.

[15] COM(2004)356 *e-Health – making healthcare better for European citizens: An action plan for   a   European   e-Health   Area* http://europa.eu.int/information_society/policy/healthsites/eh_action_plan/index_en.htm

biomedical information. Research is beginning to concentrate on innovative information and communication technologies' systems and services that process, integrate and use all relevant biomedical information for improving health knowledge and processes related to prevention, diagnosis, treatment, and personalisation of health care. They are likely to integrate data through a range of mechanisms – for example, modelling, visualization, data mining, and use of large-scale Grid technologies. The kinds of data to be manipulated will include not only information related to tissues, organs, or about the person him/herself, but could also be applied at the level of molecules and cells acquired from genomics or proteomics research.

The use of biomedical data, including molecular and proteonomic data has implications not only for the individual's health status, but also for that of his/her extended family (older relations as well as offspring). Under such circumstances, it is important to ensure that the appropriate principles of privacy, confidentiality, and control of misuse of information are maintained. In this regard, for example, the Eurostem Partnership (2004) has drafted a thoughtful ethical framework for research performance (see also, for example, Joliff-Botrel, Caro, and Sommers, 2004).

Generally, these new areas of exploration will cast light on innovative methods and systems for improved medical knowledge discovery and understanding. The proposed systems and services will undoubtedly be required to demonstrate tangible, measurable, benefits, and to remain user-friendly while at the same time respecting all aspects of confidentiality and privacy.

More specific and currently rapidly developing areas of ambient intelligence are those of *ICT implants* (which may be either medical or non-medical); *smart environments* (particularly textiles); and the use of *nano- and micro-technologies*. These three domains of the information and communication technologies that can be used in eHealth are explored here briefly, in order to give a flavour of some of the potential social and ethical considerations arising in the field.

At the start of 2005, the European Group on Ethics[16] saw it as appropriate to explore the ethical implications of both medical and non-medical *information and communication technologies implants*. In issuing a new

---

[16] The European Group on Ethics is a neutral, independent, pluralist and multidisciplinary body which advises the European Commission on ethical aspects of science and new technologies in connection with the preparation and implantation of Community legislation or policies http://europa.eu.int/comm/european_group_ethics/index_en.htm

Opinion, the Group took as its basis the precautionary principle and drew on a number of well-established, health-related principles: to 'do no harm'; to ensure informed consent, autonomy, patient choice, privacy and confidentiality of personally identifiable data; and to protect both human dignity in general and minors (children). The Group's Opinion starts from classic social science and philosophical approaches regarding forms of social control, and the nature of identity and of being.

The Opinion strongly advocated in its recommendations that: information and communication technologies implants as a form of remote control are unacceptable; information and communication technologies implants should be based on need rather than economic resources or social prestige; surveillance issues in relation to implants need to be approved and monitored by an independent court; and, finally, there should be a launch of a 'legislative initiative' in relation to the directive on medical devices in relation to implantable devices. This statement is hence a recognition of the potential ethical implications of implants, and the need for extensive discussion at ethical and philosophical levels in the field of medicine and elsewhere.

In terms of *smart environments*, the potential ethical aspects of intelligent textiles when used for health and medical purposes can be explored in greater detail (Whitehouse, *forthcoming*). Such questions can cover: the impact of the availability of self-monitoring on the wearer; the possible abuse of information; the balancing of benefits and disadvantages; equity and fair access to the benefits of smart textiles; experiments involving human and non-humans; and possible impacts of smart textiles on the environment.

In the field of *nano-technologies*, for example, it is also possible to imagine how these might be used to facilitate drug-delivery or the clearance of arteries (Klerkx, 2005).

Among other current technologies finding applications in health-related domains are those relating to wireless networks, Grid technologies, and eyegaze technologies. These cover both infrastructure and control techniques, and their social implications are increasingly well covered in recent prospective technology assessments and reports (for example, European Commission, 2005).

5.   ETHICALLY, WHERE ARE WE HEADING?

Members of the International Federation for Information Processing (IFIP) Working Group on Computers and Social Accountability (WG9.2) and others, have considered the ways in which invasive and ambient technologies will increasingly affect people's lives (Berleur *et al*, 1990; Beardon & Whitehouse, 1993; Berleur & Whitehouse, 1997; ISTAG, 2003). Some of the upcoming technologies contain tremendous potential to improve the situation of human beings, including their health and general goodwill. However, they also open up possibilities for invasion of security and privacy – if the regulations and behaviours that have been so carefully created over the decades to craft the use of technologies are not fully respected. It is certainly important to maintain a balance between "the technologies that are helping humanity to achieve greater heights and people's right to security, privacy, safety and health" (Masurkur, *et al*, 2004).

Technologies such as these can be seen as challenging, and demanding of a certain amount of ethical reflection and consideration. There is a need to show care and discretion as socially, scientifically, and technologically, shifts in opinion occur and boundaries are crossed that were traditionally protected and respected. Such dialogue is not necessarily, however, about curtailing scientific progress.

For some time, there has been a growing well of concern with regard to the ethical issues surrounding information and communication technologies. The current rapid and dynamic pace of technological change indicates that the characteristic process of 'catch-up', in legal and regulatory terms, that was prevalent in the last century will not meet the needs of the 21st century. At least three levels of commitment are required (Holvast, Duquenoy and Whitehouse, 2005, p.150):

> "First of all we have to be convinced that technique is not autonomous but can in a way be predicted and controlled. The three stages of development in social consequences of information communication technologies – awareness, scientific knowledge and political willingness – must be integrated. In controlling technique a combination of reactive, participatory and anticipatory control is necessary."

Protective approaches which rely on the uniquely legislative will be insufficient. Rather, new initiatives will have to be put into place. These include different forms of technology development, the creation of new research agendas, and various forms of user involvement and awareness-raising, dissemination, education, and stakeholder engagement

Ethical ways of thinking need to be encapsulated within the very process of the research itself, probably based on multi-disciplinary or interdisciplinary perspectives. A more informed and balanced analysis of the potential social and ethical implications of technology would, it is hoped, be the result.

All information and communication technologies-related European Union research and development proposals currently undergo a rigorous ethical review procedure. The observations which emerge from the review committee are considered to be useful in the negotiation stage of any project, and they ensure that the proper procedures are put in place during the duration of the project if they were previously missing in the research proposal.

European Member States also have their own ethics and research councils. A Forum of National Ethics Councils was set up in 2002; its membership is composed of the chairs and secretaries of national ethics committees, and it provides an independent informal platform for the exchange of information, experience and good practices on issues of common interest in the field of ethics and science. Topics covered include the ethical aspects of the life sciences, biotechnology, agriculture, food safety, and health. There are similar bodies in the countries which are considering accession to the European Union. Clearly also, on an international front, many of the leading countries throughout the globe also possess such organizations and structures.

On the industrial front, the information and communication technologies sector could do more to encourage a sense of social and ethical responsibility on the part of its member companies, especially in terms of appropriate development of user requirements and on the design side. It may be that researchers and developers are unaware of the social and ethical implications of their work. Researchers and developers should be encouraged to be more ethically aware, to recognize which areas of their work might potentially raise ethical concerns, and to embrace such questioning and awareness-raising more willingly and openly. A similar openness should be encouraged on the part of the project managers leading research programmes.

In-house within an organization, it is possible to institute approaches that raise levels of introspection and concern, as were piloted during the years 2003-2004 in the European Commission Directorate-General for Information Society and Media. These included an informal ethics network, various ethics-related seminars, and two sets of public ethics and ICT workshops that culminated in a report from external experts[17].

Large companies have also introduced such processes and procedures, although illustrations and more precise details of such cases are not furnished here. An exploration of different organizational and industrial approaches is likely to form the subject of a proposed round table or workshop to take place under the auspices of the International Federation for Information Processing in 2006.

A number of the concerns in this paper arose following a topical session on ambient intelligence in 2004 which focused on infrastructure, governance, applications, and ethics[18]. Papers were presented to an audience representing both technical and social science communities. The combination of perspectives enriched the discussions, and introduced new ideas to those involved. The benefits of these types of event should not be underestimated, as the different communities grasp opportunities to understand a different perspective. The results of the discussion were not captured in the preliminary published document (Masurkar *et al*, 2004), and are therefore summarized below in Table 4 (adapted from that document).

---

[17] http://europa.eu.int/information_society/research/ethics_141004/index_en.htm
[18] The session took place at the World Computer Congress in Toulouse in summer 2004 and was organised by Vijay Masurkar and colleagues.

Table 4: Perspectives on ambient intelligence

Area of concern	Raises issues relating to
Infrastructure	• Security • Privacy • Maintenance and obsolescence ('catch-up')
Governance	• Accountability • Professional and occupational communities • Doing science means doing politics • Pluralism • Accountability
eHealth	• Multi-agency collaboration • Stakeholder involvement • Citizen involvement
Ethics	• Political interests and negotiation the influence of the social context on designers • Giving users choice

At the end of the day, it is the process of involving all the appropriate stakeholders in an ethical dialogue which is key. These stakeholders can involve important decision-makers, industrialists, managers, researchers, all aspects of information and communication technologies professions and occupations, specialist users, generalist users, and the public at large.

6. WHAT OF THE IMMEDIATE FUTURE BOTH TECHNOLOGICALLY AND ETHICALLY?

As information and communication technologies become more invasive and ambient, they challenge many previously accepted social and ethical norms with regard to autonomy, independence, privacy, and the nature of the self. Both informed public debate and discussion in the media are of tremendous importance.

It is clear that these and other related ethical issues are likely to become increasingly more public in profile, and will not disappear in the immediate period. As patient and citizen advocacy grows, citizens are likely to become more and more involved in the debate about the ethics of technologies and to want to get clearer, more detailed, and unambiguous information. They will want to be reassured that research is conducted appropriately, and that deployment bears serious concern for users in mind.

One need only look back to the period in the mid-1990s: then, much of the media exploded with a plethora of coverage of the social and ethical issues relating to the birth of the Internet (such as the use and abuse of data, freedom of speech, and privacy of data). With this example, it is possible to recognize what may happen as new technological developments in the field of ambient intelligence emerge.

New generations and adaptations of ambient intelligence are developing, and new social and ethical questions with them. While the basic ethical questions may remain fundamentally the same, the challenge is that the work of scientists, researchers, developers, and manufacturers is entering new areas of technical and technological domains that traverse disciplines that have traditionally been separated and distinct. However, regulation should not provide an excuse to inhibit or restrain scientific advancement. Rather, it offers an opportunity for reflection on both the European continent and wider using a coherent, collaborative approach that encourages sharing of values across the Union.

In the coming decade, societies will need to optimize the benefits and reduce the risks of information and communication technologies overall, by concentrating on the advantages that can be offered to citizens. eHealth is only one example of a set of technologies that are now being used in a field that was always traditionally particularly socially oriented, and involved a great deal of human care.

Socially aware societies will now wish to pay special attention to addressing technology assessment through mechanisms like user workshops. They will wish to pay particular note of developments in specific fields, such as eHealth. There, the focus is likely to be on appropriate implementation and deployment, as well as issues of access, quality of care, the economics of care, patient safety, and reduction in medical error.

7. SUMMARY AND CONCLUSIONS

This paper offers its readers a flavour of the scope of ambient intelligence and the range of applications that are foreseen. Rather than focusing on individual applications, it emphasizes a range of roles in a networked and communicating environment. Only by taking this holistic view can the real challenges that these technologies may raise be fully appreciated. Intelligent devices – even in a network – do not operate in isolation, but are embedded in a social context and have an impact on individuals as users. Therefore, as they are introduced into the various environments and cultures within which they will be used, consideration must be given to policies and regulation, and to the rights of individuals to retain some control over their use. If these artefacts are to bring benefits to citizens rather than disadvantages, a consideration of potential ethical impact must be included in the vision.

The domain of eHealth has been paid particular attention. This paper has explored the benefits not only of immediate eHealth applications, but of longer-term developments such as biomedical informatics and the processing of large-scale health data using HealthGrid technologies.

Medical and health practice has always traditionally been an area that has been alert and sensitive to ethical behaviour and performance. So too, the use of information and communication technology implants, smart environments (particularly textiles, wearables, and implantables), and nano- and micro-technologies are generally well defined in terms of ethical principles. However, as scientists push the research envelope further – especially when technologies converge – it is always necessary to remain cautious and vigilant with regard to future directions and possibilities.

In today's construction of an intelligent world, an environment is being created with a set of dynamics and relationships that were hitherto unknown. Experience has been gained in the medical field, and more recently in the field of informatics, of the ethical implications of these constructs. It is therefore strongly recommended that previous experience is used to pursue new perspectives in the domain of ambient intelligence, that:

- advance the ethical analysis
- ensure that new organizational processes are ethically sensitive, and
- recognize that future and emerging technologies will continue to come onto the horizon and will challenge historical concepts of legitimacy and what may have been considered as 'right' or 'wrong'.

Diverse perspectives can bring different approaches, for example, from different communities (Allen, 2004). Such a multi-perspective approach is not only useful for purposes of analysis, but also provides a basis for discussion within the diverse stakeholder communities (Masurkar *et al*, 2004). As a result, it is especially recommended to creating spaces for discussion – that give consideration to the ethical perspective – as part of a proactive and yet circumspect vision of emerging and future technologies.

In the latter half of the 20th century, and particularly since the 1970s, the debate surrounding the ethics of new technologies has been considerably expanded (Holvast, Duquenoy, and Whitehouse, 2005). We believe that, at the dawn of the 21st century, an open debate on the ethics of computing is particularly pertinent. It should be conducted not simply using a theoretically-based model but in a way that is applied to technologies that are currently in development or are likely to be developed in the next 10-15-year period.

It is, therefore, appropriate at this stage of development to take a broad and multi-perspective view of such technologies – taking into account the many different interactions that will be needed to take place between the technology and the society within which it operates. From this broader view, citizens can more easily appreciate the full context of application of ambient intelligence and give consideration to its social and ethical dimensions.

ACKNOWLEDGEMENTS

The authors would especially like to thank Julie Cameron, Gérard Comyn, Sofie Nørager, Silas Olsson, and Chris Zielinski for their careful reading of various early drafts of this paper. Any errors remaining in the paper are nevertheless the responsibility of the authors.

REFERENCES

Allen, J. P. "The Social Analysis of Ubiquitous IT" in *Challenges for the Citizen of the Information Society*, edited by Bynum, T.W., N. Pouloudi, S. Rogerson and T. Spyrou, ETHICOMP 2004. 2004. pp. 7-16.

Beardon C. & D. Whitehouse, (editors). *Computers and Society: Citizenship in the information age*. Intellect Press: Oxford. 1993

Berleur J. & D. Whitehouse (editors). *An Ethical Global Information Society. Culture and Democracy Revisited*. Chapman & Hall: London. 1997

Berleur, J., A. Clement, R. Sizer, & D. Whitehouse (editors). *The Information Society: Evolving Landscapes. Report from Namur*. Springer-Verlag: New York & Captus University Publications: North York. 1990

Berleur, J., P. Duquenoy, J. Holvast, M. Jones, K. Kimppa, R. Sizer, D. Whitehouse, on behalf of IFIP-SIG9.2.2, *Criteria and Procedures for Developing Codes of Ethics or of Conduct: to promote discussion inside the IFIP National Societies*. IFIP Press: Laxenberg – Austria. 2004

Berleur, J & Y. Poullet (this volume – in press). What governance and regulation for the Internet? Ethical issues. *Landscapes: Volume 2*. Springer Verlag: Frankfurt.

Buxton, W. "Absorbing and Squeezing Out: On Sponges and Ubiquitous Computing", *Proceedings of the International Broadcasting Symposium*, November 13-16, Tokyo, pp91-96. 1996

European Commission. *Biometrics at the Frontiers: Assessing the Impact on Society*. For the European Parliament Committee on Citizens' Freedoms and Rights, Justics and Home Affairs (LIBE). Technical report EUR 21585 EN. European Commission, Joint Research Centre. February 2005. 2005

Eurostem Partnership, Draft *Ethical Framework Document*, Athens, Greece, October 7-10, 2004

Gallant, S. "It's not about the technology: legal and ethical challenges in delivering citizen-focused e-Health services" *Med-e-Tel, 2005*. 2005

Graham-Rowe, D. Smart Cellphone Would Spend Your Money, *New Scientist*, November 2003.

Holvast, J., P. Duquenoy & D. Whitehouse, " The Information Society and its Consequences: lessons from the past" in *Perspectives and Policies on ICT in Society*, edited by J. Berleur and C. Avgerou, Springer & SBS Media. 2005

Joliff-Botrel, G., Caro, S. & H. Sommers, *Stem cell research at European level*. Brussels, Belgium, pp56-58. October 2004

Klerkx, G. (2005) The immortals' club. *The New Scientist*. April 9 2005, pp38-41

Masurkar, V., P. Duquenoy, E. Mordini, & D. Whitehouse. "Perspectives on Ambient Intelligence". Topical Session 18th IFIP World Computer Congress, Toulouse, France 22-27 August 2004. In *Building the Information Society* edited by R. Jacquart, Kluwer Academic Publishers. pp. 575-602. 2004

Rosa P.F.F., S.S. Lima, W.T Botelho, A.F. Nascimento & M.S. Alaluna. "A Pervasive Identification and Adaptation System for the Smart House". *Proceedings of the 18th IFIP World Computer Congress*, Toulouse, France. 22-27 August 2004.

Simoncini, L., F. Di Giandomenico, A. Bonda Valli, & S. Chiaradonna. "Architectural challenges for a dependable Information Society" in *Building the Information Society*, edited by R. Jacquart, Kluwer Academic Publishers. pp. 283-304. 2004

Suchman, L. A. *Plans and Situated Action: The Problem of Human-Machine Communication*. Cambridge University Press. 1987

Thomas, H. "Interaction in a sensitive house: future room that senses human mood and responds to it" in *Building the Information Society*, edited by R. Jacquart, Kluwer Academic Publishers. pp. 71-75. 2004

Whitehouse, D. *(forthcoming)*. Ethical aspects. In *Smart textiles for medicine and healthcare: materilals, systems, and applications*, edited by L. van Langenhove. Woodhead Publishing Limited: Cambridge. 2005.

Wilson, P. 2005 *eHealth – Building on strength to provide better healthcare anytime anywhere*. Published in conjunction with the eHealth 2005 conference, Trømso, Norway, May 2005. 2005. http://www.ehealth2005.no

Wilson, P., C. Leitner & A. Moussalli. *Mapping the potential of eHealth. Empowering the citizen through eHealth tools and services*. European Institute of Public Administration, Maastricht, the Netherlands. 2004

SOCIAL AND ETHICAL ASPECTS OF IPV6

Chris Zielinski
Independent Consultant, Geneva, Switzerland, czielinski@supanet.com

Abstract: The Internet Protocol version 6 (or IPv6) is designed to replace the current version (IPv4), which is now over 25 years old. Three main categories of social and ethical issues arise in connection with IPv6: issues relating to the right to an IP address, issues related to the application of the technology, and issues related to governance. There are many societal benefits of IPv6, as it will enable once more to have end-to-end security of transmission. Nevertheless, the governance of this deployment now and in the coming years needs to be neutral and controlled, and the governance of the IPv6 Internet that emerges after deployment must be transparent and accountable. Any mistakes we make now will be very costly in terms of loss of existing personal freedoms. This paper will explore these issues.

1.   INTRODUCTION

Most of the ethical and social issues that arise in the use and development of the Internet have to do with access to and integrity of information (whether personal or public). It can be argued that most of these issues arise in the analogue world as well, and that they are not the products of technological advance.

Nevertheless, there are issues which have been completely transformed by the introduction of digital technology, either in their nature and scope, or as a result of a massive change in scale, such as those which, it will be argued, will be experienced in the shift from the Internet based on IPv4 and that enabled by IPv6. These issues are the subject of this paper.

In a short Request for Comments on "Ethics and the Internet" written in January 1989 by the Network Working Group, Internet Activities Board (RFC 1087), it was possible to say, "Access to and use of the Internet is a privilege and should be treated as such by all users of this system". The notion that access to the Internet was a privilege was perfectly acceptable for something which was seen as a resource used exclusively for academic research. In the scant years since the publication of this RFC, many people consider access to and use of the Internet as a *right*, largely on account of its extraordinary diffusion since then.

The RFC further endorsed a US National Science Foundation statement which "characterized as unethical and unacceptable any activity which purposely:

1. seeks to gain unauthorized access to the resources of the Internet,
2. disrupts the intended use of the Internet,
3. wastes resources (people, capacity, computer) through such actions,
4. destroys the integrity of computer-based information, and/or
5. compromises the privacy of users."

The first three of these activities would be expressed differently today. "Unauthorized access" would have to be qualified (for example, as a property right associated with a website which is compromised by a hacker), to remove the impression that someone had the authority to allow "access to the resources of the Internet". "Intended use" suggests that someone was able to state for which use the Internet was intended (now we would talk more specifically about "denial of service attacks" and the like). Even the waste of resources might now be held to be a personal or cultural choice (is the Jennycam[1] a waste of resources or contemporary art?). The issues related to integrity of information and privacy of users have persisted to this day, albeit in a greatly expanded form.

2. IPV6: OPENING THE DOORS TO THE INTERNET WORLD

Vinton Cerf and Robert Kahn published the Transmission Control Protocol/Internet Protocol (TCP/IP) in 1973. In 1978: TCP/IP was split into its separate components, TCP and IP, and in 1983, the Domain Name

---

[1] The Jennycam started in 1996 and beamed non-stop webcam pictures of Jenny's mundane doings while consuming impressive bandwidth

System (DNS) was invented, establishing the rules for associating such Domain Names as www.iwsp.org with IP addresses such as 212.234.238.114.

The IP system provides a routing address on the Internet, while domain names are ways of giving these addresses some kind of easily recognisable identity. The strings of characters used in domain names often (but not necessarily) spell out an acronym, word or words which generally convey some meaning in natural language. Websites are generally both named and numbered, but networked devices (web and mail servers, home PCs) using IP addresses do not need domain names.

The fundamental principle of the Internet Protocol is that communicating devices anywhere on the Internet have unique IP addresses, so that data packets can be carried (routed) between the devices across one or more ISP networks.

When IPv4 was designed in the 1970s, 32 bits were used to represent IPv4 addresses. Mathematically, this allows for 2^{32}, or 4.3×10^9 (4.3 billion, or 4,294,967,296 to be exact) addresses. However, the number of addresses available is actually less since the full range of IP addresses cannot be utilized. Large allocations were made per ISP or per site in the early days of the Internet. A European Commission report asserts that "74% of the IPv4 address space is already allocated to organizations in North America (15% to the US government alone); the Universities of Stanford and MIT each have more allotted addresses than the Peoples Republic of China."[2] While this may overstate the actual situation, it is still the case that the IPv4 address space is finite in size and continues to be consumed rapidly as the Internet spreads further throughout the world.

A mechanism that provides local site addressing, known as Network Address Translation (NAT), is used to "stretch" the number of IP addresses available globally under IPv4. NATs switch addresses dynamically, so that effectively you do not need to have a fixed address at either end of a communication, One effect of NATs is that they set a limit on the amount of addresses that a network can handle to 16 million addresses (and in practice,

---

[2] Next Generation Internet: Priorities for action in migrating to the new Internet protocol IPv6, Communication from the Commission to the Council and the European Parliament, COM(2002) 96 final, Brussels, 21.2.2002. This report clearly shares authorship (including entire sentences and paragraphs) with the Main Task Force Report of the IPv6 Task Force (11.02.2002, version 1.76, document number 70 available at http://www.ipv6-taskforce.org/

private networks operating under IPv4 will struggle to handle more than 5 million).[3]

Worse, the use of NATs is also one of a number of IPv4-based "fixes" that offend against the principle of "end-to-end transparency", applied since 1973. Transparency requires unique logical addresses and datagrams which do not change in transit. When end-to-end transparency is absent, the security or transmissions cannot be guaranteed from one end of the transmission to the other. There are "security blind spots" luring within NATs and intranets behind firewalls.

Coming to the rescue, IPv6, which has been in development since the early to mid 1990s, uses 128-bit addresses: it can therefore provide globally unique IP addresses to 2^{128}, or over 3.4×10^{38} (340 billion x billion x billion x billion) IP addresses. Where IPv4 allows just under 1 address per person, IPv6 allows just under 10^{29} addresses per person: enough for every cell in every human body to be a website with its own name and address.

In raising the question of internet protocol (IP) addresses in public debates, whether in developing or industrialized countries, whether among quite technologically aware netizens or among novices, some audiences start to laugh at what sounds like the boastful gigantism of future projections of Internet use. The suits with wearable chips demanding to be taken to the cleaners, the intelligent toasters adjusting themselves for each family member, the self-replenishing fridges, the implanted medicine dispensers or Big Brother-ish tracking devices. For some, all this continues to have the air of a Buck Rodgers fantasy: fanciful or foolish, unlikely or simply undesirable.

We may be amused by some of the more fanciful visions of the future, but the future will be upon us none the less. As a matter of fact, in many cases it is here already. For example, LG Electronics has been selling a "webified" kitchen in South Korea with a 15' LCD screen in the door "so you can not only download recipes but watch TV while you're cooking...'If dinner isn't coming out quite right, you can use the fridge's built-in video camera to open a video conference to your mom's kitchen' ...[With another manufacturer's Whirlpool web fridge] you can use the Web tablet in the den to preheat the oven and start the dishwasher...Xybernaut has 700 patents for wearable computing devices...Raymond Kurzweil is apparently serious

---

[3] Main Task Force Report of the IPv6 Task Force (11.02.2002, version 1.76, document number 70 available at http://www.ipv6-taskforce.org/

about retinal implants, not to correct vision problems but so you can 'enter virtual worlds'."[4]

In the European Commission (EC) paper already cited[5], the following applications of IPv6 are mentioned:

- Mobile Internet (3G mobile communications, peer-to-peer communications, wireless machine-to-machine communications and LANs)
- Novel forms of interactive multimedia services over broadband access infrastructure
- Voiceover IP (VoIP) or Internet telephony
- Homes, offices, cars and other environments may all contained many IP-enabled devices in the near future
- Remote home-management applications (multiple web cameras, or wireless temperature sensors)
- Always-on environments (such as residential Internet through broadband, cable modem or satellite)
- Rather than connecting temporarily via dialup with a temporary IP address taken at random from a pool, users and applications of the future, need permanent connectivity with dedicated IP addresses.

The paper also notes that "IPv6 projects totalling Euros 55 Million of Community funding is currently operational, including two large-scale IPv6 trials, namely 6NET and Euro6IX...The first IPv6 deployments began in 1996, from which emerged the 6bone IPv6 test bed network, now spanning over 50 countries and 1,000 sites".

Thus, whether anyone likes it or not, IPv6 is on its way, and a growing band of technologists and visionaries are mapping out the applications of the future, some of which are rolling out today.

The present discussion is not intended to speculate about or promote any one vision of the future deployment of IPv6. Irrespective of one's attitudes towards the desirability or value of the technology, it is important to explore the possible social and ethical consequences of deployment and non-deployment.

---

[4] The Webified Kitchen, Trends and Quick Takes, page 9, *Cites & Insights: Crawford at Large*, July 2002, quoting the March 2002 *Computer Shopper.*.
[5] European Commission, *op cit.*

3.   ETHICAL, SOCIAL AND POLICY ISSUES

Four main categories of social and ethical issues arise in connection with IPv6:

- The right to Internet address space
- Security
- Applications of the technology
- Issues related to governance

3.1   The Right to an IP Address

As mentioned above, IP addresses are numbers while domain names can be recognisable words. There have been extensive discussions and debates regarding domain names – particularly when two or more individuals or companies lay claim to the same or similar names. Some of these debates turn on issues related to free speech and personal identity. What relationship do such issues have to IP addresses?

First it should be appreciated that naming depends on and is constrained by language, rather than technology or IP addresses. As more people, companies and other entities seek to establish a web presence, the arguments about names will increase. If each of the 9 billion people expected to be on the planet in 2005 want to have a website (and perhaps several, for their home companies and other uses) a) they will need IPv6, as they cannot be accommodated using IPv4, and b) they will need to find satisfactory solutions to the naming problems.

Thus, providing more IP addresses only has a tangential effect on the naming problem, insofar as it enables it to get worse by removing restrictions: everybody can get on board, thanks to IPv6. But the problem does not really depend on the technology, nor is it likely that the solution will be found in technology.[6]

After satisfying the needs for billions of websites, the main uses for trillions of IP addresses will no doubt be to allow networked devices to speak with other networked devices, thus enabling the "Semantic Web", These uses and the social and ethical issues arising from them will be discussed in later sections.

---

[6] One apparently permissible solution would be to use distinct images instead of names for domains (Dominic Pinto, personal communication)

Here we will focus on the remaining subset of issues that arise in relation to the question, Do people have a right to an Internet address? This question relates to the notion that owning an Internet address is akin to having the right to free speech. In a sense, you need an Internet address to express your personality online. We will examine this assertion below.

3.1.1 The right to access the Internet and the right to have an Internet presence

Irrespective of the more fanciful possibilities of future Internet use, the need for IP addresses is related to providing equitable access to the Internet. First, let us consider if access to the Internet is a human right.

The line of argument is as follows: If education is a human right, then there must be a right to access information essential for education and human development, and thus to media providing such information, including the Internet.

The right to education is explicitly enshrined in the Universal Declaration of Human Rights (UDHR). Other related rights defined in the UDHR include those of "expressing opinions", and having access to art, culture and science.

In general, however, there is no such thing as an access right to information. Some national jurisdictions provide Freedom of Information clauses to grant citizens the right to access specific categories of government-held and/or produced information. All international and most national copyright laws and treaties allow exceptions and limitations to copyright laws allow forms of access to information for the purposes of education, citation and the like. And the public domain is growing largely thanks to proactive initiatives on the part of academics. But an explicit right of access to information essential to human development is so far absent from the international treaties and conventions.

Many declarations and manifestos have pushed the case for a right to access the Internet. This also is the explicit or implicit assumption in all the efforts to "bridge the digital divide" and eliminating the gap between the "information rich" and "information poor". This right is contained in UNESCO's Recommendation on Multilingualism and Universal access in

Cyberspace[7], which was ratified by the UNESCO Conference and tabled as a key contribution to the World Summit on the Information Society (WSIS).

Apart from the right of access to the Internet, there is the question of what you have a right to do when you get there. We have already discussed the "passive" right of access to information and education – in the sense that you can *receive* information. How about the right to *transmit* information? The right to "express opinions", in the Universal Declaration of Human Rights has been mentioned. Discussions of information provision assisted by information and communication technologies often stress the need to provide for two-way communications – an uplink as well as a downlink, the right to respond to messages received, so that the result of the medium is not just to emit advertising. This is the case in relation to the digital divide and information provision in developing countries, as well as in connection with e-government (online voting and citizen-government interchange).

If there is a right of access to the Internet, and a right to communicate on the Internet, then it can surely be argued that there is a right to have a personal presence on the Internet, up to the point of having a right to an IP address.

As the importance of the Internet in storing personal information and enabling various aspects of personal and social life expands with the roll-out of IPv6, the time will surely come when having a presence on the Internet in the form of your own web space associated with your own IP address will be considered as much a human right as the right to have a presence and occupy "meatspace" in the analogue world.

3.1.2 The concentration of addresses in industrialized countries

The core technology powering the Domain Name System (DNS) is focused at the Root Servers, which are the basic backbone of the Internet. While the concentration of DNS Root Servers is striking – there are 10 in the USA, 2 in Europe (London and Stockholm), and 1 in Japan – this is more an authority and governance question than one of restricting volume.

The shortage of IP addresses clearly arises as an ethical and societal issue in considering the scope for increasing the participation by people in developing countries.

---

[7]   UNESCO's draft Recommendation on Multilingualism and Universal Access in Cyberspace

Less than 10% of the world currently has access to the Internet[8]. Given a world population estimated at 6 billion (9 billion in 2050), it is clear that each person on the planet could not have an IP address even now. Most of these digitally disenfranchised people are currently living in developing countries. While they may have more pressing issues to face than surfing the net, even if they wanted to participate in the digital revolution, they currently could not participate to the extent of their peers in industrialized countries owing to a lack of IP addresses under IPv4.

It should be noted that, from the perspective of developing countries, the value of access to the Internet focuses is not about being on the web. As Alan Levy wrote on the GKD list[9],

> "Being 'online' is only one of the tools... the Internet Protocol itself, running over the electronic (Internet) pipeline, and that offers low-cost communications applications such as VoIP, voice/text mail, electronic ID's, electronic payments, online filings, etc., is more highly valuable to our Southern neighbors than the web itself. In fact, e-government and distance education are the only other vital requirements... which requires little bandwidth... Future growth in ICT adoption lies within the confines of the local community. This will come about not through websites, or a dozen computers in a telecenter that accesses websites, but through the beneficial (universal) access to a minimum set of basic IP-based communications applications. This is where economic development arises... this will initiate local adoption, and an equitable local e-commerce."

A crucial infrastructural issue is the cost of wiring the world, of course, but this is where mobile telephony is currently enabling the developing world to make a leap "due to their dual benefit of being faster to deploy in any area (wide-scale cabling is not required), and of 'giving wings' to the Internet with their mobility... The PC era will be overtaken by the non-PC world (PDAs, Smart Cell Phones, personal network devices, etc.)... Now, adding IPv6 to it would give the developing world immediate access to not only the Internet but to many next generation applications currently under development. Failure to provide access to digital technology to countries in the developing world would be to essentially deny them an opportunity to participate in the new economy of the 21st century."[10]

---

[8] According to NUA, 8.46% (http://www.netvalley.com/intvalstat.html)
[9] Alan Levy, 17 June 2002, Global Knowledge for Development (GKD) list (gkd@phoenix.edc.org), Re: [GKD] Proposed Open Knowledge Network
[10] Main Task Force Report of the IPv6 Task Force *op cit.*

In fact, from 1999 through 2004, the number of mobile subscribers in Africa jumped to 76.8 million, from 7.5 million, an average annual increase of 58 percent. This has happened so quickly that pundits are still found spouting the now-false comparisons equating the number of phones in all of sub-Saharan Africa to those in Manhattan or London. Asia, the next fastest-expanding market, grew by an annual average of just 34 percent in that period.[11]

Having said that, wireless access is likely to provide less bandwidth than is available through wire. Countries dependent on wireless may thus end up with less capability than those with wired with regard to absolute bandwidth and thus limitations on the applications that can be supported in the wireless context. Mobile communications would enable the developing world to get online faster, and thus bridge the digital divide, but it would still leave the two sides of the bridge at different levels.

Thus, IPv6 should be considered a benefit to the developing world, insofar as it enables those who are currently effectively disenfranchised to have equitable access to IP addresses.

3.1.3 Multilingualism and IPv6

The same can be said for the prospects for a multilingual web. Currently the fastest-growing area of web development is in Internet sites and users from developing countries and in languages other than English. More websites with more languages inevitably means more addresses.

"I believe that IPv6 will be crucial in promoting culture (which includes local languages). Today, I find recipes of Peruvian dishes on the Internet and even some of the main national dishes have "fan clubs" to discuss on how to improve traditional dishes. Not only expatriates use these addresses but local people. The different cultures should be able to fit with all others and share values in cyberspace. Somebody said, the Internet will be even more useful when people can buy a ticket to the local cinema, pay with local banking transactions (local money) and have everything explained in the local dialect."[12]

---

[11] Sharon LaFraniere, New York Times, August 25, 2005

[12] Rosa Delgado, Director of Internet Industry Relations – Société Internationale de Télécommunications Aéronautique (SITA), Geneva, Switzerland (personal communication).

Widespread use of the Internet will be dependent upon IP addresses being widely available everywhere. Encouraging local use of the Internet by providing the address bounty offered through IPv6 is thus likely to strongly favour the presence of local content, in local languages, on the Internet.

However, as the Internet Engineering Task Force has discovered, implementing modifications to the Domain Name System to accommodate domain names drawn from the rich UNICODE space is very complex and has not yet been sufficiently deployed to provide convincing evidence of its efficacy.

3.2 Security

When discussing the Internet Protocol, the term "security" usually has a purely technical sense, as exemplified in the following definition in the webopedia[13]:

(n.) In the computer industry, refers to techniques for ensuring that data stored in a computer cannot be read or compromised by any individuals without authorization. Most security measures involve data encryption and passwords.

The broader sense of the term, in which such concepts as privacy and anonymity are included, will be discussed briefly in the next section.

The technical security issues arising relate to the inherent or eventual capabilities of IPv6 to provide a secure environment for end-to-end transmission, on one hand, and the expansion of possible risks owing to the new uses to which IPv6-enabled devices will be put, on the other.

3.2.1 A culture of security

Increasingly, it is recognized that the greatest risks of destroying the promise of the information age stem from systems unable to guarantee an adequate level of security. The weaknesses of IPv4 in this regard have already provided a rich field of loopholes for malicious or criminally minded to exploit. Poor technological security invites the legislators and governments into the party. IPv6 is mandated to avoid this, and to guarantee security and quality. We will explore this further below.

---

[13] http://www.webopedia.com/TERM/S/security.html accessed 30 September 2005

The (OECD) recently drew up guidelines on the security of information systems and networks[14], identifying a clear social and ethical significance in "efforts to enhance the security of information systems and networks", and stressing that these should be "consistent with the values of a democratic society, particularly the need for an open and free flow of information and basic concerns for personal privacy". The OECD Guidelines offer the following nine principles to govern security:

1) **Awareness**: Participants should be aware of the need for security of information systems and networks and what they can do to enhance security.

2) **Responsibility:** All participants are responsible for the security of information systems and networks.

3) **Response:** Participants should act in a timely and co-operative manner to prevent, detect and respond to security incidents.

4) **Ethics:** Participants should respect the legitimate interests of others.

5) **Democracy:** The security of information systems and networks should be compatible with essential values of a democratic society.

6) **Risk assessment:** Participants should conduct risk assessments.

7) **Security design and implementation:** Participants should incorporate security as an essential element of information systems and networks.

8) **Security management:** Participants should adopt a comprehensive approach to security management.

9) **Reassessment:** Participants should review and reassess the security of information systems and networks, and make appropriate modifications to security policies, practices, measures and procedures.

It is generally accepted that IPv6 offers much greater and more robust security than IPv4 because it assures a one-to-one link between communicators. This restores the end-to-end principle violated by NATs, firewalls, and other characteristics of the IPv4 world. Nevertheless, the inexhaustible pace of development is bringing entirely new stresses to security: notably the wireless internet and internet communications mediated by mobile telephones. Proponents of IPv6 maintain that the protocol will assure security even in conditions where messages are whizzing wirelessly through ambient space in pavement cafes, but this remains to be seen. We will return to this below.

---

[14] OECD Guidelines for the Security of Information Systems and Networks: Towards a Culture of Security. 2002., Organisation for Economic Co-operation and Development, Paris. Adopted as a Recommendation of the OECD Council at its 1037th Session on 25 July 2002. Available at http://www.oecd.org/

3.3 The Application of the Technology

Some of the social and ethical aspects of IPv6 relate to the possible applications that could be enabled by, or that would be impossible without, the deployment of IPv6. These include security (aspects of privacy and anonymity), the consequences of implanting chips in animals and humans, the spectre of Big Brother (e.g., individual unique ID systems), risks associated with collection and storage of data (from issues related to the facts of your own biography, to concerns about the transience of document archives), and social impacts on employment and education.

There will be other social/ethical aspects of IPv6 based on the changes it will imply on society – hospitals, doctors, employment, etc. Will it require changes in the law? Some new or more extreme forms of data protection, for example? The concept of privacy is expanding from its "traditional" areas associated with crime, politics, sex and religion, to encompass commercial invasions of your personal space, including reading your suit/toaster/fridge chips. These issues, and legal recourses for them, have always been present, there, but the scope will expand enormously in an IPv6-enabled world.

3.3.1 Privacy and IPv6 technology

Privacy issues arise not just in the application of IPv6 but also in the technology itself. IPv4 has catered to a world in which typically a stationary PC initiates contact with the Internet by dialling in[15]. As a target for prying eyes, such PCs are not much use because they are disconnected from the Internet most of the time. Such devices do not need to have unique, stable addresses and, given IPv4's natural parsimony with addresses, it deals with such connections by temporary addresses picked at random from a pool of addresses.

However, the IPv6 user is envisaged as operating in an always-on mobile world. Such a user needs a permanent IP address for each device connected with the Internet. Extended use of the identifier over time can compromise privacy:

---

[15] This section is based on the Internet Engineering Task Force (IETF) Request for Comments (RFC): Privacy Extensions for Stateless Address Autoconfiguration in IPv6 ftp://ftp.isi.edu/in-notes/rfc3041.txt and the Statement on IPv6 Address Privacy by Steve Deering and Bob Hinden, co-chairs of IETF's Next Generation Working Group, November 6, 1999 at http://playground.sun.com/pub/ipng/html/specs/ipv6-address-privacy.html

"For example, a network sniffer placed strategically on a link across which all traffic to/from a particular host crosses could keep track of which destinations a node communicated with and at what times. Such information can in some cases be used to infer things, such as what hours an employee was active, when someone is at home, etc... The use of a constant identifier within an address is of special concern because addresses are a fundamental requirement of communication and cannot easily be hidden from eavesdroppers and other parties. Even when higher layers encrypt their payloads, addresses in packet headers appear in the clear. Consequently, if a mobile host (e.g., laptop) accessed the network from several different locations, an eavesdropper might be able to track the movement of that mobile host from place to place, even if the upper layer payloads were encrypted".[16]

Thus, the privacy risk is in disclosing the address of the individual, as this is tantamount to locating him topographically, in real space. When unique serial numbers based on IEEE identifiers are used, privacy can be compromised. To tackle this, an IPv6 address that contains a random number was introduced into the IPv6 development process.. Later, a solution was proposed to deal with the numbers based on the IEEE identifiers, as well, (essentially by letting them change over time) thus closing the door on "eavesdroppers and other information collectors".

This inherent security issue need not be considered as an insoluble vulnerability, but it is likely to remain a point of concern in the development of IPv6. The European Commission is well aware of this concern:

"...the Internet has, from the very beginning, been considered as an open network, there are many characteristics of its communication protocols which, more by accident than design, can lead to an invasion of the privacy of Internet users... The fundamental right to privacy and data protection is enshrined in the EU Charter on fundamental rights and developed in detail in the EU data protection directives 95/46/EC and 97/66/EC which both apply to processing of personal data on the Internet. In its Communication on the Organisation and Management of the Internet Domain Name System of April 2000, the Commission stated already that an IP address can be a personal data in the sense of the legal framework (for example dynamic IP addresses). Also the Article 29 Data Protection Working Party, the independent EU advisory body on data protection and privacy established by Directive 95/46/EC, draw the

[16] IETF RFC on Privacy Extensions for Stateless Address Autoconfiguration in IPv6 *op cit*

attention at several occasions to privacy issues raised by the use of the Internet. The Article 29 Data Protection Working Party as well as the International Working Group on Data Protection in Telecommunications (the "Berlin Group") consider to work specifically on IPv6. It is therefore of indispensable that the European Commission and the European Union as a whole consider privacy issues in the further development of Internet. While privacy issues are currently being taken into account in the development of IPv6, it is essential that the trust and confidence of Internet users in the whole system, including in the respect of their fundamental rights, is ensured."[17]

3.3.2 Privacy and information and communication technologies

Before considering it as an IPv6 matter, the debate on the privacy of communications should be addressed from the broader perspective of information and communication technologies (ICTs). Whatever applies to ICTs applies *a fortiori* to IPv6. A useful summary of the issues[18] was posted to a list operated by the now-defunct Internet Societal Task Force (ISTF):

- First, ICTs (and biotechnology) have produced the ability to assign an absolutely *unique identifier* for every person (e.g., a DNA-based marker). The issue here becomes who has a right to demand that unique marker and under what circumstances.
- Second, ICTs have produced the ability to engage in *non-intrusive tracking*. Walking from my residence to my office today I was recorded on 5 different surveillance cameras. ICTs mean they be fed to identity software. Who has a right to those images and under what conditions?
- Third, ICTs have produced the ability to engage in *intrusive tracking*. Consumer Relations Management (CRS) software can be used to data mine, and track, extensive personal information. Cross linking commercial data can present an individual profile which heretofore was knowable only to me. Under what conditions can that data be mined, by whom, and shared in what ways?
- Fourth, governments have both extensive information on individuals, and the legal power to engage in various forms of surveillance. This gives them the power to engage in *intrusive tracking* and construct rich individual profiles. The same questions arise. Who has the right, under what conditions, and what can be done with the information?

---

[17] European Commission, *op cit.*

[18] Edited from a message sent by Sam Lanfranco on 14 October 2001 to the Internet Societal Task Force (ISTF) Participants list (bounce-istf-participants-13688@lists.istf.org – now defunct

Clearly IPv6 can play a role in each of these: DNA-based markers, web cams with their own IP addresses, establishing stable personal profiles – all of these are among the benefits IPv6 will bring. We must ensure the conditions for these benefits are right, however, so as not to undermine the legitimate aspirations to personal privacy of the individual citizen.

3.3.3 Tagging and personal ID

Among the uses suggested for all the new IPv6 addresses is the tagging of animals with chips enabling the monitoring of their location, numbers, health status and other measurable data. Not only would this help in the husbandry and management of ecologically threatened species, it would also help to minimize the impact of zoonoses and other animal diseases – both those transmitted animal-to-animal, and those transmitted across species, including from animals to humans. The social and economic impact of outbreaks of zoonoses such as foot-and-mouth disease could be sharply reduced, as could the risks of cross-species transmission of such conditions as scabies, and perhaps Creuzfeld-Jakob ("mad cow") disease.

Clearly, the project of tagging significant proportions of the animals of the world and essentially turning them into information servers on the Internet would be impossible without the addresses created by IPv6.

Animal tagging may find resistance in animal-rights quarters, and there are ethical issues to face in this respect.

The application of such technology to the human race raises a number of further ethical questions. Apart from the human scale of tagging represented by implanting a chip, it is also possible to tag at the genetic level. "Affymetrix is…applying the principles of semiconductor technology to the life sciences.. The Company's customers include pharmaceutical, biotechnology, agrochemical, diagnostics and consumer products companies, as well as academic, government and other non-profit research institutes. Affymetrix offers … its integrated GeneChip® platform, to address growing markets focused on understanding the relationship between genes and human health."[19] The GeneChip Probe array is using the output of the Human

---

[19] See http://www.affymetrix.co.uk

Genome Project and is designed to analyse or screen for specific genetic expressions.[20]

Thus, IPv6 will enable the vast effort and address space required to tackle the human organism at genetic-code level. It is hard to overstate the importance of this, both from the perspectives of enormous opportunities in the health field, and equally significant possibilities for abuse, if the social and ethical issues are not addressed.

3.3.4 Anonymity and IPv6

Essentially, anonymity is a special case of privacy. Privacy may be an unconditional right, but anonymity is conditional – you can insist on some privacy, but you are usually allowed anonymity under certain conditions (for example, if you are participating in a medical trial under the terms of a consent agreement).

Privacy guards knowledge about a person's thoughts, activities or whereabouts, while anonymity may do all that and also cloak the person's name and identity. On the other hand, you may know everything about an anonymous communicator, except for their name. Proponents of a right to anonymity in online communications identify the following beneficial and harmful aspects of anonymous communication:[21]

Benefits	Harms
Investigative journalism	Spamming
Whistleblowing	Deception
Law enforcement	Hate mail
Self-help	Impersonation and misrepresentation
Personal privacy protection	Online financial fraud
Avoiding persecution	Other illegal activities

In the IPv6 world, anonymity depends on there being no way of identifying the individual owning or using an IP address. The problems regarding assuring privacy mentioned above would often compromise the anonymity of the address holder.

---

[20] According to Dominic Pinto (private communication), Senior Associate, Telesphere Limited (http://www.telesphere.com), to whom I am indebted for the reference to Affymetrix.

[21] Table based on Kling, Rob, Ya-Ching Lee, Al Teich and Mark S. Frankel, 1999. Assessing Anonymous Communication on the Internet: Policy Deliberations. *The Information Society* 15(2), http://www.slis.indiana.edu/TIS/abstracts/ab15-2/kling.html

It has been argued that anonymity is morally neutral and that it is a human right: "Anonymous communication should be regarded as a strong human right; in the United States it is also a constitutional right."[22]:

More broadly, the Universal Declaration of Human Rights (UDHR), contains provisions that protect the ability of individuals to communicate anonymously. Article 12 governs freedom from interference with privacy, home, and correspondence, and Article 19 provides for freedom of opinion and expression and the right "to seek, receive, and impart information and ideas through any media and regardless of frontiers."

With regard to Internet communication...recipients have the right to choose to accept or refuse anonymous messages and that individuals do not have the right to impose messages upon an unwilling recipient. At the same time, law enforcement agencies and commercial interests do not have the right to interfere with individual privacy in electronic communication, regardless of whether it is anonymous or not... Closely related to these provisions of the UDHR is the First Amendment of the U.S. Constitution, which guarantees the right of free speech to all Americans. The First Amendment applies equally to communications in which the initiator is identified and to those that are sent anonymously."[23]

If these views, expressed in the summary report of a conference of the American Association for the Advancement of Science, are to be maintained, such conditions will need to be implemented into IPv6.

Beyond that, anonymity enters the world of governance, and the rules that are agreed governing the registration of names associated with addresses. Other conditions expressed in the AAAS report are that "online communities should be allowed to set their own policies regarding the use of anonymous communications", and that "individuals should be informed of the extent to which their identity is disclosed online".

---

[22] Teich, Al, Mark S. Frankel, Rob Kling and Ya-Ching Lee, 1999. Anonymous Communication Policies for the Internet: Results and Recommendations of the AAAS Conference. *The Information Society* 15(2), http://www.slis.indiana.edu/TIS/abstracts/ab15-2/teich.html

[23] Teich, Al *et al, op cit.*

There are strong ethical arguments on both sides, and these will need to be mustered when the time comes to debate registration procedures. It is enough to place a marker here that this will need to be done.

3.3.5 Other application issues

Don Cameron[24], an IT Manager at a moderately sized rural firm with 400 staff ran a simple series of tests over a number of months in a fairly diverse cultural setting designed to determine true bandwidth requirements under a variety of Internet usage circumstances. He found that 72% of all their web-based traffic resulted from third-party web URL redirections – banner advertisements, animated GIFs, Java pop-up screens, hit counters, cookie downloads, browser & IP referrals (the information we all unknowingly send to some sites). This traffic represented nearly 40% of the total bandwidth utilisation (including e-mail) of the company. Furthermore, he determined through server logs that 20% of all inward mail traffic was unsolicited Spam.

The story continues as a technical optimization story, culminating in a win-win solution resulting in more bandwidth, faster and easier access and lower costs by switching of all the extraneous connections to the firm's traffic and tackling Spam in a systematic way.

However, from the perspective of IPv6, the fact that fully ¾ of all web traffic might be third-party web URL redirections is worth pondering. Will virtually unlimited namespace, will the flow of cookies, Spam and advertising of all kinds similarly hit exponential growth. With the remarkable growth of the good things on the Internet heralded by the application of IPv6, will the bad things grow with the same amazing vigour?

The guess is that we are reaching a critical phase in each of the applications of technology which have an abusive edge. For example, most people would acknowledge that advertising can have a positive role in the information economy (such as free-to-air television programming), turns abusive in Spam. The Internet, which has thrived on self-regulation so far, has so far failed to regulate Spam effectively. Any major expansion of what are generally seen as abusive edges of applied information and communication technology will certainly lead to a strengthening of the international regulatory framework. This by-product of IPv6 dissemination will have to be monitored carefully in relation to possible social and ethical consequences.

---

[24] Based on a message sent by Don Cameron [mailto:donc@mudgeeab.com.au] on 21 July 2002 to communityinformatics@vancouvercommunity.net

Giving in to the Internet and enabling it to do everything means that if anything goes wrong, everything goes wrong. By facilitating turning every atom of human existence into an Internet address, equal care needs to be devoted to fail-safe and security systems: "work on end-to-end security models should be pushed to achieve security for everyone as for access for everyone... Security needs not only a protocol but also a PKI infrastructure, which is an expensive investment and that is going to hinder immediate deployment of security at a larger scale to enable e-commerce and the like. The digital divide is complemented by the security divide!"[25]

Clear examples of new risks include the collection and storage of data. When you have every fact of your life stored on a tiny device, what happens when you lose it? If it is backed up, who will have the key? How will back ups be preserved? There are security issues involved, but also storage issues. Where security may be a problem (as mentioned above) storage should be facilitated by the provision of unlimited IPv6 addresses.

Extrapolating from this scenario to document archives, the proliferation of IP addresses should enable storing as many versions of archive material and any associated software in a uniquely findable way. We envisage IPv6 will be a particular bon in digital storage and archival, and thus in preserving the cultural heritage of humanity.

The massive ramping up of Internet will certainly have a cataclysmic social impact on employment and education. All technological change has such a social impact, but the scale of the impact that could be led by the extensive deployment of IPv6 has never been seen before.

3.4 Governance

The more the Internet expands its scope, the more it matters who (if anyone) is in charge, and how such a role is exerted.

As the vastly expanded name/address space offered thanks IPv6 enables the Internet to infiltrate almost every part of life, the issue of governance becomes far more significant. Whoever controls this name/address space will be very powerful – far more powerful than the managers of the IPv4 name/address space, and perhaps more powerful than elected political representatives in many countries. How will this power be allocated? Will

---

[25] Latif Ladid, Chairman IPv6 Task Force (personal communication).

the process be entirely transparent and democratic? Can everyone have a say? What is the role of developing countries? Will the solutions favour one group rather than another, one language rather than another?

Who in the end is accountable? The fact that the Internet Engineering Task Force (IETF) is not accountable to anyone is often presented as a strength and benefit. Those working on the IETF are in fact accountable to their peers. It has been argued that self-regulation is a stronger form of accountability than explicitly legislated accountability. Nevertheless, conclusions drawn from a study of self-regulating codes of ethical conduct[26] suggest significant problems with the application of self-regulation methodology, particularly in determining what the rules are in the first place, and in effective enforcement.

A number of bodies have specific roles in developing and managing cyberspace, including the Internet Corporation for Assigned Names and Numbers (ICANN), the International Telecommunications Union, the World Intellectual Property Organization, and others. Under the terms of Declaration of Principles[27], and as a part of the process of the World Summit on the Information Society (WSIS) a Working Group on Internet Governance (WGIG) was established in December 2003 to:

* Develop a working definition of Internet Governance;
* Identify the public policy issues that are relevant to Internet Governance;
* Develop a common understanding of the respective roles and responsibilities of governments, existing international organizations and other forums as well as the private sector and civil society from both developing and developed countries. [28]

It is not the purpose of this paper to review or assess these bodies, especially since at the time of writing issues of Internet governance are very fluid and it is difficult to draw any conclusions. The specific role of IPv6 in this lies in its enabling a quantum leap forward in how the internet will penetrate all of our lives. The governance structures established, their management and the assignation of responsibilities in them are, and will

---

[26] Jacques Berleur and Tanguy Ewbank de Wespin, 2002, Self-regulation: Content, Legitimacy and Efficiency - Governance and Ethics (In print).

[27] Document WSIS-03/GENEVA/DOC/4-E, 12 December 2003, http://www.itu.int/wsis/docs/geneva/official/dop.html accessed 30 September 2005.

[28] http://www.wgig.org/

become increasingly, significant as the Internet becomes increasingly significant. It is as an enabler of such societal penetration that IPv6 matters.

4.   CONCLUSIONS

The arrival and deployment of IPv6 can be seen in the classical terms of opportunity and threat. It is certainly an opportunity as it finally enables everyone in the world (and for generations to come) who might want to have use the Internet in any walk of life to do so. No one will be deprived for want of an IP address, at least – although the financial and other infrastructural aspects remain to be resolved.

At the same time, we have to ensure that the vast new possibilities afforded by the technology do not lead to vast new societal and ethical problems. It is important to raise concerns and questions as the technology is being developed, at the earliest stage possible. The development of the Internet can be seen as a giant experiment on human subjects, none of whom have been adequately warned or have formally consented.

It remains to see how the largely technical community labouring over the protocol responds to these societal demands. To develop and assure the consideration of societal concerns, an Internet Societal Task Force (ISTF) was established in 2002 under the guidance of Vint Cerf (who served as its first President) and under the aegis of the Internet Society. This group eventually disestablished as a Task Force and converted into a discussion forum. Among the reasons offered for this was that the ISTF was "unable to agree on positions" and that its process was inefficient.

To an extent the notion of having an Internet Societal Task Force to parallel the Internet Engineering Task Force (IETF) faced a confrontation between CP Snow's Two Cultures. On one hand you have a body like the IETF, which operates scientifically, issues requests for comments on technical issues and comes to black-and-white conclusions that can be adopted within specified time frames, with measurable resources and consequences. On the other you have an idea like the ISTF, which can only address issues that have no black-and-white-solution, and may indeed end up with two or more diametrically opposed points of view on a given societal issue.

The point of this discussion is to stress that the two cultures must talk to each other. A recognition of the need to address societal aspects of technological developments associated with IPv6 is overdue. The relentless focus on technology alone is not enough. We need not only to make the IPv6 enabled world work, but to make it worth living in.

Acknowledgements: All errors and opinions expressed herein are the responsibility of the author, but grateful thanks for their comments and suggestions over time (and mainly on much earlier versions) are due to Rosa Delgado, Latif Ladid, Dominic Pinto, Jonathan Robin and Vinton Cerf

TRUSTED COMPUTING, OR THE GATEKEEPER

Klaus Kursawe and Christopher Wolf
K.U.Leuven, ESAT-COSIC, Kasteelpark Arenberg 10, B-3001 Leuven-Heverlee, Belgium

Abstract: Few technologies have gained as much public attention over the last years as
the concept of Trusted Computing – while its proponents claim that this
technology may finally help overcoming the fundamental and increasing
security problems, the opponents see it as an instrument of industry to
suppress its customers. In this article, we give a short overview on what the
technology actually does, and analyse the real opportunities as well as
problems that come with its global usage.

1.   MOTIVATION AND INTRODUCTION

Recent years have seen serious attacks on the backbone of our information society infrastructure. To mention a few, we want to draw the attention of the reader to the disastrous consequences of the Slammer worm which disconnected South Korea from the Internet, knocked out ATMs, and caused an estimated damage of 7.7 billion USD for removal and down-times. On the other hand, Internet commerce grows, and every year more and more people use the Internet for business to consumer transactions. However, the consumers' confidence in the use of the Internet will drastically decrease if incidences like Slammer become more frequent. Another issue is the use of computers as a replacement of paper based voting machines, *e.g.*, in the USA or in India. Obviously, the overall outcome of these elections drastically effects at least the countries in question, and is hence a valuable asset which needs to be protected. Apart from the outcome itself, any serious doubt in the correctness of the result will shake the trust people have in their own political system. Again, the need for machines which do what they are supposed to do and nothing else is high. Finally, both the music and the film industry call for means to protect their property from being copied and distributed virtually for free, while users are getting increasingly worried about their private data being collected and electronically processed (or at least, they should).

All these items seem to be rather unconnected, but may be solved or at least eased with one development: trusted computing. The idea is rather simple: instead of trusting the correctness of software, *e.g.*, the operating system and the applications, we move the level of trust to a specific piece of hardware.

From a philosophical point of view, this "change" does actually not change anything: basically, we just move the reason of our trust to some specific token — being either software or hardware. At the moment, we have to trust in some specific software, which includes the operating system and all hardware drivers running on the machine in question. In the future, we need to establish trust in a hardware device. Before moving to a description of possible hardware devices in the next section, we start with a short introduction of the software core of trust.

1.1   The Caretakers

At the moment, all software based solutions need to trust in the core of each software, *i.e.*, the operating system. Using the picture of a large house, *e.g.*, in a university, we see that there are plenty of tasks to fulfil, and that many people work in many rooms. Once in a while, items are broken and need replacement, or just simple maintenance like, *e.g.*, cleaning. Hence, the caretakers have keys to all rooms and can go there at will. In the "real world" of a computer, the caretakers represent the different parts of the operating systems while the members of the university represent the different applications, and the rooms are the memory-protected areas of the computer. We see immediately that there are few things to do without these "caretakers" in a computer: to type a text, a word processor needs input from the keyboard and the mouse — both of them given to the word processor by two caretakers, namely the mouse and the keyboard driver. As soon as a keystroke is received, the corresponding character needs to be displayed — which again involves the work of a caretaker, in this case the driver of the graphical card and the display. At this point we did not talk about saving the text or printing it. Again, this would involve the work of even more caretakers.

As we saw, the caretakers and hence drivers are very important for the correct working of a computer today. In particular, they are necessary to ensure that the same programmes run on totally different hardware platforms and that we can easily change the configuration of our computers, *i.e.*, by plugging in a faster Ethernet card or a printer with higher resolution.

In the real world, each caretaker would have very limited power and can only do what is necessary for the fulfilment of his tasks, *e.g.*, the gardener has access to the green house, but not to the exam locker. In the computer-world, things are unfortunately different: all caretakers have equal rights and hence, can perform each others' tasks. In the model of the university this means that *any* caretaker has the keys to *all* rooms and may go there at will. While we would refuse such an arrangement in any real-world situation, this is the case in our current computer architecture — and holds for Windows, Linux, and MacOS, as all of them use a large, monolithic kernel. To come back to the chain of trust we introduced previously: we actually need to trust *every single caretaker*, *i.e.*, that this person cannot be bribed or does not lose its key or may be dishonest by nature. Translated to the computer world, this means that every single driver, in addition to the core of the operating system must be trustworthy: it may neither be a Trojan horse, *i.e.*, performing a task different from what it claims to do, nor may it have a security critical bug, *e.g.*, allows the execution of code (e.g., due to a buffer overflow). Given that we expect one security critical bug in 1000 lines of code, and the size of modern kernels (the Linux kernel in version 2.4, for example, has about 1.5 million lines of code), those operating systems are not suited for any serious security applications. Hence, to assume the security of these kernels is a rather big assumption – and given our expertise of the past years, a void one.

1.2 The Gatehouse

Hence, to overcome the problems outlined in the previous section, we need two things: first more separation, and second a trusted core on which we can base our trust in a specific computer. As we saw, this is a very risky business today, and the incidences of the previous years have shown that our doubts in the trustworthiness of current operating systems are not just an academic exercise.

From a purely logical point of view, the obvious thing to do would be to change the overall design: instead of giving each gatekeeper all keys, *i.e.*, to give each driver the credentials to perform any hardware related operation, this should be restricted to the absolute minimum per driver/gatekeeper. This way, each gatekeeper can only cause problems in its own area but would not infect others. However, reality is not that simple: given the huge amount of work already put into the architecture and the software of today's computers, we simply cannot throw all of them away. Even then, the problem arises where to start trusting ones platform — since the only way to observe the operating system without significant effort is to use a program running on said operating system, one cannot get any reliable information [Thompson, 1995]. Hence, we need a solution which is able to co-exist with current hard- and software architecture.

In the model of our university, we would fence one part of the ground, and partition it. Each partition would only allow *one* specific caretaker. If something goes wrong in this part, there can be only one person responsible for this. To allow communication between the caretakers in this new part, and also between caretakers of the old part and the new part, we install a special gatehouse: each caretaker has a mailbox there, which only he can access. The gatekeeper's task is to make sure that each caretaker gets his and *only* his mail. This way, the caretakers can communicate, but nothing else. Similarly, the outside world can ask the caretakers to perform certain tasks. In every single case, the caretaker in question can check if such a task would be allowed. Obviously, we now need to trust the gatekeeper, too. But given that there is only one gatekeeper with a very limited job, and that the hardware allows authentication of the gatekeeper, we can actually anticipate that this is possible. However, as we will see later, the role of the gatekeeper is quite critical when we evaluate the implications of the trusted computing technology. In particular, we need to know that the gatekeeper in question is legitimate and not an impostor.

2.   OVERVIEW OF TRUSTED COMPUTING

After this rather pictorial introduction we move on to a more technical description of the gatehouse, and the caretakers. We want to stress that the picture we drew on the previous pages actually is one of the most ambitious project in the area of trusted computing. Microsoft calls its internal project "NGSCB" (Next Generation Secure Computing Base, former Palladium), while the chip manufacturer Intel develops the underlying hardware under the name "LaGrande". Its direct competitor AMD is working on a similar system called "Secure Execution Mode" (SEM). We will come back to these techniques later but want to stress that we may see something different in reality.

2.1 Trusted Computing Platform and Further

Without software support, a trusted PC will not behave differently from a PC as we know it today. It will boot as normal, though a hardware module — the "Trusted Platform Module" (TPM) [Trusted Computing Group, 2004] will receive checksums of the boot sequence. However, the TPM itself is a passive module, hence some BIOS support is necessary to actually report the checksums. To this end, some part of the BIOS will be protected against manipulation and start reporting checksums to the TPM. In any case, this trusted platform module is a special chip, like a smartcard, which is bound to a specific platform — in most cases, this will be the mother board. The TPM chip will then save the current configuration, *i.e.*, the checksums of everything that in some sense affected the boot process, in a number of special registers. From a technical point of view, this is done by the mean of hash-chains, and the TPM chip will only save and later sign the last element of this chain. However, using cryptographically secure hash functions, this is actually sufficient and breaking this hash chain is far less likely than breaking the actual implementation of the TPM itself. With proper software reports, the TPM may receive another hash chain for the operating system and even another chain for the applications found on this computer. Any change in either the configuration will therefore lead to a completely different hash chain — which in turn makes it possible to detect that something has changed. Consequently, a manipulation due to a virus or a Trojan horse cannot go unnoticed anymore. Up to this point, we have the most likely scenario of trusted computing, as outlined in specification 1.2 of the trusted computing group (TCG), *i.e.*, the industry platform which brings all industrial players in this matter together.

Using LaGrande or SEM, the hardware goes one step further: now we are even able to separate the different drivers and programmes in a trusted and a non-trusted space. The operating system itself — plus all applications — are by definition untrusted: they are far too complex not to carry any security critical bug (see above). Moreover, they are usually not open source, so it is difficult for a user or even a big institution to establish any kind of trust that there is no trapdoor hidden. For all we know, Windows could be a big Trojan horse which is used to spy on all users. Even if this is not the case (we want to stress that the authors do not believe that Windows is a Trojan horse), we have no easy mean to rule this allegation out. Hence, trusting the whole operation system is simply very risky. And also for open source systems such as Linux, we have difficulties to establish the level of trust we actually need for our purpose: here, the problem is not open source, but the sheer complexity of the whole kernel, as well as a lack of people able and motivated to perform quality security audits on the code. Hence, it is simply not possible using today's methods to ensure that the kernel does not carry any hidden weakness. Hence, we need to separate the code into bygone large, untrusted area and one much smaller, but trusted area, commonly called a "Trusted Computing Base" (TCB) in the literature. There are a number of different implementations and names of a TCB that can support a legacy Operating System, such as the gatekeeper, micro-kernel, hyper-visor in the IBM model, or "Nexus" in the terminology of Microsoft. Its role has already been outlined above: deliver messages between the different caretakers, and make sure that they cannot interfere with each others tasks and in particular, that they do not steal each others secrets, e.g., the PIN for a banking application.

2.2   Trusted Computed Platform Alone

While the advantage of the latter is rather obvious, we will go back to the more short-term scenario of the trusted computing platform without any additional technology as LaGrande, SEM, or NGSCB and outline how such a system could benefit users. In this context we assume a large company which has a big number of systems — both installed in the offices of their employees, and also for some of them at their homes. The threat this company faces are employees who install Trojan horses on the system without knowing, or bring in viruses into the internal network. In both cases, trusted computing may ensure that any change of the computer system will be noticed, and hence, the system administrators can inspect this machine and determine the cause of the change. This way, it becomes easier to maintain a large number of platforms and prevent the spreading of viruses or Trojan horses. If necessary, it is even possible to "quarantine" a platform which has been changed, and deny its access to the Internet or internal databases.

However, the trusted computing platform can do more: using the technology outlined by the trusted computing group [2004], it is possible to bind a file to a specific platform configuration and only allow it to be viewed on this platform. Thus — if the system is fully utilized, installing any programme, *e.g.*, a key logger, would render the file useless as the platform will have changed. Note, however, that the TCG specification ends with verifying the master boot block — everything beyond that is up to the operating system vendor. Technically, this binding can be achieved using cryptographic techniques: each trusted computing module has a secret key which may be used to generate specific keys which only work in connection with a specific platform. If the configuration changes, the trusted computing module will simply refuse access to the key bound to this configuration and hence, the encrypted file can no longer be accessed. As we see, the role of the trusted platform module is quite prominent at this point. As we need to start our chain of trust here, we actually need to trust the implementation of the TPM. Hence, each TPM comes with a private key which is unique to this TPM. Moreover, the manufacturer issues a certificate belonging to the public key of this private key, which basically states that the TPM has been manufactured in compliance with the rules laid out by the trusted computing group, and in particular, that the trusted platform module does not contain any hidden back-door. Moreover and to fulfil its duties, a TPM has the following hardware components:

1. Hardware real random number generator
2. Public and Private Key algorithms (RSA up to 2048 bit)
3. Hash algorithms SHA-1 and MD-5

The specification does not require support for any block encryption scheme, such as AES or 3DES. The reason is that in normal PCs, the TPM is a slow device with a low communication bandwidth, and that any ability to do block encryption would cause export regulations to apply to the technology. Hence, a question to ask may be if these export regulations are justified in the first place.

In this context, (1) is used to generate cryptographically secure keys, (2) makes sure that the private key never needs to leave the TPM and hence, it is impossible for any unit other than the TPM itself to impose as the TPM, and (3) is used to compute the hash-chain for a given platform configuration, (*i.e.* the boot sequence), which is used for platform attestation. In addition to these hardware components, we also have the keys and certificates present, namely :

1. Endorsement key (EK), the identity of the TPM
2. Storage Root Key (SRK), used for key management
3. Endorsement Certificate, Platform Certificate and Conformance Certificate, with which the producers certify that the TPM has been produced and integrated according to the specification as well as some of its properties.

The endorsement key uniquely identifies a given platform, and together with the endorsement certificate can be used to prove to the outside world that a given TPM is actually genuine, *i.e.*, does comply with the specifications. To guard the users privacy, it is possible to create pseudonyms by the mean of attestation identity keys, or AIKs. With these keys, a platform can prove to the outside world that it is a genuine platform but does not need to reveal its identity. As we will see below, there are some questions to be raised in this context, but at least, the TPM specification does take user anonymity into account. Finally, the storage root key is used to encrypt user keys. This way, a TPM can use the operating system to store its keys and thus manage a virtually unlimited amount of keys, even though its amount of internal storage is limited. User keys can have a number of attributes. Most importantly, a key can be marked as *non-migratable, i.e.*, it may not leave the TPM, and the key can be bound to a specific platform configuration, which makes it inaccessible if the configuration changes. However, an optional protocol exists to move such keys to another TPM, if it is guaranteed that the new TPM satisfies the same security requirements and the old key is deleted. This protocol is rather impractical to use, though, and has not been implemented so far. Finally, the platform certificate and the conformance certificate can be used to prove the correctness of given TPM as well as additional security features, *i.e.*, in particular that a given platform does not contain any known back-doors and can therefore be considered "save" in a specific, application dependent sense.

3. REMOTE ATTESTATION

The most critical aspect of the trusted computing concept — its ability to prove statements to the outside world — requires some further elaboration. This feature allows a platform to issue provable statements, for example about the platform configuration or the properties of a key. As the verifier of that proof has no reason to trust the platform or its user, the only entity he can trust is the TPM. Thus, to establish trust in the statements, he must be sure he is talking to a real TPM that properly follows the specification. Thus,

- a TPM must be able to prove it is a genuine TPM,
- if a TPM is hacked, it must be possible to revoke its key, but
- for privacy reasons the TPM must not be uniquely identifiable.

3.1 Original Implementation

The first implementation of a system satisfying above properties, used in version 1.1b of the specification, uses a trusted third party (TTP) to establish anonymity. The user creates a pseudonym, *i.e.*, the Attestation Identity Key, and forwards it — along with the public part of the endorsement key and the certificates — to the trusted third party. The TTP verifies the certificates, and itself issues a certificate on the pseudonym. This certificate is then encrypted using the endorsement key, so that only the TPM can decrypt it. Thus, the TPM can get an arbitrary number of certified pseudonyms that prove its genuineness, but is not linked to its identity as long as the TTP remains trustworthy.

In short, the TPM uses a non-anonymous way to prove its authenticity to a trusted third party, which then certifies one or several pseudonyms the TPM can use for anonymous, unlinkable transactions.

The disadvantage of the scheme is that it requires a TTP that is trusted by both sides. This may be a trust problem, but also plain availability. For example, if TPM enabled devices want to set up an ad-hoc network, a commonly trusted TTP may not be available at that time.

3.2 Direct Anonymous Attestation

As a reaction to critics of the specification, the TCG has extended the specification with the Direct Anonymous Attestation protocol (DAA). This protocol is based on a rather complicated zero-knowledge proof which allows a TPM to directly prove its authenticity without revealing any information about its identity. To allow for key revocation, e.g. when a TPM has been hacked and its secret keys exposed on the Internet, some mechanism have been included to revoke the anonymity in case the TPMs secrets have obviously been exposed. While this protocol solves all above issues, it is rather complex, and it has to be seen if it will actually be used in practice.

3.3 Problems

Even though the issues related to the TPMs ability to prove its genuineness appear to have been resolved with version 1.2 of the specification, issues remain with the application of remote attestation. Some issues are due to the implementation. To demonstrate that an operating system satisfies certain properties, the verifier receives a log file of the entire boot sequence. This poses problems on both the privacy and the practicability side. For one, this may be more data than a user is willing to release — the BIOS version, for example, can be used to estimate the age and the price of the platform, and the operating system configuration can tell the users computer expertise. Also, it poses problems for the verifier — determining form a log file of a boot sequence if a platform satisfies a complex property may be a quite challenging task. Also, there is no transparency about the policy used. As the verifier gets all information about the platform he needs to derive his policy, he can also apply *any* policy, even those that may be considered illegal or unethical.

The second issue is that it is impossible for a user to lie about his platform configuration. Many national laws, for good reason, legalise lying in some situations. In Germany, for example, an employer is not allowed to ask a female job applicant if she is pregnant. As a refusal to answer is already giving away too much information, the applicant is allowed to lie without fearing consequences.

3.4 Owner Override and PCR Substitution

The concept of owner override and PCR substitution has independently been developed by Schoen [2004] and Kursawe and Stueble [2003]. The basic idea is to allow the owner of a TPM, hence usually the entity that paid for the platform, to modify the log-files of the boot sequence, *i.e.*, to lie about the platform configuration. While this abolishes all abuse scenarios, it also kills some of the good use-cases. There are perfect scenarios in which one does not want the owner of a TPM to be able to lie, for example, if the TPM is used to enforce a companies privacy policy. In other scenarios, it may be desirable to lie — for example, if a company tries to enforce a monopoly and lock the user to a platform configuration. For this approach to become feasible, some method needs to be developed that a human policy, *i.e.*, under which circumstances it is allowed to lie, can be enforced by a (rather simple) hardware module.

3.5 Property Based Attestation

Another approach, that addresses the above problems, is the concept of *property based attestation* [Sadeghi and Stuble, 2004, and Poritz et al 2004]. Instead of sending its log-files to the verifier, the platform receives certificates that its configuration satisfies certain properties, and binds them to the corresponding configuration. The verifier now only sees the certificates, but learns nothing beyond the fact that the platform satisfies the properties he asked for. This has several advantages. The users privacy is preserved, as the platform does not need to send out its log files. The verifier's task is rather easy, as he does not need to derive the properties himself anymore. And though lying is still not possible, this approach at least enforces transparency about the policies. The verifier must publish the properties he is interested in, which allows a judge to identify illegal requests and act accordingly.

In any case, we need to look into the question here, *where* these certificates actually come from and who pays for them — and under which authority the entity is which issues these certificates. For example, it would not help our cause if all big music distributors pool resources and set up such a certification authority. It would simply be too biased towards the needs of the music distributors in contrast to the users' and the artists' needs.

4. APPLICATION EXAMPLES

After introducing the technical specification of the trusted platform module and hence the most likely base for trusted computing in the coming years, we move on to a more case-based view, i.e., we will now outline how a trusted platform module can be used in different scenarios and how not. As a general note, it should be mentioned that trusted hardware only serves as a basis for security applications, but does not do anything on its own. There are many ways it can be used to harden existing systems, but the real strength of the concept is to serve as a foundation for a secure operating system.

4.1 Company with Computers in Different Places

We start by going back to the scenario already outlined earlier in this paper and assume a large company with computers installed in different countries and also both in its offices and at the home of some of its employees. Currently, the system administrators cannot be sure that the users really have a secure platform or — more likely — at least some of the platforms installed have a virus or a Trojan horse. The latter is a serious security risk when it comes to company secrets. With TPM 1.2, the system administrators can install the system once, and then "seal" it in its current state. Any modification of the system, *e.g.*, through a virus or a Trojan horse, could now be detected either locally by the user, or as soon as the platform accesses the company network. Moreover, the security policy can now make sure that no document can be read on a non-conforming platform. Data leaks become far less likely this way.

All in all, there are few ethical implications in this scenario and the benefits clearly outnumber the disadvantages.

While the TCG concept generally leaves the choice to the user, problems may arise if the user for some reason does need to access a certain service.

This is the case if there already is a quasi monopoly, *e.g.*, chat programs, or video distribution, or if the service is only offered by a limited number of providers, *e.g.*, Windows Security updates or high bandwidth Internet access in remote areas. This puts the user into a sufficiently weak position that the service provider can dictate the policies; another potential scenario would be that a government defines policies that may not be entirely in the users interest. This, combined with the technological means to detect policy violations or even prevent them from happening in the first place, may pose a significant problem, though it can hardly be resolved by technical means. Hence, we need a critical public here which makes sure that these scenarios do not happen to begin with.

4.2 Secure Mobile Phone

Here we move from the world of personal computers to the domain of personal electronic devices, such as PDA or mobile phones. Particularly for the latter, we may assume that the manufacturer has large control over the programmes running on these items, though phones are slowly changing into open systems. Hence, it makes sense that this manufacturer certifies that his mobile complies with certain standards, *e.g.*, music downloaded to this mobile can only be listened to on this particular mobile and not somewhere else. The same goes for the distribution of games which may now be bound to this particular mobile and not played anywhere else.

From a business perspective, such mobiles are very desirable: these days, mobiles are omni-present, and with the additional property of being "secure", they can be used to sell content securely; it is notable in this context that the same people that consider 1 Euro too much for a song are perfectly willing to pay the same price if the song comes in the form of a ring-tone. This again shows how interesting mobile phones are from a business perspective.

From a user's perspective, using trusted computing on cellular phones has two opposing effects. For one, it may be more difficult to hack a phone — thus, binding it to a service provider who subsidized it or removing the noise a phone makes while taking a picture may become much more difficult. On the other side, phones will contain a technology for anonymous authentication, which will significantly increase the users control, assuming it is used properly.

4.3 Complex Machine Replacement Parts

While technologically different, planes and cars have something in common: the need of replacement parts from time to to. Not surprisingly, there is a huge market for these items. A real problem in this context is fraud with replacement parts which do not confirm to specifications. Imagine a plane crash due to such replacement parts. To protect their image, manufacturers have a real interest in making sure that these falsified parts can be identified. As it is state of the art to have more and more computer present in any of these devices, replacements could now carry a TPM unit which states that the replacement in question is actually genuine.

As long as cars do not talk to each other, there are few privacy issues with this. Matters become different as soon as they do — or more likely will in the foreseeable future. Moreover, parts not made by the original supplier of the machine are both: a security risk and a necessary part of open market competition. Hence, we need legal procedures in place which make it impossible for a manufacturer to "lock out" competitors. From a technical perspective it would actually make sense to have several authorities in place which are allowed to certify that a hardware item does comply with specifications and may therefore be safely used in a designated complex machine. Otherwise, we are likely to face serious industrial political questions.

In any case, the current specification of TPM 1.2 would actually allow such a scenario — both the desirable and the undesirable. From a pure technical point of view, there is few what we can do to prevent either of them but need laws in place to make sure we get more security without monopolies.

4.4 Digital Rights Management

Given the prominent role digital rights management played in the whole debate of trusted computing, we felt that we should include it in this article, too. However, we want to point out that TPM 1.2 itself can do only little in this context: it is rather unlikely to assume that all personal computers on this planet will be sealed to a specific configuration and not changed from then onwards. Moreover, it is unlikely that anybody would like to testify that such a complex machine does not contain any hidden weakness. It would simply be too costly to do all the necessary tests — compared with the revenue for digital music, books, or movies.

Matters become different if Microsoft's NGSCB or any other secure operating system is in place. While the overall operating system and also the applications are not trusted by definition, this is not the case anymore for the Nexus and the secure agents, *i.e.* the gatekeeper and the care-takes from our above example. Here, we *would* have some trusted parts in which movies could be shown, music be played, or books be displayed. As soon as we are in this scenario, privacy issues become prominent: do we want companies to be able to track back the individual behaviour of a single user? While desirable from a company's perspective, it is very questionable if it is from a society point of view. Hence, as soon as later version of trusted computing emerges, we have to watch very closely if they allow digital rights management and if so to which costs of the privacy site. Again, a possible solution would be direct anonymous attestation as this makes tracing of users impossible.

5.   CONCLUSIONS

Trusted computing will become a reality as there are simply too many players in the market who do want it. For closed user groups such as companies, we see clear benefits and do not assume ethical questions which could not be resolved with our existing legal and ethical framework, *e.g.*, workers' unions.

The main open issues we see are not in the area of technology, but in the legal framework surrounding this technology [Koenig, Neumann and Katzschmann, 2004]. Given that we expect the trusted platform module being deployed on a global level with only national or (in the case of the EU) regional level legal frameworks, we can certainly expect some frictions here. The most pressing question can be expected in the near future about how to deal with monopolies of any kind. While some countries may accept these monopolies for the greater benefit of their own economy, other countries may reject them. In principal, having TPM in place might help monopolists to technically enforce their own rules, independent of legal standards set out by national governments (for example, fair use of multimedia documents may be circumvented, as it is already done with the country code on DVDs) – being only the lowest layer of a secure (or trusted) PC, one can debate about the role of the TPM in this scenario, but with higher level secure operating systems in place (which one can safely expect to happen) the risks will get concrete. Unfortunately, we cannot offer a solution for this problem but state it.

A second question is a technological one, namely how to modify the technology such that abuse scenarios become impossible, for example by allowing the users to lie about the status of their platform. By now, most proposals have serious implications also on desired use-cases, and thus the answer of the trusted computing group is negative. For example, the modification proposed to prevent a software vendor from using the TPM to bind the user to his product also prevents it from being used to secure Grid-computation. Currently, both researchers and civil rights groups such as the electronic frontier foundation actually are searching for a solution that would make both sides happy, but there is a risk that the search for the solution may take too long for it to be still practicable when it is found.

In the context of digital rights management — an often quoted application — there are still some open issues. For a highly dynamic platform such as Windows or Linux, the configuration of the system is simply too likely to change and the operating system does not provide enough security for serious DRM to make sense in the first place. However, in a embedded platform like a digital video recorder, things are different. Here trusted computing as laid down in TPM 1.2 could actually be used. And as soon as LaGrande/SEM technology or NGSCB becomes available, things may be different on a PC platform as well. Still, some privacy and consumer protection issues remain open here and need to be addressed in any solution proposed – while it is possible to implement DRM in a way that fair use and the users privacy are ensured, there is a temptation to collect user data (e.g., through an online license verification), or to use the technology to enforce policies that are of questionable benefit (e.g., that a movie bought in the United States cannot be viewed in Europe).

All in all, the technology is very interesting as it will help us to get more secure computers. Actually, it is just the next step in a trend we have since years: the first personal computers with DOS did not have any door locked: all programmes in the computer could alter any content at will. The next step was the "protected mode" in the i286 generation which shielded applications against each other. However, on the level of kernels and drivers, there was not seen any need for such a shield. But we know better now. For actual security critical applications such as Internet banking or electronic signatures, we do need to protect programs from each other, as well as a trusted path from the keyboard over the processor to the screen. Given the recent developments, we are quite likely to get them soon in personal computer. The big question is for which political and social price, As this technology can not only be used to protect the user from attackers, but also to protect some applications from the user. Here, technical solutions are void. Instead, we need a social and legal framework in place to make sure the power balance keeps intact.

REFERENCES

Hewlett-Packard. 2003. *Trusted Computing Platforms:* TCPA Technology in Context. Prentice Hall PTR.

Koenig, C., Neumann, A., and Katzschmann, T. 2004. *Trusted Computing*. Recht und Wirtschaft.

Kursawe, K. and Stüble, C. 2003.. *Improving End-user Security and Trustworthiness of TCG-Platforms*. Technical report, Saarland University. http://www-krypt.cs.uni-sb.de/download/papers/KurStu2003.pdf.

Microsoft, 2003. *Next Generation Secure Computing Base.*. http://www.microsoft.com/resources/ngscb/default.mspx.

Poritz, J., Schunter, M, Herreweghen, E.V. and Waidner,, M. 2004. *Property attestation—scalable and privacy-friendly security assessment of peer computers*. Technical Report RZ3548, IBM.

Reimer, H., 2004. Schwerpunkt: *Trusted computing*. Datenschutz und Datensicherheit (DUD), (9).

Sadeghi, A.-R. and Stüble, C. 2004. *Property-based attestation for computing platforms: Caring about policies, not mechanisms*. In New Security Paradigms Workshop.

Schoen, S., 2004. *EFF comments on TCG design, implementation and usage principles*. www.eff.org/Infrastructure/trusted_computing/20041004_eff_comments_tcg_principles.pdf.

Thompson, K. 1995. *Reflections on Trusting Trust*. Communications of the ACM, 27(8):761–763.

Trusted Computing Group, 2004. TPM Specification version 1.2. https://www.trustedcomputinggroup.org/.